TOWARD A PROCESS APPROACH IN PSYCHOLOGY

Psychological science constructs much of the knowledge that we consume in our everyday lives. This book is a systematic analysis of this process and of the nature of the knowledge it produces. The authors show how mainstream scientific activity treats psychological properties as being fundamentally stable, universal, and isolable. They then challenge this status quo by inviting readers to recognize that dynamics, context-specificity, interconnectedness, and uncertainty are natural and exciting parts of human psychology – these are not things to be avoided and feared, but instead embraced. This requires a shift toward a process-based approach that recognizes the situated, time-dependent, and fundamentally processual nature of psychological phenomena. With complex dynamic systems as a framework, this book sketches out how we might move toward a process-based praxis that is more suitable and effective for understanding human functioning.

PAUL VAN GEERT is Emeritus Professor of Developmental Psychology at the University of Groningen, the Netherlands. He is considered a pioneer in the application of the (complex) dynamic systems approach to a broad range of developmental areas, including cognitive and early language development, second-language acquisition, learning-teaching processes, and educational processes.

NAOMI DE RUITER is a developmental psychologist and Assistant Professor at University College Groningen, the Netherlands. In her research, she applies a (complex) dynamic systems approach to the study of self and identity, and to classroom interactions.

TOWARD A PROCESS APPROACH IN PSYCHOLOGY

Stepping into Heraclitus' River

PAUL VAN GEERT
University of Groningen

NAOMI DE RUITER
University of Groningen

Shaftesbury Road, Cambridge CB2 8EA, United Kingdom

One Liberty Plaza, 20th Floor, New York, NY 10006, USA

477 Williamstown Road, Port Melbourne, VIC 3207, Australia

314–321, 3rd Floor, Plot 3, Splendor Forum, Jasola District Centre, New Delhi – 110025, India

103 Penang Road, #05–06/07, Visioncrest Commercial, Singapore 238467

Cambridge University Press is part of Cambridge University Press & Assessment, a department of the University of Cambridge.

We share the University's mission to contribute to society through the pursuit of education, learning and research at the highest international levels of excellence.

www.cambridge.org
Information on this title: www.cambridge.org/9781108796651

DOI: 10.1017/9781108859189

© Paul van Geert and Naomi de Ruiter 2022

This publication is in copyright. Subject to statutory exception and to the provisions of relevant collective licensing agreements, no reproduction of any part may take place without the written permission of Cambridge University Press & Assessment.

First published 2022
First paperback edition 2024

A catalogue record for this publication is available from the British Library

Library of Congress Cataloging-in-Publication data
NAMES: Geert, Paul van, author. | Ruiter, Naomi M. P. de, author.
TITLE: Toward a process approach in psychology : stepping into Heraclitus' river / Paul van Geert, Naomi de Ruiter.
DESCRIPTION: Cambridge, United Kingdom ; New York, NY : Cambridge University Press, 2022. | Includes bibliographical references.
IDENTIFIERS: LCCN 2022016947 | ISBN 9781108490900 (hardback) | ISBN 9781108859189 (ebook)
SUBJECTS: LCSH: Psychology – Philosophy. | BISAC: PSYCHOLOGY / General
CLASSIFICATION: LCC BF38 .G38 2022 | DDC 150.1–dc23/eng/20220504
LC record available at https://lccn.loc.gov/2022016947

ISBN 978-1-108-49090-0 Hardback
ISBN 978-1-108-79665-1 Paperback

Cambridge University Press & Assessment has no responsibility for the persistence or accuracy of URLs for external or third-party internet websites referred to in this publication and does not guarantee that any content on such websites is, or will remain, accurate or appropriate.

Contents

List of Figures	*page* viii
Acknowledgments	x
Introduction: An Invitation to Step into Heraclitus' River	1

1 Change, the Final Frontier: Introducing a Process Approach to Psychology — 7
- 1.1 What Are Processes? — 7
- 1.2 Introducing the Juxtaposition: A Substance Approach versus a Process Approach — 9
- 1.3 Our Positions: Critical Realism and Plurality — 14
- 1.4 A Non-Linear Roller-Coaster Ride through the History of Process Philosophy — 19
- 1.5 It's All Greek to Me: Concluding Remarks — 23

2 A (Selected) Foundation for a Process Approach: Complex Dynamic Systems Theory — 25
- 2.1 What Is a Complex Dynamic System? — 26
- 2.2 What Is a *Dynamic* System? — 27
- 2.3 What Is a *Complex* System? — 30
- 2.4 Properties of Complex Dynamic Systems (in the Context of Psychological Constructs) — 32

3 The Goal of Socrates: Philosophical Foundations for a Value-Laden, Action-Based Praxis of Research — 44
- 3.1 A Memorable Soccer Game — 44
- 3.2 The Philosophical Foundations of Doing Science: Aristotle's Scheme of Knowledge — 45
- 3.3 Psychological Science and Arendt's Notion of Praxis: Thinking, Doing, and Producing — 47
- 3.4 The Constructivist, or 'Practice Turn', in the Theory of Science — 53
- 3.5 Foundations Set — 60

4 Esteeming Entities: Enacting a Substance Ontology in Self-Esteem Research   61
   4.1 A Critical-Realism Stance toward Praxes   61
   4.2 Self-Esteem Research as a Case Study   63
   4.3 Reflecting on the Enactment of a Substance Ontology in Self-Esteem Research   77
   4.4 Conclusion: The Enactment of a Substance Ontology in Self-Esteem Research   84

5 A Person Acting amongst Persons: Enacting a Process Ontology in Self-Esteem Research   86
   5.1 On the Nature of Self-Esteem from a Process Philosophy   86
   5.2 Descriptions and Conceptualizations of Self-Esteem as Processes   92
   5.3 Separate Roads of Knowledge Construction?   108
   5.4 Self-Esteem in the Real World: Experiencing the Stability and Flux of Self-Experience   110
   5.5 Conclusion: The Enactment of a Process Ontology in Self-Esteem Research   112

6 Cliffhangers and Utilitarian Infants: On How Classification and Science Communication Create Worlds   115
   6.1 Crossing the Visual Cliff and Failed Experiments   115
   6.2 Text and the Creation of Infant Economists   124
   6.3 Conclusion   134

7 Causes, Kings, and Interventions: Causality and Explanation in Mainstream Psychological Theory and Research   137
   7.1 The Effectiveness of Psychotherapies: Questions for a Health Insurance Company   137
   7.2 Causality and the Wish to Make a Difference   142
   7.3 Causality and the Wish to Explain   153
   7.4 Toward Processual Explanations: Tinbergen's Framework   157

8 (Compl)explanation and King Alfonso's Lament: Complex Dynamic Systems and Causal Explanation   160
   8.1 Playing a Simple Tune   161
   8.2 Process as Cause   163
   8.3 Process Characteristics Relevant for Causality   164
   8.4 Features of Complex Process Causality   164
   8.5 From Abstract to Concrete: Specifying Causality in Complex Systems through Models   171
   8.6 Conclusion: Causality Is Interaction and Interaction Is Causality   187

Contents

9 What's in a Name?: On the Ontology of Psychological Measurement — 189
  9.1 Understanding (Psychological) Measurement — 190
  9.2 The Ontology Enacted in Standard Psychological Measurement — 194
  9.3 Psychological Measurement and the Enactment of a Process Ontology — 202

10 (Un)Certainties: Epistemological Issues of Psychological Measurement — 215
  10.1 The Colours of Uncertainty — 215
  10.2 Observation and Measurement as Processes of Uncertainty Management — 225
  10.3 Vagueness and Ambiguity as Forms of Uncertainty — 229

11 Troubled Waters of Heraclitus' River?: A Process View on Reproducibility and Generalization in Psychological Research — 251
  11.1 The Reproducibility Crisis — 252
  11.2 Picking Apart the 'Crisis' — 254
  11.3 A Process Approach to Generalization and Reproducibility — 260
  11.4 Conclusion: Stepping into the River — 264

12 Psychological Science as a Complex Dynamic System: From an Entrenched Substance-Oriented Praxis to the Emergence of a Process-Oriented Praxis — 266
  12.1 Mechanisms of Praxis Development — 267
  12.2 Created Ontologies Accepted as Realities — 279
  12.3 Bringing about Change to the Mainstream Praxis — 281
  12.4 A Multi-Stable Praxis: A Tug of War — 286
  12.5 Conclusion — 289

Glossary — 292
References — 303
Index — 353

Figures

2.1 A state space consisting of connected variables 'amount of help given by a teacher' and 'number of maths problems solved during a lesson by a student' — *page* 28
2.2 A two-node-network representation of the state space model — 29
2.3 A depiction of a psychological property (here, well-being) as a straight line, representing a typical linear approach — 33
2.4 An attractor landscape demonstrating an attractor state with its local minimum with surrounding slopes that constrain the variability of the system's movements (i.e., the ball) — 34
2.5 A deep and narrow attractor (top) contrasted with a shallow and wide attractor state (bottom) — 35
2.6 The cusp catastrophe is a folded geometric plane — 41
2.7 A simulated developmental trajectory (a) showing typical features of self-organized criticality — 42
4.1 A cloud of data points representing a general relationship between variable A and variable B — 74
5.1 Time series for adolescent autonomy, adolescent self-affect, and parental connectedness during one parent–child interaction for one dyad — 98
5.2 Significantly different combinations of self-esteem cues observed for one adolescent, transposed onto a time series for the adolescent's average valence of self-esteem during one parent–child interaction — 103
5.3 Circular causality between trait and state self-esteem — 105

List of Figures

5.4(a)	A state space grid for one adolescent, showing that the trajectory of 'trait self-esteem clusters' corresponds highly with the trajectory of 'state self-esteem level'	107
5.4(b)	A state space grid for one adolescent, showing that the trajectory of 'trait self-esteem clusters' does not correspond with the trajectory of 'state self-esteem level'	107
7.1	An imaginary causal graph focussing on a core node, namely post-therapy symptoms	145
8.1	Circular causality between two parts of a system, A and B, over the course of time	165
8.2	The causal fan, that is, the totality of interactions contributing to the current interaction between two components	170
8.3	A two-dimensional state space based on locally smoothed trends in physical contact and fretting during the first year of life in one child	178
8.4	A simple and generic network representation of coupled dynamics between components	179
8.5	A basic and generic causal-loop graph, showing how components cause each other and themselves	181
8.6	The variable well-being, represented by a straight line, ranging from high to low, and a ball representing the current position of an individual on the well-being dimension	183
8.7	A system with two local minima, that is, stable states	184
8.8	A visual representation of the effect of forces such as interventions	185
8.9	A change in the attractor landscape due to a change in a control parameter across time	186
10.1	A fuzzy representation of a child's MLU as a degree of membership	247
12.1	A simple and generic network representation of coupled dynamics between components in a scientific praxis	268
12.2	Basic continuous causal loops between two high-level interacting components (psychological research and the subjects and topic of research)	280
12.3	A change in the attractor landscape of the psychological praxis, from a substance orientation to a process orientation	287

Acknowledgments

A Word from Naomi de Ruiter

It was an absolute pleasure to work on this book, and to do so together with Paul van Geert. Paul has been a huge inspiration for my ideas about psychological phenomena as fundamentally processual in general, and it was he who inspired me to enter the vibrant world of complex dynamic systems some fourteen years ago. When he asked me to co-author this book with him, I was absolutely honoured, and I am grateful for having had that invitation. This book, with its emphasis on critical reflection on the field of psychology at large, and its meta-theoretical and philosophical perspective, has been nothing short of a dream project. I have always known Paul to be the embodiment of creativity, and he brings a freshness and an eccentricity to his work that breeds innovation. Co-writing with him was a joy. Indeed, collaborating with such a person is something that all young academics should be able to enjoy. This kind of collaboration affords passion and intrinsic motivation to scholarly work that is, unfortunately, often given little room to breathe in the current context of academia.

Being given the opportunity to delve into the creative and intellectually stimulating process of writing this book was a refreshing and exciting experience. It was a deep-dive into Heraclitus' river. This is not to say that the process of writing was smooth sailing. Working on this book began during the post-doc phase of my career (where far too much of my time was dedicated to writing and applying for grants to support the next steps in my career) and continued into the assistant professor phase (where I was developing new courses and establishing myself as a new member of faculty). The latter phase was also the period in which my second child was born, and in which COVID-19 took hold of our lives. Working on this book in these times, with the work insecurity and pressure that came with it, and with the demands that come with new parenthood during lockdown, was a challenge, to say the least. The reason I was able to negotiate this challenge and to persist was a network of supportive colleagues, friends, and family members. The situated nature of productive activity was clearly evident in my case, and I would like to thank those who supported me.

First, thanks to Paul, who demonstrated an admirable level of patience and flexibility toward me as a co-author. He demonstrated a deep understanding of the vast differences in life stages in which we were working. For this, I am deeply grateful, in addition to my gratitude for our collaboration itself. Next, many people encouraged me to continue writing this book when I felt overwhelmed by the times I found myself in: I am grateful to Helen and Allan Wilcox for their enthusiasm and encouragement, and especially to Helen for frequently offering her guidance, support, and advice. My mother, Joyce Witten, was a constant source of positivity and support, and I am grateful to her for the detailed feedback she gave on chapters. In the final stages of completing this book, Alette Smeulers was immensely helpful in offering assurance and support. I am very thankful for the time she invested in reading chapters and offering advice. Most of all, I would like to thank my husband, Tom Wilcox, for being my soundboard and offering critical feedback and practical support, and for taking on so much of the childcare when deadlines approached so that I could press on. I am deeply grateful for his endless and unwavering enthusiasm and encouragement.

A Word from Paul van Geert

I can only agree with my co-author, namely that it was an absolute pleasure to work on this book in the form of a truly joint project. I have always felt, from our earliest meetings on, that Naomi de Ruiter has an exceptional talent for theory, and has the ability to find the connecting threads in the often chaotic and incoherent multitude of publications, ideas, and facts that are so typical of the science of psychology. As I know she also has a healthy portion of self-critical self-confidence as well as a willingness to practise intellectual bungee jumping, I felt no hesitation when I asked her to co-author this book with me.

The lifespan circumstances of our writing couldn't have been more different. As Naomi had just started an academic career and a family, with all the opportunities and limitations that are typical of this generative stage of life, I had retired as Professor of Developmental Psychology at the University of Groningen (which was so kind as to give me an honorary appointment that facilitated the writing of this book). In fact, the idea to write this book arose in the context of my farewell speech in April 2015, which I called 'Time for a change, said Heraclitus, as he tripped over his short legs'. It's a title with many layers (and I feel a strong urge to elaborate on them, but won't, given the limited space), but the most obvious is the message that it is time for a change in psychology, namely for shifting the focus toward the study of real processes. In pursuing the ambitious goal of our book, I felt that some irony was required here and there, although Naomi justifiably used the scissors when I let myself be led astray in the amusing trivialities of associative thought. The generational differences between us may have indeed been instrumental in the fruitful collaboration between Naomi and myself, allowing us to bridge generations, as well as meaningfully invite young academics to the drawing table that is our praxis.

During my long career as a professor of developmental psychology, I have had the deeply rewarding opportunity of accompanying many talented young scholars for a while, on their paths toward academic or applied careers. 'Supervision' of PhD students, as it is called, is also a form of being supervised, of looking at oneself and being reflected in so many different mirrors. I thank all of my previous PhD students for being a mirror that kept me self-reflecting.

I thank my wife, Leen Waegeman, for her support during the writing of this book. In fact, fifty years of married life have resulted in an ecology of comfortable co-existence, where the writing of a book 'goes with the flow'. 'Support' is an example of enactment as well as complementarity: it is provided primarily in deeds rather than words, and it is natural and obvious as well as deliberately given and maintained. Leen's rather down-to-earth and sobering view on the importance of abstract theorizing is a welcome preventive medicine against taking one's theoretical side all too seriously.

A Collective Word from Us Both

We represent two generations of process-oriented researchers, and it is our hope that this book solidifies a bridge between generations of researchers working to explore, develop, and refine a process-oriented psychology. To this end, this book was written as a truly collaborative project, stemming from our shared enthusiasm for how a process approach can positively transform the field of psychology. Within this, a number of chapters (i.e., 4, 5, 7, 9, and 10) were written as single-authored contributions to our joint goal.

Together, we would like to thank Janka Romero, our commissioning editor at Cambridge University Press. It has been a pleasure to work with her throughout this process, and we greatly appreciate the enthusiasm and patience that she showed while shepherding our book through the publication process. We would also like to thank the anonymous reviewers of our book proposal and final manuscript, whose comments and suggestions most definitely helped to improve the book.

Our book sets itself a rather high, maybe somewhat impossible, standard, namely to present an alternative for the current major praxis of psychology, including its hidden philosophical foundations, research methods, communication practices, concepts of measurement, and forms of explanation. We hope that the book will open up discussion and provide inspiration, in particular to young scholars.

Introduction
An Invitation to Step into Heraclitus' River

> One cannot step twice into the same river, nor can one grasp any mortal substance in a stable condition, but it scatters and again gathers; it forms and dissolves, and approaches and departs.
> Attributed to Heraclitus by Plutarch, from Kahn (1979, p. 52)

Psychology is an enormously prevalent discipline. It finds its way into the curious minds of an ever-growing body of psychology students, the homes of struggling parents, and the rambunctious classrooms led by caring teachers. Across many pockets of society, individuals are eager to gain and apply knowledge from the field of psychology. As a discipline that aims to achieve 'the understanding of behavior' (American Psychological Association, 2015), it makes sense that the knowledge that flows from psychology is ferociously consumed for personal and public use.

But this knowledge is not just an accumulation of simple facts. It is the product of a vast and moving collection of institutions, lecturers, and researchers, as well as the methodological tools, rules, values, and norms that bind them together as acting members of a discipline. In this book, we refer to this dynamic network of people and their activity as a *praxis*.[1] We aim to show the ways in which psychological knowledge is contingent upon the praxis from which it emerges. In our analysis, we specifically probe the ways that mainstream research-practices emerge from as well as simultaneously construct underlying assumptions about the nature of reality. These assumptions are often implicitly held, and are referred to as *ontologies*. They are relevant for 'the study of being', which belongs to the branch of philosophy called metaphysics.

---

[1] Our notion of *praxis* bears similarities to Bourdieu's concept of *habitus*, which plays an important role in sociology (Bourdieu, 1977; a particularly clear and extensive definition is given in Maton, 2008, p. 52). We prefer the term 'praxis' because of its explicit connotation with the notion of 'doing'.

Drawing on major concepts from ontology and metaphysics, we reveal the many ways in which mainstream praxis in psychology corresponds with a particular ontological commitment, called a *substance ontology*. This relates to the existence of fundamental properties of reality as independent, isolable, stable, and enduring 'things'. We discuss how this underlying substance ontology is apparent in the specific ways that psychological phenomena or groups of people are studied. In short, psychological phenomena and groups of people form a world consisting of variables. To grasp this world, researchers are concerned with the measurement, manipulation, controllability, explanation, causal powers, and generalization of variables. Throughout the book we unpack these, and other, practices and analyse the various enactments of a substance ontology.

But why is it important to reveal the specific ontologies enacted by these practices? Firstly, for those that take part in the construction of knowledge – such as researchers – revealing underlying ontological commitments is crucial so that we can reflect upon what exactly our praxis is doing: what kind of knowledge are we constructing? How does this knowledge lead to a certain way of construing reality? What are the consequences of this particular construal for the people living these realities?

We show that a research praxis that is committed to a substance ontology creates facts about populations and subpopulations (and more specifically, populations consisting of independent and static individuals or properties). As a field that is primarily concerned with 'the understanding of behavior', this poses a problem. While it is plainly clear that behaviour is fundamentally dynamic and individual, both the dominant research praxis and the resulting knowledge enact a commitment to an ontology of fundamentally stable and isolated things. There is thus a disconnect between ontology and epistemology in psychology. Here, we are thus faced with a threat to the overarching endeavours of our field. While other disciplines, such as biology, physics, and the humanities are largely moving toward both an ontology and an epistemology that are process oriented, psychology seems to be left behind, stuck in a pursuit of stable and universal entities.

Secondly, how does this substance-oriented praxis and knowledge construction influence the construal and lived experience of reality? It creates substance ontologies. The communication of substance-oriented knowledge through textbooks, blogs, podcasts, and scientific articles means that the users of this knowledge construe themselves, others, and their psychological realities as substance oriented. Low self-esteem is viewed as something that we 'have', that makes us act in defensive ways, and that we need to boost. High intelligence is seen as something that we 'have', and that will bring us success. Depression is perceived as a 'thing' that certain groups of people are more likely to 'have', and Cognitive Behavioural Therapy as a corresponding 'thing' that is most likely to mitigate this depression. These phenomena are construed as predictable, fixed, universal, and isolable from each other. Therefore, people are left to navigate their fundamentally messy, fleeting, and interconnected psychological and social realities through this overly simplified, static, and generalized lens. This can only lead to unrealistic expectations of ourselves, others, and the interventions we seek out in life.

Moreover, this knowledge comprises facts that do not actually refer to individual processes, but to populations. This means that such knowledge cannot be validly used to understand, improve upon, or predict how any particular person, or their abilities and traits, will function. For users of psychological knowledge, it is thus important to understand how the psychological knowledge they consume is contingent upon a research praxis that assumes a substance ontology. This is crucial in order to gauge what this knowledge means and how it can be used to help us make sense of the world and to make decisions. These issues are explored in various contexts throughout this book.

We challenge the underlying substance ontology that pulses through the veins of the dominant psychological praxis and which can be observed from advice columns to scientific articles. We advocate for an alternative, which we believe is beneficial to individuals and the field of psychology at large: a commitment to a *process ontology*. This involves the study of people and phenomena as inherently time- and context-dependent and as fundamentally processual. With a commitment to a process ontology, researchers do not study (stable, isolable, enduring) things, but (dynamic, interconnected, fleeting) processes, which have the potential to change and stabilize. Psychological phenomena, in other words, are similar to a river: they are ever flowing, and moving, never the exact same at different moments in time. This notion stems from the ancient philosopher Heraclitus, and it embraces the complexity, variability, and dynamics of human functioning. In other words, it takes the messiness and interconnected nature of lived experiences seriously, and it recognizes that human functioning and action 'emerge through interrelated individual, social, and cultural processes' (Raeff, 2016, p. 227).

We will illustrate throughout this book why championing a process approach is desirable. We argue that it is advantageous for a more accurate scientific understanding of behaviour and psychological phenomena, and thus benefits the core endeavour of our field. We also argue that the knowledge gained from a process-oriented praxis constructs knowledge that is suitable and readily applicable to individuals and their lived experience of reality.

While our starting point is to challenge the status quo, our final aim is to support the ongoing development of our discipline. Accordingly, we treat psychology as a collective process of activity with a hopeful future, rather than a stable discipline that is essentially deficient. As such, we emphasize how the scientific aims and goals that currently characterize our field can still be realized through a different set of practices, and we sketch a concrete picture of what the resulting process-oriented praxis might look like.

In our attempt to encourage a process-oriented praxis for psychology, we present complex dynamic systems as a means for substantiating a process approach. We argue that the meta-theory of complex dynamic systems provides a practical and workable model of a process ontology, both theoretically and methodologically. While we focus on complex dynamic systems as our process model of choice, there are many different approaches, models, disciplines, and theories that are committed to a process ontology. It should therefore not be understood as a monolithic framework (Rescher, 1996), but as a pluralist one (also highlighted in Overton's 2015 scheme).

In Chapter 1, we lay down the conceptual foundation for a process approach by describing processualism, including the characteristics of a 'process' and a process ontology (or metaphysics) and its philosophical roots. We describe how this approach contrasts substantialism and a substance ontology. Here, we introduce what our envisioned process approach implies for realism, where we discuss the stance that the representation of reality is constructed. Accordingly, we position ourselves as critical realists, an approach that comes into play throughout this book.

In Chapter 2, we provide an overview of the foundational aspects of complex dynamic systems. This chapter serves as a reference for many of the following chapters, where we explicitly apply complex dynamic systems concepts and methods to concrete topics in order to illustrate the utility of a complex dynamic systems approach in realizing a process approach.

After laying the conceptual groundwork for the book, we begin our analysis of the mainstream psychological praxis and our vision for a processual alternative. In Chapter 3 we do so by discussing the broad organizational power structures that regulate the virtues of doing science, the values upheld, and the introduction of novices into the scientific community. We discuss these ideological issues in the context of classic philosophical notions put forth by Hannah Arendt (and her work on action) and Bruno Latour (and his work on praxis, actor networks, and inscription devices).

This chapter thus serves as a broad foundation for our later analyses of the ways in which scientific virtues are deeply intertwined with the activities of psychological science.

With Chapters 4 and 5 we provide a broad, but applied, analysis of a whole praxis (from definition and operationalization to aims, methods, and practical knowledge-use). Here we demonstrate how concrete practices align and form a praxis. For this, the field of self-esteem research is used as a case study – as one of the most popular concepts in both academic and pseudo-psychology. With these two chapters, the aim is to concretely illustrate the juxtaposition between a substantialist (Chapter 4) and processual (Chapter 5) praxis before further unpacking specific research practices in the context of psychological research more broadly.

The first specific psychological-research practice that is broadly tackled is science communication (Chapter 6), and the ways that our words, definitions, and descriptions (of experimental studies) create a world of categories, called 'natural kinds'. In this chapter, we describe how these natural kinds are constructed by our communication practices and subsequently serve as targets for social action, which then further construct the meaning of the natural kinds.

Next, Chapters 7 and 8 focus on the notion of causal explanation. Chapter 7 examines psychology's deeply rooted practice of explaining psychological phenomena based on the model of manipulation or intervention causality. Here, we reveal and unpack the assumption of isolable factors that bring about a specific effect, and of unidirectional pathways from cause to effect. The chapter then dives into specific forms of causal explanation, including psychology's tendency to explain the relationship between separate universals.

Chapter 8 contrasts the mainstream explanatory practices with forms of causality that are processual: complex causality. Here, complex dynamic systems are used as a framework, incorporating principles such as emergence, self-organization, circular causality, and perturbations. With this alternative, processes themselves are seen as causes, making causality a moving and dynamic phenomenon. The chapter is concluded with descriptions of various concrete causal models that can be used to help researchers understand causality via processes.

Chapter 9 discusses the practice of measurement, where we cast doubt on the basic assumptions and endeavours underlying the act of measuring. Next, we introduce the processual alternative, which stresses the study of activity as situated and coupled with an environment. This chapter explains how a process approach to 'measurement' is thus fundamentally different from the standard one, and can remedy existing issues related to non-ergodicity and the ecological fallacy. These ideas are illustrated by means of the concept of intelligence, which is undoubtedly one of psychology's show-pieces of measurement.

Chapter 10 deals with the problem of uncertainty – how it is defined and dealt with in the standard praxis. It stresses that the idea of measurement 'error' (in the sense of variability) is predominantly valid under a substance ontology. The processual alternative is described, again stemming from a complex dynamic systems framework, which embraces variability, a fuzziness of category boundaries, and multiplicity. As the notion of uncertainty is also inextricably linked with the fundamental concept of probability, we present a processual framework for understanding probability.

After the deep dive into specific practices central to our discipline, Chapter 11 broadens up again. It reflects on the relative 'success' versus 'failure' of our field, and challenges the widely held notion that we are in a reproducibility (or replication) crisis. At the centre of our discussion is the question: Does psychology have a future, qua science, if the phenomena it studies are changing all the time and contingent on fleeting contexts or historical conditions? This chapter describes how there is only a reproducibility crisis if we adopt assumptions and expectations that enact a substance ontology. In contrast, we describe how variability is to be expected if we adopt a process ontology. This is Heraclitian fluidity. We argue that the way out of the current 'crisis' is therefore not necessarily more methodological and experimental rigour, but a fundamental shift in what we should expect from psychological phenomena. We call for a prioritization of understanding the ways in which phenomena are socially situated and context-contingent, rather than an unrealistic need to replicate.

Finally, in what serves as our concluding chapter, Chapter 12 sketches a picture of a future process-oriented praxis. We describe what is required to instigate a theoretical shift toward a process commitment, and what that shift might look like for the psychological praxis. To flesh this out, we conceptualize psychological science as a complex dynamic system whose behaviour is currently dominated by a substance-oriented attractor state. We describe the dynamic mechanisms that serve to integrate the layers of practices into a living, breathing praxis. And we describe how the current praxis might be perturbed, such that a new process-oriented praxis might emerge.

With this book, we hope to invite readers to step into Heraclitus' river, by diving into the conceptual world of flux and flow and by exploring what it might feel like if our discipline were to take this dive: possibly a bit of a cold shock at first, but ultimately an exciting and refreshing experience.

CHAPTER I

Change, the Final Frontier
Introducing a Process Approach to Psychology

> *Turn, turn, my wheel! All things must change*
> *To something new, to something strange;*
> *Nothing that is can pause or stay;*
> *The moon will wax, the moon will wane,*
> *The mist and cloud will turn to rain,*
> *The rain to mist and cloud again,*
> *To-morrow be to-day.*
>   From *Kéramos*, a poem by Henry Wadsworth Longfellow

1.1 What Are Processes?

What exactly are processes? Researchers often use this term in psychological studies: psychological processes, developmental processes, social processes, schooling processes, clinical processes, and so forth. Johanna Seibt, an eminent process philosopher, provides a non-technical definition: 'What holds for all dynamic entities labelled "processes", however, is that they occur – that they are somehow or other intimately connected to time, and often, though not necessarily, related to the directionality or the passage of time' (Seibt, 2020, p. 1; for a technical definition see Seibt, 2004; for a comparison with the substance view, see Winters, 2017).

In this section, we will unpack the definition of processes provided by Seibt (2020), outlining six specific characteristics of processes. These characteristics further draw upon the scholarship from several process theorists, including Nicholas Rescher, Mark Bickhard, and Johanna Seibt, as well as John Dupré and Daniel Nicholson's (2018) book entitled *Everything Flows: Towards a Processual Philosophy for Biology*. Note that the meaning of process is later unpacked via its juxtaposition with the notion of *substance*, where we draw on the foundational work of Willis Overton.

First, and most broadly, a process is any temporal sequence or flow of events. This sequence of events can only be called a process, however, if there is *process causality* or *process conditionality* between the events. That is, processes are 'integrated series of connected developments unfolding in programmatic coordination: an orchestrated series of occurrences that are systematically linked to one another either causally or functionally' (Rescher, 2000, p. 23). This means that any event in the sequence is conditioned or constrained by the preceding events. In other words, the process must be characterized by *iterativity*: an event at $t+1$ is dependent on the event at t (Van Geert & Steenbeek, 2005a). Second, any truly iterative process will occur within concrete, particular subjects (i.e., a thing or person to which the process applies). An example of such a subject is a concrete individual person, a dyad, family, group, or culture. This requirement is relevant for living systems, and as such, we should be careful to avoid the misunderstanding that all processes require a particular subject. There are many examples of subject-less processes: rain, wind, electricity, light, osmosis, fermentation, adaptive radiation (Dupré & Nicholson, 2018, p. 12; Seibt, 2018). Subject-less processes pertain to the interaction of many components that, for the duration of the process, constitute an interactive whole that may resemble a subject (water molecules, gaseous molecules moving with a particular direction and speed in the case of rain, for instance).

Third, processes (as occurring within a subject) function separately *and* simultaneously in relation to their material, social, and cultural context. Processes are thus embedded in their (layered) context, such that the iterativity of a process is intertwined with that of the context.

Fourth, iterative sequences of events or occurrences involve change that is underpinned by activity (Raeff, 2016). Activity forms the basis of change for a stone that changes its position as it rolls downhill. Activity supports the changes in your perception as your eyes move along this sentence. Processes are therefore *action-based*. The action-based nature of processes has two important implications for how we approach them: one, actions necessarily move in a certain direction. This direction comes from capacities, potentials, and (for living systems) intentionality (Campbell, 2010; Gill, 2003). Two, actions do not have sharp boundaries, such that it is unclear where one action stops and the next begins (Raeff, 2016): 'They are individuated not so much by where they are as by what they do' (Dupré & Nicholson, 2018, p. 13). The iterative steps that make up a process are therefore characterized by a certain fuzziness or indeterminacy.

Fifth, processes have temporal properties or structure (Dupré & Nicholson, 2018; Seibt, 2004). These properties and forms of structure emerge over the course of the process, and they structure the action of the process in some way. This structuring may relate to how affordances (i.e., possibilities for action) are created by interactional events, to coherent patterns and their recurrence across the process, and to mechanisms of change that occur across the process. For pragmatic and descriptive reasons, these properties or structures allow us to observe them as 'things' (or 'subjects', as mentioned), as they allow for a level of stability on a larger timescale (Dupré & Nicholson, 2018).

Sixth, a process involves multiple timescales (Dupré & Nicholson, 2018). On the smallest timescale, we can observe fluctuations in the content of events as situated in concrete contextual changes. For many (but not all) processes that we are likely to study in psychology, the micro-level timescale occurs across seconds, minutes, or hours. However, the units of time that characterize the micro-level timescale (and any timescale for that matter) depend on the phenomenon in question. Some phenomena, such as an individual's identity narrative, will likely not demonstrate variability from minute to minute, but will require weeks, months, or years to show fluctuations (De Ruiter & Gmelin, 2021). As we move up in timescales, from meso- to macro-level timescales (obviously across increasing units of time), the variability that we might observe in smaller timescales becomes patterned. We may observe self-sustained stability or developmental change, for example. Each timescale corresponds with a specific scale of the organization, from the level of quantum physical processes to the level of organisms and societies. This characteristic is crucial, as it signifies that 'the world is process (relations) all the way up and all the way down' (Bickhard, 2011a, p. 13).

Seventh, processes that occur on different timescales – while separate – are intrinsically interconnected. Micro-level processes of variability emerge into the patterns and their development that occur on the meso- and then macro-levels, and the patterns that emerge at these higher levels constrain the variability of micro-level activity.

1.2 Introducing the Juxtaposition: A Substance Approach versus a Process Approach

In order to fully grasp what the study of processes entails, it is useful to contrast it with what it does *not* entail. This is because the process approach deviates from the approach adopted in mainstream psychological science. As such, the process approach can be positioned outside what is deemed conventional. To understand what is non-conventional, it is necessary to first grasp what is conventional. This introduction to the substantialist and processualist perspectives will be recursively revisited in later chapters, each chapter describing how these perspectives are manifested in – or are relevant to – the specific area or aspect of psychological research in question.

1.2.1 Mainstream Substantialism

The current dominant approach in psychology entails the study of psychological constructs as stable and enduring 'substances'. This concept has a long and complicated philosophical history, which the interested reader can read more about later on in this chapter. What we wish to focus on here is that the concept of substance pervades so much of our thinking and reasoning in present-day psychological science, and science more broadly. Bracketing the philosophical history of the concept for a moment, the basic meaning of the concept can be easily retrieved from its etymology, that is to say, from the meaning of its original components. The word is derived from the Latin verb *substare*, which is composed of *sub* (under) and *stare* (stand). Substance then means the stable, permanent, and enduring essence (the latter word derives from 'being') that underlies, or literally under-stands, the fleeting, non-enduring, ephemeral, and impermanent appearances that are the content of our observations: 'Substances are that which can exist on their own, where accidents require a support from substances in order to exist' (Smith, 1997, p. 108; where 'accidents' are events, see also Hoffman & Rosenkrantz, 1997). From a substance approach then, to understand something means to grasp its underlying permanent, independent, and universal essence.

To illustrate this substance approach in action, think about how psychologists tend to explain behaviour. For instance, a researcher can understand a particular child's restless, agitated, and nervous behaviours by referring to their under-lying (or under-standing) attention deficit hyperactivity disorder (ADHD). ADHD is commonly assumed to be a stable and enduring psychological condition that explains the child's observed behaviour. Similarly, a researcher can understand a person's solving of a series of questions and problems by referring to that person's intelligence, which – like the case of ADHD – is viewed as the stable and static factor underlying and explaining the person's (variable) performance. In many ways, a substance approach reflects the norms that we adopt in society at large. For example, adopting a substantialist perspective of the world is obvious. Doing so is consistent with the grammatical habits of many Indo-European languages, with their distinction between nouns and verbs. We usually refer to ourselves and the things that are important to us in terms of nouns, referring to a-temporal objects. We may refer to these nouns as undergoing changes, in the form of verbs (e.g., the student's ADHD is improving), but we are quick to refer to nouns as the underlying thing of interest (Raeff, 2019). In addition, according to Michael Billig (2013), scientific communication practices tend to over-emphasize the use of nouns, replacing process descriptions with nouns. By doing so, they amplify the habit of substance reasoning in the sciences (see also Chapter 6).

Substance reasoning is also comforting, and the most obvious habit of explanation. When we look at the world around us, we don't necessarily see processes. Any phenomena will be stable at a small enough timescale. Arguably, one of the smallest timescales is that of the current moment, where we will, of course, perceive stability. Our experience of ourselves and our world may resemble stable things, such as an emotion, a loving relationship, a conceptualization of ourselves, a doubt, a skill, or the oak tree in our garden. However, if we zoom out a little in time (or a lot, depending on the object), we will see that any of these 'things' are not actually stable (and thus not 'things'). Instead, they are all in a state of flux. The emotion evolved from pride to guilt (from one *hour* to the next), the relationship is moving toward a new level of commitment (from one *day* to the next), the self-conceptualization is evolving from novice to expert (from one *month* to the next), and that tree is growing larger (from one *year* to the next). We simply need to look at a large enough timescale in order to see ourselves and our world as continuously changing (De Ruiter & Gmelin, 2021).

The stability that we perceive in any given moment is real of course, and it can be useful and comforting to take stock of the current state of things. However, the perception of stability should not be used to inform our understanding of the ontology – the nature – of the thing we are perceiving (Seibt, 2020). As Rescher (1996) described, doing so would be 'at best a useful fiction and at worst a misleading delusion' (p. 28). This brings us to the processualist perspective that we wish to support.

In developmental psychology, the distinction between substance versus process ontology is most explicitly made by Willis Overton (2015), who refers to it as the Cartesian-split-mechanistic ontology (contrasting a process-relational ontology). The distinction can best be explained in terms of Overton's own summarizing scheme:

> Atomism versus Holism; Fixity versus Activity of nature; Stasis and Being versus Change and Becoming; Nature as substance versus nature as process; Uniformity versus the Necessary organization of nature; Dualism versus a Pluralistic Universe; Realism versus Constructivism; Either/or Split understanding versus Relational understanding; Dualistic split between objectivism and subjectivism versus Multiple perspectives; Efficient/material causal explanation versus Multiple forms of explanation. (Overton, 2015, p. 12)

The substance-oriented or Cartesian-split/mechanistic ontology (in the former of each of the above distinctions) is typical for mainstream psychology (Witherington et al., 2018). This is not to say that a hardliner substantialist approach is the only explanatory perspective that psychology actually adopts. Some notable exceptions are the many researchers that are devoted to a person-oriented approach (Bergman & Wångby, 2014), for example, those who develop differential equation techniques (e.g., Boker & Laurenceau, 2006; Felmlee & Greenberg, 1999; Gottman, 2003; Steele & Ferrer, 2011). Differential equations present a basic mathematical representation of change, and the rate of change of some variable. In addition, but from a completely different methodological perspective, psychologists who adopt a discursive approach to psychological phenomena also distance themselves from a substance approach (Te Molder, 2015). In approaching psychological phenomena as socially constructed and situated processes, these qualitative scholars also adopt a process approach. Finally, those who adopt a complex dynamic systems approach demonstrate a commitment to process ontology (as a 'group', they are widely divergent, for example, Howe & Lewis, 2005; Lewis & Granic, 1999; Overton, 2013a, 2013b; Thelen & Smith, 1994; Van Geert, 1994; Witherington, 2011).

1.2.2 *Emerging Processualism: Process Metaphysics*

Contrasting the substantialist approach is a processualist approach. An approach that (summarizing from Overton's (2015) scheme) stresses holism, activity, change, becoming, process, organization, pluralism, constructivism, and relationalism. This approach stems from process philosophy (or *metaphysics*, more precisely – which is the branch of philosophy that examines the fundamental nature of reality).

Rescher (1996) described two premises of a process philosophy, which may also function as a philosophical summary of the properties of processes described in Section 1.1. One is that a process is something for which change is essential, meaning that the process ceases to exist if it can no longer change. There is a dynamic and active self-maintenance involved in this property, which is why Dupré and Nicholson (2018, p. 13) prefer the term 'dynamicity' above 'change'. This is apparent in many everyday examples of processes: a river is no longer a river if it does not flow, a dance is no longer a dance if the dancers do not move, and we as humans are no longer *living* human beings if we do not act, think, engage, breath, feel, or move. In fact, we are at all moments human *becomings* rather than human *beings* (Prigogine, 1980).

The second premise of a process philosophy, noted by Rescher (1996), is that stability is *derived* from dynamics and change. This means that stability emerges out of processes that occur on smaller timescales. Stability, from a process perspective, is thus secondary to dynamics and change. This premise is an ontological one: phenomena cannot be reduced to some stable essence or substance. This ontological premise is pivotal in the process notion that a phenomenon is process all the way down, as Bickhard (2009a) and as others have stressed (Dupré & Nicholson, 2018; see also Section 1.1).

Classical process philosophy is represented by Alfred North Whitehead's *Process and Reality* (1929; see also Rescher, 2000; note that a historical overview is provided in Section 1.4). Whitehead's work has had relatively little direct influence on scientific research, however, probably due to its rather opaque character. Modern process theorists thus often turn to different scientific foundations for process thought. Bickhard, for instance, consistently refers to fundamental theories of physics, quantum physics in particular. Others, such as Dupré and Nicholson or Overton, base their processual ontologies primarily on organismic biology. When applying these broad perspectives, these physical and biological foundations often converge on complex dynamic systems theory. This is a meta-theory that is lower in abstraction than the highly abstract perspectives of organicism and relationism (Overton, 2013a, 2013b). This meta-theory, which the mentioned scholars also endorse, serves as the foundation of this book (see Chapter 2).

The premises of a process philosophy encase a crucial epistemological argument: a process philosophy argues that making processes the primary focus of our endeavours as researchers and scholars is the most appropriate and effective way of understanding our world. Bickhard (2003, p. 294) formulates this quite explicitly, stating that 'one of the major themes of the history of science is the replacement of substance assumptions about the phenomena of interest with process models'. He notes, however, that the 'most significant exceptions to this historical pattern are found in studies of the mind. Here, substance assumptions are still ubiquitous, ranging from models of representation to those of emotions to personality and psychopathology. Substance assumptions do pernicious damage to our ability to understand such phenomena'.

While psychology of course accepts and aims to understand how humans change, in mainstream psychology change is treated as secondary to stability, and to phenomena as substances. All too often, change is treated like a mist that looms in front of an observer, something that conceals the true properties – the substance – that they are actually trying to observe. The observer needs to get through that mist, carefully avoiding the auxiliary obstacles, in order to arrive at the real objects that the mist conceals. In this view, change is seen as something that gets in the way of studying something's essence, represented by measurement error or noise. As the observer passes through it, they will reach the final frontier – the substance or essence.

We hope to convince you that *change* should be the final frontier. The importance of adopting a process approach in psychology, and understanding the resistance to doing this, forms the core aim of this book. To do this, we will unpack the various ontological and epistemological assumptions and practices that mark the substance approach so dominant in mainstream psychology, as well as those that characterize the kind of process approach we envision for psychology.

1.3 Our Positions: Critical Realism and Plurality

1.3.1 Critical Realism

When discussing questions of ontology, questions of realism automatically become relevant. While a substance approach aligns quite easily with realism, the relationship between a process approach and realism is more complex. For a substantialist psychologist, the nature of psychological domains can be reduced to fixed, underlying things – whether they are factors, traits, genes, or any other 'essence'. Such a perspective thus stresses the *intransitivity* (Pilgrim, 2019) of psychological domains and assumes that these domains are not influenced by us as researchers, as outsiders to these 'things'. Under this assumption, a substantialist would adopt a positivist approach to this reality, whereby scientists 'discover' the predictable characteristics and laws of a fixed reality that awaits said discovery; a *naive-realist* stance.

If a substance approach contrasts a process approach, does this make a processualist anti-realist? No. Or at least, not from the processual approach that we adopt (recall that a process approach can be applied in an array of different ways). We will describe here the line between realism and anti-realism that we attempt to walk in this book – *critical realism* (the following description of our critical-realism stance draws heavily from Pilgrim (2019). This is a meta-theoretical stance that informs much of our analyses in this book.

Let us make it clear that we do not wish to reject realism (adopting a strict anti-realist approach), nor do we wish to adopt a naive-realism stance that adheres to positivism (i.e., where reality is considered to be fixed and independent of changing contexts, such that our interaction with it is primarily a matter of *discovering* or *confirming* it; Pilgrim (2019)).

However, with this it is important to stress that the things that make up reality are not static. Instead, they are transient. This means that reality (or at least some domains of reality, such as the psychological) is changeable, and that this change comes about because we are part of reality, interacting with it. We are not simply passive observers or consumers of our reality, but active agents in the creation of the reality in which we live and with which we interact (see Chapter 12 for an in-depth depiction). Therefore, we reject the 'intransitivity perspective' of reality. Instead, a critical-realist stance places emphasis on the fact that we influence reality as we interact with it. Note that this does not necessarily imply that we literally *construct* reality, making reality relative (as is the case from a strong subjectivism perspective). Instead, the critical-realism perspective acknowledges and explores the influence that we have on the development of reality and its characteristics, processes, features.

If we influence reality as we move through it, the critical-realist stance works from the premise of *epistemological relativism*. This is the notion that – because any understanding of reality is situated in time and space – there are necessarily different ways of *construing* reality. All knowledge bears the signs and properties of its constructive activity. As such, we believe that – while reality itself is not necessarily relative to the knower – the knowledge that one obtains *about* reality *is* (see Chapter 6 on how language creates perceived realities). With this, we stress the importance of *epistemic humility* for psychological science. In acknowledging that we construct the knowledge that we are pursuing, our knowledge is fallible. It is influenced by the biases and limitations of our scholarly actions and practices, which we must try to make explicit.

This last characteristic of our critical-realist stance brings us to an important implication: room for pluralism. As critical realists, we are 'concerned with mapping the ontological character of social reality' (Archer, Decoteau & Gorski, 2016, p. 3). Since the character of social reality is multi-faceted and multi-layered, we acknowledge that a complete understanding of social reality requires a culmination of different (levels of) explanations (Potochnik & De Sanches, 2020).

The ontology of some aspects of social reality is that of individual psychological processes, while others are population distributions. These different levels of ontologies require different approaches to adequately 'map' the entirety of social reality. In psychology, critical realists emphasize the importance of studying processes, including complexity and emergence (Pilgrim, 2019; Pratten, 2013). However, a critical-realist stance does not imply that a process approach must replace all instances or aims of a substance approach in psychological science. This is also something that we do not wish to convey in this book. Instead, we wish to clarify that a process approach (and its corresponding theories and methodologies, which we will delve into in Chapters 2, 5, 6, 8, 10, and 11) is most useful and appropriate for understanding psychological processes, while many practices within a substance approach are useful when interested in population distributions. We illustrate these differentiated aims and their relation to a substance versus process approach in Chapters 4 and 5 for the case of self-esteem research.

Here, an additional element of our critical-realism stance becomes apparent – *judgmental rationalism*. This is the premise that some accounts about the world are more likely to be true than others, in a particular context. Context, here, refers to a specific phenomenon being studied and a specific scientific aim. For the substance and process approaches to peacefully co-exist in psychology – reaching true pluralism – it is crucial that we critically assess the suitability of a given epistemological approach in relation to a given phenomenon and aim (Chang, 2019).

We must therefore acknowledge that a processualist has specific aims, which necessitate certain meta-theoretical accounts and methodological approaches. Generally speaking, the most pivotal questions to ask from a process approach are of *becoming* rather than *being*, and of *how* rather than *what* (Rescher, 2000). It should be clear that studying 'becoming' and asking 'how' by no means excludes the study of 'being' and the asking of 'what'. Therefore, a suitable aim for the substance approach is to understand distributions of relatively stable dispositions (i.e., the 'what' of 'being'). This aim is compatible – but separate from – the process-approach aim to understand 'how' these dispositions came to be and are evolving (i.e., the 'how' of 'becoming'). The key difference, then, between a substantialist and a processualist at work, would then be one of 'significance, centrality, priority, and emphasis' (Rescher, 1996, p. 31) of substances versus processes, respectively (we describe how the interests of substantialist psychologists *and* processual psychologists may be integrated into a common and pluralist psychological-science practice in Chapter 12).

With this in mind, our aim is to show that a process approach is more suitable than a substance approach for explaining (Chapters 7 and 8) and measuring (Chapters 9 and 10) phenomena, and establishing validity in our field (Chapter 11) in the context of studying *psychological processes*.

In Section 1.3.2 we provide a general description of how a substance and a process approach differ with regard to how they perceive and engage with phenomena. We do so via the different construals of the reality of a roller coaster.

1.3.2 Timescales and the Illusion of Stable Things

What we understand or come to know about a given phenomenon – even something as seemingly self-evident as a roller coaster – is highly dependent on the approach we take when looking at it. We show here that, to see the processual properties of a given thing, one must look at that thing in the context of time: its temporal order.

At first glance, one may argue that the understanding of a roller coaster requires – and supports – a substance approach. It is counterintuitive to call a roller coaster a process, as the event of a roller-coaster ride entirely depends on the presence of an enduring, static, and a-temporal physical structure, instantiated in the form of an *object* called the 'roller coaster'. And indeed, the characteristics of this structure can clearly be the object of study. Such an approach, however, negates some important properties of the roller coaster, which can only be understood when considering how the roller coaster is situated in multiple timescales.

First, one might consider that an important property of the roller coaster is the *event* of the roller-coaster ride. The function of the roller coaster is to enable an activity, a very dynamic one at that. This property is a process-based one, where the roller-coaster ride takes place at the relatively small timescale of minutes.

Second, the event of the roller-coaster ride itself demonstrates flux. Interestingly, the speed of the roller-coaster carts increases over the course of the day due to greasing of the wheel bearings, which warms them up.[1] Come evening, when the roller-coaster ride is closed, the carts do not move, and the wheel bearings cool down again. There is thus a daily cycle of warming up that gives rise to a slow increase in speed; a process that takes place at the timescale of a day.

Third, even the structure of the roller coaster itself cannot be fully understood based on its static features, as this structure was of course physically *constructed*. This property is one of *becoming*, and takes place at the relatively large timescale of weeks and months.

Fourth, once constructed, the roller coaster is not static. It requires constant maintenance and upkeep. It needs to be constantly checked and greased, and worn out parts have to be repaired or replaced entirely. This process of *maintenance* takes place at the timescale of months and years.

---

[1] For further details, see www.coaster101.com/2010/09/27/coasters101-what-influences-train-speed/ and www.youtube.com/watch?v=zi4piO1gK7g.

And finally, these timescales are intimately intertwined. For one, the time that it takes to design and construct the structure of the roller coaster will be partly determined by the ride that it is intended to provide, whereby a simple ride will require a shorter and more basic structure than a roller coaster that is intended to send its passengers in loops and free falls. The former will thus require less time to design and to construct compared to the latter. In addition, the repairs and maintenance that must take place may be a function of how intensely the roller coaster is used. And, of course, the ride – in the sense of a temporal sequence of events – is dependent on the physical structure of the roller coaster. Any obstruction of the structure will immediately halt the activities of the roller coaster.

Therefore, to an observer of the roller coaster at any given moment, the roller coaster may appear to be a static, unchanging metal structure. The timescale of that observation is too small to notice the dynamics of the roller coaster, such as its wear and tear and repair thereof. Moreover, for a passenger of the roller-coaster ride, there is no point in worrying about the intrinsic dynamic nature of all the materials that make up the roller-coaster structure, or about the external forces that are required to maintain its safety. Essentially, it is perfectly normal for an observer or passenger of the roller coaster to *bracket* the process characteristics of the roller coaster. This bracketing (or *Einklammerung* in German, which sounds much more interesting) was described in Edmund Husserl's phenomenology as the suspension of engagement with the processes underlying a stable substance or structure. It is a form of reductionism, whereby the long-term processes of emerging stability are reduced to the short-term experience of the here and now: the roller-coaster ride.

As we will explore in Chapters 4, 6, 7, and 9, it is common to bracket the process nature of things that we interact with, especially when we want to characterize them via quantified measurements. Bracketing the process nature of something may free us from worrying about the state of flux of our reality that we rely on, live with, and attempt to measure. However, any apparent stability results from past and ongoing constructive and maintenance processes, much like the roller coaster. Moreover, our interacting with that reality influences the stability of these structures (like the cumulation of passengers riding on the roller coaster). And while the apparent stable features of our reality – physical or psychological – can be understood at any given moment using a substance approach, it would be incorrect to claim that this approach fully elucidates the ontology of these things. Indeed, underlying any apparent stability is a dynamic interconnection of short- and long-term processes, which require a process approach to understand.

1.4 A Non-Linear Roller-Coaster Ride through the History of Process Philosophy

1.4.1 Philosophical Origins

Thus far, we have given a general description of what a process approach is, where it fits in with a pluralist approach (allowing for epistemic relativity) to the understanding of reality, and why it is necessary to delve into the process nature of phenomenon. We explained how these epistemological arguments stem from process philosophy. Here, we provide a brief historical account of process philosophy.

The father of process philosophy is the Greek philosopher Heraclitus of Ephesus, who lived around 500 BCE (c.535–c.475 BCE) and was called the 'dark' or obscure philosopher because his – very scarce – writings are indeed very hard to understand if you take them literally.[2] Heraclitus is probably best known for the statement *panta rhei*, which means *everything moves*. However, we owe this statement to a passage in the *Cratylus*, which is a book written by Plato describing a dialogue between Socrates, Cratylus, and Hermogenes (three Athenian philosophers who lived around the fifth century BCE). Heraclitus' statement is embedded in the following passage, written almost like a modern-day comedy sketch.

SOCRATES: My friend, I have thought of a swarm of wisdom.
HERMOGENES: What is it?
SOCRATES: It sounds absurd, but I think there is some probability in it.
HERMOGENES: What is this probability?
SOCRATES: I seem to have a vision of Heracleitus saying some ancient words of wisdom as old as the reign of Cronus and Rhea, which Homer said too.
HERMOGENES: What do you mean by that?
SOCRATES: Heracleitus says, you know, that all things move and nothing remains still, and he likens the universe to the current of a river, saying that you cannot step twice into the same stream.
HERMOGENES: True.[3]

This passage reveals Heraclitus' ideas about how things are always moving, and as such, that any two instances of observing (or interacting with)

---

[2] If you speak Dutch and you have sufficient knowledge of *Star Wars*, you'll probably understand why Heraclitus is the Dark Vader of process philosophy.
[3] Plato, *Cratylus*, 401e and 402a. http://data.perseus.org/citations/urn:cts:greekLit:tlg0059.tlg005.perseus-eng1:402a.

something will not be the same. Since all thoughts of Heraclitus have come to us through the reconstruction of his ideas by other, later philosophers (as illustrated), there is a lot of debate on what Heraclitus truly would have said. According to Kahn (1979), the most directly Heraclitean of all river fragments is the one that says 'as they step into the same rivers, other and still other waters flow upon them' (pp. 166ff., see also Graham, 2008).

The main philosophical point is that things obtain sameness in their identity through their changes, or from the way they change. The identity or sameness of a particular individual person – Paul Van Geert, Naomi De Ruiter, or the current reader of these lines – is that of the individual's patterns and processes of change. We are our processes, all the way down to the timescale of the processes that go on in the cells and molecules that constitute our bodies. This philosophical premise was described in Section 1.2.2.

The metaphor of the river – and the broader issue of change and identity in flux – is in fact part of Heraclitus' major doctrine of the unity of opposites, such as sleep and waking, warm and cold, delight and disgust, approach and avoidance, and so forth. If such opposites were enduring[4] substances, if they were separate 'things' with an unchanged and fundamental essence, a doctrine of unity of opposites would be irrational or illogical. For Heraclitus, the unity consists of their being linked by processes of change or transformation: warm turns into cold and cold turns into warm, approach turns into avoidance and avoidance into approach. There is thus a cycle of transformations from one opposite to another, thereby uniting them. For Heraclitus, the world is 'a manifold of opposed forces joined in mutual rivalry, interlocked in constant strife and conflict' (Rescher, 1996, p. 9). In the same way, individuals may leave behind old qualities or characteristics, while others are more of a cyclical transition between recurring qualities. This brings us back to the notion of humans as 'becoming' rather than as 'being', introduced earlier in this chapter.

The typical antagonist of Heraclitus is his near contemporary Parmenides of Elea, who developed a metaphysics of timeless, unchanging and uniform existence, denying the existence of change. For him change is an illusion resulting from the working of our perception. Parmenides' view on the unchanging nature of existence led to the atomism of Leucippus and Democritus, stating that the world ultimately consists of unchanged and

---

[4] There is quite some discussion on the meaning of the word 'perduring' versus 'enduring', see for instance Seibt (1997, pp. 148ff.) and Noonan and Curtis (2018).

unchangeable elementary building blocks, the atoms, the configurations of which form all the objects and properties that we can perceive in the world. Parmenides had a strong influence on Plato, whereas Aristotle was influenced by Democritus' ideas.

As Plato and Aristotle had a great influence on Western metaphysics and science, the tacit opinion of current science – and by implication also of psychology – about the ultimate nature of reality is primarily an inheritor of Parmenides, rather than of Heraclitus. The heritage consists of the role of time and change, which are treated as added, secondary properties instead of fundamental and defining features. A belated echo of the Parmenidean view on change as a basically deceptive feature is the way psychology commonly treats variability and fluctuation, namely as measurement error, or as a phenomenon caused by other factors than the underlying, measured factor (think, for instance, about the distinction between 'trait' and 'state' self-esteem; see Chapter 4).

If you travel upstream the river of thought that originated in pre-Socratic philosophy, you will find that it splits into two tributaries, one representing the metaphysics of change, the other the metaphysics of enduring substance or essence. A philosopher such as Aristotle, who has been so important for the development of Western science, is rowing his boat just before the river forks, although it seems as if he is going to opt for the substance- rather than the process-branch.

To illustrate this somewhat ambiguous nature of Aristotelian philosophy,[5] let us look at the important distinction between *potentiality* and *actuality*. Potentiality is the possibility of something to do a particular kind of thing, to change in a particular way, or to do a particular sort of 'work' that can affect certain things. The Greek word for potentiality is *dunamis*, which we recognize as the root of the word dynamic. It refers to the concept of forces as the potentiality of doing a particular kind of work (as in thermodynamics, studying the work that can be done by heat). If it is applied to persons, it refers to these persons' ability to do something, to change in particular ways. That is, it refers to the abilities, which are defined as a potential for change or activity that is an intrinsic property of some sort of thing. In this sense, we come close to the concept of an ability as a substance, an enduring essence, a stable property or component in the

---

[5] On this ambiguity – or rather, richness – of Aristotle's philosophy, see among others Seibt (2002) and Gill (2003), who defends the position that Aristotle was in fact a dynamicist, and that the notion of substance needs to be understood in dynamic terms, as the dynamics that 'stands under' all natural phenomena.

person, that can be expressed in the form of doing certain things (such as giving a right answer to an item in an intelligence test).

The complementary term of potentiality is actuality. For Aristotle, actuality had two sides. One was what he called *energeia*, which means something like 'being in a state of doing what one is supposed to do', for instance, like when an intelligent person is solving a difficult problem that requires a lot of intelligence, or when a depressed person is ruminating and entertaining negative thoughts. Psychologists would probably call this *behaviour*, which is the actualization of a particular disposition (for example, an ability, capability, or psychopathology; Von Wachter, 2009). The other side of actuality is *entelechy*, which is the realization of a particular potentiality. This is the notion of actuality that features in psychological ideas such as self-actualization, but also in the concept of development (de-velop goes back to a Latin stem that means unwrapping, and in Germanic languages such as Dutch or German the word for development is *ontwikkeling* or *Entwicklung*, which is literally unwrapping or unfolding). Aristotelian distinctions thus continue to run through the discourse of modern psychology.

A perennial problem with the distinction between potentiality and actuality, or disposition and behaviour, is that one cannot be defined without the other. The only way to know about the potentiality of a thing or person is by the actual expression of that potential through behaviour. On the other hand, the actual expression derives its meaning from the disposition that it is thought to represent (for example, sleeping badly is only a symptom of depression if there is an underlying depression). The two are intimately and circularly connected. Therefore, a dualistic perspective of the two is likely not complete or accurate and most likely grounded in a reductionistic belief that 'real' explanations require underlying enduring essences, substances or qualities.

1.4.2 *The Branching Off of the Forked River: Process Philosophy*

After Aristotle's somewhat ambiguous commitment to a process versus substance ontology of things, we find many philosophers who explicitly developed a more radical process philosophy. Here, there are roughly two main bodies of literature that demonstrate a commitment to process philosophy. The first body of literature comes from the sciences of the living, biology in the first place, with its discoveries of the process of evolution, development of the individual organism and human history. It is the basic justification for philosophers such as Hegel (in human history), Bergson (biological growth and evolution), Dupré and Nicholson (2018), and arguably one of the most important process philosophers, Alfred North Whitehead (see also Rescher, 1996 and Seibt, 2020, who have further explained and clarified Whitehead's account of process philosophy).

The second body of literature comes from the physical sciences, and the recent developments in quantum physics in particular. As Bickhard (2016, p. 24) describes, at its foundation the world consists of 'quantized excitations in quantum fields', not particles or enduring substances that are reminiscent of the pre-Socratic atoms. The Russian-born, Belgian chemist and Nobel Prize winner, Ilia Prigogine, has been an important advocate of the idea that modern physics, thermodynamics in particular, supports a process rather than a substance view of nature. As the title of one of his best-known books testifies, we must change our view of reality as a matter of being to a matter of becoming (Prigogine, 1980).

In his overview, Rescher (1996) provides an account of process philosophers that jumps from the ancient Greeks to Leibniz (1646–1717), and goes on with Hegel (1770–1831), Peirce (1839–1914), James (1842–1910), Bergson (1859–1941), Dewey (1859–1952), Whitehead (1861–1947) and finally Sheldon (1875–1981). Readers might notice that this list includes two psychologists, James and Dewey (and we believe it should include Bickhard, as a radical process theorist and interactionist; Bickhard, 2009a, 2009b, 2016). This contrasts with the relative lack of process accounts in psychology that we outlined throughout this chapter (where some more recent exceptions are, for example, Dafermos, 2020; Hibberd, 2014; Witherington & Heying, 2015). The scarcity of process philosophy in psychology is despite the fact that human experience has quite classically been conceptualized as a continuous and complex flow of events, for instance, in the process philosophy of William James.

1.5 It's All Greek to Me: Concluding Remarks

While it may be easy to dismiss metaphysics or ontology as ancient or obscure philosophical accounts that no longer have a place in modern-day psychology, we believe that these accounts show their face in all layers of psychology today. What we aim to show with this book is how psychological research is an ongoing *praxis*, or a whole of practices, ways of doing, ways of asking questions, patterns of communication, interacting researchers and applied practitioners. Furthermore, this praxis enacts particular accounts of metaphysics and ontology – of 'the way the world is'. Beliefs or assumptions about metaphysics and ontology are likely to be implicit in this praxis, in that they almost completely escape reflection. Yet despite this implicitness (or perhaps because of it), these underlying metaphysical or ontological assumptions are robust, self-perpetuating, self-reproducing and thus very hard to change.

We will show throughout this book that the underlying metaphysics and ontology enacted by the standard practices of current psychological research amounts to an ontology of substances: assumptions about 'things' (e.g., psychological constructs) as a-temporal and enduring, and we show how complex dynamic systems can aid a shift toward a process-ontology praxis. This shift will necessarily include the re-conceptualization of psychological constructs, the nature of the questions asked, research methodology, and research norms.

In line with our pluralist, critical-realist view we argue for a thorough reflection on the implications of a substance- versus process-oriented ontology. What does this contrast reveal about the nature of psychology's subject? What is it that psychology focusses on, tries to understand and eventually change? The questions will be answered via our own reflections throughout this book.

The emergence of a processual alternative to the dominant substance-oriented praxis of psychology leads to various possible scenarios. One scenario is that the 'best' praxis – in terms of explanatory value and success of applications and interventions – will replace the other one. Another scenario is that a processual praxis branches off from the current praxis and both continue without any significant form of interaction, more or less like two biological species that originated from a common ancestor and that are no longer capable of interbreeding and producing viable offspring. Both scenarios would run against our pluralistic beliefs, namely that the subject of psychological science can most fruitfully be approached from distinct perspectives, including different ontologies. However, this pluralism implies an awareness of the ontological choices implicit in the different praxes involved. A third scenario is that of an integration into a larger praxis – and its associated ontology – of complementarity (e.g., Kelso & Engström, 2006). This is a kind of Hegelian synthesis of antithetic positions. This book invites the reader to reflect on these possible scenarios and their implications for the nature of psychological science (and we offer an imaginary possibility in our final chapter of the book, Chapter 12).

CHAPTER 2

A (Selected) Foundation for a Process Approach
Complex Dynamic Systems Theory

> I think the next [twenty-first] century will be the century of complexity.
> Stephen W. Hawking, '"Unified Theory" Is Getting Closer,
> Hawking Predicts', interview in *San Jose Mercury News*
> (23 January 2000)

The process approach that we wish to advocate for in psychology (briefly introduced in Chapter 1) is not a method in itself, nor is it a theory. Instead, it is a praxis: a family of theories, metaphysical assumptions, methods, scientific goals and values that, together, argue for and create a specific worldview: a process-relational worldview. In such a worldview, phenomena are conceived of as fundamentally processual, embedded in and emerging from interactions across nested levels of a system (Bickhard, 2009a; Overton, 2015).

This worldview encompasses, and can be realized via, a wide range of meta-theories. Each of these meta-theories will necessarily lean on and prioritize slightly different aspects of this worldview. These meta-theoretical differences, in return, will afford and require different methodologies, including quantitative, statistical, hermeneutic, qualitative, empirical, theoretical, computational (and more) methods. Finally, these different methodologies will be better suited for application to some theories or some questions over others. There is thus a plurality of meta-theories, theories, and methods that are equally interesting and suitable for what we are ultimately trying to achieve with this book: the adoption of a process approach for psychology (and the social sciences more broadly).

In this chapter, we provide an overview of one such possible meta-theory: complex dynamic systems theory, which we will describe here. With this chapter (and this book more generally), we do not wish to privilege complex dynamic systems over other meta-theories that align with a process-relational worldview. Instead, we suggest that it is one of many meta-theories that can provide a solid foundation for pursuing a process approach. That being said, we do believe that this meta-theory is an ideal candidate for a process approach, as it is itself a theory, an approach, and a methodological toolkit (depending on the researcher and their disciplinary background). As our (personal) selected foundation for a process approach, we will return to this meta-theory throughout this book, applying the concepts introduced in the current chapter in order to unpack or illustrate various themes related to psychological science as a praxis that enacts particular ontological views.

2.1 What Is a Complex Dynamic System?

It is hard to think of a phenomenon that is of interest to psychology that is not an example of a complex dynamic system. To us, this seems apparent when faced with the etymologies of 'dynamic' and 'complex', as they are intuitive characterizations of the kinds of phenomena that psychologists study.

Etymologically, 'dynamic' means that forces are at work, and that such forces produce change. Instead of 'forces', psychologists are likely to talk about abilities, influences, dispositions, and so forth. 'Complex' is derived from 'being woven together, entwined'.[1] This implies that there must be things, elements, processes, or components that are interwoven or entwined. The elementary form of this is when some element A (a variable, process or component) has an influence on, or affects, another element, B, *and vice versa*, in the sense that A causes B, and B causes A, to change (or do something).

'Complex', then, is different from 'complicated'. Etymologically, the latter means 'folded together', without the connotation of being entwined. The distinction between 'complex' and 'complicated' might be a key point of divergence between what we (the authors) see as intuitive and what mainstream psychology sees as intuitive. A standard approach to psychological phenomena, for example intelligence or self-esteem, is that of unitary, independent entities or properties that affect each other in an additive cause–effect manner. The common conceptualization is that phenomena are *complicated*, and the aim is to *unfold* these complications in order to reveal a neat array of causal or constitutive factors. This contrasts our starting point, which is that phenomena are in fact *interwoven*, and can therefore not be unfolded into independent contributions. Unfolding would undo a phenomenon, such that it ceases to be complex and *dynamic*.

---

[1] www.etymonline.com/search?q=complex.

2.2 What Is a *Dynamic* System?

Below we further delve into the definitions and characterizations of what makes a system *dynamic*, and what makes it *complex*.

2.2.1 Change Across Time

A dynamic system can be defined as something whose present state develops into a next state over the course of time (Weisstein, 2020; Van Geert, 2019). The state of a system is conceived of as a particular position in a larger *state space*, that is, a space consisting of possible properties that we use to specify the system (e.g., the magnitudes of a depressed person's sleeplessness and pessimistic thoughts, or words and syntactic forms in a child's language).

2.2.2 Rules for Time Evolution

Additionally, the development from one state to the next involves some kind of 'rule for [the] time evolution on a state space' (Meiss, 2007). This rule is some kind of function that specifies a principle of change. In a formal or mathematical dynamic systems model (which is where the notion of *dynamic systems* originated), this function is defined by means of a differential (or difference) equation.

At the bare minimum, the rule for time evolution is iterativity (see Chapter 1), where every next state is a function of the preceding one, given some chosen state of departure:

$$x_{t+1} = f(x_t); \ x_{t+2} = f(x_{t+1}); \ x_{t+3} = f(x_{t+2}); \ x_{t+4} = f(x_{t+3}); \ \ldots$$

The function f is an operation on the current state of the variable that transforms it into the next state. It represents the so-called *evolution term*, specifying the principle of change, and x is the dimension of the state space (e.g., a child's current vocabulary).

The timeline notation of the above formula therefore looks like this:

$$x_t \to x_{t+1} \to x_{t+2} \to x_{t+3} \to x_{t+4} \to x_{t+5} \to \ldots$$

The sequence of such points is a *trajectory* (i.e., a path) in the state space. In this particular case (above), the state space is one-dimensional, as it applies only to the variable x.

A multivariate iterative process specifies a process in an n-dimensional (2, 3, etc.) state space. These dimensions (or variables, e.g., x and y) are

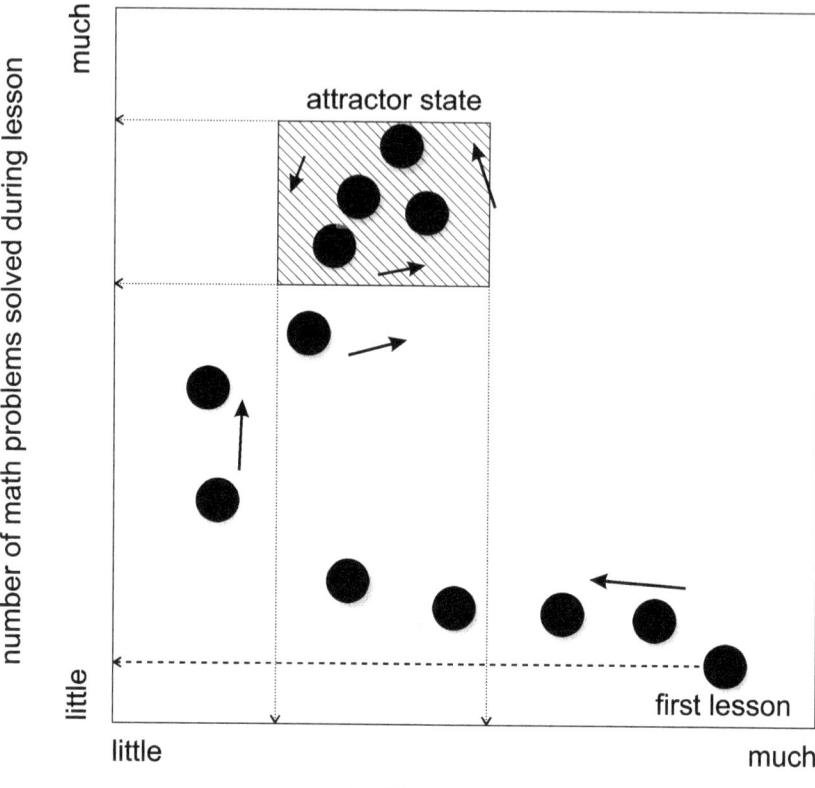

Figure 2.1 A state space consisting of connected variables 'amount of help given by a teacher' and 'number of maths problems solved during a lesson by a student'. The dots represent steps from an initial state (bottom right) to an attractor state (see further for explanation).

coupled: x and y affect or influence one another over time. The dynamic system representing this relationship for a two-dimensional state space (i.e., x and y) is as follows:

$\{x_{t+1} = f(x_t, y_t); y_{t+1} = g(y_t, x_t)\}; \{x_{t+2} = f(x_{t+1}, y_{t+1}); y_{t+2} = g(y_{t+1}, x_{t+1})\}; \ldots$

This is visually portrayed in Figure 2.1, where x = the amount of help given by a teacher, and y = the number of maths problems solved by a student during a lesson.

A trajectory of a dynamic system can of course include more dimensions, as we add variables to the system. Another way of representing a

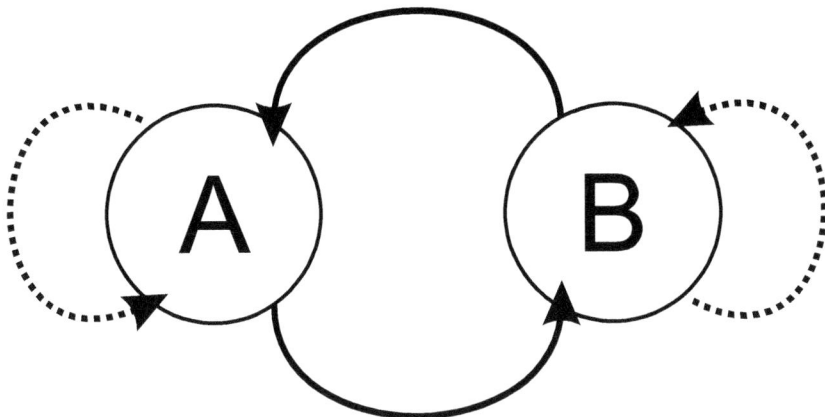

Figure 2.2 A two-node-network representation of the state space model from Figure 1. The system's evolution rules are represented by the arrows ('vertices' of the network).

trajectory within a state space is via networks consisting of nodes, which are useful for displaying systems with many variables (where every node corresponds with a dimension in the state space). Above (Figure 2.2) a simple two-dimensional system is shown, where the relationships are dynamical (i.e., they pertain to the change in the variable or component to which they apply).

Crucially, the function or rule of development is not the same thing as being *governed* by some central coordinator or controller. Coordination and control, instead, emerge from the dispersed and continuous interactions between the components. The totality of these interactions form what is called the collective behaviour of the system.

Dynamic models such as the basic ones shown above represent a meta-theoretical framework that can be applied to any system, and thus any domain-specific theory of change. For example, they have been used to describe the change that occurs in language development (Bassano & Van Geert, 2007; Robinson & Mervis, 1998; Van Dijk et al., 2013; Van Geert, 1991), cognitive development (Van Geert, 1991, 1998, 2000), meaning making in identity development (Kunnen & Bosma, 2000), dyadic play (Steenbeek & Van Geert, 2007, 2008; Hesp, Steenbeek & Van Geert, 2019), major life decisions and career choice (Van der Gaag & Van den Berg, 2017; Van der Gaag et al., 2020), risk behaviours in adolescence (Schuhmacher, Ballato & Van Geert, 2014), colour preference in young children (Van Geert, 2014a), scaffolding in educational processes (Van Geert & Steenbeek, 2005b), learning-teaching trajectories

(Steenbeek & Van Geert, 2013), life span trajectories of excellent performance (Den Hartigh et al., 2016), and classroom aggressive behaviour (Abraham, 2014; Van Geert & Steenbeek, 2004).

2.3 What Is a *Complex* System?

With the above statement that a dynamic system can be described as a network of (many) connected components, we basically enter the realm of *complex* dynamic systems. The number of books on the basic properties of complex dynamic systems, or complexity for short, is quite overwhelming (to name just a few that might be of particular interest to psychology: Érdi, 2008; Holland, 2014; Hooker, 2011; Jörg, 2011; Juarrero, 1999; Ladyman & Wiesner, 2020; Mitchell, 2009). The recent book by Ladyman and Wiesner (2020) provides a particularly accessible and up-to-date introduction. We shall loosely follow their overview of properties of complex systems (Ladyman & Wiesner, 2020, p. 10) as a guideline for our own short overview, which will be more thoroughly discussed in the remaining sections of this chapter, and in the various chapters in this book.

2.3.1 *Many Interacting Components*

A complex system is a network of *many interacting components*. 'Many' varies between two (like the one described in the previous section) to virtually uncountable (like the 100 billion interacting neurons in the human brain).

Furthermore, the network of components is an *open* network. First, it is not bounded, in the sense that its exact boundaries are often impossible to determine. Second, complex systems are open to their environment: they exchange energy and information with their environment, and by doing so, they are able to 'survive' as a system, that is, they are able to maintain their internal structure over the long term. Because complex systems are open to their environment, they are *adaptive systems*. This means that they are capable of changing their internal composition (their components and the way in which they interact) to match the exigencies of their environments, enabling their survival.

Although one might expect that an uncontrolled and open system like this would give rise to totally chaotic and disorderly behaviour, the collective behaviour of complex systems displays *spontaneous order and structure* (which we will describe in Section 2.4).

2.3.2 Nested Timescales

Importantly, the components of a complex system are complex systems themselves, resulting in so-called *nested* structures (e.g., Bechtel, 2009; Ellis, 2016). Hence, describing a complex process always requires a particular focus on a specific level of a nested system. It is important to note that no nested structure (or level) of the system can be reduced to another. For example, molecules are the components of water (and thus a lower-level structure than 'water'). The many interactions between water molecules thus generate properties of water: liquid, frozen, or gaseous states. However, these properties (or states) are in no way present in the water molecules themselves. It is through the *interactions* between components that higher-level structures emerge. A system is therefore 'processes all the way down' (Bickhard, 2011a; see Chapter 1).

Different levels of a system's structure necessarily develop across different timescales, from very short events to long-time processes. These timescales are not discrete, but instead, feed into each other. The short-lived interactions on the level of components generate processes or temporal patterns that can last for a long time (and these temporal patterns form components that interact across larger timescales, and which generate even larger-scale patterns across larger time intervals). For instance, interactions between neurons are very short lived, but the totality of interactions gives rise to long-lasting memories. Individual memories may then be communicated and shared across individuals across much larger timescales, giving way to even longer lasting and self-maintaining cultural memory.

The nested-time aspect of complex systems means that processes occurring much later in time are still influenced by processes that occurred a long time ago. Complex systems therefore have 'memory', in the sense that they are history dependent.

2.3.3 Non-Linear Relationships

The fact that emergent properties are not reducible to those of components or a sum of components is also referred to as *non-linearity*. The relationship between components[2] is, instead, *discontinuous* because it is a dynamic relationship that is open to changes. Two (or more) components may then

---

[2] In particular, those components that *typify* the complex system, such as the nagging and the other person's reaction in the following example; as a complex system entails many interacting components, continuous, and discontinuous relationships may co-exist, a condition typical of complex systems (e.g., Kelso & Engström, 2006).

interact in such a way that they maintain a certain stable state, until their interaction can no longer maintain this state. The relationship between the components then changes, resulting in a transition in the behaviour of the system as a whole. For example, imagine that someone is nagging you, and you are ignoring this behaviour. At first, there is a simple continuous process, whereby the person nags and you remain calm. After a while, this (continuous) process will likely change after a certain threshold is reached (because the acts of the other person are also recursively influenced by the person themself). For instance, you suddenly lose your temper and react with an emotional outburst (a discontinuous change from ignorance to fierce reaction). Discontinuities typically mark transitions between relatively stable states of the complex system, namely states that are actively self-sustained (e.g., you remaining calm, or the liquid state in water). During those transitions, systems show typical, erratic forms of fluctuation and variability.

2.4 Properties of Complex Dynamic Systems (in the Context of Psychological Constructs)

2.4.1 *Emergence*

The concept of emergence is the topic of an extensive body of literature (e.g., Bedau & Humphreys, 2008; Bickhard & Campbell, 2000; Campbell, 2015; Clayton & Davies, 2011; Corradini & O'Connor, 2010; English, 2017; Gibb, Hendry & Lancaster, 2019; Goldstein, 1999; Holland, 2000; Humphreys, 2016). While Sawyer (2002) suggests that emergence has had 'a longstanding influence on psychological thought' (p. 2), Antonietti (2010) noted that the 'term "emergence" is seldom used by psychologists' (p. 266).

Psychology's reluctance to use the concept may be due to its being notoriously difficult to define, in particular because it is used with a variety of meanings and connotations. However, what most of the definitions of emergence have in common is that an emergent property is a *higher-order property that cannot be reduced to the sum of its parts* (Campbell, 2015; O'Connor, 2020; Santa Fe Institute, 2021).

Emergence implies that the interactions between components of a system obtain or create new (and non-reducible) qualitative properties. This makes an emergent property autonomous, in a sense that it can influence the interactions between components that it depends upon, and can interact with other emergent properties (Humphreys, 2016; O'Connor, 2020; De Wolf & Holvoet, 2004). However, this autonomy

2.4 Properties of Complex Dynamic Systems

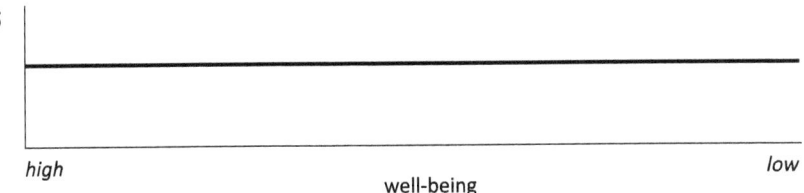

Figure 2.3 A depiction of a psychological property (here, well-being) as a straight line, representing a typical linear approach. An individual adopts a position on this line (i.e., a level of well-being on the x-axis) depending on the current environmental affordances, such that each position on the line requires an equal amount of energy (i.e., the y-axis, and every change is proportional to the amount of external energy invested (e.g., a particular clinical intervention).

is limited, in that emergent properties exist only by virtue of the underlying interactions between the components. This apparent ambiguity or tension makes the concept of emergence in the context of psychological constructs difficult to understand. Yet, it is indeed key to understanding complex dynamic systems. The following sections unpack the *limited-autonomy* ambiguity further.

2.4.2 Attractors

Higher-order emergent properties are the *attractors* of the complex system: given a current set of interactions between its components, temporarily self-sustaining states will emerge. This 'self-sustaining' property clarifies why emergence is both *autonomous* and *limited*.

Attractor states are self-sustaining because they actively resist external influences (up to a certain level and for a certain duration, think about the 'nagging' example), making them robust. This can be depicted by means of an *attractor landscape* (or *epigenetic landscape*, *potential landscape*, depending on the context of application, see Figure 2.4). The notion of epigenetic landscapes was introduced in biology by Conrad Waddington (1957) (for a developmental example, see Newell, Liu & Mayer-Kress, 2003). To explain the attractor landscape, it is useful to begin with the classic conceptualization of psychological constructs. Most variables can commonly be depicted as a straight line with measurement units on the x-axis, from high to low, much like a Likert scale (see Figure 2.3, applied to well-being). A particular person's value for that variable (here, well-being) is then a single point on this line, which may vary across circumstances.

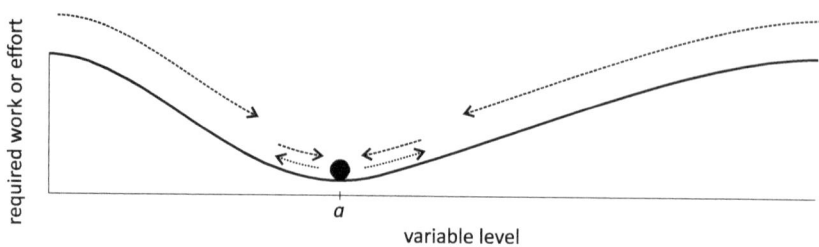

Figure 2.4 An attractor landscape demonstrating an attractor state with its local minimum (*a*) with surrounding slopes that constrain the variability of the system's movements (i.e., the ball).

A complex dynamic systems conceptualization of properties such as well-being is that there are certain states that require less energy (or effort) to maintain. If we add *effort or energy* to our depiction of the well-being property (on the *y*-axis), our figure (Figure 2.4) depicts a valley. This is the point on the *x*-axis (i.e., the state of well-being) that is most easily maintained for this particular individual (called the *local minimum*). It is the individual's most 'natural' state to which they are 'attracted' to (not in the sense that it is preferable, but in that they are pulled toward this point).

The 'pull' toward this state can be depicted by the affordances provided by the slopes of the valley to a ball, which is rolling around the attractor landscape (see the long arrows in Figure 2.4). The ball will 'naturally' roll to the local minimum, that is, only very little effort is needed to make the ball roll from the highest point to the lowest point. The steeper the slope, the less effort is needed to arrive at the local minimum, and the more effort or energy is needed to move the ball out of this local minimum (to make the ball roll uphill). The wider the slope, the more possibilities there are for moving toward the local minimum. In Figure 2.4, all possible starting points of the ball, except point *a* itself, will make it roll toward point *a*. The vertical dimension of the landscape corresponds with potential energy: if the ball is on the highest point, there is a considerable amount of energy available to make it move downhill. If it is on the lowest point, there is no energy available to make it move spontaneously, and the ball will only move if some external action or force is applied (e.g., a clinical intervention to make the system move out of a state of depression).

This attractor landscape demonstrates not only why an emergent property demonstrates self-maintenance, but also why it is that a system will always show variability over time. Specifically, the system's behaviour is not *determined* by the local minimum, it is not fixed to that point. Instead,

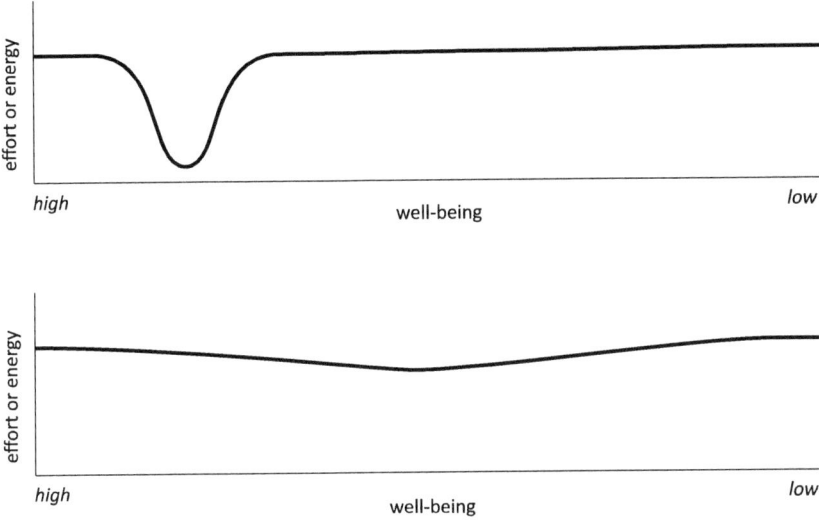

Figure 2.5　A deep and narrow attractor (top) contrasted with a shallow and wide attractor state (bottom).

the system moves around this local minimum as it interacts with the environment (or other properties), see the smaller arrows in Figure 2.4. Some external forces will be strong enough to move the system out of the local minimum, and toward alternative well-being potentials (elsewhere on the x-axis). These forces are then *perturbations* to the system. Note that this requires a landscape with several local minima (not shown in Figure 2.4, which has only one local minimum).

The amount and form of variability experienced by the system depends on both the size of the external force and on the width and depth of the attractor (i.e., how entrenched the property is). Figure 2.5 shows two different attractors, characterized by different basins of attraction. In the shallow and wide attractor (below), any relatively small perturbation can have a noticeable effect on the system's behaviour, resulting in a high level of variability. In contrast, in the deep and narrow attractor (top), only a very strong perturbation will have a noticeable effect on the system's behaviour. In this case, where the attractor has a narrow basin of attraction, the ball must be very close to the attractor well in order to make a spontaneous movement toward the deepest point.

A system's attractor state provides a counterforce against possible perturbations. It does this via *feedback loops* between components of the system.

Some interactions demonstrate negative feedback loops (which work to inhibit changes, bringing the system back to its original state), while other interactions demonstrate positive feedback loops (which amplify changes). Together, positive and negative feedback loops maintain a system.

In the attractor landscapes discussed above, attractors are single points, represented by the one attractor basin (a valley). This visualization falls short of the real complexity of a system's attractor landscape. An attractor, in the form of emergent patterns of activity, is often characterized by long-term recurrence of *multiple* stable states, that is, of multiple attractors (e.g., Marwan et al., 2007). For our discussion of a person's well-being, they may then demonstrate robust feelings of positive well-being (i.e., a deeply entrenched attractor state) alternated by periods of relatively low well-being sensitive to accidental influences (i.e., a shallow and wide attractor state). For complex systems such as humans, it is highly unlikely that the system will settle into only one particular attractor. Instead, it is more common and likely that human phenomena will flexibly move between semi-stable states (e.g., Spivey, 2008; Tognoli & Kelso, 2014).

Furthermore, the attractor landscape is not fixed, but malleable. Its form (i.e., where the attractor point is, how many attractor points there are, how deep or wide the slopes are) is shaped by the movements of the ball: by the system's actual behaviour in response to its interactions with the environment. Attractor landscapes can thus also be used to visualize entrenchment of attractor states, or transitions between one attractor state to another, as described by synergetics and coordination dynamics (we will describe this in-depth in Chapter 8).

2.4.3 Emergence as 'Soft' or 'Strong'

Years ago, one of us (PvG) had a PhD student with whom a visit was made to Esther Thelen, the author (together with Linda Smith) of a frequently-cited book on dynamic systems in human development (Thelen & Smith, 1994). We (PvG and the PhD student – Els) were having pizza when Esther asked what kind of research Els was doing. Els amply explained that she was studying the development of theory-of-mind (Blijd-Hoogewys & Van Geert, 2017). Esther listened very attentively and then spoke the unforgettable words: 'very interesting, but, you see, we don't believe theory of mind exists'.

Esther Thelen's remark represented a broader view on the nature of psychological constructs that she and her collaborators were defending, namely, an *argument against design* (Thelen & Smith, 1994; see

Witherington, 2011, for a critical account). Witherington (2011) describes this as follows: 'Pattern does not presuppose design and consequently does not presuppose a designer; instead, complexity arises in genuinely novel fashion from simpler components, without its being prefigured in those components' (p. 67). This argument contrasts the classic representationalist view, whereby individuals 'have' mental structures (such as abilities or conceptual understanding) that are conceived of as internal entities that cause specific behaviours. In place of mental structures, Thelen and Smith (1994) shifted the dialogue to the emergence of patterns out of interactions between situated components.

The 'interactions between situated components' are thus key for understanding psychological constructs as emergent properties. Some go so far as to suggest that the emergent psychological construct is actually secondary to these lower-order components (as argued by Witherington, 2011). From this account (which is called *soft emergence*), the emergent properties are seen as *epiphenomenal*, or as by-products of the processes from which the pattern emerges. This perspective is 'soft' in the sense that an emergent property or pattern is thought to ultimately be dependent on, and is reducible to, the 'local process dynamics that engender it, maintain it, and into which it falls out of being' (Witherington, p. 70). With this, the 'forces or laws that govern emergents exist solely at lower levels of explanation … not the reverse' (p. 70). Soft emergence, then, is that emergent properties are merely patterns of lower-order interactions. For instance, when an infant searches for an object, a typical pattern of activity emerges, leading to successful or unsuccessful retrieval of the object. According to soft emergence, what emerges is merely (i.e., is reducible to) the moment-to-moment dynamics of action and perception. There is no 'new' or 'novel' property (such as an understanding of 'object permanence'). The emergent property then 'doesn't exist', as Esther Thelen remarked years ago.

Soft emergence is thus radically different from the classic representationalist perspective of mental structures, and this radical juxtaposition was important for changing the way that developmental psychologists think about phenomena (for more on the divergent conceptualizations, see Chapter 6, where we discuss the classic A-not-B error and its different interpretations).

Witherington (2011) argues that 'this antistructuralist stance conceptually undermines the very principle of emergence through self-organization upon which the approach is built, jeopardizing its process focus' (p. 66). In fact, emergent properties are temporal and transient organizations of activities that *influence and constrain* the activities that the organization depends upon. In contrast with soft emergence, *strong emergence* then stresses that patterns are not mere end-products of lower-order interactions, but that these patterns offer explanation. As such, strong emergence suggests that emergent properties are ontologically real. This conceptualization 'endows the emergent organization of a system – its structure, form, pattern – with causal significance and removes it from the throes of epiphenomena, thereby rendering the novelty such organization represents in real rather than illusory terms' (Witherington, 2011, p. 71). For instance, during repeated instances of infant object-search, a stable pattern of visual-motor coordination emerges, which then constrains the visual-motor activities of search itself. This stable, recurrent pattern can be conceptualized as an 'object concept'. Strong emergence can ultimately be explained by *circular causality*, which we will describe in more detail in Chapter 8; see also Witherington (2011); Emmeche, Køppe and Stjernfelt (2000); Haken (1992); McClelland (2010); Antonietti (2010).

A strong-emergence stance is important for understanding how emergent properties can be conceived of as 'autonomous' and 'self-sustaining' (see previous sections), while still stressing that emergent properties do not exist outside or independent of the activities from which they emerge. Importantly, then, 'vertical separation' is rejected, which is the belief that, once these emergent properties have emerged from particular developmental processes, they obtain the existence of an independent entity (Van Orden & Holden, 2002). By rejecting vertical separation, emergent properties remain 'soft-assembled' (Humphreys, 2016; O'Connor, 2020; Thelen & Smith, 1994): the emergent property cannot be detached from the actual behaviours and their interactions as they take place in a concrete activity context (Emmeche, Køppe & Stjernfelt, 2000). This non-detachability is a very important feature as far as psychological constructs are concerned, which clearly separates the standard praxis of internally represented, measurable constructs from the process-oriented praxis we are advocating for.

2.4.4 Self-Organization

In complex systems, emergent properties result from underlying processes and interactions between components of a system. The patterning that arises from those interactive processes is the result of *self-organization*. Self-organization occurs when many interacting processes coordinate spontaneously, without external guidance, to form self-maintaining, temporarily stable, patterns or structures (i.e., organizations or coordinations of components). Self-organization is a form of drive, a drive toward (temporary) stability that dissolves tensions or minimizes energy or effort (Juarrero, 2000; Riley & Turvey, 2001; Swenson & Turvey, 1991). Self-organization in organisms – including human beings and their complex psychology – is a direct consequence of the fact that organisms are material organizations, structures or patterns of interacting processes that depend on energy exchange with their environments (Prigogine, 1980). Self-organization can be conceived of as an umbrella term for (and consisting of the collective action of) the above mentioned properties of complex dynamic systems (Halley & Winkler, 2008).

In psychology, research on self-organization has been inspired by various theories that we will discuss in some detail below. These theories provide a picture of the many different approaches to self-organization adopted in different (sub)fields, and by extension, the wide-spread application of complex dynamic systems thinking.

2.4.4.1 Synergetics and Coordination Dynamics

Self-organization has been extensively studied by synergetics, a branch of complex dynamic systems theory: 'Synergetics asks about the general principles of self-organization of such complex systems, irrespective of the nature of the individual entities' (Hutt, 2020, p. 1; for a recent and comprehensive overview, see Hutt and Haken, 2020). The word synergetics stems from the Greek *synergein*, meaning 'to work together, cooperate'. It is a theory about the spontaneous emergence of coordinated patterns with emergent and self-sustaining properties, caused by interactions between components.

Synergetics was described by Herman Haken as an offspring of studies on the dynamics of laser light, which led to the discovery of universal properties of self-organizing systems. In the fields of neuroscience and behaviour, this theory has been transformed into a general theory of coordination dynamics (Bressler & Kelso, 2016; Kelso, 1995, 2013). Synergetics and coordination dynamics are primarily interested in the features of discontinuities (e.g., a sudden switch between walking and running when a person increases the speed of movement; see Section 2.3).

The concept of synergetics is universal, and hence, can be applied to any system, from laser light to human activities, allowing us to conceive of any system as a self-organized processes with the associated properties (e.g., the variability typical of discontinuities) (Bickhard, 2009a; Molenaar & Campbell, 2009; Juarrero, 1999, 2000; Witherington, 2011; see also the series of papers in *Humana Mente*, January 2011, among others Bickhard, 2011a, and Silberstein & Chemero, 2011).

Synergetics, and the resulting self-organization, have been applied in many domains of psychological research. Examples concern perception and cognition (e.g., Haken, 1992), motor coordination dynamics (Kelso, 1995, 2013), brain dynamics and neurocognitive processes (Tognoli & Kelso, 2014), psychotherapeutic processes and clinical psychology (Goudsmit, 1989; Tschacher, Schiepek & Brunner, 2012), social and business organizations (Guastello, 2013), policy making (De Greene, 1993), long-term cognitive change (Van der Maas & Molenaar, 1992), social psychology (Vallacher & Nowak, 1997), self-esteem (De Ruiter, Van Geert & Kunnen, 2017; see Chapter 5).

2.4.4.2 Catastrophe Theory

Another major theory explaining the dynamics of self-organization toward stable states and transitions between such states is catastrophe theory, developed by the mathematician René Thom (Thom, 1989). 'Catastrophe' means a sudden transition from one stable state to another, a discontinuity. The theory has been influential in research on discontinuous changes in psychological systems (Van der Maas & Molenaar, 1992; Wagenmakers, Van der Maas & Molenaar, 2005).

Similar to synergetics, catastrophe theory is based on the notion of *control parameters* (i.e., variables to which a system is particularly sensitive). Examples of control parameters in the context of maths performance in a child are the difficulty of the maths problems, the child's motivation and stamina, fatigue and boredom, and so forth. In psychological research, much attention has been given to systems that are sensitive to the effect of two control parameters. These systems undergo discontinuities that can be described by the so-called *cusp catastrophe*, which is a form of discontinuous change with typical, identifiable properties (see Figure 2.6). This typical form of discontinuous change has been applied to development, work and organizations, education and clinical change (Guastello, 2013; Hartelman, Van der Maas & Molenaar, 1998; Hayes et al., 2007b; Stamovlasis & Tsaparlis, 2012; Wagenmakers, Van der Maas & Molenaar, 2005; Witkiewitz et al., 2007).

2.4.4.3 Self-Organized Criticality

Another generic theory for dealing with the combination of stability and instability that is typical of the propensities of complex systems in general, is the theory of self-organized criticality (Bak, 1996; Ramos, Sassi & Piqueira, 2011; Tonello, Giacobbi & Pettenon, 2018; Van Geert, 2008; for applications to brain activity, see Haimovici et al., 2013). The theory

2.4 Properties of Complex Dynamic Systems   41

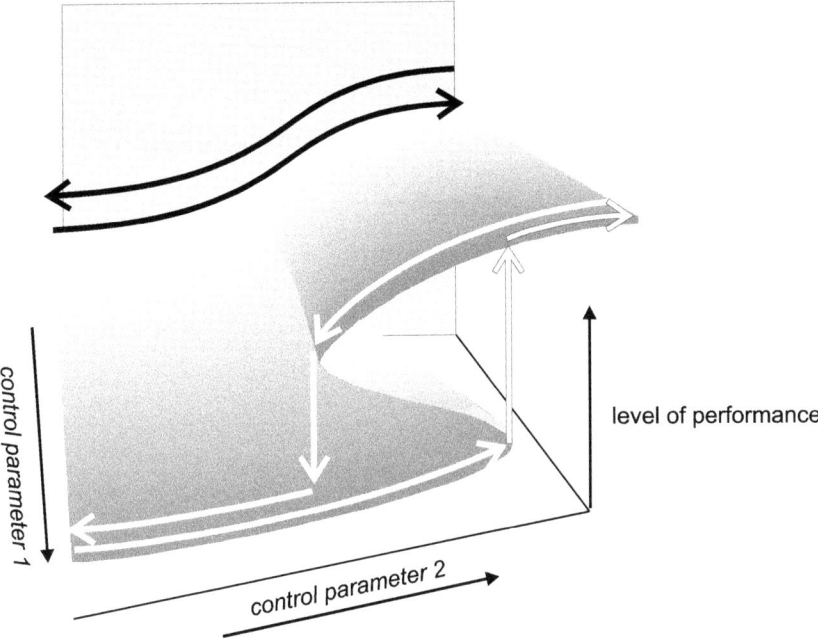

Figure 2.6   The cusp catastrophe is a folded geometric plane (represented in gray shades) that shows the solutions of dynamic systems governed by two control parameters (1 and 2). The height of the plane corresponds, for instance, with a level of performance. For low values of control parameter 1, the changes governed by control parameter 2 are continuous (back), for high values the changes are discontinuous (i.e., a sudden jump either to the lower or to the higher level; front).

focusses on complex systems that undergo slow, relatively weak, continuous influences. Think of a developing child, undergoing a constant stream of activity-based experiences. Self-organized criticality implies that the continuous stream of experience will drive the system, through processes of self-organization, toward a critical state where any minor influence (e.g., another experience) will cause a sudden change of highly variable, basically unpredictable magnitude (see Figure 2.7a).

Figure 2.7a represents development by means of a single y-variable. In this simulated trajectory (Van Geert, 1998), change over time occurs in four clusters (basically like Piaget's stage-theory). Within these clusters, changes occur, but only minimally (i.e., small distances between consecutive dots). The jumps that occur between clusters are premised by points of self-organized criticality: the system becomes unstable, and suddenly settles into a new

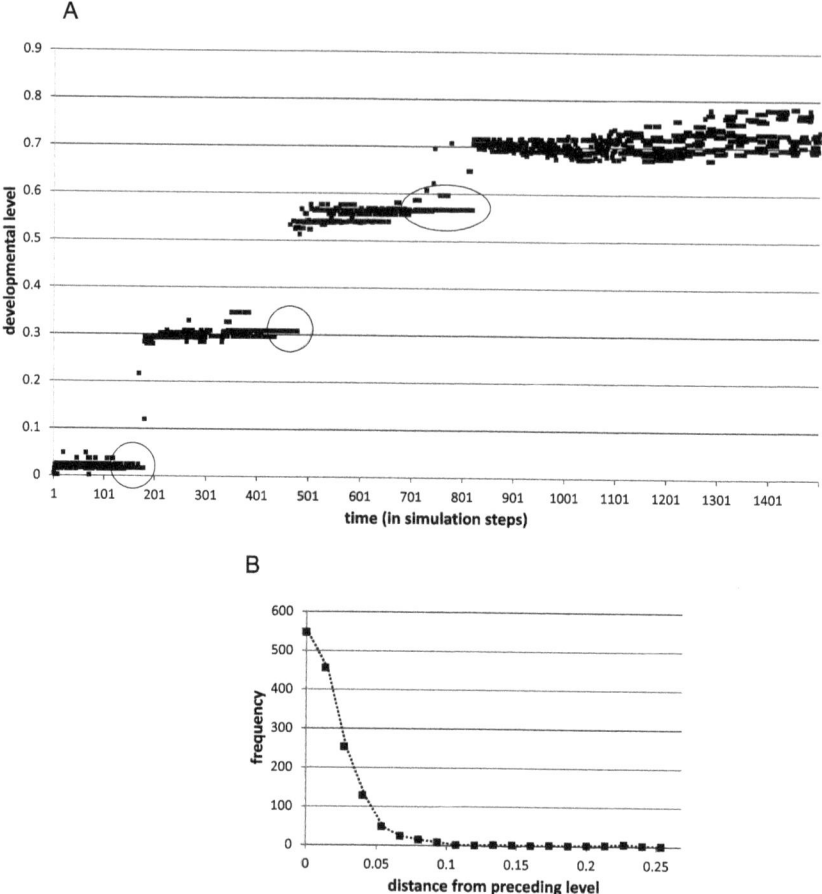

Figure 2.7 A simulated developmental trajectory (a) showing typical features of self-organized criticality: minor changes (distances between the dots) occur in the overwhelming majority of cases, and are interspersed by (very few) major steps (i.e., jumps to a higher level; circles and ellipse represent self-organized critical regions). The magnitudes of the changes (from very small to very big) are distributed according to a power law (b).

equilibrium (i.e., a new cluster at a higher developmental level). Over time, small changes and (fewer) larger changes occur interchangeably.

Together, this pattern of changes follows a *power-law distribution* (Figure 2.7b). It represents a quantity, the frequency of which decreases as a power of its magnitude. For example, the quantity refers to frequencies of soccer players, or frequencies of fluctuations in a developmental process. The magnitude refers to the number of goals made by a soccer player during the player's sporting career, or the difference between a child's number of different words used today and the number used tomorrow. In a power-law distribution, very small magnitudes (e.g., no goals made during professional soccer games, or very minor daily fluctuations in the number of different words used by a child) occur in very large numbers, and very large ones occur with very small frequencies. Power-law distributions are scale invariant: every arbitrarily chosen smaller piece of the distribution has the same form as a larger piece, including the distribution as a whole. This distribution typically results from non-linear behaviour (e.g., two types of event amplifying each other's probability of occurrence) and is characteristic of complex systems.

The counterpart to power-law distributions are symmetric distributions (e.g., the *normal* or *Gaussian distributions*). The majority of cases occur at the middle values (e.g., average IQ), and scale invariance does not apply (a small piece of a normal distribution does not have the same form as the whole distribution, for instance). Normal, symmetric distributions are typical of linear systems, where events contributing to the frequency of occurrence are added up (additivity of factors or influences of events is a major feature of linearity, characteristic of standard psychological research).

CHAPTER 3

The Goal of Socrates
Philosophical Foundations for a Value-Laden, Action-Based Praxis of Research

> The philosophers have only interpreted the world in various ways; the point is to change it.
> Inscription on Marx' tombstone at Highgate Cemetery, London; from Marx (1845) *Theses on Feuerbach*: II, VII, XI

> In theory there is no difference between theory and practice. In practice there is.
> Benjamin Brewster, *The Yale Literary Magazine*, 47 (5) (1882), p. 202. But consequently attributed to many others including Yogi Berra, Albert Einstein, Richard Feynman and Jan L. A. Van de Snepscheut, former professor at the University of Groningen, whose dramatic death illustrates the practice of an existential *Grenzzituation* (limit situation)

3.1 A Memorable Soccer Game

In 1972, Greece and Germany played a soccer game in the packed Olympic stadium of Muenchen. The German lineup consisted of players such as Leibniz (goalkeeper), Kant, and Nietzsche, while the Greeks, led out by their veteran centre-half Heraclitus, counted illustrious players such as Plato, Aristotle, and Socrates. This historical and beautifully played soccer game (which we can thank Monty Python for sharing with the world[1]) provides insight into how soccer is done – or at least – when philosophers are the ones doing it.

The game begins with the usual warming up: a little jogging around, dribbling, kicking the ball to one another. Then the referee – Kung Fu Tse, better known as Confucius – blows the whistle. Immediately, the philosophers start to do what philosophers are supposed to do: the Germans turn away from the ball, hands on chins, in deep contemplation. A pan to the other end of the

---

[1] Monty Python (1972). *International Philosophy* sketch, commonly referred to as *the Philosophers' Football Match*.

field shows that the Greeks are also thinking deeply, occasionally gesticulating. Meanwhile, the ball stays untouched in the centre of the playing field. There is no doubt, however, that the philosophers are indeed playing a soccer game. They are doing so in their own way, the way any philosopher so obviously would. As we come to the closing minute of the match – it's absolutely not clear where all the minutes between the opening and the closing minutes have gone – Archimedes shouts 'Eureka', runs toward the ball, kicks it, passes to Socrates, Socrates back to Archimedes, Archimedes to Heraclitus, Heraclitus easily passing Hegel who is still thinking, passes the ball to Socrates, Socrates heads it in! A beautifully orchestrated chain of passes, made possible by the quiet contemplations and reflections of the players.

According to the British philosopher Julian Baggini, the Monty Python comedy sketch 'represents a coherent, Anglo-Saxon take on existentialism. French thinkers such as Camus and Sartre recognized the absurdity of life, but it took the English Pythons to show that the right response is to laugh at it' (*The Guardian*, 10 April 2010). Although we do not contest either the legitimacy of this interpretation, or the observation that life is quite absurd, we see the Philosopher's Football Match as a commentary on philosophy. Put differently, the sketch illustrates the praxis of philosophy – including individuals (mostly old, white men) deep in thought, contemplating, debating, seemingly separate from the world around them and the practical tasks at hand (whether Monty Python's comedic interpretation of this praxis is stereotypical or actually quite accurate is, of course, up for debate). At the same time, the sketch also illustrates the utility of a 'philosophical approach' (i.e., the praxis) for accomplishing a goal (pun intended). As the sketch demonstrates, the philosopher soccer players were able to cut through the dramatics and time-wasting tactics that often typify soccer games, leaving only the bare bones of the game and an elegant outcome. So, too, can philosophy help us cut through the dramatics of academics, revealing its bones. In the case of this chapter, the bones of science: the scientific praxis.

3.2 The Philosophical Foundations of Doing Science: Aristotle's Scheme of Knowledge

What are the bare bones of doing science, the praxis that we are part of and aim to discuss in this book? To begin, the scientific praxis is built on the pursuit of knowledge. This involves both the level of activity and the level of that which activity produces. The activity relates to Aristotle's concept of *theoria*. While the meaning of this term was never explicitly articulated, it can be described as *the actualization of knowledge* (Roochnik, 2009). A parallel can be drawn here with the act of *doing* science. The concept of *theoria* is, for Aristotle, actually intimately related to issues of ethics, and in particular, the study of how human activities can lead to happiness, to life in a good spirit (*eudaimonia*). Aristotle described how pursuing knowledge, *theoria*, can include various virtues of thought (Kraut, 2018).

One of these virtues is *techne*, which can be translated as 'craft'. This is 'the making of' (or *poiesis*) and is thus done in the service of a specific outcome. For *techne*, then, the end is the product. Techne is a sort of knowledge that can, at least partly, be inferred from *theoria*. Relating this to the field of psychology, we aim to 'infer' a clinical intervention from the knowledge we've 'actualized' from science. This clinical intervention is created in order to 'produce' mental health. There are thus layers of *poiesis* here: the production of interventions, which in turn, are produced in order to make happy individuals. Taking this further, producing these clinical results is done (in part) in the service of new scientific publications, promotions, or academic status.

Related to *techne*, Aristotle also described the virtue of *episteme*, often translated as 'knowledge' (Parry, 2020). This is the accumulation of eternal, context independent certainty, of truths, of universal facts. *Episteme* can be conceived as another goal – or end – of *theoria*. These virtues of thought – *techne* and *episteme* – are thus highly characteristic of modern science: we take part in science for the sake of producing universal truths and favourable results of various kinds.

These virtues of thought, for Aristotle, should be complemented by the virtue of *phronesis*, which is 'practical wisdom'. This is 'doing' (as opposed to 'making'), where the end is the activity itself. *Phronesis* thus refers to doing things well for their own sake, and for the sake of excellence. Excellence, here, is more than a methodological issue (i.e., conscientiously and thoroughly conducting research), and is more of an ethical issue (although the first would of course imply the latter). The virtue of *phronesis* is typically related to happiness and the wilful activity of free men (and women, but unfortunately not in the historical description of the term). This is a far cry from doing science for the sake of building a long list of publications and having an impressive h-index, which unfortunately represent the shackles of many researchers trying to reach the intellectually free and safe state of tenure.

The virtue of *phronesis* is thus value oriented. As complementary virtues of thought, then, *episteme* and *techne* cannot (and should not) be seen as separate. In his book, *Making Social Science Matter: Why Social Science*

Fails and how it can succeed again, Bent Flyvbjerg (2001)relies heavily on the notion of *phronesis*, describing how 'truths' of the social sciences are highly context- and history-specific (see also Kristjánsson et al., 2021). The social sciences often cling to instrumentalist and functionalist forms of reasoning, often artificially separating scientific results from the researchers behind these results and from the *doing* that produces the results.

In line with our critical realist approach (see Chapter 1), the act of doing science (*theoria*) should not be seen merely as the production of knowledge or results, but as highly interconnected with the values, culture, policy making of those who are doing the science. A fact-oriented approach can therefore be integrated with a value-oriented approach. The praxis – the doing – of science is just as fundamental as the outcomes of science. If we consider the *doing of* science as equally fundamental to the *techne* and *episteme* – the outcomes – of science, it then becomes imperative that we make all parts of this praxis explicit and reflect upon them.

3.3 Psychological Science and Arendt's Notion of Praxis: Thinking, Doing, and Producing

In the mid-20th century, the concept of *praxis* was revived by the influential philosopher Hannah Arendt (1906–1975), who is probably best known for her analyses of totalitarianism, but whose work on the notion of praxis in *The Human Condition* (Arendt, 1958) should be of interest to scientific researchers.

In this book, she makes a distinction between the *vita contemplativa* and the *vita activa*. Regarding the latter, she introduces a distinction between *labour*, *work*, and *action*. Labour is the activity that serves the needs of human subsistence and survival, work is about the production and fabrication of things ('to build and maintain a world fit for human use', Passerin d'Entrèves, 2019, p. 14). As such, the term *work* comes close to the Aristotelian concepts of *poiesis* in relation to *techne*. It is a form of activity that is entirely determined by the goal or product itself, rather than the activity. It is a means to an end. As such, if a particular end can be more easily achieved by other means, a rational person should prefer those other means. If science would only be work, related to the production of publications appearing in high-ranked journals having passed the critical reading of expert reviewers, alternative ways of producing these publications should in fact be preferred by rational scientific people. For example, if focussing on one research topic over another would make one's research more publishable, the wise researcher (again, assuming that doing research is about work, about *poeisis* in relation to *techne*) would select the 'sexier' topic. Another example would be for managers of a lab or department to make decisions about academic contracts (i.e., fixed term versus tenure) based on which arrangement will ultimately result in the largest number of publications. Arguably, hiring fixed-term employees is likely to elicit the perfect amount of anxiety and external pressure to ensure that young employees spend all their available hours on publishing. Heaven forbid they use their time to read, learn, discuss, and explore! Of course, the most effective strategy – which does require a skilled level of deception and concealment – is cheating and fabricating data (for an analysis of a highly illustrative and recent case, see the entry *Diederik Stapel* in Wikipedia, and if you are in the lucky circumstance that you can read Dutch, the book by cultural psychologist Ruud Abma, *De publicatiefabriek* (*The publication factory;* Abma, 2013) is highly recommended).

All these strategies relate to a self-referential utilitarian view on the praxis of science, which entails that the ultimate goal of scientific work is in the production of scientific publications. The quality of this particular product, the publication, is then defined by the number of times it is quoted in other scientific publications. Unfortunately, this slightly absurd, autopoietic scenario comes eerily close to the daily reality of many researchers, especially (but not limited to) young academics in the tenure track or stuck in a series of fixed-term contracts. Researchers in these situations are far too often judged (of course not solely, but often primarily) by their number of publications, and the level of their impact (i.e., impact factor of the journal, or citation rate of the article).

We (and many others, of course, e.g., Moosa, 2018) wonder what kind of limitations these values are placing on the praxis of doing science? Are we not witnessing a drift toward psychological science as purely work (i.e., the production of publications)? We worry that, if scientific activity becomes too focussed on iterative cycles of work, we will increasingly lose sight of the intrinsic value of action, of *phronesis*.

Indeed, the current praxis of science is becoming imbalanced. But it is becoming imbalanced, not because of some external force, but because of the various agents that make up the praxis: us, you, our actions, and choices. The praxis itself is both a result of these agents and their interactions, as well as a battleground of values (see Chapter 12, *Psychological Science as a Complex Dynamic System* for an in-depth illustration of this). We believe it is crucial that we recognize we are taking part in a battle of values, everyday, via our actions. Doing so encourages us to stop, reflect, and stear (where possible) the self-reproductive process of our praxis and the values that become so deeply ingrained in it.

3.3.1 Praxis and the Importance of Appearing: The Responsibility of Free Scientists

A praxis thus includes the products, the drives or values behind these products, and the virtues of doing the actions themselves. In addition, pivotal in all of this is the people themselves that are doing the praxis. People are part of, and create, a community. This is why Arendt's analysis of praxis remains so relevant for our perspective of psychological science. While her analysis was primarily aimed at political action and praxis, the Greek word *polis* that forms the stem of the word *political* originally referred to the structure of the community.

The structure of a community, in the view of Athenian democracy, is the active responsibility of all free men (we would currently say 'of all *members* of the community', the freedom and equality of whom is now, at least in principle, a foundational human right). The community we are focussing on in this book is a community of academics in psychology. This community may of course not be so clearly defined, it may be a rather complex, and fuzzy community, but it is a community nevertheless. The community is, what Arendt called, *the space of appearance*: 'the space where I appear to others as others appear to me, where men … make their appearance explicitly' (Arendt, 1958, pp. 198–199). Hence, as a community of academics, we make our appearance explicit to each other. Appearance, in this case, refers to all actions of academics that are, in some way or another, visible to, perceived by, or affecting others.

This appearance necessarily brings a level of plurality with it, that is, a plurality of researchers who represent a plurality of – equal but separate – views and values. Action is inextricably related to speech. That is to say, every action communicates a certain view or value. While academics in the psychology community often strive hard to keep these views and values separate from their actions, it is mainly the *disclosure* of these views or values that is removed.

As hard as we may try, our actions are speaking to certain realities, reinforcing certain views. Accepting, and indeed embracing, this plurality by means of disclosure, opinion, and debate, allows us to do more with our freedom, and reminds us to be responsible with it. We may thus appear to others in indirect ways via our actions, or more explicitly and openly in answering the question 'researcher, who are you, what do you stand for?'.

If the structure of our academic community is the responsibility of all free members appearing to each other, it is imperative that we – who are free – exercise that responsibility (on the relationship between the praxis-related notion of *habitus* and freedom, see Hilgers, 2009). It is our responsibility to use our voice and actions as tools, as forces, to create and maintain the kind of structure that we value. While it might sound a bit odd to speak of 'free members' in our academic community (there are of course no academic slaves or prisoners, in the literal sense, in our community), there is value in pausing to reflect on this more deeply.

The fundamental property of freedom, in Arendt's sense, is in many ways in conflict with numerous characteristics of current academics. There are indeed many ways in which individual members are not free to pursue the research actions they wish to pursue, to collaborate with whom they wish to collaborate, and to produce the kinds of research output they wish to produce. We are bound and restricted by notions of academic hierarchy and authority, by the pursuit of fame and status, by gender inequality, and by political and societal pressure.

In this way, not all members of our academic community are equally free to take part in the praxis of academics in the same way. Some can move in limited spaces – appearing to fewer or only certain kinds of members. Some are limited in the kinds of virtues of thought they can enjoy – exercising only work and *poiesis* of *techne*, rather than action and *phronesis*. Some have less freedom to act upon the current praxis than others, constrained to iterations of the same type of actions rather than innovating and changing the praxis.

In this way, it truly is the role of free members of the community to take advantage of that freedom – appearing to others and actively creating the structure of the praxis that has the most value. Action thus requires free participants to be involved in communication, collaboration, debate, creation of ideas and practices, education and initiation of new members of the community, scientific virtues, societal responsibility, accountability and so forth. The pressure of production (i.e., publish or perish) is already a force that stands in the way of freedom for too many members of the academic community.

Therefore, it is the right and the responsibility of those who are free to uphold Arendt's fundamental principle of *natality*, which means the introduction of new researchers and scholars into the existing community. According to Arendt, human activities – labour, work, and action – are 'intimately connected with the most general condition of human existence: birth and death, natality and mortality' (Arendt, 1958, p. 8). Of the three forms of activities, 'action has the closest connection with the human condition of natality; the new beginning inherent in birth can make itself felt in the world only because the newcomer possesses the capacity of beginning something new, that is, of acting' (Arendt, 1958, p. 9). In the polis of academics, the newcomer is of course not the newborn child, but the PhD student and early-career researcher. These are the individuals with the quintessential promise and possibility for something new (which does not stand in the way of the existing members of the community to innovate, but instead, can carry the load of their personal histories and the relative closure that inevitably comes with that). In light of Arendt's emphasis on the notion of natality, the education and introduction of new members, new researchers, are crucial aspects of action – praxis – in science (for a critical analysis of how young scholars are introduced in their scientific community, see Billig, 2013, Chapter 3).

The current drift in psychological science (and other scientific disciplines for that matter) toward the mode of work and production threatens to transform natality from that which promises the unexpected and the creative, to yet another product of *theoria*. We risk treating PhD students and postdocs as commodities that contribute to academic CVs and to departmental output – thereby actually preventing fundamental innovation from occurring.

3.3.2 A Community Within a Community: The Responsibility of Science in Creating Worlds

A scientific community, for instance of academic psychologists, exists as part of the larger public community. The actions of the scientific community are always in close interaction with this public community. This interaction is often viewed as including 'practice' or 'applied science', such as applications in the form of psychotherapies and educational technology. This relationship between science and the public community resembles the typical product-related part of scientific activity (the work aspect, or *techne*, the making of things such as tests or therapies). Of equal, if not greater, importance, is the 'inter-action' with the public community.

A scientific community 'inter-acts' with, or on, the public community in its ability to establish and reinforce a particular ontology – type of reality – of psychological matters. Psychology in particular has played an enormous role in the formation of public ideas, concepts, and values since its rapid spread that began at the start of the past century. We are referring here to the ideas that are held about the nature of psychological phenomena and properties; about mental illness, about personality, about intelligence, about success and talent, about what makes us similar to each other and what makes us different. In that sense, psychology has had a direct formative influence on the self-disclosure of the members of the public community, on their identities as psychological beings. What we are today, as members of a larger community, is (to a very considerable extent) equal to what the psychological-science community has told us to be, and by implication, what we think we have always been as humans.

Concepts such as intelligence, personality, depression are not just discussed and used in our academic community, they pervade public life, manifested in advice, criticisms, aspirations, and explanations. This kind of osmosis of concepts is, in itself, a positive thing. Indeed, the last thing that the scientific community should be is an isolated community – the ivory tower metaphor. However, as we shall explore in Chapters 4 and 6, concepts and facts (their meaning and implications) are not simply straightforward or objective things. They are the result of a particular way of construing reality that informs (and is informed by) *how* knowledge is constructed. This process of knowledge construction is entangled in a particular ontology. Facts are not just facts, they carry with them an implicit network of beliefs and assumptions about the way the world is, about the nature of reality.

As we wish to make explicit in this book, the particular ontology that psychology has imposed on the public community is that of substance ontology (i.e., an ontology of enduring, a-temporal entities) (see Chapter 1 for our introduction to substance ontology). With this comes a certain disregard for, or ignorance to, notions of change, of transformation, and of individual development as a complex and creative sort of process (we use the term 'individual' in the generic sense, thus also in the sense of particular families, schools, and so forth). As we will discuss in Chapter 6, researchers create and reinforce these ontologies through their communication and presentation of their research results.

All this concerns 'ethical' matters, in Aristotle's sense of the word, and matters of scientific virtue that are deeply intertwined with the way psychological science is done, the questions it asks, and the methods it uses. In the following section, we wish to make the case that any praxis of science is in fact constructivist: we construct norms, values, knowledge systems as we take part in this thing that we call psychological science. The norms, values, and knowledge systems that make up a particular praxis, in return, can take on different forms (which we explore in the remainder of this book). To understand the foundations of a constructivist praxis, we examine the science-action relationship in the science and technology studies (STS) literature, and in particular in the work of Bruno Latour.

3.4 The Constructivist, or 'Practice Turn', in the Theory of Science

In some ways, the above emphasis on the virtues of doing science, of action, sketches a picture of an atypical praxis for science. For many, the aim of science is quite obviously to produce facts – true facts – about our world. Period. For some, the aim of science is 'to discover the relations among the natural kinds in the universe that exist independently of our minds and ways of coping' (Dreyfus, 2005, p. 159). This particular stance is called robust realism, and is a strong variant of realism (there are, of course, thus also lighter variants) – obviously not held by all psychologists. For psychologists, the dominant view is scientific realism (Stedman et al., 2016). Shortly, scientific realism entails 'an epistemically positive attitude toward the outputs of scientific investigation, regarding both observable and unobservable aspects of the world'. (Chakravartty, 2017, p. 1). That is, it entails a belief in the reality of the things that we observe, such as a person struggling with items on an IQ test, and things that we infer from those observations, such as intelligence.

In line with our own personal views about realism (described in Chapter 1), we further sketch our preferred praxis as one that acknowledges the embedded nature of our facts and our actions, of the constructive processes of generating truths. As such, we propose a deviation from the norm – from strict scientific realism. Specifically, a deviation in the direction of, what Dreyfus has called, deflationary realism (Dreyfus, 2005; and for a discussion of the relationship between deflationary realism and the dynamics of scientific knowledge, see Chapter 7 in Rouse, 1996). This view stresses that the constructs we study are close enough to reality because the process of producing and understanding these concepts was done as an interactive process, between real people, real problems and suffering, in real social and cultural contexts. Instead of the somewhat derogatory predicate 'deflational', we prefer the term *critical realism* (explained in Chapter 1). This viewpoint thus places all knowledge in the context of our actions as researchers, and all our interactions with material and immaterial actors. These interactions, and their part in the construction of a praxis, are made clear by Bruno Latour's notion of a praxis as a network of actions, interactions, material, and people.

3.4.1 Bruno Latour and a Praxis as Actor Network

Bruno Latour (born 1947) is a French philosopher, who is probably best known for his work in science and technology studies. Law (2017) describes that this field of research seeks to answer the following questions: 'How do science and technology shape the world? Or medicine and engineering? How does the world in turn shape them? And how, if at all, might we intervene in these processes? ... STS authors tackle them by asking how *science (and technology) work in practice*'. (Law, 2017, p. 31; italics by current authors.)

Latour conceives of science as an actor network, or to use a more precise term, an *actant* network, since the actors need not be persons (Harman, 2009; Latour, 1996, 2005; Law, 2004, 2017). We will use the word *agent* instead of *actant*. In a psychology lab, for instance, the researchers are of course agents, but so are their computers, the people they call the 'subjects' of experiments, the articles that the researchers are reading and writing, the theories on which the articles contribute, the coffee cups and the occasional house plants, the books on the shelves, and so forth. Agents exist by virtue of their being *active*, that is to say of their acting with other agents. For this reason, all agents are in principle on the same footing, in that they can become important or unimportant for the main course of the process depending on what they actually do in the context of what other agents are doing in the here and now. All agents are processes, events, and the way they are interacting with others changes over time.

With this in mind, if one wishes to understand the nature of a particular scientific fact, for instance, one must study the process of interactions between agents connected to that fact. Doing so reveals the historical and cultural processes that gave rise to the fact, as well as the ways in which the fact, itself, is an actor in this network. A fact, then, is not a static thing, but a process that is dynamically interconnected with other dynamic agents (or processes). This line of logic can be extended from one single fact to an entire praxis.

Latour's position is constructivist in the sense that he considers scientific facts (or truths, or theories, or whatever else one sees as the outcome of scientific research) as being constructed by agents. This implies that the form, content, meaning and effect of such scientific facts must be understood in the context of these constructive processes (note the critical-realist stance implied). As such, there is no scientific 'outcome' that is free from the agents that were part of the constructive process, no 'truth' that is separate from the reality in which it was constructed. In this way, a 'truth' does not have an obligation to be universally true, as it is only compliant with the constraints put upon it by the agents and the reality in which they act.

A constructivist stance, in particular that of actant network theory, is often criticized for its being indifferent to the distinction between truths and falsehoods, of being an 'anything goes' theory. The worry, often, is that acknowledging the constructed nature of our truths (again, results, or theories that emerge from research) legitimizes the denial of empirical facts, such as global warming and COVID-19. This criticism, however, is flawed because it denies the totality of interactions upon which truth and facts are built. Indeed, just because parallel truths exist (in their respective networks of agents) does not mean that they are equally feasible and worthy of wider belief. To assess which truths are worth believing, one must understand the network from which a certain truth emerges – a stance that is central in Latour's reasoning.

To make a comparison, a bridge made of straw and bridge made of metal are both examples of social constructions (we could also use the three houses of the little pigs here, as an equally illustrative example). It is obvious that there's no place for 'anything goes' when it comes to putting weight on, indeed *using* these constructed objects for our subsequent decisions. Obviously, the straw bridge will collapse once we set foot on it, while the metal bridge will not. In deciding which bridge to 'believe in', one must explicitly reckon with how its agents interact with and support one another, with the constructive process that gave way to the structure, and with their likely ability to resist gravity or pressure. In the same way, if 'alternative facts' are maintained solely by virtue of their interactions with political power agents, then they are, by definition, facts of political power. If, instead, the process of construction takes place within the interactions between empirical agents, such as persons – 'subjects' and 'researchers' – and the materials used in laboratory experiments, then the facts are empirical facts. The two lines of facts can co-exist as parallel processes of knowledge construction (which will be demonstrated in the following two chapters, which reveal and contrast two praxes of self-esteem research). This comparison clarifies why people, things, and actions are all part of the actor network, and why all of the agents need to be considered when determining which facts we want to rely on: 'Microbes, neutrinos or DNA are at the same time natural, social and discourse. They are real, human and semiotic entities in the same breath' (Latour, 1996, p 369).

It should be clear at this point that some truths are stronger (i.e., resting on more expansive networks of agents and the checks between them) than others. Constructing a viable truth, therefore, requires a considerable amount of – mostly collective – effort. Latour relates the strength or power of scientific facts to the relationships they bear with their *allies*, that is, supporting agents. In the case of global warming or COVID-19 for instance, the scientists' allies consist of an intricate network of relationships between observations, readings of instruments, statistical calculations, many other researchers, and so forth. There are thus more allies (both in numbers and in types) of global-warming facts than there are for global-warming deniers (for whom the allies are primarily political) (for discussion see Stengers, 2015).

Latour's notion of co-existing truths, entangled in dynamic networks of actants that keep these truths in place and further reinforce them, is compatible with the Complex Dynamic Systems concept of attractor states co-existing in the same attractor landscape, and of the interaction between components and the intrinsic dynamics that strengthen certain attractors (see Chapter 2 for our introduction of these terms). We focus explicitly on this idea for psychological science, and the co-existing process and substance praxes that belong to it, in Chapter 12.

3.4.2 Inscription Devices as Active Agents

In their book *Laboratory Life: the Construction of Scientific Facts* (1979), Latour and Woolgar describe the processes of scientific research as they were observed by Latour at the Salk Institute in San Diego in the mid-1970s. Researchers rely heavily on the use of tools or instruments that transform particular types of phenomena into inscriptions, which can be numbers, graphs, categorical terms, and so forth (see also Law, 2004, for an insightful analysis). These tools are called *inscription devices* and they are necessary to construct scientific facts.

In psychology, such inscription devices typically take a wide variety of forms, for instance measurement or categorization instruments in the form of tests, such as intelligence tests, or self-esteem questionnaires. Other examples are devices for stimulus presentation and response time measurement. Still others are categorical assessment systems, such as DSM-V for psychiatric and psychological assessment, consisting of checklists and clinical questions to clients. The list goes on with coding systems for video-recorded events, including lightweight wireless video cameras and microphones, or smartphone apps for experience sampling.

These devices allow for, and constrain, certain types of truths. Smart phones, for example, made the experience-sampling technique possible in a way that was not possible before this technological advancement, which in return has made truths pertaining to the day-to-day dynamics of psychological experiences possible. Questionnaires, as another example, constrain the answers that participants can provide, and thus the kind of information that forms truths about the concept in question. Inscription devices are therefore not just a means to an end, instead they create affordances for the end; they are meaningful agents in the network of facts and their construction.

The use of such inscription devices is of course closely related to the term 'measurement', which is the assignment of numbers or categories to a particular phenomenon. We do not wish to use this term here, however, as 'measurement' implies, first, the existence of something that can be measured, and second, that the properties of the measurements taken reflect the nature of that which we are measuring. Applying the word *measurement* to a particular activity therefore implies a great number of assumptions. We will delve into the assumptions behind measurement and the implications for the praxis of psychological science in Chapters 9, 10 and 11. What we would like to stress in the current chapter is that the concepts, tools and theories of psychology can be understood only by focussing on the processes by which they are created, used, given meaning, transformed, made public, and so forth. Put differently, the question of 'true' facts and our collective 'knowledge' must be understood in a processual framework.

3.4.3 An Anti-Reductionist View of Truth and Meaning

Latour's philosophy of science is anti-reductionist in the sense that no phenomenon, agent (or 'actant'), or event can (or must) be reduced to another. This contrasts the reductionist thinking that can be observed in psychology at times. For example, it is common to view mental properties as causes of underlying biological-neurological-material properties, implying that what a person does (the pathological behaviour, for example) can be reduced to what their brain does (also known as the mereological fallacy, see Smit and Hacker, 2014). While promoting irreducibility is not necessarily new, Latour's view of irreducibility goes as far as to suggest the irreducibility of basically every event. For example, a child solving a particular simple science problem at one moment in time in the classroom is seen as different from solving another simple science problem at a later moment. There is no reducibility to an underlying 'cognitive structure' or 'knowledge'. These things are radically different, they are what they are.

Yet, for our understanding of reality, connections must of course be made. We aim to understand how concepts and events relate to each other – connect. Latour referred to this 'connecting' as *translation*. While most modern-day researchers would of course state that they too are making connections between concepts, theories, or events, it is often the case that, once a pivotal connection has been discovered, the intermediary steps (i.e., interactions between agents) are discarded as transient means to an end. The ultimate aim, then, is all too often to discover a *direct* relationship between two things; for example, between consciousness and the brain – ultimately reducing consciousness to the brain. All intermediary translation steps and interactions between agents, to do with measurement, concrete events, or experiences, are just ways of discovering these immediate (unmediated) real and timeless relationships between objective phenomena. This kind of connection is different from Latour's, where the aim is to connect various sorts of phenomena, which are then also connected to other networks. This *whole* network, for Latour, constitutes the true knowledge of a phenomenon, such as a conscious thought.

3.4.4 The Enactment of Ontologies

If our knowledge and truths are socially constructed, embedded in networks of people, material, actions, and interactions, it then becomes pertinent to consider the *nature* of that knowledge. What we hope to show in this book, more generally, is that a praxis represents, creates, does, and maintains certain ontologies – certain realities. A praxis, in this way, *enacts* ontologies. The term *enactment* stresses two things. First, how each action (and the larger praxis of which it is part of) demonstrates a process of the 'bringing forth of meaning from a background of understanding' (Varela, Thompson & Rosch, 2016, p. 149). We take 'meaning', for our current purposes, to refer to what we know to be true in the field of psychology: how we define concepts, what it means to know or understand them, what valuable knowledge or understanding is. Let us then think about a 'background of understanding' as the knowledge and assumptions we – as psychologists – have thus far developed about what psychological phenomena are and how they can be 'known'. With this, to 'enact an ontology' might first and foremost mean that a research action brings forth these basic assumptions that have thus far emerged; it displays them and generates a concrete manifestation of them.

To 'enact' is so much more than simply *reflecting* a certain ontology, however. If our actions as scientists were solely reflections of a substance versus process ontology, or of the overarching praxis that correspond with these ontologies, we would be mere 'cogs and wheels in the machinery of the "mental institution"' that is psychological science (p. 21), as De Jaegher (2013) described in her arguments against an extended-mind account of institutions. With this description, De Jaegher argued against viewing individuals – and our actions – as passive and static, and as reduced to following ready-made rules, guidelines, and a general structure. Therefore, the second part of the notion of enaction is dynamic and active – in line with Latour's 'actants': while our scientific actions emerge within the constraints of assumed and practiced ontologies (and thus 'reflect' ontologies), our actions also construct and maintain ontologies.

To fully understand the dynamic and active aspect of enaction, it is useful to refer back to the original use of the term enaction in psychology. The notion of enactment was introduced to mainstream psychology in 1991 by Varela, Thompson & Rosch (2016), who focussed on cognition and perception. Varela and colleagues, and now many others (e.g., Thompson, 2007; Di Paolo, 2005, 2009; De Jaegher & Rohde, 2010; Di Paolo, Rohde & De Jaegher, 2010) proposed that cognition is not the internal processing of objective information that exists outside of the individual. Instead, cognition is an ongoing activity that is shaped by experiences in the world. From an enactivist perspective, we do not ever come to know an objective reality. In line with critical realism, enaction seems to follow the tenets of epistemological relativism; that our knowledge about a reality is dependent on our interactions with the world. Enactivism, therefore, contrasts the intransitivity assumption that underlines positivism (for more discussion on positivism, see Chapter 1). Instead, enactivism emphasises that to 'enact' knowledge is not to retrieve information about an objective and true reality, but to create a subjective experience of a reality. The reality that is experienced can thus never be universally known because it is always changing based on our interactions with it thus far. Knowledge never 'is', but is always 'becoming'.

To summarize, we *enact* ontologies in two ways: on the one hand, scientific actions emerge within particular ontologies and thus display its basic assumptions. On the other hand, scientific actions also create (or further solidify, or work to deviate from) the basic ontological assumptions and idiosyncrasies of constructs.

While much of the enactivist literature concerns the construction of knowledge at the individual level, where knowledge is seen as being more than static representations of an objective reality that exists and can be known (i.e., positivism), we are thus expanding the term 'to enact' to the context of a broader psychological science. Indeed, 'science is a particular form of social knowledge construction' (Rohde, 2010, p. 30).

The concept of enaction thus stresses that our scientific actions are more than internalizations of rules that stem from 'the' correct way of doing science. The concept of enaction, to us, stresses that scientific actions are our (i.e., psychologists') way of engaging with, making sense of, and establishing basic assumptions about psychological phenomena; assumptions about what a concept is and what it means to 'know' it. We may think of our actions as a means to an end – namely, to generate knowledge – but these actions themselves are so much more than just this, as they belong to a larger praxis that reflects or demonstrates what we assume about the ontology of that knowledge. At the same time, these very actions are also creating the very fundamentals of said knowledge.

3.5 Foundations Set

In this chapter we have laid the groundwork for the rest of the chapters in this book, to a practice-theoretical view of psychological science as a process of connected activities. Our choice to refer to 'praxis' in this book, rather than to 'paradigms', for example, stems from the rich philosophical history that stresses the processual and action-based nature of what we do in psychological science and how we do it, and our wish to revive this perspective. To this end, we started with philosophical foundations of action, practice, and productivity of human agents. We then discussed Latour's theory of actant networks, highlighting how basically all researchers, members of the public, inscription devices, actions, and events are potentially contributing to the praxis of psychological science as a whole. In the chapters to follow, we explore in more depth what these agents may be, and how their interactions can reflect and emerge into two very different types of praxes: one that enacts a substance ontology and one that enacts a process ontology, and how these have substantial consequences for agents within and outside of psychological science.

Social and professional structures, methodologies, concepts, rules and habits, facts, knowledge, applications are constantly created and re-created by the activities of all participants in a particular type of practice, that is, a community of practitioners. In Chapters 4 and 5, we explore the notion of *enacting an ontology*, and illustrate how agents that we often assume to be the 'norm', 'correct', or the 'best' are actually part of a complex web of practices, assumptions, and values. In Chapter 4, we describe the mainstream web of practices for a concrete topic of research – namely self-esteem, and explain how it enacts a substance ontology, and in Chapter 5 we describe how this is the case for the enactment of a process ontology.

CHAPTER 4

Esteeming Entities
Enacting a Substance Ontology in Self-Esteem Research[*]

> In an age where there is much talk about 'being yourself' I reserve to myself the right to forget about being myself, since in any case there is very little chance of my being anybody else. Rather it seems to me that when one is too intent on 'being himself' he runs the risk of impersonating a shadow.
> Thomas Merton, 'Day of a Stranger', *The Hudson Review*, Vol. 20, No. 2 (Summer, 1967), pp. 211–218

Most psychologists do not deeply contemplate the philosophical foundations of their everyday *doings*. As we plan, conduct, and interpret empirical results, we are unlikely to ask ourselves 'what are the philosophical assumptions implied by my choice of methodology'? or 'what does my research question assume about the nature of reality'? Indeed, to many it may seem that abstract philosophies have little relevance to our individual process of doing empirical research. This chapter (and the following chapter, Chapter 5) illustrates the critical realism stance adopted throughout this book (described in Chapter 1): investigating the ontologies we – as psychological scientists – are operating with when we empirically study psychological phenomena, and thus how philosophical assumptions are interwoven into our everyday research actions – whether we are aware of them or not. In this chapter and the next, I will also evaluate the consequences (for our research output and our everyday lives) of adopting certain ontological and epistemological assumptions.

4.1 A Critical-Realism Stance toward Praxes

When we go about selecting literature, developing our next idea for an empirical study, developing research designs, and selecting methodological

---
[*] This is a single-authored chapter written by Naomi De Ruiter. For this reason, the chapter makes use of first-person singular pronouns.

methods, these choices reflect, construct, and constrain the kind of knowledge we generate about reality. In other words, with our seemingly minute, arbitrary, or inconsequential actions, we are taking part in a collective process of knowledge construction that construes our psychological reality in a particular way.

A choice for any specific research action then, should not be viewed as only the result of our individual considerations in the moment, but as part of a larger praxis shared across many individuals and having evolved over time. As we first discussed in Chapter 3, a praxis refers to psychological science as a community of academics, their interactions, and their patterns of activity. Activity includes actual acts (types of things people do), but also the values, hierarchies, routines, structures of power and influence, learning and education (i.e., the introduction of novices to the praxis of psychological research), actual products (findings and bits and pieces of knowledge), as well as applied practices (psychological testing, clinical therapy, and so forth). A praxis thus occurs on all possible (highly connected) timescales, from minutes to centuries. At the smallest timescale, we emphasize or neglect facts and theories each time that we select an article to read or teach, and within this, when we select the most relevant sections of the article. Across years, we neglect whole lines of research and put others in a focal position. Over decades, schools of thought become fundamental to how we see ourselves and our goals as scientists, while other scientific disciplines are forgotten or discredited. Moreover, a praxis can be conceived of as a *living* praxis, in the sense that it is continuously changing (whether the change is that of reinforcing and solidifying itself or evolving and adapting, which we explore more in Chapter 12). The praxis to which each individual action of each individual scientist belongs, can then be seen as having an emergent and constructivist function.

Irrespective of the praxis that we enact with each of our discrete action(s), researchers are generally trying to do what is 'correct' in the context of gaining knowledge. As researchers, undertaking 'correct' actions is thought to bring us closer to the truth. A psychology student, for example, is taught how to correctly conduct inferential statistics so as to avoid Type I or Type II errors, among other things. Prescribed actions may then include being conservative in selecting a significance level, using a large sample size, checking assumptions of homogeneity, linearity, or normality. Most psychology students will go through an entire trajectory of statistics courses thinking that these actions ensure that they will conduct their research 'correctly' and that their research will thus generate 'true knowledge'.

What is often referred to quite generally as 'psychological research methodology', is, however, part of a very specific praxis, the mainstream praxis. As I will show in this chapter, this particular praxis enacts a deeper metaphysical assumption of a substance ontology. This assumption is enacted in the variable-oriented and nomothetic focus of psychological research, and in the large-scale sampling and inferential statistics that go with this focus. The enactment of a metaphysical assumption, however, is not a reflexive process; it is not a choice per se. Instead, educators teach a certain type of knowledge system and methodology frameworks because these are the ones that are collectively acknowledged as the most 'correct'.

While there is nothing inherently wrong with a psychological praxis that puts a strong emphasis on inferential statistics, for example, teaching solely within this praxis neglects the fact that there are disparate ontologies that can be assumed when doing psychological science. Each assumed ontology corresponds with its own assumptions about how we should go about trying to understand reality. Thus, engaging in 'correct' actions (i.e., following the rules that were taught to us in our undergraduate studies) will lead to true knowledge within a very specific set of ontological assumptions. The actions are then 'correct' insofar as they generate truth and knowledge within a specific understanding of what the nature of psychological reality is.

4.2 Self-Esteem Research as a Case Study

To make my analysis of praxes as concrete as possible, I will take self-esteem research as a case study in this chapter and the next. In both chapters I will analyse the concrete *doings* of self-esteem research (from research aims, operational definitions, measurements, analyses, to empirical findings) to elucidate the underlying ontological assumptions that are enacted. In this chapter, I will examine mainstream self-esteem research, showing how it enacts a substance ontology across each step of the research cycle. Afterwards, in Chapter 5, I will examine the praxis of alternative self-esteem research, showing that it enacts a process ontology.

Self-esteem is an ideal candidate for such an analysis, as it is an exceptionally prevalent construct in modern psychology (Zeigler-Hill, 2013). Self-esteem continues to gain immense academic attention as a relevant correlate for traits and behaviour, from leadership style (Matzler, Bauer & Mooradian, 2015) to binge drinking (Bartsch et al., 2017). It also remains a key target in therapy, from treatment of ADHD (Castelnau et al., 2017) to anorexia nervosa (Adamson et al., 2019). Levy (2019) has even suggested that we continue to be 'obsessed' with self-esteem. Interestingly, for a phenomenon that receives so much attention we also have a very poor understanding of it. Levy (2019) suggests that a key reason for why we still don't quite understand self-esteem is 'a deficit in critical thinking' (p. 330). Specifically, he suggests that we are not sufficiently critical of the words we use to define and characterize self-esteem, of the ways in which we measure self-esteem, and how we communicate findings about self-esteem. As a result, we have many facts about self-esteem, but little in-depth understanding about what self-esteem is and how it functions.

Like Levy's (2019) critique, others have stressed that self-esteem is a relatively atheoretical field, including Scheff and Fearon (2004) and Strandell (2017). Self-esteem research is thus a useful context for making the implicit *explicit*, and for making the atheoretical *theoretical*. Theoretical and critical questions that deserve to be explicitly discussed concern the ontology and epistemology of self-esteem; questions like: What are our assumptions or beliefs – implicit or explicit – that we have with regard to what 'self-esteem' really is? In what way is it experienced, or known, by us in our everyday lives? And how does our empirical research contribute to these expectations and experiences? In my critical-realist analysis of self-esteem, I hope to touch upon such questions. In doing so, I hope to contribute to the understanding of *why* we know what we know (or don't know) about self-esteem. With these chapters, I hope to invite readers to adopt a critical-realist stance in the context of their own research actions; to ask the kinds of reflexive questions illustrated in the opening of this chapter.

With these chapters, I argue that much of what self-esteem researchers are ultimately interested in necessitates a process-ontology perspective, but that there is also room for a collaboration between this perspective and a substance-ontology perspective. As such, this chapter contributes to the idea of a pluralist approach to scientific aims and methodology, as argued by Chang (2017), in this case for self-esteem research. For this to be possible, I argue that self-esteem researchers must be cognizant about the assumption they adopt going into their research, and the relationship between these assumptions and their scientific aims and methodology.

It is important to stress that the following descriptions of ontological assumptions, connected to the common practices in self-esteem research, are not necessarily explicitly held by researchers. Throughout the chapter I will examine how linguistic norms, measurements, and analyses of self-esteem *reflect* or *imply* certain assumptions about the ontology of self-esteem. The 'ontology' of self-esteem is generally not the focus of common self-esteem research, nor are theories of self-esteem ontology used explicitly to inform methodological choices. These assumptions are therefore not necessarily views that mainstream self-esteem researchers would endorse or even recognize (although perhaps they would upon further reflection). It is therefore not my

4.2 Self-Esteem Research as a Case Study

intention to describe how self-esteem researchers explicitly think about self-esteem. Instead, I intend to show how their practices enact certain ontologies.

4.2.1 On the Nature of Self-Esteem from a Substance-Ontology Perspective

The praxis that I will first unpack with regard to its enactment is that which enacts a *substance ontology*. A substance ontology was described in Chapter 1, but for the sake of completeness, I will reiterate it here. This ontology implies that psychological phenomena are independent, stable, permanent, universal and enduring entities. Moreover, these entities are thought to *underlie* any fleeting and non-enduring appearances of the phenomenon that we might observe. Fleeting observations are thus *expressions* of the entity and are thus separate from the entity itself.

A result of implicitly enacting ontologies is that the enactment of a substance ontology in mainstream self-esteem research does not resemble some kind of formal theoretical model that coherently connects all mainstream self-esteem research. As we will see in this chapter, the various details around this ontology can thus often be characterized as 'fuzzy' reflections of a substance ontology. Few assumptions that I will discuss below reflect the foundations of a substance ontology, while others loosely enact some version of a it.

The boundaries of what belongs to a particular 'substance' is a topic of historical debate (for a concise overview, see Robinson, 2020). At the foundation of discussions of *substances* is Aristotle's distinction between *primary substances* and *secondary substances*. Primary substances are individual entities (i.e., Naomi's self-esteem), and secondary substances are kinds of entities with universal laws (i.e., self-esteem). As I will show, some research practices enact (aspects of) the former, some enact (aspects of) the latter, and some enact a relationship between the two. There are various conceptualizations for how primary and secondary substances relate specifically (e.g., MacBride, 2013), and research practices are similarity divergent in the exact relationship they enact. In Aristotle's scheme, primary substances are also called *particulars* – for example, a particular person, or a particular person's self-esteem. Secondary substances are called *universals*, because they are common to every particular instance (every person with particular self-esteem shares the universal self-esteem; Mahlan, 2019; Vella, 2008).

Furthermore, research practices differ in how they enact the relationship between a substance (primary or secondary) and its *property*; for example, the substance 'self-esteem' and the property 'stable'. An Aristotelian perspective of primary substances is that an individual entity is separate from its properties. The entity thus *under-lies* its properties. This is the literal meaning of the term *substance* (i.e., 'under'-'stand', as described in Chapter 1). The term 'substance' therefore does not refer to a physical substance, but to the thing that underlies (under-stands) ephemeral instances or events (Bickhard, 2009a). To avoid confusion, I will therefore use the term 'entity' to refer to the primary substance of self-esteem (or an *individual's* self-esteem).

In contrast, Locke's account of primary substances was that these properties are part of these individual entities, such that the entities' properties make it what it essentially is. Even the interpretations of what Aristotle and Locke believed to be true of primary substances remains a matter of controversy amongst philosophers of science (Robinson, 2020).

In my analysis, I will show that the various enactments of an ontology in mainstream self-esteem research form a conceptual family, one of a broad substance ontology. It is of course logical that each discrete enactment of a substance ontology in self-esteem research is only loosely connected to the next, given that common research practices are not explicitly grounded in reflections of self-esteem ontology, nor are these studies explicitly aimed at understanding the ontology of self-esteem. Indeed, as described above, self-esteem research has been characterized as uniquely *lacking* critical self-reflection and strong theoretical foundations (Levy, 2019; Scheff & Fearon, 2004; Strandell, 2017).

In my analysis of self-esteem research, I will begin with the ways in which researchers operationalize and measure individual instances of self-esteem (i.e., primary substances), and I will then describe how this is then used to reveal a universal self-esteem as a secondary substance.

4.2.1.1 Conceptualizing Self-Esteem: Self-Esteem as a 'Thing' That We 'Have'

A conceptualization of self-esteem as a secondary (i.e., universal) substance is most broadly enacted when researchers *reify* self-esteem, meaning that an abstract thing is regarded as a concrete thing that exists universally. Self-esteem thus becomes a kind of 'thing', a thing that we all 'have'. As Schiff (2017) described it, 'it is as if the person were the vessel for a plethora of substances, like vapors or liquids, that are concealed inside them. We all have more or less shyness, motivation, self-esteem, or prejudice' (p. 3).

This reification is demonstrated in the common linguistic approach to the construct of self-esteem. Self-esteem is often referred to as a noun. For example, a psychologist might say 'I study self-esteem'. Self-esteem is implicitly treated like an object, some kind of disembodied thing that can be studied as an objective variable with quantitative dimensions (Raeff, 2019). Moreover, this reified disembodied object that is self-esteem is often thought to *do* things, for example, Brown and Marshall (2001) state that the 'function of self-esteem is to regulate feelings of self-worth' (p. 582). With this conceptualization, self-esteem is not the act of feeling something about one's self and its worth, it is the thing that *regulates* this process of feeling. It is as if self-esteem 'somehow becomes an inanimate object that is capable of complex human activity' (Raeff, 2010, p. 36, where Raeff was originally referring to 'self' rather than 'self-esteem', although the description remains equally applicable). Cigman (2004) refers to this view of self-esteem as the *simple* self-esteem: an attribute of minds, quantifiable, a project of boosting, and having causality (which she contrasts with *situated* self-esteem, discussed more in the next chapter).

Similarly, Levy (2019) points out that 'it's easy to forget that self-esteem is not some objective *thing* that an individual actually "has" (although it can be tempting to regard it as such); rather, it is a hypothetical concept that we have created to help us organize and make sense out of people's behavior' (p. 325).

The following sections unpack the details of the primary-substance ontology as enacted in research practices.

4.2.1.2 Capturing Self-Esteem: Questionnaires

When conducting research, *inscription devices* are necessary (introduced in Chapter 3, also discussed in Chapter 9). These are tools for transforming phenomena into inscriptions, such as numbers, graphs, categorical terms, and so forth, so that researchers can communicate their findings to each other. In psychology, inscription devices are most often scales, which are thought to capture some kind of *quantifiable* immaterial substance that can be measured with some margin of error (Schiff, 2017; see also Chapter 11).

This is certainly the case for self-esteem, which is treated as something that we can measure in the same way as we might try to measure someone's height or weight (Cigman, 2004). Mainstream research on self-esteem predominantly relies on questionnaires, such as the widely used Rosenberg Self-esteem Scale (Rosenberg, 1965). This self-esteem scale, like most others, provides a unidimensional measure of self-esteem. The scale ranges from 0 to 30, with higher scores representing higher self-esteem.

Scales such as these are often utilized with the assumption that self-esteem exists independently of us measuring it. The point-like values that are derived from these scales (i.e., a 'high' score of 25) are thought to be meaningful in the sense that they represent something that *is*. Mainstream self-esteem researchers thus aim to tap into this property via the self-esteem scale, such that the scale should offer a valid and reliable measurement irrespective of where or when they are filling in the questionnaire (i.e., at home, in a laboratory). When self-esteem scales are used in this way, the researcher is adopting an *objectivist* perspective, which is the notion that facts – and knowledge in general – correspond directly to reality (i.e., *direct* or *epistemological realism* as opposed to *epistemological relativism*) (Holden & Lynch, 2004). This level of self-esteem is thus *there* waiting to be measured, as it were, and the measurement corresponds with that which was waiting to be measured.

While self-esteem scales are frequently used, they are also frequently criticized by mainstream self-esteem researchers (e.g., Paulhus, 2002). Specifically, the concern is that these scales may elicit a reactivity effect, where they 'may stimulate [participants] to consider the topic [of self-worth] in a new way, or even prompt them to formulate an opinion when they previously had none' (Levy, 2019, p. 316). Moreover, this is worrying to many self-esteem researchers as it suggests that these scales 'might fail to express [their self-view] due to self-presentational pressures that tempt them to inflate their self-evaluations' (Buhrmester, Blanton & Swann, 2011, p. 365). This criticism clearly reflects the objectivist stance toward self-esteem, namely, that there is a real, underlying self-view that researchers are attempting to measure.

Next to the assumption (or hope) that self-esteem scales are objectively tapping into something that is independent of us measuring it, these scales directly imply the nature of the 'something'. Specifically, researchers use these scales to determine 'how much' self-esteem someone has; a question that assumes that self-esteem has a quantitative structure; that it exists in static quantities (Maul, 2013). Researchers thus measure the level of someone's self-esteem in the same way that they would measure how much money someone has, where both are seen as desirable substances to have. Having 'a lot' of self-esteem is thus better than having 'little' self-esteem.

Moreover, this 'amount' is assumed to be relatively stable, such that the researcher is measuring a persistent and true level of self-esteem (perhaps with some measurement error). The amount of self-esteem that individuals have is thus treated as an essence of who they are. Person A and Person B are thus different from each other in that Person A has a high self-esteem score of 25 and Person B has a low self-esteem score of 10. Furthermore, Person A is similar to other individuals who have high self-esteem, and Person B is similar to others who have low self-esteem. Because self-esteem scales assume that individuals have a true amount of self-esteem that is directly quantifiable, this inscription device is a clear and quite direct enactment of a substance ontology.

The act of measuring self-esteem using self-esteem questionnaires is perhaps the most strictly protected self-esteem-research 'action' within the substance-ontology praxis. While researchers can of course examine an almost endless array of associations between self-esteem and other variables without their theoretical assumptions being attacked too heavily, there is little to no tolerance of operational definitions of self-esteem other than the rules and procedures surrounding self-esteem questionnaires. This highlights the assumption of a substance ontology, as it implies that any other way of communicating about self-esteem is in fact not communicating about *real* self-esteem.

To illustrate, a reviewer of an empirical paper of ours (which aimed to capture observable experiences of self-esteem during parent–child interactions) questioned our 'self-esteem measurement' and suggested that 'this research is not focussing on self-esteem but rather on what a child experiences with his parents' (the article in question is De Ruiter et al., 2015). To us, this comment represented the common view that self-esteem is a universal essence – substance – that must always be treated as a point-like property that can be measured only in one specific way (not to mention negating the relevance of approaching self-esteem as a situated experience of the self).

Self-esteem researchers thus generate and communicate substance-related knowledge of self-esteem in a number of pivotal ways: the way in which they talk about self-esteem as a thing that people 'have', with their aim to reveal underlying true levels of this psychological substance, with their use of a specific set of scales for measuring self-esteem, with their aim to explain how self-esteem changes across time or differs across individuals depending on various other independent variables, and with their reliance on questionnaires to inscribe objective point-like properties of self-esteem.

4.2.2 In search of 'True' Self-Esteem: Central (Trait) Tendencies and Random (State) Variability

Pivotal to a substance-ontology perspective is the notion that there is an essence, or entity, that underlies observed variability. Moreover, a primary-substance ontology implies that this underlying essence remains the same (remains *there*) even if fleeting contexts result in temporary departures from that permanent underlying essence. From this perspective, the goal of self-esteem researchers is to dig through the 'mess' of the fleeting contexts and temporary deviations from the 'true' level of self-esteem. This 'true' level of self-esteem is thus an individual's underlying self-esteem entity.

4.2.2.1 Trait Self-Esteem

Classically, self-esteem is approached as a point-like property: *trait self-esteem*. The trait self-esteem level is thought to be a reflection of an individual's fundamentally stable 'baseline' level to which they return after deviations (Kernis et al., 1992, Savin-Williams & Demo, 1983). This property is assumed to be ontologically separate from incidental fluctuations (Alessandri et al., 2016). This form of substance ontology thus resembles the Lockean interpretation of a substance ontology, such that an individual's self-esteem entity has a core property. The entity is *not* separate from its property. For example, individual A's true self-esteem is high (i.e., the entity *is* high self-esteem).

There is a growing interest in how this entity is expressed over time, indicating a non-static approach to trait self-esteem. The general assumption here is that trait self-esteem 'under-lies' (i.e., persists amongst) these ups and downs (e.g., Alessandri et al., 2016; Donnellan et al., 2012). This assumption is directly reflected in the methodological choice to assess participants' baseline or stable level of self-esteem by averaging across the ups and downs of self-esteem that individuals experience across contexts (e.g., Oosterwegel et al., 2001). These contextual fluctuations are assumed to result in a kind of 'noise' around (what is assumed to be) a meaningful baseline level of self-esteem (DiDonato et al., 2013). The temporally aggregated self-esteem level is a *central tendency* of self-esteem.

4.2.2.2 Self-Esteem Stability

Aside from the 'average' central tendency, mainstream self-esteem researchers are also interested in another central tendency of self-esteem; *self-esteem stability*. This property refers to the degree to which someone's self-esteem is pushed or pulled away from their stable level of self-esteem in response to contextual information or experiences (Kernis, Grannemann & Barclay, 1989, see Kernis, 2005 for a review). It is the 'bandwidth' of context-dependent fluctuations around the baseline level, and it is used to categorize people as having 'fragile' (or 'insecure') self-esteem versus 'secure' self-esteem. Specifically, this central tendency is referred to as an individual's *self-esteem stability*.

Stable versus unstable self-esteem are treated as properties of self-esteem (e.g., Franck & De Raedt, 2007; Kernis et al., 1993, 1989; Oosterwegel et al., 2001). For example, Kernis et al. (1993) referred to the stability of self-esteem as a 'component of self-esteem' (p. 1203) and as a 'dispositional quality'. Furthermore, Kernis described this disposition as having an 'essential nature', where 'the essential nature of unstable self-esteem involves the propensity to exhibit variability in self-feelings across time' (p. 1190).

4.2 Self-Esteem Research as a Case Study

This aspect of self-esteem research enacts a substance ontology yet further, where 'stable' or 'unstable' self-esteem are seen as universals that are common to a certain group of people. Kernis et al. (1993), for example, referred to people as 'posess[ing]' unstable self-esteem (p. 1191) and describes how this disposition leads them to seek out self-enhancing experiences. People who exhibit unstable self-esteem are thus assumed to be a *kind* of person; a group of individuals who are expected to follow the same universal law (e.g., self-enhancement behaviour) because of the secondary substance that they share (i.e., unstable self-esteem).

4.2.2.3 State Self-Esteem

Related to the notion of stable or unstable self-esteem is the concept of *state self-esteem*, being someone's experience of self *in the moment*. State self-esteem is commonly viewed as a 'barometer' that fluctuates around one's baseline as a function of current contextual cues (Kernis et al., 1993; Leary et al., 1995; Rosenberg, 1986). Indeed, according to a prevailing theory in self-esteem research – the Sociometer Theory (Leary et al., 1995) – trait self-esteem is viewed as the resting level of self-esteem in the absence of contextual information, and state self-esteem is thought to fluctuate around this resting level of self-esteem as a function of social cues of inclusion or exclusion from the immediate context (Leary, 1999). State self-esteem is thus thought to be an expression of the individual's trait, but deviations from the trait level (i.e., variability of state self-esteem) are then thought of as indicators of social inclusion and exclusion (where the person is motivated to minimize the probability of exclusion).

The underlying assumption is therefore that, without the presence of contextual events, state self-esteem would be equal to the baseline level of trait self-esteem, like pure or uncontaminated expressions of the underlying trait (for further analysis of these assumptions and their conceptual validity, see De Ruiter et al., 2015). They are ephemeral and peripheral experiences of that entity, an experience that fluctuates around the underlying stable entity.

4.2.3 Individual Particulars of Self-Esteem as Enduring over Time

While the enacted substance ontology described above views self-esteem as a stable and enduring entity, this does not exclude the possibility of development. The most common way of analysing self-esteem development in mainstream research may be through growth-curve analyses of self-esteem trajectories. For these studies, large time intervals separate one self-esteem assessment from the next, for example intervals of one to seventeen years between measures (e.g., Baldwin & Hoffmann, 2002; Birkeland et al., 2012). Development, then, is conceptualized as increases or decreases in self-esteem across time.

If the assumption is that the researcher is capturing 'underlying' and real growth curves, then it is directly implied that no *significant* (i.e., qualitative or non-linear) changes are occurring in between self-esteem assessments (at least no more than the gradual changes necessary to move from the levels assessed at t_x and t_{x+1}). The implication then is that the self-esteem entities being studied change in a slow and monotonous fashion, such that the underlying entity (e.g., high self-esteem) remains *essentially* the same. There seems then to be an assumed self-similarity over time, reflecting the assumption that self-esteem is primarily an enduring and stable entity.

The study of enduring entities and their monotonous decreases or increases over time is also reflected in studies of *rank-order stability* of self-esteem, which (based on test-retest correlations) is the degree to which the relative ordering of individuals is maintained over time (e.g., Trzesniewski, Donnellan & Robins, 2016). A high rank-order stability indicates that an individual who is high (or low) in self-esteem relative to others at one point in time remains high (or low) in self-esteem relative to others at another point time (this is often found to be the case for self-esteem; e.g., Chung et al., 2017; Trzesniewski, Donnellan & Robins, 2003).

Thus, while the assumption is that increases or decreases in self-esteem will occur over the lifespan (largely due to the common external experiences that occur in normative development), individuals maintain their self-esteem entity. Comparatively speaking, a 'high self-esteem' person will remain a 'high self-esteem' person and a 'low self-esteem' person will remain a 'low self-esteem' person. This particular enactment of a substance ontology seems to align with the notion that a property of an individual entity is *in* (i.e., ontologically part of) the entity.

4.2.3.1 Individual Self-Esteem as Instances of Esteem as a Universal

As is the case in most lines of mainstream psychological research, individual self-esteem scores or the development thereof are not, in themselves, deemed informative. Facts regarding primary substances are ultimately used to establish secondary substances (i.e., shared universal substances and their universal laws) – discussed in Chapter 6 as well in the context of developmental psychology research.

In classic self-esteem research, the ultimate goal is to understand what self-esteem (as a consistent, separate, disembodied, de-conceptualized variable) does for people and what its function is (e.g., as a monitor of psychological needs; Howell, Sosa & Osborn, 2019; also discussed in Pomagalska, 2005; Strandell, 2017). This shared goal amongst mainstream self-esteem research highlights the positivist perspective that is often adopted. With positivism, the emphasis is placed on the aim to verify or confirm the underlying and essential properties of a phenomenon. Furthermore, from a positivism stance, these properties can – and should – be confirmed by empirical evidence (Pilgrim, 2019) – see also Chapter 1.

Self-esteem is thus treated as a universal thing (a secondary substance) that exists in the world, in the same way for all individuals (or *kinds* of individuals, such as male Dutch students, Magro et al., 2019; for a discussion of how *natural kinds* are communicated in mainstream psychological research, see Chapter 6). It is assumed to be measurable as fundamentally separate from other universal secondary substances, personality for example (e.g., Kelly, Desiree & Stephen, 2015).

4.2.3.2 Relationships as Universals

This broad and pervasive practice of searching for universals is commonly referred to as the *variable-centred approach.* For this approach, 'the focus of interest is the relation between individuals' positions on latent dimensions, statistically studied across individuals' (Magnusson, 2003, p. 14). While there are various aspects of this approach that are important to discuss (e.g., the fact that the result of such an approach is a description of the non-existent average person, rather than real individuals within the sample and how this relates to the conditions of *ergodicity* – for more on this, see Chapter 9), what I wish to highlight in the current chapter is that the aim of this approach is ultimately to establish universal laws between substances in the generic sense (rather than understanding the particulars, or individuals, themselves). An *average* calculated across a particular sample represents a universal self-esteem for a particular *kind* (e.g., female academics), which is used to unearth a universal relationship between this universal and another (Arocha, 2020).

The variable-centred approach enacts the philosophical standpoint that particulars are equal instantiations of a real universal. Quite simply, this is implied when researchers try to discover a relationship between self-esteem and another variable (such as financial risk taking, Sekścińska et al., 2021, or age and gender, McMullin & Cairney, 2004) based on data that are representative of a given population. The 'relationship between two variables' is the universal and the 'data' are the particulars.

The universal is thus assumed to exist in every individual that makes up the sample, which is another way of saying that each individual within a sample are all expressions of the same general principle (putting aside the

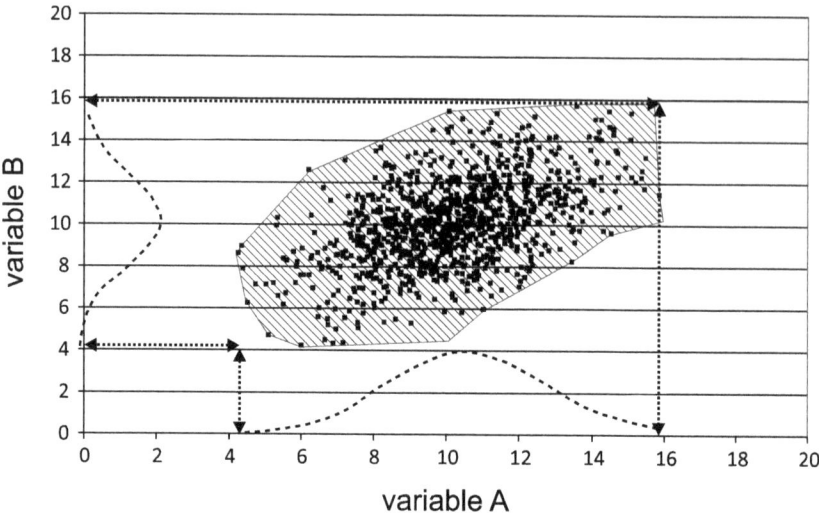

Figure 4.1 A cloud of data points representing a general relationship between variable A and variable B. From Van Geert (2014b). Every point on a variable maps onto a whole range of points on the other variable, e.g., value 10 on variable A maps on a range of values on B (roughly between 6 and 16). Reproduced with permission from Enfance, 3, 2014, 283–312.

question of whether this assumption reflects an ergodic principle or not). A particular data point is then only different from any other data point with regard to where it falls within a general relationship. Figure 4.1 shows a standard scatterplot, where the cloud represents the general relationship that is of interest to the researcher. The spatial differences between individual data points are useful in as far as they help reveal the 'underlying' universal law that each individual instantiates.

The variable-centred focus on universal laws between self-esteem and other variables has remained dominant in mainstream self-esteem research. This is of course the backbone of correlational and experimental studies, which are often viewed as being essential to research programs in psychological science (Tracy, Robins & Sherman, 2012).

The centrality of self-esteem's predictive ability is illustrated by the fact that a review-study published by Baumeister and colleagues in 2003, revealing that self-esteem does not predict nearly as much (with regard to positive or negative life outcomes) as researchers assumed, was cited 5,271 times at the moment of me writing this (December 2020). Articles like this have single handedly resulted in 'psychologists' faith in self-esteem [to be] deeply shaken' (Levy, 2019, p. 307). The shaken faith, here, does not refer to a belief in the existence of self-esteem as a secondary substance, but in its predictive ability in relation to other universal substances.

Self-esteem's failure to predict outcomes has culminated in far more criticism and scholarly doubt than any careful critiques of the theoretical or conceptual foundations of self-esteem (i.e., the ontology of self-esteem itself). For example, Scheff and Fearon's (2004) account of the 'dead end of self-esteem research' has, in comparison, been cited only 76 times at the time of writing this. Scheff and Fearon's theoretical blow to mainstream self-esteem was a more direct criticism of the very nature of self-esteem, yet, its citation rate does not compare to the empirical blow from Baumeister and colleagues (2003). This discrepancy illustrates the kind of threats that mainstream self-esteem researchers find worrying.

4.2.3.3 Explaining Development
Self-esteem researchers have traditionally not only been interested in what self-esteem predicts, but also in what predicts self-esteem. Indeed, much self-esteem research has been dedicated to whether self-esteem (i.e., central tendencies of self-esteem or decreases/increases therein) can be explained by other central-tendency properties, such as a sense of mastery (Erol & Orth, 2011), the occurrence of life events such as employment status (Orth, Maes & Schmitt, 2015), and by age itself (e.g., Robins et al., 2002). In this form of self-esteem research, the aim is to understand when, for whom, and why self-esteem develops. The form of explanation that is used is called *causal interventionism*, which is that the value of a variable will change if there is an intervention on – or manipulation of – another causally relevant variable (this form of causal model is discussed in depth in Chapter 7).

Understanding how self-esteem – as a secondary substance, or a universal – develops is thus based on establishing universal relationships with other secondary substances. Often, these secondary substances are not other trait-like variables, but contextual variables. For example, contextual variables such as social inclusion during studies abroad (Hutteman et al., 2015) or school transition (Schaffhuser, Allemand & Schwarz, 2017) are examined as predictors of specific properties of the self-esteem universal. The situated nature of self-esteem is thus often reduced to the study of 'context' as context-free variables.

In an operationalizing 'context' as a static variable that *intervenes* on self-esteem in a universal way (i.e., looking for *the* relationship between context X and self-esteem), an opportunity is missed. Namely, the opportunity to gain a richer, deeper, and person-specific understanding of self-esteem as intrinsically situated. The variable-focussed approach to context may be useful in directing our attention to certain contexts, but these efforts should ultimately be combined with studies of self-esteem as person-specific, as processes, and as situated in contexts. This alternative for self-esteem research is discussed in depth in Chapter 5.

4.2.3.4 Self-Esteem in the Real-World: The Pursuit of High Self-Esteem
In the preceding sections I sketched a picture of how the various elements of a mainstream self-esteem praxis sketch a picture of self-esteem as a substance (i.e., underlying entity). The substance-oriented facts generated in mainstream self-esteem research (regarding, for example, cause–effect causality or groups of individuals, i.e., kinds, having a common self-esteem property) do not remain within the metaphorical walls of academia. Knowledge generated by mainstream self-esteem studies seeps into the realities of lay people, often via popular texts that communicate these facts (see Pomagalska, 2005 for an extensive study of self-esteem discourse in self-help literature).

Despite the fact that many self-esteem scholars are losing their faith in the relevance of self-esteem (with regard to its predictive validity) and are concluding that efforts to boost self-esteem are of little value (Baumeister et al., 2005), self-help blogs and books abound, offering quick and easy methods to gain self-esteem or fix low self-esteem (for example, see *The Self-Esteem Workbook,* Schiraldi (2001) or *Ten Days to Self-Esteem*, Burns, 1993).

In her analysis of the reification of self-esteem in popular texts, Pomagalska (2005) demonstrated how popular texts about self-esteem clearly rely on language that reifies self-esteem, and she highlights the implications of this reification for readers. She described how a central objective of self-help books about self-esteem is to encourage readers to work on their self-esteem (illustrated by the titles alone of the above-mentioned self-help books). Pomagalska described that, for this to be a worthwhile practice, the self-help authors describe self-esteem as a reified entity (even an anthropomorphized entity) in order to enhance its importance as a real thing that has weight – and control – in our lives. Pomagalska explained how these attempts to help readers ultimately places an obligation on them; an obligation to pursue high self-esteem. Moreover, she described how this obligation is often communicated as a kind of moral obligation to work on ourselves.

Ryan and Brown (2003) described that 'as long as one remains invested in a specific self concept ("I am X"), there will inevitably be times when one is not X or one does not live up to the image one has created' (p. 75). Indeed, the culturally ingrained incentive (moral or otherwise) to boost one's self-esteem might be an important result of the reified account of self-esteem. At the very least, people run the risk of interpreting an inability to boost their self-esteem as a personal failure (Levy, 2019), in line with Pomagalska's analysis.

Aside from feelings of failure, pursuing self-esteem is of course also associated with more narcissistic tendencies, namely, intrapersonal and interpersonal strategies to protect one's positive self-perceptions (Geukes et al., 2017). The way that self-esteem research communicates facts about self-esteem might then be vital for our everyday relationship with 'self-esteem'. Because facts about self-esteem implicitly communicate a substance reality, a substance ontology is created for the people who experience (or *have*) self-esteem, ultimately leaving them with the burden to pursue 'it'.

4.3 Reflecting on the Enactment of a Substance Ontology in Self-Esteem Research

The praxis described above generates substance-related facts that are *empirically true* (or well-defined empirical truthmakers, as we discuss in Chapter 11): individuals have self-esteem scores (quantities of self-esteem) as measured by self-esteem questionnaires, invariant relationships exist between self-esteem variables and other central tendencies (in the form of correlations, for example). These facts sketch a kind of psychological reality that is substance based, which then necessitates further substance-based methodologies. The dominant praxis therefore not only *reflects* deeply held assumptions of a substance ontology, but it also *entrenches* a substance-based reality that may not be *ontologically true*.

Even though self-esteem is acknowledged as a *hypothetical variable* (a concept that researchers have created to make sense of, to study, and to communicate about an observed psychological phenomenon; Levy, 2019; Tafarodi & Ho, 2006), it has become generally accepted that, to study this phenomenon *correctly*, it must be quantified with validated self-report questionnaires. Therefore, the dominant praxis of quantifying self-esteem and its correlates or predictors generates substance-based facts about self-esteem as a quantifiable thing, which then create a substance *reality* for self-esteem, which then further necessitates a substance-ontology praxis.

4.3.1 *Natural-Science Envy*

Why is the study of self-esteem as an immaterial substance, as an entity or latent trait that takes on the form of variables, so dominant? Why do so many self-esteem researchers continue to enact this substance ontology in their decisions regarding research questions, in their choice of inscription devices and analytical methods? A full discussion and analysis of this goes beyond the scope of the current chapter, but it may be useful to highlight a few contributing processes that are themselves part of the larger dominant praxis adopted in psychological science.

First, 'psychologists believe that disciplines can be ranked in a prestige hierarchy of "scientificness" according to how close they are to physics, as follows: physics, chemistry, biology, psychology, sociology, anthropology, education' (Fish, 2000, p. 553). This ranking, and the need to be seen as close to the natural sciences, is pivotal in understanding why psychologists adopt the general praxis of referring to *variables* rather than people who act and do, and of looking for universal relationships between variables (Fish, 2000; Raeff, 2019). Note that this particular way of responding to a sense of natural science envy is based on inaccurate perceptions of the natural scientists, as being substance-oriented (when in fact they are highly process-oriented, see Chapter 1).

I assume many psychologists will recall receiving comments from others about psychology not being a 'real science' – most likely when they were psychology students. One can only assume that these comments correspond with the belief that science, in its purest form, involves the use of objective measures (things like test tubes that accurately measure substances that are manipulated in the laboratory). When I think back to my responses to these types of comment when I was a student, I remember feeling the need to defend psychology, to prove that we *also* measure things objectively and manipulate them in controlled environments in order to test objective relationships between variables. This is indeed a common experience for psychologists (Howell, Collisson & King, 2014).

For psychologists then, validated questionnaires are our test tubes, experimental settings are our labs, and manipulating independent variables in order to test the outcome of our dependent variable is our mixing of substances in the test tube. The same process can be seen in psychological research that is biologically oriented (studying specific genes, the brain, or hormones as independent variables that predict psychological phenomena). 'Biologized methodologies', as Fish (2000) refers to them, are sexy. They are the ones that lead to grants and media coverage; arguably because they are seen as the closest to being 'scientific'.

From the perspective of the self-esteem researcher who adopts a substance approach, it may then seem as though enacting a substance reality is necessary for bringing psychology closer to 'the ideal model for all science', namely, 'physics, with its admirable precision and quantification' (Fish, 2000, p. 553). Doing so calms our collective fear of being viewed as 'non-scientific'.

Furthermore, enacting a substance-ontology is also preferable for many as it is strongly rewarded in psychological science. Studies that adopt large-scale designs and rely on inferential statistics heavily dominate high-impact psychology journals. The drive to publish in high-impact journals thus motivates researchers to continue down this road. This is of course especially true in our current climate of temporary contracts and competitive tenure-track positions, where (young) researchers run the risk of sacrificing their careers if they pursue lines of research that are off the beaten track and associated with lower-ranked journals. Our entire institution of psychological science thus reinforces the enactment of a substance ontology through hierarchical and power systems (note, we will explore this notion of reinforcing a praxis in depth in Chapter 12).

But is the enactment of a substance ontology the only way to do 'science'? And what are the consequences of knowledge construction from a substantialist perspective? These are questions that I believe more self-esteem researchers should reflect on.

4.3.2 An Alternative Praxis for Self-Esteem Research?

Fish (2000) described how science 'involves the systematic study of observable phenomena, uses evidence and logic to further that understanding, and chooses its methods based on the problem investigated' (p. 553). Similarly, Overton (1991) described that the general aim of science is 'to bring order and organization to the chaos of everyday experience' (p. 7). These conceptualizations of science are quite distinct from the description that mainstream psychologists evidently hope to abide by: 'clearly defined terminology, quantifiability, highly controlled experimental conditions, reproducibility and, finally, predictability and testability' (Berezow, 2012).

Fish (2000) and Overton's (1991) definitions do not enact a substance ontology, and therefore, do not constrain scientific pursuits to controlling and manipulating, objectifying, and quantifying. Indeed, adopting a substance ontology in order to emulate the natural sciences is neither necessary nor accurate, as much of modern biology and physics also adopt a process ontology (Bickhard, 2009a; Dupré & Nicholson, 2018; Koutroufinis, 2017). Fish suggests that, in focussing on science as the controlling and measuring of substance-like variables, psychology 'excludes or disparages both (1) consideration of important questions and (2) the use of qualitative, field, and descriptive methodologies. In addition, it places a value on biologized explanations for behavior (closer to the physics end of the prestige hierarchy) over social ones (closer to the education end)' (p. 554).

If self-esteem researchers (or any academic psychologist) were to let go of the notion that doing science means controlling and manipulating static and disembodied variables, as entities that individuals have, we would open up a rich and varied array of research aims. Currently, treating self-esteem like a universal substance that has universal relationships with other substances directs researchers' focus toward quantifying these substances and discovering the specific *intervening* variables (e.g., age or personality) that determine (i.e., predict) self-esteem, or vice versa (Raeff, 2019).

To 'understand' self-esteem then (and to help people with self-esteem issues) commonly comes down to pinpointing which variables need to be manipulated in order to increase self-esteem. If the dominant ontology enacted remains a substance ontology, then this will ultimately remain the main goal of self-esteem researchers (and thus also the bearers of 'low' self-esteem). Self-esteem research will then remain populated by nouns (as opposed to verbs), quantities of self-esteem, and strengths of universal relationships.

There is of course value in facts about quantities of self-esteem and relationships with other variables. Knowing how self-esteem is distributed across individuals (such as men versus women, ten-year-olds versus fifteen-year-olds, the employed versus the unemployed) is useful, especially for those that need to identify group tendencies, such as policy makers. A policy maker may want to know which groups tend to have low self-esteem if they need to decide which populations require extra attention or support, or what the general trend in self-esteem level is as children move from primary to secondary education to determine when psychoeducation should be introduced into the curriculum (Boker & Martin, 2018).

However, I think it is safe to assume that – in most cases – it is not the group differences per se that academic psychologists are interested in. Instead, it is what these differences presumably tell us about how the construct in question *works*, its general laws (Hamaker, 2012). Indeed, the ultimate aim is often to understand dynamic and individual realities. This involves questions like: How does a person's self-esteem change as they grow older? How is self-esteem affected by our relationships with others, or how can we deal with self-esteem issues that arise in adolescence? I believe that many academic psychologists studying self-esteem are then ultimately more interested in the *processes* involved in self-esteem than the strictly group-based distributions of self-esteem scores.

As mainstream self-esteem researchers are interested in questions pertaining to how self-esteem works, it is then not the *question* that enacts a substance ontology. Instead, it is how the question is answered that enacts a substance ontology, the methods used, the facts that are generated, and the assumptions that are held in order to generate these facts. These types of question are answered with central tendencies, static descriptions of self-esteem, and predictive relationships between variables based on group averages. These are the practices that enact a substance ontology.

4.3.3 Studying Processes despite a Substance Ontology

The issue with studying processes within the dominant substance-ontology praxis becomes salient when we ask questions such as 'How does a person's self-esteem change as they grow older? How is self-esteem affected by our relationships with others? Or How can we deal with self-esteem issues that arise in adolescence?'. These questions a) pertain to the level of the individual, and b) involve some kind of process. The substance-oriented answers to these questions (i.e., starting with the empirical facts) pertain to the level of groups or between-individual differences. This is a mismatch between ontology and epistemology (a discussion that exceeds the scope of this chapter) that highlights an issue with the current substance-ontology praxis (for more on this, see Chapters 8, 9 and 10; and Boker & Martin, 2018; Hamaker, 2012; Molenaar, 2004).

Shortly, models of *inter*individual associations stemming from large-scale research studies are 'non-ergodic' (Molenaar, 2004), meaning that they do not apply to the level of the individual (see also Chapter 9). If self-esteem is found to be higher for individuals who are employed compared to those that are not, this group-level finding cannot be *individualized* (for a discussion on the difference between individualization and generalization, see Chapter 11). Specifically, it would be false to conclude that if a person who is currently unemployed were to become employed that their self-esteem would increase. In order to understand these kinds of *individual* processes, they must be studied at the level of the individual. This is especially true for empirical facts of processes (Molenaar, 2004).

The point here is that if we are interested in processes that ultimately take place at the individual level (which self-esteem researchers generally are) then we must be sure that the assumptions held by our dominant methodologies do in fact allow us to study individual processes. Studies have demonstrated that this is not the case (e.g., Fisher, Medaglia & Jeronimus, 2018). This means that the dominant praxis of relying on large-scale research, group-based variables and inferential statistics of between-individual central tendencies is not suitable for studying individual processes, even if researchers who enact this praxis are ultimately interested in these processes and indeed ask empirical questions about individual processes. This is an important step for psychologists, because 'once we lay bare some of those assumptions, we can question them, and subsequently we can articulate an alternative theoretical framework that provides a basis for understanding human functioning in terms of acting and active processes' (Raeff, 2019, p. 316).

What might such an alternative theoretical framework look like? Many researchers have focussed on alternative *methodological* frameworks specifically, such as multilevel models that consider variability at the individual level (Level 1; time) as well as the between-individual level (Level 2; individuals) (Hamaker, 2012). These kinds of statistical model account for the non-ergodic nature of psychological processes and are thus able to accurately say something about how individual processes work.

While multilevel models based on time series are process-oriented, self-esteem researchers who use them often communicate their facts in substance terms. For example, conclusions like 'self-esteem appears to have a significant stable core. This core may represent the essence of how people evaluate themselves. This core is modelled as independent of previous self-esteem-related perceptions and also independent of occasion-specific conditions or experiences' (Wagner, Lüdtke & Trautwein, 2016, p. 531). Thus, we are faced again with assumptions of a universal (i.e., the universal trait that all individuals in the sample have) and its distinct properties (i.e., the specific score of each individual's stable trait entity and the fleeting variability around it). With these kinds of methodological advancement then, the underlying assumptions of a substance ontology remain the same as in classical models of self-esteem, where the universal trait self-esteem and the variable state self-esteem are treated like distinct things (Leary et al., 1995).

Moreover, statistically advanced studies that take group *and* individual trait and state variation into consideration still reveal a reality that is described by central tendencies, and thus a description of quantities as 'high', 'low', 'stable', or 'unstable'. For example, the main empirical facts generated in Wagner, Lüdtke & Trautwein's (2016) study are that self-esteem is a relatively stable and enduring construct, that women have lower self-esteem than men and higher state variability than men. The communication of these facts thus treats processes like entities. The practical relevance of these facts, however, does not imply ontological privileges (Rohde, 2010); it does not say anything about the *nature* of these processes. To illustrate, while a study may operationalize state variance and trait variance as two distinct things, the results do not necessarily contribute to our understanding of the nature of state versus trait self-esteem. Wagner, Lüdtke & Trautwein (2016), for example, wrote in their abstract that they found 'evidence for the general pattern of a major proportion of stable and autoregressive trait variance and a smaller yet substantial amount of state variance in self-esteem'.

I would argue that this does *not* reveal anything about the 'stable' nature of self-esteem, because the methodology was not sensitive enough to capture variability. The evidence for the above finding stems from a repeated measures design in which self-esteem was measured six times across the span of two years with a questionnaire. This kind of design, therefore, cannot logically say much about the nature of variability if variability is only investigated based on six static measures. 'State self-esteem' is, after all, a *momentary* experience by definition. Here we see that state self-esteem is forced into an entity substance, where it is assumed that it is the same underlying entity over time that will change only in a slow and gradual way. The practices of measuring self-esteem this way, therefore, *create* an ontology of stable entities via the facts generated.

Conclusions such as the one above concerning the 'stable' nature of self-esteem are directly refuted by studies that *have* measured the variability of state self-esteem across a more suitable interval (which I will describe in more detail in Chapter 5). These studies, in short, found that self-esteem is best described as highly variable, where variability is not characterized as a stable-bandwidth of fluctuations around a stable core. Instead, state self-esteem variability demonstrates intrinsic dynamics, and these intrinsic dynamics *give way* to a stable tendency that we might call trait self-esteem – suggesting that 'trait' and 'state' are not distinct or separate from each other (De Ruiter et al., 2015; Fortes, Delignières & Ninot, 2004; Ninot, Fortes & Delignières, 2005).

What I wish to highlight here is that these mainstream self-esteem studies (even those with elegant and sophisticated multi-level modelling) are ill-equipped to study the specific set of questions that refer to the ontology of processes and *how* self-esteem processes occur. To understand more about the reality of self-esteem as a process, a process ontology is more suitable (see Chapter 5).

4.4 Conclusion: The Enactment of a Substance Ontology in Self-Esteem Research

With this chapter, I hope to have demonstrated that the various components that make up the mainstream praxis of self-esteem research enact a substance ontology. At the very foundation of mainstream self-esteem research lies the aim to capture participants' *true* level of self-esteem – reflecting the assumption that there is something that is 'under-lying', permanent, and universal to be captured. This is demonstrated when researchers speak of 'latent' 'trait' self-esteem, which is assessed by means of static self-esteem questionnaires, or by collapsing repeated measures of state self-esteem across time in order to obtain the central tendency – the baseline level of self-esteem.

Furthermore, a substance ontology is enacted when researchers assume that self-esteem is a *universal* essence (i.e., a secondary substance), something that exists universally, as the same 'thing', across individuals. This assumption is evidenced by the fact that mainstream self-esteem researchers deem it necessary to exclusively use self-esteem questionnaires as *the* way to tap into the *real* essence of self-esteem, namely as a quantifiable immaterial substance. Any other methods are therefore assumed to measure 'something else'.

Self-esteem is treated as a universal substance of which there are different *kinds* – primarily 'high' and 'low', 'stable' and 'unstable' (Baumeister et al., 2003). As a universal secondary substance, common research practices then enact a substance ontology in which the (secondary) self-esteem substance adopts different properties depending on the bearer of the particular instance of the substance.

Self-esteem is most often investigated in terms of the universal relationships that it has with other variables – predictive relationships, explanatory relationships, or correlational relationships. Individuals are treated as particulars of these universal relationships, based on their particular self-esteem property. For example, the relationship between 'self-esteem' and 'taking initiative' is a universal one (Baumeister et al., 2003), where individuals differ as to where they fall within this relationship: those with 'high' self-esteem demonstrate 'higher' initiative, and those with 'low' self-esteem demonstrate 'lower' initiative.

In summation, this chapter assessed how mainstream practices in self-esteem research enact (some form of) a substance ontology in the common operational definitions of self-esteem (quantified scales), empirical investigations of self-esteem (relationships between variables), and the kind of knowledge generated about self-esteem (distributions of central tendencies across individuals). These enactments are implicit and implied by the practices adopted. The practices, therefore, do not stem from an explicit metaphysical *theory*. The substance ontology enacted in mainstream self-esteem research is not a formalized ontology like those described in the field of philosophy of science. Instead, it is an enacted one: it is a particular way of making meaning about a reality as we interact with it. In self-esteem research, the enactment of a substance ontology is a fuzzy one.

Nevertheless, the enactment of a (fuzzy) substance ontology in self-esteem research has a number of consequences, both for lay people and for self-esteem research. Regarding the former, a substance ontology of self-esteem reifies self-esteem, which affects the everyday lives of the 'bearers' of self-esteem. If individuals are to understand that self-esteem is an underlying thing that they 'have', this compels them to, first, assess the property of their own particular instance of self-esteem. They take a *self-as-object* perspective toward their core 'self' and evaluate it; do I esteem myself positively or negatively (Ryan & Brown, 2003)? Next to this, this approach to 'self' leads many to either try to pursue 'higher' self-esteem or to protect high self-esteem from becoming 'lower'. These motivations can then ultimately lead individuals to engage in dysfunctional self-esteeming behaviour and to feelings of failure, respectively.

All of this is not to say that recent efforts to improve the statistical rigour of large-sample studies are useless. Not at all. These efforts should be applauded, as they allow researchers to study general tendencies and relationships between variables, and to do so in a way that these findings can be 'individualized'. These efforts indeed demonstrate that a process approach can be adopted to understand populations. In addition, however, these population-focussed efforts (which can be subsumed under a process approach) should be accompanied by more process-oriented efforts to understand the truly within-person processes of self-esteem, as embedded in contexts and variable over time (this pluralist take is discussed more in Chapter 5, and in Chapter 12).

In the next chapter (Chapter 5), I will outline what the processual praxis looks like, how exactly it enacts a process ontology, and what this means for self-esteem research and our everyday experience of self-esteem. With this, I hope to demonstrate the unique value of a process-oriented research praxis for self-esteem.

CHAPTER 5

A Person Acting amongst Persons
Enacting a Process Ontology in Self-Esteem Research[*]

> *Two roads diverged in a wood, and I—*
> *I took the one less traveled by,*
> *And that has made all the difference.*
> From *The Road Not Taken*, a poem by Robert Frost

In this chapter, I continue with self-esteem research as a case study for demonstrating how a research praxis enacts a certain ontology. Whereas Chapter 4 analysed how the mainstream praxis of self-esteem research enacts a substance ontology, here I will analyse the ways in which alternative research approaches to self-esteem reflect and construct a process ontology of self-esteem. While the substance-ontology praxis forms the mainstream approach to self-esteem, the process-ontology praxis is arguably in its infancy. This chapter thus discusses a small body of research that demonstrates a road less taken. As I will show, the operational definitions of 'self-esteem' adopted in these studies are highly divergent, which may be a defining feature of the process-oriented research praxis. I will assess the contributions that this praxis has to offer the field of self-esteem, and how a processual approach to self-esteem might be advantageous for laypeople and the everyday experience of self-esteem.

5.1 On the Nature of Self-Esteem from a Process Philosophy

A research praxis ties together concrete practices, output, and researchers with respect to a common ontology that is enacted, as well as in the epistemic values implied. In a substance-oriented praxis, the nature of a psychological phenomenon like self-esteem is that of an enduring universal substance, and individual entities that instantiate this universal (Aristotle's *primary* and *secondary substances*, respectively; see Chapter 4).

---
[*] This is a single-authored chapter written by Naomi De Ruiter. For this reason, the chapter makes use of first-person singular pronouns.

5.1 On the Nature of Self-Esteem from a Process Philosophy

The epistemic values enacted in this praxis are then of establishing the universal laws that correspond with 'self-esteem' as a secondary substance.

But some scholars have begun to bring 'into question the idea that there is some personal property, "self-esteem", which is other than, and explanatory of, people's expressed beliefs about themselves. This "property" is supposedly a causally efficacious cognitive state which would bring about these beliefs' (Sabat et al., 1999, p. 11). Rather than assuming that an underlying property, a thing, exists that is generating people's narratives (and eventually, their self-reports) about their self-worth, some researchers have turned toward the process of acting, experiencing, and narrating itself. In a process-oriented praxis, the nature of self-esteem is characterized by processes of change and variability, and of movement and action, toward temporary or maintained stability or to novel forms. In such a praxis, *processes* are the explanatory default (Bickhard, 2009a). Epistemic value is placed on understanding the processes that constitute a phenomenon such as self-esteem, as well as how, when, and why stability occurs (Rescher, 1996). To do this, the epistemic stance of a process researcher is to follow these processes as closely as possible. With this diverging epistemic stance, processual investigations of self-esteem often *explicitly* build on, investigate, or assume a process ontology of self-esteem. Process studies of self-esteem are thus highly theory driven, which is in stark contrast to the standard atheoretical approach often adopted in self-esteem research (Scheff & Fearon, 2004; Strandell, 2017).

5.1.1 Observing Self-Esteem: Descriptive Methodologies of Actions

Similar to a substance philosophy, a researcher with a processual perspective assumes that it is a viable undertaking to try to understand reality. Both perspectives thus assume that self-esteem is real. In other words, a realist stance is adopted in both cases. The two perspectives differ, however, with regards to what the ontology of that reality is assumed to be and how we should try to study it.

5.1.1.1 Subjective and Socially Constructed Processes

A processual approach to self-esteem rejects the *objectivist* perspective that underpins the substantialist approach. That is, the properties of self-esteem can be objectively known in the sense that they are independent and inherent properties of the secondary substance (i.e., the universal 'stuff' of self-esteem). Instead, the process approach asserts that these properties are constructed by the individuals that experience self-esteem as they move through their everyday interactions, including a research context. Any empirical assessment of self-esteem processes is thus uniquely shaped by constructive processes that take place between the individual and their environment (including the material space, tools, and modes of communication utilized by a researcher).

In this sense, I argue that processual researchers of self-esteem are more inclined to adopt a *subjectivist* stance, or an intermediate version thereof. This stance does not focus on the *measurement* of a psychological phenomenon, but the *understanding* of the phenomenon (Holden & Lynch, 2004). This understanding necessitates an (ideally explicit) appreciation for how the phenomenon is embedded in the context (Bickhard, 2009a; Dupré & Nicholson, 2018), and an appreciation of a pluralist approach to how understanding can be gained.

A commitment to context dependency necessitates an understanding of the ways in which each context affords a different quality of self-experience (e.g., sitting alone at one's desk, interacting with peers, being interviewed about one's self-conceptions, writing in a diary). An operational definition of self-esteem will then depend on how the specific context affords self-experiences (Bickhard 2009a). People will be likely to 'do' self-esteem in a different way depending on the context in which they are experiencing themselves and the world. A diary or interview setting will elicit more self-reflections, whereas working alone at a desk or interacting with someone else will elicit more emotional and behavioural experiences. In this sense, in the process-ontology praxis, the researcher develops a method for understanding self-esteem as situated in a specific context – rather than studying the entity 'self-esteem' as if it were a context-free thing that individuals take with them.

As Raeff (2010) described, when people refer to 'Bob's self-esteem' they are in fact (or they *should be*) referring to 'Bob's evaluation of Bob, or how… Bob felt about … Bob' (p. 38). Self-esteem is thus not a thing that exists independently from the person, but a series of *actions* that the person does. In Strandell's *self-motivated behaviour* model of self-esteem, he also highlights that action ('how and what people try to become, maintain, or avoid being' p. 78) is pivotal to understanding self-esteem processes.

The task of the process researcher is then, first, to develop ways in which we can grasp how people *perform, construct,* or *express* self-esteem: how they experience and *do* self-esteem (Bortolan, 2018). A shift to a process approach for self-esteem thus requires a shift to verbs, rather than nouns (Raeff, 2019). For example, Susan can do 'high' self-esteem when she speaks up and defends her position in a committee meeting, when she is expressing pleasure in her own joke, and pride when she is able to formulate a thought, when she tells her father that she has come to appreciate her

5.1 On the Nature of Self-Esteem from a Process Philosophy

own to-the-point demeanour and that she thinks she deserves a place in management, when she feels comfortable stepping into difficult situations, or when she sees others valuing and appreciating her input or entrusting her with important tasks.

In contrast (and as discussed in Chapter 4), referring to *self-esteem* as a noun (e.g., 'I study self-esteem', 'Naomi's self-esteem') often reflects and contributes to the substance-oriented approach to this action-based process. That being said, it should be acknowledged that rigidly avoiding the use of nouns need not be the goal. Obviously, replacing the noun 'self-esteem' with 'the *valenced and action-based processes of experiencing, becoming, maintaining, avoiding, or feeling a specific enaction of self*' is obviously unwieldy. For pragmatic purposes, I will simply refer to *self-esteem* in this chapter. This should be interpreted within the context of my wish to distance myself from the common noun-based linguistic norms that characterize classic self-esteem research.

5.1.1.2 Research Contexts as Affordances for Experiences of Specific Forms of 'Self'

Every particular context thus affords (suggests, triggers, shapes) *what* people can try to become, maintain, or avoid being. A research context should then be cognizant of the particular experience of 'self' that the context affords: a static reflection of self-as-object? A dynamic narrative of self-as-object? A situated negotiation of self-worth?

A study in which a participant fills in a classic self-esteem scale while isolated in a laboratory room, for example, provides a very specific and unique context. The scale (including the explicit terms used, the repetitive nature of the questions, the total length of the questionnaire) affords the act of directing one's focus to the *self-as-object*, directing one's gaze to the self in general and one's worth and value relative to others (Ryan & Brown, 2003). This research context must thus be understood as affording certain constructive processes, for example it 'may stimulate them to consider the topic [of self-worth] in a new way, or even prompt them to formulate an opinion when they previously had none' (Levy, 2019, p. 316).

While this *reactivity* effect is often viewed as a validity issue for the use of classic self-esteem scales (e.g., Buhrmester, Blanton & Swann, 2011; Levy, 2019; also discussed in Chapter 4), a process perspective would simply see it as a particular constructive context for the enactment of one's identity (in Section 5.2.1, I discuss an example of how this can be explicitly used to the researcher's advantage). Therefore, there is no need to deem some contexts or measurement tools as 'wrong' or invalid and others as 'right' or valid, under the condition that the affordances provided by the context or tool (for the constructive process of self-esteem) are explicitly taken into consideration. Self-esteem can thus be situated in any context. The key is that it is examined as such, as situated.

Cigman (2004) stresses that this conceptualization of self-esteem, which she refers to as *situated self-esteem*, is crucial for a practical and applied perspective of self-esteem. Educators, for example, should busy themselves (not with simply and generally trying to increase the *level* of children's self-esteem, but) with the complexities of when and how children feel competent and lovable (and especially when this is not the case) in concrete social contexts, and with the way that they negotiate these feelings in those contexts. Cigman highlights that it is the everyday (i.e., lived) experiences of self-esteem that matter.

Self-esteem scales, while perfectly useful for studying certain constructive processes of self-esteem, are of course a very specific and unnatural context for studying the everyday lived experiences of self-esteem. While I would not go so far as to say that they are 'not valid', as other critics of mainstream self-esteem research have (Scheff & Fearon, 2004, p. 79), it is clear that they do not suffice as a general method for studying all possible contexts for the enacted process of self-esteem. This is because they 'confound thoughts (such as egotism) with emotions (such as authentic pride)' (Scheff, 2015, p. 205), 'tapping the cognitive component of self-esteem, but ignoring or confounding the social and emotional components' (Scheff & Fearon, 2004, p. 79). Indeed, for most lived experiences of self, additional research contexts and tools must be used that allow us to observe these emotional and social features of self-esteem processes. Appreciating this as a logical consequence of studying self-esteem allows researchers to capture the processes that we have come to know as 'self-esteem' in different ways.

Moving away from the use of self-report questionnaires is thus pivotal (but not necessary) for process-oriented researchers to differentiate their research from the standard substance-ontological approach to self-esteem. Inscription devices (i.e., an umbrella term for all tools used to transform observed phenomena into inscriptions) that can capture *processes* of self-esteem are necessary for the complete and in-depth study of how people negotiate, develop, maintain, or resist certain self-esteem experiences.

5.1.1.3 *Characteristics of Process Description*

The above discussions regarding how self-esteem should be approached from a process ontology can be summarized in the following points.

5.1 On the Nature of Self-Esteem from a Process Philosophy

First, a descriptive methodology is required. Utilizing a descriptive methodology enacts a process ontology because the researcher is *describing* observations of self-esteem in action, rather than *capturing* an independent entity that is self-esteem (Raeff, 2010; Ryan & Brown, 2003; Scheff & Fearon, 2004; Strandell, 2017).

Second, describing how self-esteem *is done* requires the examination of how it is done *in situ* as a 'person amongst persons' (Cigman, 2004, p. 96; Schiff, 2017). The situation considered can vary in size, duration, and frequency, and can thus include intrapersonal or interpersonal situations (Cottrell, 1941, p. 259). In studying self-esteem processes in a specific situation, the researcher enacts the assumption that individuals exhibit self-esteem-related experiences in relation to something or someone else, rather than seeing self-esteem as a disembodied and independent attribute that individuals *have*.

Third, the consideration of the context should be more than a reference to contextual variables as static entities, such as 'the family context', or 'school'. Instead, it should ideally be a consideration of the temporal association between self-esteem experiences and the context, and thus how the *moment-to-moment* changes in self-esteem relate to the *moment-to-moment* changes in the context. According to Cottrell (1941), with the rigorous study of how a system behaves *in a specific situation*, researchers will be able to fully understand, and indeed predict, behaviour using case-study methods. A processual approach is thus highly Gibsonian, in its emphasis on studying organism-environment interactions as the unit of analysis (Bickhard, 2009a). As such, the unit of analysis should not be 'an individual's self-esteem', but 'an individual's (negotiation of, expressions of, construction of) self-esteem in situation X'. In the following illustrations of processual studies of self-esteem, we see that the extent to which this is done in *explicit* terms varies.

Fourth, approaching self-esteem with verbs in mind means looking past the conceptualization of self-esteem as primarily a cognitive appraisal (Scheff, 2015; Scheff & Fearon, 2004), and broadening the scope of processes to include actions and emotions (Raeff, 2010; Ryan & Brown, 2003; Scheff & Fearon, 2004; Strandell, 2017).

These characteristics collectively draw from the Relational-Developmental Systems perspective (Overton, 2013a, 2013b) and the 4E perspective (*embodied, embedded, enactive, extended*; each of which represents its own perspective on the nature of phenomena; e.g., Varela et al., 2016). Positioning self-esteem research characteristics within these frameworks 'frames an ontology of becoming that allows the construction of meaning through the embodied activity of the individual' (Marshall, 2016, p. 248).

5.2 Descriptions and Conceptualizations of Self-Esteem as Processes

Here I will describe some characteristic ways that the above characteristics have been incorporated in process-oriented research of self-esteem thus far. Note that the following descriptions of methods, analyses, and results are not intended to be complete descriptions of each study, as that is beyond the scope of this chapter. The below descriptions are general highlights, drawn from published research. Interested readers are encouraged to read the original work for more complete and detailed descriptions of methodology and results.

5.2.1 *Self-Esteem as Processes of Negotiation and Performance: A Qualitative Account*

While a qualitative approach is frequently adopted within the praxis of identity research (which is of course conceptually related to self-esteem), this is not the case in self-esteem research. There are a handful of exceptions to this, such as Sabat et al. (1999) and work by Scheff and Fearon (Fearon, 2004; Scheff & Fearon, 2004), where discursive tendencies are observed based on how individuals talk about themselves in an interview setting.

In Fearon's 2004 study, for example, participants filled in a self-esteem scale and were subsequently asked to reflect on their answers – both in writing and by interview. These reflections were then analysed discursively. Here, the self-esteem scale *Texas Social Behavior Inventory* was used, but Fearon noted that any other standard measure of self-esteem could have been used. The scale was, therefore, used as a tool for evoking self-constructive and performative actions and emotions, not to tap into or measure an underlying self-view. This sentiment was elegantly described by Sabat et al. (1999): 'Questionnaires are not instruments in the sense that thermometers are. They are invitations to a conversation' (p. 13).

This study thus explicitly examines the situated nature of self-reflections, where the self-report scale and the researcher form the context, and the researcher is the audience of the performative actions of self-esteem. Following the use of the self-esteem scale, the researcher asked participants to explain their choice for particular responses and were asked to describe

5.2 Descriptions and Conceptualizations of Self-Esteem

specific instances of problematic social situations related to the items. This interview process revealed how the participants presented themselves with respect to others, how they negotiated their experience of closeness versus separateness among people to protect their sense of self-worth, and how they managed the emotions that were elicited during this constructive process.

Using conversation-analytic methods, Fearon (2004) found that participants quickly directed attention (or 'oriented' themselves) toward 'bond threats', which refer to evaluations of self in the context of (relationships with) others. 'Others' can range from a specific person who has a long-standing relationship with the participant, to the researcher, to generalized others. Threats include evaluations of self or associations with others as negative, threatened, or isolated. Fearon found that an orientation toward bond threats was followed by expressions of shame, as evidenced by 'hiding behaviours', where the participants used actions such as nervous laughter or lowering eyes, for example, to deflect or distract from the threatening aspect of what was being said. Finally, the expression of shame was then followed by discursive attempts to mitigate, repair, or alter information that led to the threat. An expression of shame thus functioned as a signal of a bond threat and the need to repair it. For example, participants would shift the way that they referred to themselves or alter attributions. This sequence (of 1. Orientation toward bond threat, 2. Expression of shame, and 3. Repair of bond threat) was termed the 'bond threat sequence'.

This study demonstrates how researchers can shift their attention from measuring how 'much' self-esteem individuals have (in general, or even within a particular context, i.e., trait and state self-esteem, respectively) to the rich texture of how people 'do' self-esteem. Here, individuals 'do' self-esteem via performative emotional and behavioural acts as they move through the typical sequence of evaluating issues with regard to the social self, expressing shame that signalled the presence of the 'issue', and performativity repairing the issue.

The use of self-report questionnaires used in Fearon's (2004) study offered specific affordances and constraints to how the participants were likely to do self-esteem, such that questioning participants about their self-report answers likely produces explicit self-reflections, which the participant must then manage in some way. Moreover, the study reveals the way in which individuals might negotiate the discursive conventions specific to the context of talking about one's self to unfamiliar others – here, the social bond sequence. Findings such as these should be seen as part of a larger collection of observations, done in disparate contexts, of how individuals do self-esteem when specific contextual and social affordances are provided.

Another example of a discursive approach to studying self-esteem is Sabat et al. (1999), in their account of how sufferers with Alzheimer's disease managed their self-esteem in the context of the changes that come with having Alzheimer's. In their study, the authors found that individuals' sense of self-worth reflected a 'complex interaction between the person's attitudes and beliefs about his or her attributes, and the opportunities the person had to make manifest his or her valued attributes and minimize potential embarrassment in the social world' (p. 27). The context of 'Alzheimer's disease' was crucial here, as it highlighted how individuals tried to distance themselves or mitigate 'negative' attributes of Self (here, derived from having Alzheimer's) in order to maintain a positive self-regard (here, which hinged on their personal attributes that were primarily salient in their past). Moreover, the authors found that distancing oneself from activities and individuals associated with Alzheimer's disease and aligning oneself with non-sufferers of Alzheimer's was a typical way of managing this self-protective process. This study and Fearon's (2004) study utilized different research contexts and tools, yet both illustrate how individuals actively construct a sense of positive self-regard during their interactions with the researchers, and how this involves a complex negotiation of conflicting and confronting information regarding the Self.

Unfortunately, the use of discursive methodologies is rarely adopted in self-esteem research. Methodological practices that are interpretive and pattern-seeking can uniquely shed light on patterns of human experience such as self-esteem, demonstrating the ways in which they are intrinsically situated in the world that an individual is engaging with and co-constructing through this engagement (Sugarman & Martin, 2020). Sugarman and Martin refer to these methods of enquiry as methods of 'psychological humanities', which are adopted by scholars who believe that 'psychology needs to draw on the knowledge and practices of the humanities to access extensive content and material, as well as a long tradition of research on the processes and products of human mental life' (Teo, 2017, pp. 3–4). Discursive methods thus contribute to a different vision of the way psychological phenomena can be understood in psychology compared to the mainstream approach adopted in self-esteem research. They can be used to understand phenomena such as self-esteem as shifting, and in flux as the individual engages in the immediate moment with other individuals. It can be used to study how phenomena such as self-esteem are traceable in interactions by examining what can be *seen* (from the vantage point of

5.2 Descriptions and Conceptualizations of Self-Esteem

the interaction partner, for example, and thus also the researcher) (Stokoe et al., 2012). In interaction settings, discursive methods can thus be used to examine the ways that self-esteem is *enacted*; performed, claimed, and repaired via concrete and situated actions.

5.2.2 Self-Esteem as a Self-Organizing and Self-Maintaining Processes: A Time-Series Account

A number of time-series approaches have also been developed that study the flux and flow of self-esteem as a pattern rather than a measurable and stable property. Time series obviously involve *quantification*. However, it is important to highlight that these types of studies do not claim or aim to 'measure self-esteem' in the classical sense of capturing someone's true level of self-esteem. Measuring the *processes of self-esteem* is thus distinct from measuring self-esteem.

What is common across many time series approaches to self-esteem is an attempt to demonstrate and further understand the self-organizational processes that give way to the experience of self-esteem as self-maintaining, recurring, and stable alongside evident day-to-day or moment-to-moment flux. The aim then is often to explicitly describe the processual nature of self-esteem as consisting of nested levels of a system that interact across different timescales.

This aim is firmly embedded in a key assumption of a process metaphysics: that phenomena are 'constituted by processes all the way down' (Dupré & Nicholson, 2018, p. 13) and 'all the way up' (Bickhard, 2011a, p. 13), see also Chapter 1. Applying this to self-esteem, valenced experiences of the self (which we may observe to be stable) are both derived from processes (rather than from underlying entities) and are themselves processes. Conceptualizing self-esteem as processes all the way up and all the way down means that there is *no* level, irreducible component, or sum of components that ultimately define(s) self-esteem. Instead, self-esteem only comes into existence via self-experiential dynamic interactions; emotions interact with thoughts, individuals interact with their environment, thoughts interact with subsequent thoughts, and current interactions feed into the development of entrenched patterns.

Here it may be helpful to introduce a commonly used illustration of process ontology, namely, the swarm behaviour of flocks of birds. The swarm (being the ebb and flow of the flock in the sky) cannot be reduced to any internal causal components (i.e., in individual birds), nor to an external driving force (such as the wind). Instead, the swarm is an emergent behaviour that arises from the interactions (i.e., processes) at various levels or scales. On the largest scale, we see the twists and twirls of the entire flock – the phenomenon that we recognize as 'swarm behaviour'. These characteristic twists and twirls are a process. One can of course measure central tendencies of this phenomenon, such as the average height, or diameter of the swarm behaviour across the time span of minutes or even days. Indeed, there is nothing wrong with doing so. Such results would be useful for things like comparing how central tendencies of swarm behaviour differ across seasons or countries. Importantly, however, these static descriptions would not represent, or allow for the study of, the inherently process-based nature of the swarm behaviour. For this, it is vital that we describe the process of the swarm behaviour in processual terms.

Moving down to a lower level, we might see local processes: the interactions between the components of the emergent swarm (i.e., birds). These are the processes that give rise to emergent swarm behaviour. At this level, one would necessarily describe behavioural rules that characterize the interaction between *individual* birds in the form of *if-then* relationships (e.g. follow the nearest bird, but if it comes too close, move away from it). Moving even further down, the 'components' of these interactions are of course not actually the birds themselves, but their own individual movements (e.g., fast, slow, up, down, left, right). These movements are of course dynamic too, and thus processes, created by internal processes of muscle action and sensory perception (et cetera).

In this way, the swarm is made up of nested levels of processes. It is this 'processes all the way up and all the way down' notion that makes the swarm, what is called, *soft-assembled* (Thelen & Smith, 1994); a term which we introduced in Chapter 2 to describe how a phenomenon emerges in a specific context in the here and now. The swarm behaviour will cease to 'be' when the birds stop interacting with each other, or when the birds stop moving.

This is what the handful of studies described below have done. Collectively, they describe the nature of these nested processes. At a low level of the system, they reveal how self-esteem related actions or experiences emerge into a coherent and recurrent experience of self-esteem in the current moment (De Ruiter et al., 2018; Wong, Vallacher & Nowak, 2014, 2016). Moving higher up, they describe the self-maintaining property of self-esteem that emerges across the span of many days, weeks, and months (Delignières et al., 2004; Fortes, Delignières, & Ninot, 2004; Ninot, Fortes & Delignières, 2005).

As we will see, these studies demonstrate an array of disparate operational definitions of self-esteem, the majority of them work to elucidate the

5.2 Descriptions and Conceptualizations of Self-Esteem

process ontology of self-esteem, united not by their method but by their meta-theoretical perspective – namely, the Complex Dynamic Systems approach. Fearon (2004) and Sabat et al.'s (1999) studies (see Section 5.2.1 above) resonate with this approach while not explicitly adopting it.

5.2.2.1 Time-Series Account of Behavioural and Emotional Cues

In our own research on self-esteem processes, we analysed participants' verbal and nonverbal self-esteem cues, such as eye contact aversion, nervous laughter, or autonomous actions (De Ruiter et al., 2015; De Ruiter et al., 2018). Rather than analysing these cues as occurring in the context of self-reflection – as the qualitative studies above did, we studied naturally occurring self-esteem cues of adolescents in dialogue with a parent. This allowed us to investigate the situated nature of self-esteem processes as well as the intrinsic dynamics of self-esteem processes in real-life relationships (which we will describe in the section *Higher-order soft-assembled recurrent patterns*).

The process of categorizing and quantifying what is observed in real-life dyadic interactions requires a coding scheme; an inscription device that comes with its own praxis (see, e.g., Hennessy et al., 2020). The deductive method of coding attempts to create a kind of pre-defined state space for a potential dynamic trajectory of a self-esteem process, in that it provides the researcher with a set of potential behaviours that an individual system can do. Such a 'set' will always be for a specific context, as different contexts afford different experiences (described earlier). In our case, we developed a coding scheme for observing expressions of self-esteem in the context of adolescents talking to a parent in their home (see De Ruiter et al., 2015 and De Ruiter et al., 2018). These expressions were categorized into different categories of self-esteem cues for adolescents: self-affect and autonomy. We also developed a coding scheme for mapping parents' regulatory cues: autonomy support and connectedness.

The dyads were asked to discuss a topic that had recently resulted in conflict; such as the adolescent not cleaning up their room or having inappropriate friends. These interactions were videotaped for later analysis. The richness of facial expressions, posture, physical position, intonation, and speech content was turned into multidimensional time series representing the coded categories (Figure 5.1).

This approach thus demonstrates that ways of *doing* self-esteem (i.e., autonomous actions and expressions of self-affect) can be mapped as processes situated in time and context (the context of parental behaviour and affect). This processual mapping was used to further analyse the

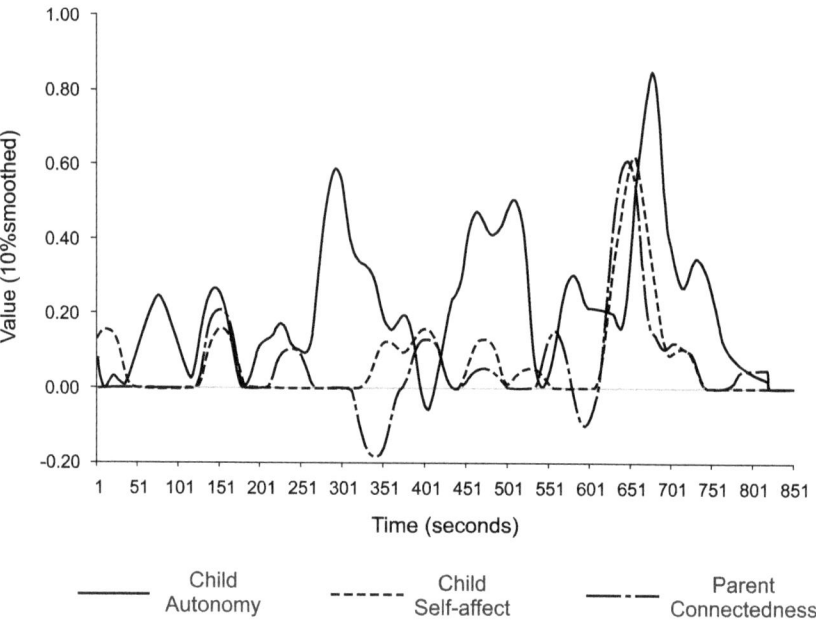

Figure 5.1 Time series for adolescent autonomy, adolescent self-affect, and parental connectedness during one parent–child interaction for one dyad.

intrinsic dynamics of self-esteem as a moment-to-moment situated process (which will be described below in Section 5.2.3).

5.2.2.2 Time-Series Account of Narratives

The next processual study of self-esteem that I will discuss is different from the others described in this chapter in that self-esteem processes were not studied in a social context, Specifically, Wong, Vallacher & Nowak (2014, 2016) used an unstructured narrative form, where participants were asked to describe themselves for three minutes while sitting alone, resulting in a kind of stream of thought narrative about their personality, preferences, goals, and social life.

This qualitative data was then quantified by the participants themselves: The narratives were played back to them, and they were asked to rate the content on a moment-to-moment basis as being positive or negative in self-evaluation by moving a cursor across a screen (the *mouse paradigm*). This resulted in a uni-dimensional time series of self-evaluation. This method, like the previous one discussed, was used to demonstrate the intrinsic dynamics of self-evaluation, which will be described later on in Section 5.2.3).

5.2 Descriptions and Conceptualizations of Self-Esteem

This approach, while not explicitly interested in the *socially* situated nature of self-esteem processes, examined individuals' self-evaluations in the context of the research task: taking a *self-as-object* perspective. This context is something that is commonly created when participants fill in a self-esteem questionnaire and are forced to take their 'Self' as the object of reflection (Ryan & Brown, 2003). The free-narrative nature of Wong, Vallacher & Nowak's (2014, 2016) studies thus effectively affords the same kind of experience of 'self' as classic self-reports, but in an unstructured way.

This task thus allows for self-evaluation (and the corresponding valence) to wax and wane based on the natural intrinsic dynamics of the individual's self-evaluations – that is, the system of self-evaluation, rather than based on an interview or questionnaire structure determined externally. The advantage of studying self-esteem in the context of this affordance is that the researchers were able to examine this process of self-evaluation in terms of the moment-to-moment structure and dynamics that emerged. This approach to self-esteem is thus one that relates to the question 'what kind of self-esteem processes occur when individuals are instructed to take a self-as-object perspective'? What Wong, Vallacher & Nowak's (2014, 2016) operational definition of self-esteem contributes to is, therefore, the understanding of self-esteem when individuals adopt a self-as-object perspective and thus 'perform' self-esteem to themselves on demand.

5.2.2.3 Time-Series Account of Self-Report

The last operational definition of self-esteem used in process research (to the best of my knowledge) can be seen as the closest to the standard questionnaire approach, while still clearly enacting a process ontology. Ninot and colleagues (Delignières, Fortes & Ninot, 2004; Fortes, Delignières, & Ninot, 2004; Ninot, Fortes & Delignières, 2005) used self-report measures of self-esteem that were adjusted to measure self-esteem *at the current moment*, thus tapping into the current self-evaluations (i.e., state self-esteem). The authors gathered high-frequency data by asking individuals twice a day to reflect on their self-esteem (i.e., 'globally, you have a good opinion of yourself') in the current moment using a visual analogue scale, and they did so for 228 consecutive days. These self-report measures were filled in while the participants were taking part in their everyday lives. As such, they are situated – although the authors did not explicitly explore the role of the context.

This approach, while using self-report questions similar to those used in the standard substance-ontology praxis, enacts a process ontology because of the way that the repeated measures of state self-esteem were used in subsequent analyses. Instead of using them as a means for capturing a central tendency (i.e., an average self-esteem score, or the standard deviation) as is done in the mainstream use of repeated state self-esteem measures (e.g., Kernis et al., 1993), the authors analyzed the *time evolution* of the self-evaluations (the results of this analysis will be described in Section 5.2.3).

Aside from the obvious focus on *processes* (instead of aggregated central-tendencies), all of the above time-series approaches enact a process ontology in that they assume that a) there is not a persistent self-esteem entity that underlies the observed and variable properties of self-experience; b) the variability or fluctuations of self-experience are the main properties of interest, and are thus *not* viewed as random noise; and c) the assessment of self-esteem processes does not resemble an attempt to *measure* a central tendency – or stable property – of self-esteem, but to describe processes of self-experience. All of these studies attempted to study the process nature of self-esteem by following these processes (across varying timescales) as closely as possible.

5.2.3 A United Analytical Framework: Complex Dynamic Systems

The complex dynamic systems approach (reviewed in Chapter 2) provides conceptual principles and methodological tools that can help to clarify what the nature or quality of processes are at each level of a complex system and how they interact, so that we might have an understanding of what *self-esteem as nested processes* really means. Because a complex dynamic systems approach provides both conceptual and methodological tools, it lends itself particularly well to the development of a comprehensive process-oriented praxis of self-esteem research (Olthof et al., 2020a).

5.2.3.1 Intrinsic Dynamics of Self-Esteem Variability

From a complex dynamic systems approach, interactions between the processual components of a system are the building blocks for the emergence of higher-order and self-maintaining patterns of self-experience that we might call 'self-esteem'. For self-esteem, these components are the concrete emotions or actions that relate to one's experience of Self in a positive or negative way. As such, the *temporal structure* of variability observed in these components is informative. Importantly, it is not the components as such that are central here, but the interaction between them. A process ontology, therefore, implies *interaction-dominant causality*, which means that it is the interactions between components of a system that cause its behaviour, not the existence of a specific set of components (Van Orden, Holden & Turvey, 2003).

This contrasts the substantialist approach in self-esteem research, where only the aggregate structure of variability is seen as informative (i.e., the average bandwidth of the variability, for example). This is based on the assumption that the in-the-moment experience of self-esteem (often called *state self-esteem*) is a function of the individual's 'underlying' level of self-esteem (called *trait self-esteem*) plus deviations due to the current context. The temporal structure that this corresponds with would thus be that of *white noise*, which is noise with a stable bandwidth that varies randomly (with regard to the temporal structure) around a stable baseline.

A major empirical goal within a process-ontology praxis for self-esteem research has, therefore, been to demonstrate that the *nature of the self-esteem variability* is not that of white noise, but instead, it demonstrates intrinsic dynamics that resemble interaction-dominant causality. In other words, the various moments of situated self-esteem are being carried forward, such that the previous moment affects the next (i.e., iterativity and recursiveness), so that something emerges, over time, out of the variability demonstrated across the moments. The 'something', here, is a pattern of self-esteem (which I will discuss more below).

To examine the nature of this temporal variability, process-oriented researchers studied the temporal structure of the time series generated in the various ways described in the previous sections (time series of behavioural and emotional cues during dyadic interactions, of narratives related to Self, and of self-report across a large span of days). The studies described above used different statistical tools to characterize the nature of the temporal variability in these time series, but they all did so in a within-individual manner. This means that the time series were not averaged together and then analysed as an average, but kept separate. The analyses included Auto-Regressive-Intregration-Moving-Average (ARIMA) procedures (e.g., Fortes, Delignières, & Ninot, 2004), fractal analyses (Delignières, Fortes & Ninot, 2004; Wong, Vallacher & Nowak, 2014), and Detrended Fluctuation Analysis (De Ruiter et al., 2015). Note that it is beyond the scope of this chapter to describe the features of these analyses, so interested readers are encouraged to read the original papers for more statistical information.

What is important here, is that all of the studies showed that the within-individual variability of self-esteem components did *not* resemble white noise around a stable mean or constant (De Ruiter et al., 2015; Ninot, Fortes & Delignières, 2005). Instead, the temporal variability (within individuals) – in all cases – gave way to intrinsic dynamics. Different aspects of this intrinsic dynamic were revealed, such as a short-term adjustment (Ninot, Fortes & Delignières, 2005), a dynamic interplay between 'preservation, which tends to restore the previous value after a disturbance, and adaptation, which tends to inflect the series in the direction of the perturbation' (Fortes, Delignières & Ninot, 2004, p. 12), and pink noise or fractal dynamics (De Ruiter et al., 2015; Wong, Vallacher & Nowak, 2014).

What all of these results showed is that there is, indeed, historicity across the points, such that what happens at one moment is related to what happens at the next moment and moments much later on. Together, these findings directly support the assumption of interaction-dominant causality in self-esteem by showing that the process of self-esteem is self-organizing, rather than simply a reaction to the immediate contextual cue. The iterations of self-experience that occur from moment to moment are thus not simply temporary deviations from a baseline level, but they are interacting across time to give rise to a larger pattern.

5.2.3.2 Higher-Order Soft-Assembled Recurrent Patterns of Self-Esteem
Any self-esteem researcher will acknowledge that there is some kind of 'stability' (i.e., patterning) relevant to self-esteem, in the sense that something persists through time. As Bickhard (2009a) described, there are at least two broad types of stability. One is 'that in which an instance of the organization remains stable unless some above-threshold amount of energy impinges on it', and the second (which is more characteristic for psychological phenomena) is 'dependent on its being maintained' (p. 554). For this second type of stability, stability can be maintained by external sources and by processes of recursive self-maintenance. Recursive self-maintenance means that the system continuously changes its activities or those in its environment in order to maintain its own existence. A central aim for process-oriented self-esteem researchers has thus been to demonstrate that self-esteem is a recursively self-maintaining system, where its own activity (i.e., moment-moment intrinsic dynamics) maintains the existence of a stable property of self-esteem that shows recurrence. The property of self-esteem thus recurs over time.

The methods adopted by process-oriented self-esteem researchers for capturing a recurrent stable property of self-esteem that emerges out of its own intrinsic dynamics have been just as heterogeneous as the operational definitions of self-esteem themselves described above. Nevertheless, the findings from these various studies tell a coherent story. They have all

5.2 Descriptions and Conceptualizations of Self-Esteem

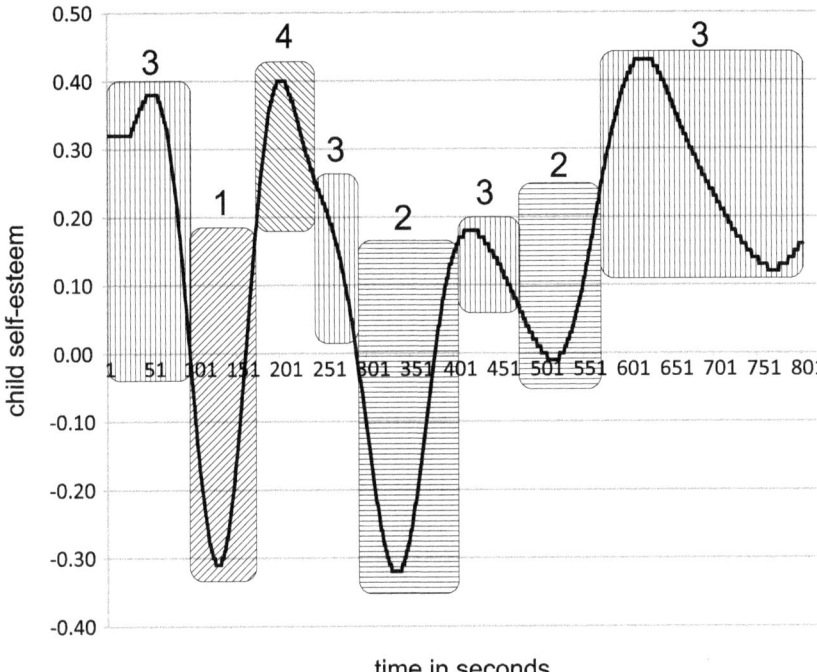

Figure 5.2 Significantly different combinations of self-esteem cues observed for one adolescent (represented by the numbered boxes), transposed onto a time series for the adolescent's average valence of self-esteem cues (averaged across the cues simultaneously occurring at one moment). Both trajectories took place during one parent–child interaction.

found evidence of recurring self-esteem qualities that have self-organized across the time series.

For example, in our (De Ruiter et al., 2018) study, we used a data-mining technique called Kohonen's Self-Organizing Maps to find re-current qualities (within individuals) in time series (for more information on this technique, see De Ruiter et al., 2017). With this method, we found that each adolescent repeatedly returned to certain combinations of self-esteem cues (i.e., autonomous actions and self-affect) while interacting with their parent. Figure 5.2 shows the average valence of the adolescent's self-esteem cues (averaged across the cues simultaneously occurring at one moment) across the discussion (*y*-axis). Transposed onto this line are numbered boxes. These correspond to the content of the self-esteem cues, where each numbered box is a unique combination of self-affect and autonomy (i.e., a different pattern, or *way of doing*, self-esteem). For example, In the language adopted in the Kohoen's Self-Organizing Maps technique, each of these combinations is referred to as a 'network' of components, and each one is statistically significantly different from the rest (in Figure 5.2, these are Network 1, 2, 3, and 4). For example, Network 3 is a combination of a positive expression of self-affect (e.g., upright posture, voice projected, or eye contact) with an autonomous behaviour toward the parent (e.g., proposing a new idea, confronting the parent, defending themself). As the name of the technique suggests, each network emerged from the interactions between the components, that is, the discrete moments of self-affect and autonomy from one moment to the next (*self-organization*).

What is primarily interesting for the processual aims of this study was that Network 2 and 3 were recursive, recurring more than once across the interaction (with Network 2 recurring twice, and Network 3 recurring four times). This recurrence of specific ways of doing self-esteem demonstrates the *self-maintaining* stability of self-esteem during the interaction. These self-organizing patterns of self-esteem-related actions thus demonstrate properties that are typical of *attractors* (introduced in Chapter 2), which are emergent patterns that a system is drawn to, away from alternative modes of system behaviour.

Aside from the temporal structure observed in this data, one could of course also focus on the qualitative information available in the recurrent patterns of self-esteem. While this was not the focus in the published work (De Ruiter et al., 2018), investigating the qualitative make-up of the networks would bring this analysis closer to the discursive approach described earlier (in Section 2.2.1). For example, some networks were internally 'coherent', where both self-affect and autonomy share the same valence: either positive self-affect (e.g., smiling) combined with autonomy (i.e., proposing an idea) or negative self-affect (e.g., downward gaze) combined with *heteronomous* behaviour (e.g., relinquishing one's turn to give input). Other networks, however, were internally 'incoherent' (true for Network 2, here), such that the valence of self-affect and autonomy were opposite. These 'incoherent' ways of doing self-esteem may be interesting to explore as, for example, potential 'unsuccessful' attempts to perform positive self-esteem. Patterns of self-presentation such as these may be an interesting avenue to explore in terms of the discourse conventions afforded by parent–adolescent interactions, and as part of identity negotiation in this context (Lichtwarck-Aschoff et al., 2008).

While the above study focussed on recurrent patterns of qualitatively distinct combinations of self-esteem cues, another way of investigating the emergent stability of self-esteem is to study the recurrence of certain valences. Wong, Vallacher & Nowak (2016) examined the valence of self-evaluation that the participants returned to the most during the free-flow

5.2 Descriptions and Conceptualizations of Self-Esteem

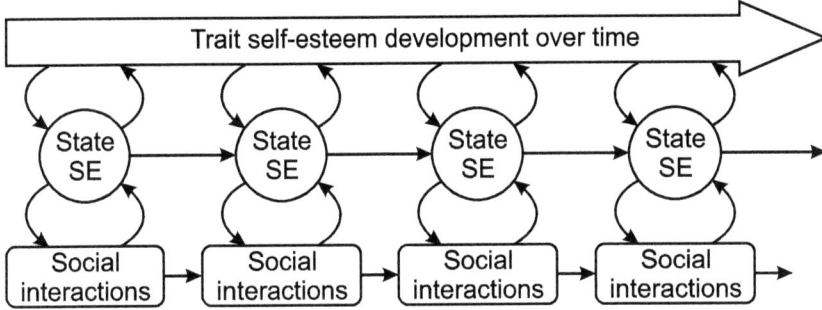

Figure 5.3 Circular causality between trait and state self-esteem, stemming from the SOSE model from De Ruiter et al. (2017).

narrations about the Self. The authors found that, while the valence of the self-narrations varied across the experiment, each participant gravitated to certain valences (e.g., neutral and very positive), and quickly moved past and did not settle on other valences (e.g., moderately high). Valences that participants were drawn to repeatedly were characterized as recurrent and self-maintaining *attractors*, and valences that were avoided were characterized as *repellers* (i.e., unstable points that cannot be maintained).

These studies (De Ruiter et al., 2018 and Wong, Vallacher & Nowak, 2016) showed that individuals settle on *multiple* self-esteem patterns, characterized either by their quality (i.e., types of self-esteem cue) or their general valence. This suggests that self-esteem is likely multi-stable. In revealing this multi-stability in self-esteem processes, the above studies contrast the traditional perspective of individuals having one baseline level of trait self-esteem.

Both studies showed the recurrent nature of these patterns, where this recurrence was interpreted as evidence of attractor properties. This is an important part of re-conceptualizing self-esteem as a system that is capable of self-maintenance, and thus stability, via its own intrinsic dynamics. This recurrence, according to complex systems theory, is due to the 'pull' that attractors have on the system. This 'pull' is the process of *downward causation* that is typical of emergent higher-order structures in complex systems (which, together with the *upward causation* involved in self-organization, result in *circular causality*; see Chapter 8). Downward causation is the process of constraining the variability of lower-order interactions, such that lower-order components resonate with the attractor.

The process of circular causality for self-esteem is depicted below in Figure 5.3. In our Self-Organizing Self-Esteem (SOSE) model (De Ruiter et al., 2017), we conceptualized state and trait self-esteem as two separate but reciprocally dependent processual parts of the self-esteem system, whereby they are interlinked by means of constant upward causation, or emergence (upper arrows between state self-esteem and trait self-esteem development) and downward causation, or constraint (downward arrows between trait self-esteem development and state self-esteem).

In our (De Ruiter et al., 2018) study, we used the State Space Grids (SSG) method to explicitly examine the dynamic relationship between these two levels of self-esteem. In this study, we re-analysed the data described above, based on adolescents interacting with their parents. 'Trait self-esteem' (as the relatively stable aspect of self-esteem) was operationalized as the emergent 'networks' of adolescents' self-esteem cues (described above, see Figure 5.2). State self-esteem (as the momentary and fleeting experience of self-esteem) was operationalized as the average valence of their self-esteem cues for each moment in the interaction. We then used the SSG technique to map the temporal variability of adolescents' state self-esteem and their trait self-esteem. This mapping is shown in Figures 5.4a and 5.4b, showing two SSGs for two different adolescents.

Both grids consist of a two-dimensional space, with one dimension being the adolescent's two most recurrent 'trait self-esteem clusters' (i.e., two separate 'networks' of self-esteem cues, shown on the y-axis), and the second dimension being the adolescent's 'state self-esteem level' (i.e., the average valence of their current self-esteem cues, shown on the x-axis). The lines on the grid show how these two trajectories intersected. In Figure 5.4a, we see that when the adolescent experienced Trait self-esteem cluster 1, this corresponded with relatively low state self-esteem (i.e., 2) and neutral state self-esteem (i.e., 3); whereas experiences of Trait self-esteem cluster 1 corresponded with relatively high state self-esteem (i.e., 4) and neutral state self-esteem. This kind of grid thus shows that the trajectories of higher- and lower-order self-esteem processes corresponded highly with each other across time.

In contrast, this temporal correspondence is not present in Figure 5.4b. This grid shows that the adolescent experienced (roughly) the same range of state self-esteem levels during Trait self-esteem cluster 2 *and* 1.

These differences were interpreted as indicative of two different types of trait self-esteem attractors. The adolescents that had grids resembling that in Figure 5.4a were thought to have highly entrenched, or 'strong', trait self-esteem attractors, such that the experience of a specific trait self-esteem attractor (i.e., called 'cluster' in the figure) means that lower-order variability (i.e., state self-esteem) was constrained within a certain range. Adolescents that had grids resembling that in Figure 5.4b, however, were thought to have 'weak' attractors that are less entrenched, such that experiencing one trait self-esteem attractor resulted in only weak, or no constraint

5.2 *Descriptions and Conceptualizations of Self-Esteem* 107

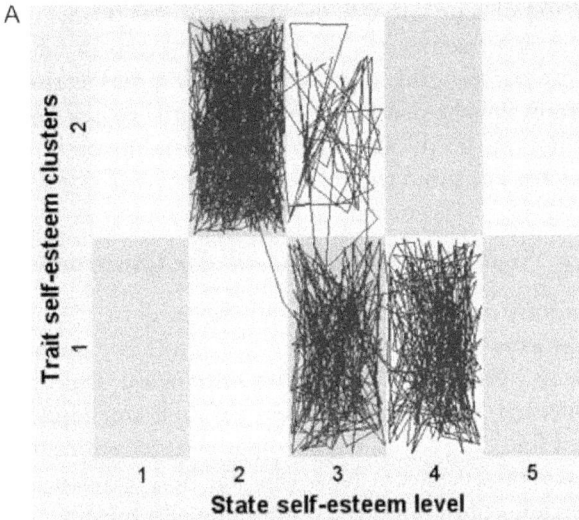

Figure 5.4a   A state space grid showing a for one adolescent, showing that the trajectory of 'trait self-esteem clusters' (i.e., statistically different combinations of self-esteem cues that frequently recurred) corresponds highly with the trajectory of 'state self-esteem level' (i.e., the average valence of their current self-esteem cues at that moment).

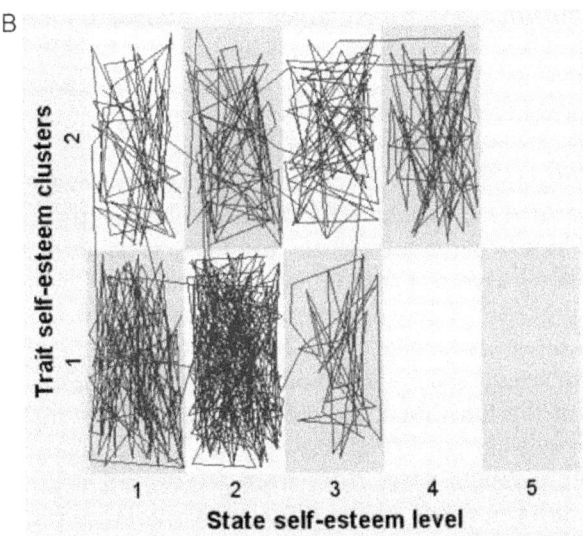

Figure 5.4b   A state space grid showing a for one adolescent, showing that the trajectory of 'trait self-esteem clusters' (i.e., statistically different combinations of self-esteem cues that frequently recurred) does not correspond with the trajectory of 'state self-esteem level' (i.e., the average valence of their current self-esteem cues at that moment).

on the direction of state self-esteem movement (for further description of weak and strong attractors, see the section *Attractors* in Chapter 2). The difference between the grids of these two profiles was statistically significant. This study thus helped to further conceptualize self-esteem as characterized by person-specific attractors that, depending on how entrenched the attractors are, constrain the variability of state self-esteem.

5.3 Separate Roads of Knowledge Construction?

The above process-oriented studies of self-esteem illustrate how the 'enactment' of a process ontology in self-esteem research is in many ways an explicit process. Whereas many of the ontological assumptions in the substance-oriented praxis of self-esteem research are implicit, and indirectly implied (see Chapter 4), the ontological assumptions in the process-oriented praxis of self-esteem have thus far been explicit and form the theory-driven aims of the empirical endeavours. In this way, philosophical assumptions about the nature of reality are not just *reflected*, but actively examined in the process-oriented praxis of self-esteem research. The results of these studies then also offer direct evidence for the process ontology that is examined.

Are we now left with two disparate realities of what self-esteem is and what it means for individuals? Perhaps not. Because the driving forces between the substance-ontology praxis and the process-oriented praxis are in many ways different, it may be possible to contextualize the two praxes and to see how they may be able to coexist. Specifically, while the aim of process-oriented self-esteem researchers has been theory-driven (with a specific emphasis on establishing a process ontology), the aim of substance-oriented self-esteem research has predominantly been to establish relationships between self-esteem and other variables (i.e., universal laws related to self-esteem as a secondary substance, see Chapter 4). These are separate processes of knowledge construction, for which one need not threaten the other (as long as group-based results are not used to make ontological or causal statements about psychological processes relevant to the level of the individual, see the *ergodicity problem* in Chapter 9). Results from substance-oriented research can be informative about relevant group differences, while those from process-oriented research can then inform us of how self-esteem processes work for individuals within these groups.

To demonstrate how a substance- and process-oriented self-esteem praxis may work collaboratively on two separate, but related, processes of knowledge construction, let me take *self-esteem stability* (Kernis et al., 1993) as an example, described in-depth in Chapter 4. This term is used to describe the magnitude of short-term fluctuations that people experience in their current, contextually based feelings of self-worth. As described above, it is a concept that is derived from substance-oriented research, based on the assumption that individuals have a true level of self-esteem, and that state self-esteem fluctuates (with a stable bandwidth) around this baseline level in response to contextual cues.

Studies from process-oriented research have provided direct evidence *against* this ontology, showing that state self-esteem has its own intrinsic dynamics and that there is not a baseline of self-esteem that individuals return to after deviations pass (see Section 5.2.3.1).

However, the group-based findings are of course still valuable, as long as we do not use those results to inform us of the ontology of self-esteem. For example, group-based research has shown that some individuals have, what is called, *fragile* (or insecure) self-esteem (i.e., lower self-esteem stability; Kernis et al., 1993). On average, these individuals demonstrate higher levels of self-esteem contingency (where self-esteem is contingent on what others think of them; Harter & Whitesell, 2003) when compared to individuals with *secure* (or stable) self-esteem, i.e., higher self-esteem stability (Kernis et al., 1993). This research has highlighted the theoretical relevance of 'self-esteem stability', suggesting that stable self-esteem provides individuals with a solid foundation for their feelings of self-worth, such that feelings of self-worth are 'well-anchored' (Zeigler-Hill, 2011). For example, these studies suggest that individuals with 'secure' self-esteem are more likely to be able to handle ups and downs in their daily lives than those individuals with 'insecure' self-esteem (Greenier, Kernis & McNamara, 1999). This research highlights the relevance of 'stable' versus 'unstable' self-esteem as a property of self-esteem.

A possible association between two variables at the group level, however, does not reveal how these properties relate within individuals, or *why* individuals may be more or less reactive to contextual cues (i.e., where this 'anchor' comes from). Process-oriented research on self-esteem can provide an explanation for these underlying mechanisms and processes that function at the individual level. For example, in our (De Ruiter et al., 2018) study, we also found that adolescents with 'strong' attractor profiles showed fewer perturbations from their parents' autonomy-management behaviour and expressions of connectedness. This is of course in line with the general attractor properties that the study aimed to show, where strong attractors mean that the system is not easily perturbed. In the context of

Zeigler-Hill (2011) and Greenier, Kernis & McNamara's (1999) suggestion that individuals with secure self-esteem are more able to handle ups and downs in their daily lives, our results offer an explanation as to why this is: If individuals' self-esteem is conceptualized as processes of self-esteem experiences that self-organize attractors, then these attractors become further entrenched (and thus stronger) when patterns of self-experiences are repeated over time, whereas they become less entrenched (and thus weaker) when they are not repeated over time. Thus, as individuals develop a solid sense of self (by virtue of certain patterns of self-esteem showing recurrence), their self-esteem attractors become more entrenched. As this happens, the self-esteem attractors provide a strong anchor for self-experiences, thus resulting in less variability of self-esteem and more resistance to external perturbations (i.e., ups and downs in daily life).

In a similar way, processual results regarding the properties of entrenched self-esteem patterns can explain why mainstream studies have found that individuals' self-esteem levels become increasingly similar to their previous levels as they transition from adolescence to adulthood (i.e., increased autoregressive stability longitudinally; Donnellan et al., 2012). During adolescence, individuals typically explore various Selves and have yet to develop an entrenched and stable pattern of self-esteem. As a result, their self-esteem will necessarily be less constrained, and more sensitive to perturbations – resulting in more variability. This might account for the relatively low autoregressive stability of self-esteem evaluations during that period. As the transition from adolescence to adulthood is typically the period in which individuals solidify their sense of self, an increase in self-esteem consistency over time may be explained by the formation of increasingly strong (i.e., entrenched) self-esteem attractor states as individuals develop a stronger sense of self.

As we can see, processual research that has focussed largely on reconceptualizing the ontology of self-esteem can explain group-based findings that stem from substance-oriented research, with those related to 'stability' as a prime example.

5.4 Self-Esteem in the Real World: Experiencing the Stability and Flux of Self-Experience

While a process ontology of self-esteem denies the existence of an underlying or true self-esteem in the form of a baseline or a trait, it is not antirealist. Self-esteem is real. It is the *doing* of self-esteem, and the *experience* of that doing, that is real, rather than the *having* of self-esteem.

This chapter illustrates the different ways that researchers can study how people do or experience self-esteem, including responding in various ways to threatening or affirming social cues, reflecting on one's own abilities and attributes, or protecting or maintaining how these attributes are presented to the world. These are all self-related experiences that can be seen as having a valence and can thus be characterized as self-esteem experiences.

These experiences are not simply momentary passive reactions to our context, however. They have their own intrinsic dynamics, which is necessarily embedded in the current context and bi-directionally connected to it, emerging into attractors of valenced self-experience. These attractors are also *experienced*. For example, consider a moment in which someone feels deeply ashamed and inferior after receiving some feedback that is arguably quite neutral. The disproportionately negative self-experience may come as a surprise or frustrate this person. The experience of this frustrating *pull* to negative self-experiences is thus the experience of the higher-order self-esteem attractor. It is the experience of the 'attraction' to a certain pattern. We thus experience the lower- and higher-order levels of self-esteem simultaneously, both in the here and now. We experience a concrete emotion, action, or thought, and we experience how this enacts a personal history of patterned self-experience. Moreover, these attractors are not something that individuals *have* in the sense that they are static properties that are isolable from the context. These attractors are *done* in the sense that they emerge as individuals act in interaction with the current context (i.e., *soft assembly*) and are constantly evolving (i.e., they are *enacted*).

This conceptualization corresponds with the framing of Self as *self-as-process*, as opposed to *self-as-object*. Ryan and Brown (2003) described the conceptualization and engagement of self-as-object as the having of (and appraisal of) a representation of 'self' (described in Chapter 4). In contrast, self-as-process was described as the process of engaging with our actions and experiences that occur as we interact with the world. Ryan and Brown claimed that people do not need self-esteem, in the sense that they do not need a positive appraisal of 'the Self'. They argue that the very act of asking 'how worthy am I?' (which is necessary for a positive appraisal of self-worth) suggests that 'worth' is not a given and that there is a more fundamental lack of happiness or fulfilment of basic psychological needs. In this way, if individuals 'have high self-esteem' in the classic sense (such that they have a representation of their 'self-as-object' as being 'worthy'), they will necessarily have been preoccupied with their 'worth', which suggests that it was up for debate in the first place.

Instead of encouraging people to be preoccupied with the worth of their Self (as self-as-object), Ryan and Brown (2003) suggested that engaging with a self-as-process is key to being fundamentally and non-contingently happy. They explained that engaging with such a conceptualization relieves us from the obligation to esteem the self. Instead, it enables us to simply engage in 'ongoing activities of extending, assimilating, and bringing meaning and coherence to life experiences' (p. 71). Indeed, 'when standards are not met, failures occur, or rejections are experienced, one can experience disappointment, feel sadness and loss, or question and re-evaluate one's actions – but the self as a whole is not made into an object, and then disparaged … [to operate without concern with self-esteem] entails taking interest in what one has been up to and what has occurred, including its effects and meaning' (p. 74). This is in line with Cigman's (2004) notion of *situated* self-esteem. In this way, a process ontology of self-esteem encourages us to engage with the situated flux and patterning of self-experiences without implicating what these might reveal or mean for a (non-existent) underlying entity that is *self-esteem*.

5.5 Conclusion: The Enactment of a Process Ontology in Self-Esteem Research

In summation, the study of self-esteem can be grounded in two very different praxes: the mainstream substance-oriented praxis (see Chapter 4), and the process-oriented praxis (the current chapter). Both praxes enact diverging ontologies of self-esteem. The mainstream praxis enacts an ontology of a universal self-esteem substance, instantiated in individuals as separate self-esteem entities, where these self-esteem entities underlie daily waxing and waning of self-experiences. The process-oriented praxis enacts an ontology of nested processes of self-experience that are always *becoming*, and never reducible to a static 'thing'. These ontologies are enacted in the ways that researchers *measure* versus *describe* self-esteem, their analyses of *predictive relationships* between decontextualized variables versus *patterns of situated* self-esteem, which are based on *group-based* versus *individual* data, respectively.

The facts that are generated by these two praxes all have practical value. I do not wish to claim that one has more practical value over the other, as the two (should) have value for very different purposes. The

5.5 Conclusion

substance-oriented praxis is useful for establishing general group averages for self-esteem, whereas the process-oriented praxis is useful for elucidating *how* self-esteem works, develops, or stabilizes in particular contexts.

What I hope to have highlighted with my analyses of self-esteem praxes in this chapter and the previous one is that we need to be aware of the kind of knowledge that the two praxes can validly contribute to, and the specific ontology that the knowledge enacts. Knowledge stemming from group-based studies of self-esteem should not be assigned '*ontological* privileges and a universality which it does not deserve' (Rohde, 2010, p. 30). Just because we *can* quantify amounts of self-esteem and relate these amounts to other variables should not imply that self-esteem *is* a quantifiable underlying entity that *has* universal relationships with other variables (for more on measurement in psychology, see Chapter 9).

A process-oriented approach to self-esteem stresses, firstly, that 'self-esteem' is a human-made construct developed by researchers in order to aid our communication about how people experience themselves in a certain (positive or negative) way (Levy, 2019). Secondly, the construct of 'self-esteem' itself is processual by nature: it is process all the way up and all the way down (Dupré & Nicholson, 2018; Bickhard, 2011c). These are processes of *doing*, such that people *do* self-esteem in their moment-to-moment actions, as well as in their tendencies that they develop and enact over time. As such, all levels of self-esteem processes are dynamic, and cannot be reduced – on any level – to a static substance (*under-standing*) or entity.

Approaching self-esteem as ontologically processual has important implications for the kind of realities that our research praxis creates for people in general. If self-esteem is not perceived as a true essence that we have, then we can shift our attention *away* from boosting or protecting this true level, and *to* our actual context-bound actions and experiences as we move through the world (Ryan & Brown, 2003; Cigman, 2004).

As demonstrated in this chapter, the complex dynamic systems approach provides both theoretical and methodological tools for studying the process ontology of self-esteem. It helps us to develop a concrete idea of what the nature of self-esteem processes might be at various (nested) levels, as well as how these levels of processes interact. Together, the comprehensive meta-theoretical principles from this approach provide a strong and unifying framework for various (processual) operational definitions of self-esteem.

With this chapter and Chapter 4, the goal was to provide a broad picture of what a praxis does, which necessitated a specific research topic as a case study. In the following chapters, we delve more deeply into how a complex dynamic systems approach can provide a workable model for a process approach to specific and pivotal parts of the psychological praxis, including communication of results and the role of linguistic norms (Chapter 6), causal explanation (Chapters 7 and 8), measurement (Chapters 9 and 10), and establishing general validity in our field (Chapter 11).

CHAPTER 6

Cliffhangers and Utilitarian Infants
On How Classification and Science Communication Create Worlds

> The fact of the matter is that the 'real world' is to a large extent unconsciously built upon the language habits of the group.
>
> Edward Sapir, 'Language, Culture and Personality'
> (1949, p. 69), from a lecture delivered in 1928

> Hopi, with its preference for verbs, as contrasted to our own liking for nouns, perpetually turns our propositions about things into propositions about events.
>
> Benjamin Lee Whorf, 'Language, Thought and Reality'
> (1956, p. 63), from a paper probably written in 1936

6.1 Crossing the Visual Cliff and Failed Experiments

In virtually all first-year psychology textbooks, the visual-cliff experiment (Gibson & Walk, 1960) is presented as a device to measure or demonstrate an infant's ability to perceive depth at an early age, basically before the infant could have learned about depth by means of extensive experience. In this experiment, a baby is placed on a transparent horizontal plane. Under this plane is a 'cliff'. The baby is placed on the highest point of this cliff. The baby is faced forward, such that they would see the cliff declining in front of them. On the other side of the cliff, the mother stands facing the baby. The mother is instructed to encourage the baby to cross the 'cliff'. In this experiment, the criterion of *depth perception* is the infant's 'freezing' at the edge of the cliff, before the decline.

Years ago, a colleague of ours[1] was hired by a television production company to assist in the making of a documentary series where the highlights of early child development would be shown by means of the

---

[1] Marijn van Dijk, who has published extensively on intraindividual variability and detailed process studies in language development, scientific reasoning in young children and the transition from breast or bottle feeding to spoon feeding in babies; see also the section Spoon Feeding and Conversations (Van Dijk & Van Geert, 2014; Van Dijk, Hunnius & Van Geert, 2009, 2012).

classical developmental-psychology experiments, including the visual-cliff experiment.[2] The experimental conditions were meticulously reconstructed in the form of a construction of wood and safety glass, the size of a small room. The crew invited one mother and baby pair, despite the fact that our colleague – being an expert on intra- and inter-individual variability – warned them that real experiments of this sort do not always succeed and thus usually involve a number of babies. But as the producer had read that it is scientifically proven that twelve-month-old infants 'can do the visual cliff', it was assumed that a normal baby, above the age of twelve months, in good health and mood, in the child-friendly experimentation room would demonstrate the appropriate visual-cliff behaviour: freezing.

The experiment began: the mother took a position at the deep side of the visual cliff, and the infant – who was held by his aunt with whom he clearly felt comfortable – was put on the shallow side. The mother placed a toy, a soft cube with pictures on it, in front of her and began to gently urge her baby to crawl to her side in accordance with the protocol of the visual-cliff experiment. The baby looked at his mother, and then, against expectations, did what she asked. Rather than freezing, the baby crawled over the Plexiglas cover of the deep side, reached for the toy, and proceeded to play with it together with the mother. After playing with the cube, the baby then looked down for a while (inspecting the deep side of the cliff) and proceeded to crawl back to the shallow side of the visual cliff.

How is one to communicate and interpret these results? Was the baby unaware of the cliff underneath him? Could he not perceive its depth? Was he in fact aware of it, but not scared, as he was with his mother? Did the baby crawl back to the shallow side out of fear after finally perceiving the cliff's depth? Or did he crawl back to his aunt, who had held him in her arms before the experiment started? We don't know of course.

We could interpret this as evidence that the baby did not perceive the cues of depth, and therefore, the baby does not have depth perception. Such an interpretation would be in line with the standard use of this experiment. However, we find this an extremely narrow and specific notion of what depth perception means, and of what infants are actually doing when

---

[2] By presenting and discussing this example we follow two important recommendations from Michael Billig: the first is the importance of examples in psychological writing to counter the adverse effects of too much focus on theoretical terms (Billig, 2019), the other is a focus on a process or event description instead of using nouns (e.g., depth perception) to describe phenomena of interest (Billig, 2013). Both recommendations are directly in line with our process-oriented view.

6.1 Crossing the Visual Cliff and Failed Experiments

they take part in this experiment. This is because infants – when placed in such an experimental setting – are doing much more than simply demonstrating a (lack of) depth perception by freezing or not freezing at the beginning of the cliff.

The complexities of what infants are truly doing are not, however, habitually treated as relevant scientific information (we will discuss 'what counts as facts' in more depth in Chapter 11). But let us take a closer look at this particular visual cliff as a context of movement affordances. For reasons of safety, the deep side (but not the shallow side) of the visual cliff was surrounded by a plastic screen considerably higher than the infant's line of vision during his crawling position. This means that, one, as the infant approaches the deeper side of the visual cliff, he also approaches an obstacle (one which seems to grow visually bigger as he approaches it). Two, as his mother was standing behind this wall, once he reaches the end of the visual cliff, it is directly obvious that it is possible for him to actually get to his mother. Three, moving over a slippery Plexiglas cover (where soft baby clothes and socks provide almost no friction), requires quite some effort. Moreover, this increased effort makes it considerably more difficult than usual to change into an upward sitting position so that he could actually reach over the Plexiglas edge to his mother. With these factors in mind, returning to the side of the cliff that is not surrounded by Plexiglas might have looked like the most obvious possibility. This example illustrates the complex intertwining of affordances and constraints provided by this type of experiment. The infant's actions emerge in the context of these affordances and constraints, and are, most likely, not simply the result of some explicit prior deliberation of depth perception.

Instead of studying these contextual affordances and constraints on how infants navigate experimental settings, the non-random probability with which 'freezing' occurs in a group of infants is used to justify the presence of a depth-perception ability in infants. The practice of the experiment, including the data reduction and generalization, turns the visual-cliff apparatus into an inscription device for this specific ability. The visual cliff is a context stripped of all the confounding aspects of real or normal contexts, including the ability to learn (which would require repeated practice and conditions of intentional activity). But because of this 'purification' of the visual-cliff experiment, it is believed to be capable of directly assessing the real depth-perception capability of infants.

We could say that this type of explanation is typical of a substance philosophy, focussing on substances or essences in the form of isolable abilities (depth perception) associated with certain categories of people (infants) (for a discussion of the basic features of substances or essences, see Chapter 4; Robinson, 2016; Smith, 1997, 2003).

The way that we describe these research settings and outcomes – the language we use – is an integral part of how we come to understand or explain experiments like the visual-cliff experiment and its outcomes. The way we talk about research is thus a far from superficial issue.

The visual-cliff experiment, as it is presented to students in introductory psychology textbooks, avoids language use that might point toward contextualization, change, adaptation, or learning. Instead, textbooks describe abilities, age ranges, and static behaviours (freezing or not freezing). In fact, this is an example of teaching students 'to write badly', as Michael Billig (2013) has called it, that is, of teaching them to focus on thing-like abilities described by nouns ('depth perception ability') and to eschew concrete, event-based descriptions of real activities (Billig, 2019).

However, like many such inscription devices in psychological research (see the discussion on questionnaires in self-esteem research in Chapters 4 and 5), the visual cliff is actually a strange, unlikely, and extremely specific context, to which an infant is confronted only once and for a very constricted time window. Rather than describing what an infant can or can not do at a particular age, researchers could also describe what infants do as they interact with this uncommon and singular context. What they do, here, involves sensory-motor loops, with the infant's body as the central agent of these loops (and where depth perception is an intrinsic, inseparable aspect of these loops). In order to understand what infants do, researchers need to consider the phenomenological characteristics of such an experiment, describing what the infant is likely seeing, feeling, and wanting from one moment to the next as the specifics of the context change while they move. Such a phenomenological description places the reality of autonomous agents (here, the infants) in the foreground, and thus deviates from the sort of standard linguistic description of 'depth perception ability' (e.g., Grush & Springle, 2019). This was done in 2012 by Adolph and Kretsch, who revisited the extensive literature on the visual-cliff experiment. They came to the conclusion that the visual cliff should be reinterpreted as a context for studying the processes of exploration, adaptation, learning, and development in infancy (see also Adolph, Kretch & LoBue, 2014). This is in line with Gibson's later introduction of the ecological approach, where perceptual systems (embedded in acting organisms), coordinate perceptual information with bodily movement in an ongoing process. Visual information about movement affordances, for instance, is directly given in the form of a rich optical flow directly dependent on the organism's motion itself.

6.1 Crossing the Visual Cliff and Failed Experiments

From this perspective, the focus can be shifted from the static presence (or absence) of an ability that does or does not statistically depend on age as a correlate of the amount of experience, to the dynamics of exploration and activity in a complex context. In the classical visual cliff, the infant explores an environment offering a mixture of coherent and conflicting visual, tactile, emotional, and social information. Individual depth information conflicts with the tactile information of a solid surface. The social information in the form of the mother inviting the infant to come to her side is at the same time the prime determiner of the infant's intention to try to cross the visual cliff and to neglect potential conflicts with the visual information of an edge and a cliff. The interesting question is then how individual infants find their own, flexible ways of solving the visual-cliff problem, and whether and how they learn from repeatedly doing so. Adolph and Kretch (2012) showed that, when these intertwining processes are reduced to static effects of age, experience, or social factors, we are often left with seemingly contradictory results and replication issues. From the viewpoint of replicability, the visual-cliff literature provides a rather messy picture if researchers are hoping to find coherence with regards to the predictability of 'depth perception' based on age, experience, or social factors (see our discussion of the replicability issue in Chapter 11).

To conclude, the classical visual-cliff experiment can be described in largely divergent ways: as an ideal and iconic example of sound methodology in scientific research on developmental milestones, or as an ideal context to study how infants explore, adapt, and learn in complex environments with contradictory cues. These two descriptions of what an experiment is (or can do) enact two different pictures of 'the way the world is'. Language, therefore, is an important part of psychology's praxis.

6.1.1 On Words, Kinds, and Entities

The scientific terms, but also the colloquial words that we use, are ways of 'carving up' the world into what appears to be its natural categories or its 'natural kinds'. These are any categories deemed to be useful for understanding reality, such as 'men versus women' or 'children versus adolescents'. In his dialogue with Phaedrus (an Athenian aristocrat) about the forms of madness related to love (the modernity of those Greek philosophers is striking), Socrates says that there are two things that are worth taking into consideration if one deals with a particular topic. The first is 'bringing things which are scattered all over the place into a single class by gaining a comprehensive view of them, so that one can define any given thing and so clarify the topic one wants to explain at any time' (Phaedrus, 265d[3]). The second is to be 'able to cut things up again, class by class, according to their natural joints, rather than trying to break them up as an incompetent butcher might' (Phaedrus, 265e). The commonalities that we perceive in spite of all the particularities of appearance must be natural, they must be properties of the world (i.e., *natural* kinds).

In the philosophical literature, the definition of natural kinds varies from the true components of reality to pragmatic distinctions featuring in causal explanations and explanatory strategies (Bird, 2018; Bird & Tobin, 2018; Magnus, 2018; Beebee & Sabbarton-Leary, 2010; Hawley & Bird, 2011; Kendig, 2015). The *communis opinion* on natural kinds, in particular in the social and behavioural sciences, is that the natural distinction – based on empirical criteria of distinctive properties – is always both natural and interest-based. This means that what we come to see as separate natural kinds (i.e., ten month olds versus twelve month olds, for example) is intertwined with what we are interested in and what we deem as relevant. According to Boyd (2003, p. 538) 'natural kinds are features, not of the world outside our practice, but of the ways in which that practice engages with the rest of the world'. Hacking (2007, p. 203) takes this further, with a rather radical stance: 'Some classifications are more natural than others, but there is no such thing as a natural kind'.

Natural kinds thus serve as targets for social action, and through this targeted action we modify the meaning of the natural kinds (i.e., their significance as well as what counts as their properties). What is deemed a useful target and what is not is, firstly, domain specific. In psychology, the distinction between subjects with straight and curly hair does not coincide with a natural kind, as it is virtually never the basis of sampling into distinct research groups. But for a hairdresser, it forms a very obvious natural kind. These two natural kinds require different treatment, skills, and styling norms. At this most fundamental level, we can see how natural kinds are not features of the world per se, but of the way that we engage with our world.

Second, many if not all of the natural kinds that form the subject of psychological research are *constructs*, that is to say, categories resulting from human and research activities (Hacking, 2007). A construct is developed (i.e., becomes a target of our research) when we observe something of relevance, identify its unique features, and give it a label. Natural kinds of this type are thus not immutable and fixed features of our world, as we can come to identify or understand a given construct in a new way if

---

[3] www.perseus.tufts.edu/hopper/text?doc=Plat.+Phaedrus+265e&fromdoc=Perseus%3Atext%3A1999.01.0174

we change the way that we interact with it. The way that we interact with natural kinds therefore can change them as constructs.

Importantly, human beings are the only object of scientific research that 'talk back' (Kouwer, 1963). We observe classifications that are set upon us, and we proceed to assimilate and adapt to them. As such, the mere fact that we (not as humans more broadly, but as men or women, or as educated or uneducated individuals) are targets of psychological research means that we ('men' or 'women', 'educated' or 'uneducated') evolve alongside this human activity of targeted research. Hacking (1995a, b) has called the interaction between psychological science and the objects of research 'looping effects'. Classifications or categorizations are not independent descriptions of reality: in fact, they change the people who are thus classified, and the changes they bring about feed back onto future classification revision (Hacking, 1995a; 2013, Haslam, 2016). This was illustrated in-depth in Chapter 4, where the features of 'high self-esteem' versus 'low self-esteem' are construed as natural kinds and will be explored more broadly for the general psychological praxis in Chapter 12.

In identifying natural kinds ('one-year-olds', 'two-year-olds', 'children with autism spectrum disorder', 'girls' in comparison to 'boys', and so forth) and trying to identify features of these natural kinds (such as abilities) researchers are thus creating a world that is increasingly characterized by these natural kinds. The distinct kinds (ten month olds versus twelve month olds) are represented as increasingly divergent. This is because studying these natural kinds is typically done with a distinctive purpose: ascertaining whether a general property (i.e., ability) applies to one category and not to another (for instance, is depth perception characteristic of 'one-year-olds' or of 'infants with ample depth experience'?). If such distinctions hold, they will contribute to interpreting the population categories as meaningful and significant natural kinds.

Examining the world through natural kinds treats them as universal entities. The word *universal* means that they are treated as the common element shared by particular instances. For instance, what is common in every two-year-old infant is the age category 'two-year-old-ness'; what is common in every particular instance or actualization of depth perception in a particular infant is the universal entity 'depth perception'. They are universal substances or entities to which properties can be assigned. This assignment is often of a probabilistic nature, but this probabilistic meaning itself is subject to a whole range of problems related to the way we define the concept of probability (see also Chapter 10).

6.1.2 Extensional and Intensional Definitions and the Logic of Experiments

The standard practice of experimentation, and psychological research in general, heavily relies upon *extensional* definitions related to universal entities and classes (for a historical account, see Ostertag, 2020). A particular universal category or entity – let's say 'six months old', 'autism', 'depth perception', or 'intelligence' – is *extensionally* defined by the collection of all concrete instances to which this categorical definition applies. An *intensional* definition specifies the meaning of a term (e.g. autism) as an enumeration of its necessary and sufficient properties. Extensional definitions of universal entities can refer to kinds of individuals or to concepts related to abilities or dispositions. When referring to kinds of individuals, psychologists do not routinely speak about 'extensional sets', but of *population* and *sample*. The populational extension refers to the set of all six months olds or to the set of all people with autism, for instance. In the case of dispositions or abilities, such as depth perception or intelligence, the extensional set is a collection of all concrete instances where these dispositions or abilities occur or are displayed in the activity of organisms.

If we take the example of the visual cliff experiment, researchers are thus interested in two types of extensional definition of natural kinds: the populational extension of infants of ten months versus twelve months (extending to all individuals of these ages) and the conceptual extension of depth perception (extending to all concrete instances where depth perception is displayed). This particular experiment thus focusses on the intersection of these two extensional definitions of universal kinds. The problem with most extensional sets that are of interest to psychological research, however, is that they are in principle infinite, or indeterminate, to be more precise. For instance, the extensional set 'six months old' consists of all *current* six month olds, but also of all *former and future* six month olds. We are thus dealing with sets (of types of people or demonstrations of a concept) that are not immutable and static things, but changing across time and contexts (see also Section 10.3). How can one then claim to be studying a certain extensional set if that set is always changing?

The common pragmatic solution for this infinity or innumerability problem is to replace the infinite extensional set by a finite set that is said to 'represent' (i.e., stand in the place of, the infinite set). In psychology, researchers thus use samples of a population (e.g., a representative sample of ten-month-old infants). All members of the sample are known and countable, and will remain '10-month olds' for the duration of the study. The extensional set, therefore, is not going to change and is thus measurable. Furthermore, since depth-perception is not a stable set (i.e., it is displayed differently in different contexts), the standard solution is to replace it by a single representative condition, which is used as the measurement instrument. For instance, all possible instances of depth perception are represented by a single instance, namely the visual cliff.

The issue with the above solution (i.e., using finite and restricted representative samples and conditions to study extensions of kinds) is that researchers are assuming a substance ontology for natural kinds that cannot be characterized by this ontology. The information that might be gained about '10-month-olds' and their 'depth perception' may be representative in the traditional sense (representative samples and conditions were chosen), but not of the actual ontology of the entity we wish to understand. First, depth perception is not something that either is 'there' or 'not there'. Instead, it is part of ongoing action-perception loops bound up in the various contextual factors that the infant interacts with from moment to moment (as described in the previous section). Second, any specific ten-month-old infant is not the same tomorrow as it will be next week or three weeks from now. The way that this infant displays depth-perception, for instance, will not remain stable across the eleventh month of its life. By studying highly constrained and static versions of depth-perception for specific populations researchers are studying this ability in a way which is not actually, or naturally, displayed.

Processual approaches, in contrast, tend to turn this strategy upside down. First, they tend to focus on individuals, based on the idea that, on the one hand, the processes of interest occur in individual cases, and on the other hand, such processes are often highly idiosyncratic. A processual researcher may gather a collection of individual properties that can then be clustered on the basis of similarities and differences between these individual cases. Therefore, the processual researcher is not interested in the average abilities of ten month olds, but in a holistic description of how individual ten year olds (and perhaps a collection of them) *do* depth perception. With regard to contexts in which abilities or dispositions are displayed, process approaches tend to focus on the variability of contexts, as abilities or dispositions are defined as intrinsically context-determined. This is in stark contrast with the mainstream approach, where considering phenomena in a variety of natural (uncontrolled) contexts would be seen as contaminating the measurement condition. We can see, therefore, that specific approaches to extensional definitions of natural kinds enact significantly different ontologies. Below we discuss how, after establishing extensional definitions, researchers then create worlds via linguistic tools.

6.2 Text and the Creation of Infant Economists

6.2.1 *Infants Inferring the Value of Goals from the Cost of Actions*

In 2017, *Science* published an article showing that ten-month-old infants are capable of *inferring the value of goals from the costs of actions* (which is the title of the article). Infants were described as expecting an agent to prefer the goal that the agent attained through costlier actions. The article described that infants could thus make a distinction between activities of agents requiring various levels of effort as related to the difficulty of attaining a particular goal, such as jumping over a low versus a high fence (Liu et al., 2017).

By way of introducing the study, the abstract is as follows:

> Infants understand that people pursue goals, but how do they learn which goals people prefer? We tested whether infants solve this problem by inverting a mental model of action planning, trading off the costs of acting against the rewards actions bring. After seeing an agent attain two goals equally often at varying costs, infants expected the agent to prefer the goal it attained through costlier actions. These expectations held across three experiments that conveyed cost through different physical path features (height, width, and incline angle), suggesting that an abstract variable – such as 'force,' 'work,' or 'effort' – supported infants' inferences. We modeled infants' expectations as Bayesian inferences over utility-theoretic calculations, providing a bridge to recent quantitative accounts of action understanding in older children and adults. (Liu et al., 2017, p. 1038)

As the production of texts (i.e., manuscripts) is one of the major explicit goals of scientific research, the analysis of the way such texts enact ontologies might contribute to our understanding of the praxis-ontology relationship (the approach of discursive psychology, Edwards, 2005; Wiggins & Potter, 2008; Wiggins, 2016). With this analysis of Liu et al. (2017), we hope to illustrate how the language used in scientific articles work to transform the events that occurred in the context of a research activity – an experiment for instance – into data, which are then transformed into facts, which are then finally transformed into truths – or ontologies.

6.2.2 *Texts as Producers of Genericity*

Here, we shall focus on the use of *bare nouns* and *implicit quantifiers* in *generic statements* (e.g., Zahnoun, 2020). Although these terms do not sound terribly inviting, they are of considerable importance in scientific communication in psychology. They are linguistic tools for transforming concrete and specific data into general truths and constitute typical ways of constructing a particular substance-focussed reality. The abundant use of these linguistic tools is an example of 'nominalization', that is, the habit of representing phenomena that exist in the form of events and processes by nouns, thus hampering their understanding as contextual activities of concrete agents (e.g., infants) (Billig, 2013; see also Brian Arthur, 2021, in the context of economics).

6.2.2.1 Does 'Infants' Mean 'All Infants'? On Bare Nouns and Implicit Quantifiers

A bare noun is a noun without a determiner or quantifier. For instance, 'infants' is a bare plural noun, whereas 'the infants', 'three infants', 'an infant', 'some infants', 'all infants' are not, as they appear with a determiner such as *the* or *a(n)*, or appear with quantifiers such as *all*, *some* or *three*. Determiners thus specify what the noun is referring to. In empirical studies, the most relevant determiners are quantifiers, as they indicate how many concrete cases the noun refers to (e.g., all, many, some, none). Without these determiners, it remains unclear what the noun (e.g., infants) refers to, and the reader is left to use common linguistic practices to decipher the implicit meaning of these bare nouns.

Bare nouns often carry an implicit meaning of determination or quantification, which is most often dependent on the linguistic context (e.g., the verb and noun phrase construction of the sentence in which they appear; Gillon, 1990; Newstead, 1994; Glanzberg, 2004). Bare plural-nouns typically appear in *generic statements*, which are statements that *express general truth, generalization, characteristicness, regularity, normality*, and so forth. The study of generic statements is of particular importance for understanding how scientific communication constructs worlds of facts and truths (Mari, Beyssade & Del Prete, 2012; Carlson & Pelletier, 1995; Pelletier, 2009a, b; Nickel, 2016).

Generic statements come in two variations. First, they refer to kinds; for instance, 'infants' refers to the class or category of infants. Second, they refer to general properties, meaning that they 'report a regularity which summarizes groups of particular episodes or facts' (Krifka et al., 1995, p. 2; see also Pelletier, 2009b; Mari, Beyssade & Del Prete, 2012 and Carlson & Pelletier, 1995).

Let us take the mammoth for examples of generic statements:

1. Mammoths are pachyderms (by implication, all and every individual mammoth is a pachyderm).
2. Mammoths roamed the Siberian tundra (which is a statement about a typical feature of the Siberian tundra, namely that Mammoths roamed it, but Mammoths roamed so many other places).

3. Mammoths are extinct (which implies that the genus Mammuthus is extinct; it is not a property of any or all individual mammoths, as an individual cannot go extinct: it lives or dies).
4. The mammoth lived on a diet of tough grasses (which is either another way of making a generic statement similar to saying 'mammoths lived on a diet of tough grasses' or it is a statement about a specific mammoth, mammoth Yuri, who features in a yet to be written novel *Mammoth Yuri and the Tundra of Doom* who was forced to live on a diet of tough grasses while his children ate all the tender shoots).

These four examples represent only a few of the many possible meanings one can convey by using generic statements. Note that generic statements can of course also be put in the form of questions or assumptions, in which case they directly relate to the notions of hypotheses and expectations in scientific research (e.g., 'Are Mammoths extinct?').

Let us now take a look at generic statements in Liu et al.'s (2017) article on infants inferring the cost of goals. The article contains statements such as

1. *'infants first saw an agent move to and refuse to move to each of two target goals under conditions of varying cost. Then, infants watched test events'* (page 1039; statement 1).

In this particular case, the implicit quantifier in the plural bare noun 'infants' is totally clear: it is the universal quantifier *all*, which is applied to a *determinate extension* of individuals, namely all the individual infants participating in the researchers' subject sample (the number of infants participating in the three experiments is twenty-four, twenty-four, and thirty-two, respectively). In this case, this quantifier is made clear through the linguistic context, where it is clear that the authors are describing a part of the procedure, which all infants necessarily will have followed. A statement like this means that each and every infant of the representative sample first saw the agent move, and then watched the test event.

In other instances, the quantifier of the plural bare noun is unclear and must be interpreted based on its implicit meaning. For example:

2. *'infants expected the agent to prefer the goal it attained through costlier actions'* (statement 2, p. 1038); or
3. *'infants are sensitive to the relative value of different goal objects for an agent who chooses to approach one object over another'* (Statement 3, p. 1039); or

6.2 Text and the Creation of Infant Economists 127

4. '*Do infants apply the logic of cost-reward reasoning?*' (Statement 4, p. 1039).
5. And interpreting the findings, the authors say things like '*This finding further suggests that infants understand agents' actions in accord with abstract, general, and interconnected concepts of cost and reward*' (statement 5, p. 1040).

In all these cases, 'infants' is used as a bare noun carrying an implicit quantifier. Intuitively, a reader would assign the universal quantifier – *all* – to the generic term *infants*. For instance, Statement 3 is likely to be intuitively interpreted as '*all infants* are sensitive to etc.', eventually with specifying adjectives, such as in the phrase: 'all [normal, healthy, typically developing] infants are sensitive to … etc.'. While this interpretation may be common, other interpretations of the implicit quantifier are also possible. For instance, '*most* (normal, healthy …) infants are sensitive to etc.', or '*the typical* infant is sensitive to etc.' (where one would then need to specify what is meant by 'typical').

These plural bare nouns and the various ways in which they can be interpreted with regard to their determiners require vigilance from the reader. If the quantifier 'all' is not explicitly given by the authors, it remains unclear what the plural bare noun actually refers to. These types of plural bare nouns make it easy to interpret them as referring to the indeterminate set of 'infants', that is, all past, current, and future infants. In other words, plural bare nouns often seem to refer to the natural kind *infant* (see Section 6.1.1). This is problematic given (as we described earlier) that infants change over time and across contexts, and often do not follow such strict rules that define their properties.

6.2.2.2 'Do Infants Look Longer at Test Trials?' On Individuals, Sets, and Kinds

Let us focus on a typical statement from the results section from Liu et al. (2017):

6. '*Infants looked longer at test trials in which the agent chose the target for whom it had jumped a lower barrier*' (statement 6, p. 1040).

Given the linguistic context of this statement (i.e., a description of events that took place during the experimental procedure), it is clear that Statement 6 applies to the determinate set of infants from the sample in experiment 1. But looking at this further, should the reader conclude that this statement refers to all twenty-four infants in this sample? Such an interpretation would be incorrect, as the graphs show highly variable individual looking times (Figure 3 on p. 1040). The astute reader is able to see this because, unlike most other published studies on group data, this particular study shows the *individual* data as well as the mean. However, given that most studies do not provide the individual data, and given that it is uncommon for readers to cross-reference results statements such as Statement 6 with graphs provided, plural bare nouns are likely to be interpreted as referring to all cases of infants in the sample (and likely also the universal kind 'infants').

Statements such as Statement 6 actually refer to the calculation of an average: The group average of looking times of individual children is greater in condition A than in condition B, with a small, calculable probability that this difference is due to chance alone. What we see, then, is how the bare noun – *infants* – has undergone a shift in meaning from Statement 1 (describing the concrete events that infants undertook in the concrete experimental context) to Statement 6 (describing the findings of the experiment). We see that 'infants' shifted from referring to *members of a set (a specified collection of individual agents)* to a *set of members*. The property 'look longer at' is treated as a property of the set, and not as a property of its members. The reality of the individual processes of looking is swapped for an allegedly deeper reality of 'true', 'essential', 'typical' or 'characteristic' looking time for the natural kind 'infant'. The property 'look longer at' becomes an essential property of the natural kind 'infant'.

These semantic shifts from properties of individuals to properties of sets or samples, and from samples to categories or kinds, are often implicitly made and seen as perfectly fine and obvious. This reasoning was originally explored by the nineteenth-century Belgian statistician, sociologist, and astronomer Quetelet,[4] who pioneered the use of averages over many individuals as a way of specifying the nature of the corresponding kinds or categories into which these individuals could be classified (e.g., his notion of the average man, or 'l'homme moyen'; Quetelet, 1869).

The interpretive shift from *members of a set* to *set of members* (occurring in Statement 6) *replaces* the individual idiosyncrasies (of unique processes

---

[4] To contribute to the knowledge of trivia: Quetelet was among the first doctoral students of the then newly founded University of Ghent in Flanders, Belgium, which is also the alma mater of the first author of this book and the only Belgian university founded by a king of the Netherlands; he developed the Quetelet index, currently known as the body-mass index, which every health-conscious person is expected to constantly monitor. Quetelet became the doctoral supervisor of Pierre François Verhulst, who developed the logistic function, which played such an eminent role in the studies on chaos and chaotic dynamics and which can be used as a universal growth equation featuring in dynamic models of development (e.g., Van Geert, 1991).

of looking back and forth and away, and visual scanning, in the context of actions and a specific environment) with a central tendency and dispositional properties of a natural kind. The idiosyncrasy is transformed into a secondary issue, namely the mathematical dispersion indicator, which is typically the standard deviation. This is in contrast to a processual point of view, where the primary issue is that of the individual processes of temporally and conditionally connected action-perception loops.

The automaticity of transforming individual sequences of connected action-perception events into dispositional properties of categories or kinds ('infants'), and the corresponding shifting between extensional and intensional readings (from actual collections of individuals to defining properties of natural kinds) is a distinctive feature of the standard praxis of psychological research. This feature is clearly reflected in the way that nouns undergo transformations in the process of a textual discourse describing a particular experiment in the form of a scientific article. It characterizes the praxis as the enactment of a basically substantialist ontology.

6.2.2.3 Sensitive Infants, Generic Statements and Individual Cases

In the preceding section, we discussed the transformation of observations of individuals to general statements about properties of kinds ('infants'). Another important shift that occurs in the way that we use bare nouns is that statements about general scientific facts are subsequently used to refer to individual members of those kinds (i.e., any individual infant).

Take an example of a statement from Liu et al. (2017) that represents a general fact, such as:

7. *'infants are sensitive to the relative value of different goal objects for an agent who chooses to approach one object over another'* (Statement 7)

Does Statement 7 mean that each and every individual infant is sensitive to the relative value of different goal objects each and every time it is presented with a contextual situation where relative values of different goal objects are present, or that each infant does it *most* of the time? Does it mean that *most* infants do it most of the time, or that more infants than babies do it (assuming infants and babies represent different age-related kinds, with different characteristic properties)? These questions concern the extent to which generic statements *individualize*, that is, how they apply to individual cases and tolerate exceptions across those individuals.

Generic scientific statements referring to a bare noun ('infants') imply the universal quantifier, meaning that the statement is true of *all* infants (with eventual specifications such as 'all healthy and typically developing infants'). This, however, is not realistic. One needs only to think about counter examples, such as those infants in the sample who did *not* show different looking times (i.e., those who deviated from the mean). What then might an alternative interpretation be of bare nouns used to report on findings?

A common strategy is for researchers to choose a *probabilistic interpretation* of generic statements: The probability that a specific infant will be sensitive to the relative value of different goals, or the difference in such probabilities between individuals from different age groups. We shall go deeper into the various meanings of 'probability' in Chapter 10 on uncertainties in psychological measurement, but in the current discussion, we would like to highlight that probabilistic interpretations can have either an epistemological or an ontological meaning.

From an *epistemological* perspective, it could mean that the general statement is true for all individuals (e.g., all infants look longer), but that the probability of actually *observing* this property is considerably lower than 100 per cent, as the actual behaviour is believed to be confounded by all sorts of accidental influences. For instance, children who do not demonstrate a difference in looking time in different experimental conditions might be taken to indicate *measurement error*, or as evidence of accidental influences that conceal the 'true' property in question.

Note that this assumption is also the standard justification for aggregating over individual cases, i.e., across the experimental sample). Any accidental factors are thought to cancel each other out, resulting in the observation of the real property (i.e., the real 'signal' transmitted through the observations). The assumption works well in cases where observations of a particular phenomenon are indeed polluted, so to speak, by the effects of accidental factors intervening in the observation, thus resulting in random variations of the observed signal. For instance, Quetelet's astronomical observations of the night sky were disturbed by the Belgian cloudy skies. Quetelet no doubt understood how the observation of a celestial body was a combination of its own light and noise coming from a range of disruptive sources. But this reasoning does not work the other way around: random variations of some observed signal, such as the variations in looking times across a number of individual infants, are not necessarily caused by the intervention of random, accidental factors that conceal the real signal. The random variation has indeed been found to be a property of the phenomenon itself (e.g., the infant's behaviour) (e.g., Thelen & Smith, 1994; De Weerth, Van Geert & Hoijtink, 1999;

Van Geert & Van Dijk, 2002; Van Dijk & Van Geert, 2014; Van Dijk, Hunnius & Van Geert, 2009). The point is that, without a good theory explaining why this interindividual variation is either a form of measurement error or an intrinsic feature of the observed phenomenon, the epistemological or measurement error interpretation of variation remains unclear.

The other alternative interpretation of a probabilistic message is the ontological interpretation. This is that the general property applies only to a certain – big or small – percentage of infants. That is, some infants will show it (look longer), while others won't. The probability thus refers to the presence of the phenomenon itself, rather than our ability to observe it. This ontological interpretation poses several problems from the viewpoint of generalization, which we will discuss in the next section.

6.2.2.4 Are Generic Statements Necessarily Majority- or High-Probability-Statements?

The first problem of probabilistic interpretations of results that are communicated using bare nouns is that it is an unspecified probability. Does 'infants looked longer' imply that *most* infants looked longer? The intuitive answer is yes. Statement 7 and comparable statements from Liu et al. (2017) referred to dispositions of infants, for instance, the disposition to show sensitivity to differences in goal values. These dispositions were described as being triggered or expressed under certain conditions (see also Chapter 10). As a disposition that characterizes the natural kind 'infants', with the probability interpretation, we would expect that *most* of the infants display this disposition *most* of the time (when confronted with the right information, as in a particular experiment).

However, majority statements do not necessarily equate to generic truths about a natural kind. An interesting illustration concerns sea turtles. For instance, 'sea turtles die before they can reproduce' is true of the overwhelming majority of individual sea turtles,[5] as only one out of 1,000 to one out of 10,000 survive to adulthood (let us, for simplicity, say they have a probability of 0.02 per cent of reaching an age at which they can reproduce; this is really way below the 5 per cent probability that researchers customarily use to decide that some result is statistically significant). Nevertheless, it would be incorrect to infer a general truth from this probabilistic statement. We cannot infer that *sea turtles die before they can reproduce*. This is obviously not true because there are still sea turtles

---

[5] Sea Turtles: Fascinating Facts – NOAA's National Ocean Service; https://oceanservice.noaa.gov/news/june15/sea-turtles.html

for us to comment upon. Therefore, it must be the case that sea turtles lay eggs. The correct generic-truth statement, therefore, is that 'sea turtles lay eggs'. This statement, then, refers to adult sea turtles (i.e., those that survived past infancy). Interestingly, this generic truth-statement stems from an extreme-minority probabilistic statement: sea turtles have a probability of 0.02 per cent of reaching an age at which they can reproduce. Here, we define the kind 'sea turtle' by a very small minority of all sea turtles. Given that biological reproducibility is a *conditio sine qua non* for the concept of *biological species*, this is warranted.

The point that we hoped to make with the above sea turtle statements, is that probabilistic majority interpretations of results using bare nouns might seem like the most accurate interpretation. Delving deeper, however, it is obvious that it can also be unclear whether such interpretations can be used to formulate generic truths about a certain natural kind.

What we have shown, then, is that an epistemological, ontological, and a probabilistic interpretation of results communicated via bare nouns is problematic. For all these interpretations, we can not correctly assume that the statements made invoke the universal operator '*all*', or that they invoke non-trivial majority probabilities.

The core problem arises because of the substantialist ontology assumed in these kinds of experimental studies. First, the main intention of these studies is to access an internal knowledge entity, here infant goals and utility perception. Second, this is done by privileging a particular experimental condition that is assumed to represent the entire range of possible activity conditions where such mental entities are implied. As such, the substantialist assumption is that an infant's concepts, knowledge, or abilities exist independently of the conditions that trigger them, and these concepts, knowledge, or abilities act as internal causal agents for the infant's actions. The concepts, knowledge, or abilities are thus treated as substances, or static entities, residing – so to speak – inside the infant (Overton, 2015; Witherington et al., 2018).

6.2.2.5 On Generic Statements and Their Use for Practical Applications
In his thorough discussion of the meaning of generic statements (using bare nouns), Nickel (2012, 2016) defends the view we have described above, that generic statements are statements about characteristic properties of kinds. Nickel also describes how understanding generic statements requires an analysis of the metaphysics of *normality* and *characteristicness*; an analysis that is certainly not present in articles that demonstrate such generic statements, nor is it a common task for readers of such articles. Thus, the

common communication of facts is likely misleading, where readers will erroneously assume that the facts being reported are referring to characteristic properties of all members of a certain natural kind and in all contexts.

This poses serious problems when individuals attempt to apply these facts in clinical or educational settings, where they are concerned with concrete cases (i.e., individual clients, families, and so forth) living and acting in concrete contexts and circumstances. For instance, in the DSM-V, characteristic properties (e.g., 'a tendency to avoid interaction') are treated as probabilistically related to the class or kind at issue (autism). A specific individual belongs to the class of autistic children if this individual has most of the properties mentioned in a checklist. There will also be many autistic children that have none, or at best just a few, properties in common with many other autistic children (see Chapter 10, the section on vagueness and ambiguity and the praxis of psychiatric categorization). This problem has been solved by subcategorization, such that all members of a particular subcategory have more in common with other members of the subcategory than with members of another (e.g., subcategories such as Asperger, classic autism, or PDD-NOS). In the case of autism, this solution has now been abandoned in favour of a so-called 'spectrum-oriented view', recognizing that differences between autistic children are too considerable to justify sub-classification (e.g., Volkmar, Reichow & McPartland, 2012). But in this and comparable cases, the question is: What is it that binds this spectrum together? What is it that unites all the different manifestations under the natural kind autism? There is a famous quote from Wittgenstein's Philosophical Investigations that addresses this question:

> §66. Consider for example the proceedings that we call 'games'. I mean board-games, card-games, ball-games, Olympic games, and so on. What is common to them all? Don't say: 'There must be something common, or they would not be called "games"' – but look and see whether there is anything common to them all ... And the result of this examination is: we see a complicated network of similarities overlapping and criss-crossing: sometimes overall similarities, sometimes similarities of detail. (Wittgenstein, 2006, §66, pp. 27–28, originally published in 1953)

Wittgenstein thus noted that most of the semantic categories that we use in language refer to extensional sets, the members of which have nothing overall in common (despite our inclination to assume that this is the case). Some members of a category share properties with some others, but there is no single defining property that is shared by all (a view, by the way, which is considerably older than Wittgenstein's formulation and has been a recurrent theme in semantics since Aristotle's *Metaphysics*; see Fortis, 2015).

This family-resemblance theory of meaning – dealing with what Wittgenstein so beautifully called *Familienähnlichkeiten* – is hard to reconcile with the naturalistic essence-interpretation that the standard research praxis bestows on psychological and clinical categories such as infancy or autism. The common praxis treats categories as natural kinds, where the 'naturalness' of kinds or categories is typically justified on the basis of characteristic properties that often directly relate to specific genetic and neurological causes (Haslam & Kvaale, 2015; Racine et al., 2010), and are implicitly supposed to apply to the 'normal' individual from that category, that is to say the great majority of cases. The reality of the situation is that members of these 'natural kinds' may potentially have nothing in common except for the fact that they comply with classificatory criteria of the kind in question, which is more or less the same as saying that they are of a similar kind because they carry the same label.

6.3 Conclusion

6.3.1 *The Tip of an Iceberg*

We can summarize the discussion on the implications and semantics of general statements, or generics, by quoting Nickel (2016, p. 244):

> A generic is the tip of an iceberg. It rests on a large theoretical structure that provides the explanatory resources to distinguish the normal from the abnormal, all the while floating beneath the surface of our conscious awareness. As it turns out, some of the superficially simplest linguistic constructions out there are theoretically extremely complex.

Put differently, the unambiguous use of bare nouns and generic truths in psychological research requires that all assumptions are made explicit and are empirically verified; something that is not likely in the foreseeable future. The issue here is not the use of large-scale studies, but in the communication of the facts derived from these studies. Similar to the analyses in Chapter 4 (on common praxes in self-esteem research), these large-scale studies are perfectly reasonable – and necessary – for providing information about populations, but they should not be communicated as being relevant for individuals within the sample studied or for variations on contexts. For instance, the effectiveness of a particular intervention on the level of the population is defined by the percentage of the population that fares better with the intervention. However, in the preceding sections we have seen that if populations are explicitly viewed as extensional definitions of a specific natural kind, and if individuals are seen as representatives of this natural kind, population-based information is often, wrongly, interpreted as information about individuals (see our discussion on the ecological fallacy or the fallacy of the ergodicity assumption, Chapter 9).

6.3.2 Processualizing Science Communication

How then might researchers communicate about facts that inform us of individuals, and of the way that 'dispositions' manifest in different contexts? The answer is quite simple: researchers can describe the actions of concrete individuals and their interactions with concrete contexts. What this provides are facts that are much more descriptive than claims of universal truths (or of having versus not having certain mental entities). Processual communication of research involves the description (qualitatively or quantitatively) of processes, when and how they occur. These descriptions are usually not meant to characterize all members of a kind, but possible processes that can be observed in members of a kind or of mental kinds (see Chapter 5 for a description of processual communication of research on self-esteem). A similar plea is made by Michael Billig, who argues for much more focus on examples of concrete events in psychological writing (Billig, 2019), and on avoiding nominalization (turning process descriptions into nouns) and the use of passives to conceal that events are concrete activities (Billig, 2013).

An example of a focus on the processual description is the study by Smith et al. (1999) on the so-called A-not-B error, which refers to a task aimed to demonstrate the infant's current object concept (see also Clearfield et al., 2006). The task originated in Piaget's (1954/2013) work on the object concept and is described in his 1954 book on *The Construction of Reality in the Child*. In the task, an infant is seated in front of two covers, for instance two towels, and a small attractive object is repeatedly hidden under one of them, for instance under the towel on the right. Mainstream (substantialist) studies typically show that ten-month-old infants typically retrieve the object from the hiding place, thereby demonstrating an early form of object permanence. Put differently, they demonstrate the knowledge that the object, although hidden and out of sight, is still there and can thus be retrieved. But if, after repeating the same hiding place for a while, the object is then hidden under the other cover while the infant is watching, most ten month olds will nevertheless search under the first towel, on the right, where the object had been hidden several times before. The standard interpretation is that this indicates the infant's *lack* of a fully developed object concept, according to which an object is an entity that is independent of the activities that are carried out with it.

Smith et al. (1999), however, described that there is no way that the *object concept*, or any other concept for that matter, can be separated from the activities in or by which it is displayed. They objected to the communication of the *object concept* as an internal entity underlying performance in all these tasks. Instead, these authors described how the context provides the framework for the activity, and that, as soon as the activity starts, the context itself necessarily changes (e.g., by lifting one of the towels, or putting it back), which then changes the affordances offered for further action. In other words, the primary interest was the action-perception loops from the perspective of the agent (the infant). What this descriptive communication taught us (the scientific community) was of great significance. Their processual descriptions taught us that perception, action, and memory are embodied and embedded processes; soft-assembled phenomena, which refers to the processes of self-organization and emergence (described in Chapter 2). In other words, they were able to elucidate something vital about the ontology of infant phenomena, something that has – thankfully – been taken up by most introductory developmental psychology textbooks.

CHAPTER 7

Causes, Kings, and Interventions
*Causality and Explanation in Mainstream Psychological Theory and Research**

> The law of causality, I believe, like much that passes muster among philosophers, is a relic of a bygone age, surviving, like the monarchy, only because it is erroneously supposed to do no harm.
> Bertrand Russell, 'On the Notion of Cause', *Proceedings of the Aristotelian Society* 13 (1912), 1–26 (but with regard to causality, Russell changed his view quite considerably in 1948)

> Incidentally, I once asked Russell if he was willing to die for his beliefs. 'Of course not,' he replied. 'After all, I may be wrong …'
> Columnist Leonard Lyons in the *New York Post*, June 1964
> (https://quoteinvestigator.com/2016/03/07/never-die/)

7.1 The Effectiveness of Psychotherapies: Questions for a Health Insurance Company

7.1.1 The Cases and the Questions

How does a particular research praxis – theoretical or applied – enact an ontology regarding causality? To answer this question, we shall focus on a praxis where causality is a major issue and concerns the question of the effectiveness of psychotherapies. The praxis in question involves the complex network of actual psychotherapies given in the context of psychotherapeutic or mental health companies, the businesses structure of such companies or institutions, the role and activities of mental health insurance companies, effectiveness assessments on the work floor and academic effectiveness research, practices of scientific and applied communication about effectiveness between professionals, clients and researchers, the role and activities of clients, public and media, and so forth (see Dalal, 2018, for a case study regarding the praxis of Cognitive Behavioural Therapy (CBT)).

---

* This is a single-authored chapter written by Paul van Geert. For this reason, the chapter makes use of first-person singular pronouns.

A striking property of this praxis is that the daily work of psychotherapy is concerned with individual clients, whereas the dominant discourse focusses on the *effectiveness of a particular psychotherapy*, which typically pertains to (very) large statistical ensembles of clients. The effectiveness discourse takes place on the level of decisive power, for instance, the power of health insurance companies to decide which type of psychotherapy will be paid for with insurance money (interestingly, the insurance industry itself can be modelled as a complex dynamic system, Owadally, Zhou & Wright, 2018). For an insurance company, the actuarial level – that is to say, the addition of profits based on large numbers of compiled individual cases – is the natural or logical level of decision. The line of causal reasoning applies, by definition, to the aggregate, population level: does the application of therapy X for all clients with diagnosis A yield more cumulative profit than therapy Y?

But what about the line of causal reasoning on the level of scientific efficacy-research (i.e., research on effectiveness in scientifically controlled conditions) (Nathan, Stuart & Dolan, 2000; Rosqvist, Thomas & Truax, 2011)? What is the cause of the treatment effect? Is it the therapy as such (i.e., the universal category, or kind, 'CBT')? Or is the cause of the treatment effect the actual, particular therapeutic process, as it occurs in recurrent interactions between a concrete client and a concrete therapist? We shall try to clarify this issue by means of a thought experiment.

Suppose that we are employees working for a health insurance company and we have to decide on the following case. A particular client, P, suffers from mental and behavioural problems seriously hampering his personal, family, and job functioning. P consults Dr N, a registered and qualified psychotherapist. After a thorough intake assessment, they both decide that Angel Therapy will be the best therapeutic intervention to cure P's problems. Unfortunately, Angel Therapy is not recognized by P's insurance company as an effective psychotherapy, and the costs will thus not be reimbursed (see Norcross, Koocher & Garofalo, 2006, on discredited psychological treatments). As Dr N is thoroughly trained in methodologically and statistically sound n=1 studies, she first conducts a series of observational, diary, and experience-sampling assessments, to determine P's problems. During the Angel Therapy sessions, Dr N meticulously and repeatedly registers client P's mental and behavioural symptoms. It seems there is relatively rapid improvement. Suddenly, Dr N has to interrupt the therapy for a while. A clear aggravation of P's symptoms occurs. After the interruption, the therapy is continued, resulting in noticeable improvement again. After five months of therapy, client P and Dr N decide that the problems have gone, and that therapy can be stopped, with the exception of short check-up meetings every six months. After two years, P is still free from all symptoms, has re-entered his job and has restored a positive relationship with his spouse, indeed the happiest of therapeutic endings.

After therapy, Dr N and former-client P discuss practicalities, and they decide that P should be able to claim the costs of the therapy with P's health insurance company. However, the health insurance company declines the claim, on grounds of the fact that there is no scientific evidence whatsoever that Angel Therapy is an effective form of treatment. Dr N and P contest this decision, and their case involves all the empirical data collected by Dr N and is based on counterfactual causality reasoning. *Counterfactual* means that without this cause (the therapy) the effect (the improvement) would not have occurred (in all likelihood, given the current facts described above). Thus, Dr N demonstrates that P's symptoms occurred for many years, that P has undergone several established, evidence-based therapies that were not successful at all, that improvement clearly co-varied with the intensity of the Angel-Therapeutic encounters, with a relapse during N's absence, and that the improvement after treatment has been stable for at least two years.

Let us imagine another case, with client N and highly experienced and competent psychotherapist Dr P. After a thorough intake procedure, Dr P decides that the best form of therapy would be CBT, an evidence-based treatment for the cluster of problems described by patient N, and which the health insurance company has accepted as highly effective. The therapy is carried out skilfully and in full compliance with the rules, prescriptions, and therapeutic protocols, but there is no serious evidence of any form of significant improvement. Even worse, as the therapy proceeds, severe and persistant side effects begin to occur that N does not disclose to her therapist, such as 'suicidality, breakups, negative feedback from family members, withdrawal from relatives, feelings of shame and guilt, or intensive crying and emotional disturbance during sessions' (Schermuly-Haupt, Linden & Rush, 2018, p. 223). These symptoms decrease when, due to purely accidental circumstances, the therapy is put on hold for a while. However, the symptoms then increase again, and after the termination of therapy, they remain persistent. N loses her job and marriage, followed by two suicide attempts (note that this example is meant to be as dramatic as possible).

In spite of the devastating results of these – imaginary – CBT sessions, the insurance company reimburses the costs, as CBT is an evidence-based effective treatment. The effectiveness is probabilistic. In the behavioural sciences, cause-effect relationships are virtually always probabilistic (Hausman & Woodward, 2004), which implies that exceptions prove the rule.

7.1.2 *The Likely Answers from the Insurance Company*

Let us try to reconstruct the insurance company's line of reasoning in the successful Angel Therapy case.

Premises:

1. There is scientific evidence that Angel Therapy is not effective, it does not make a consistent change (i.e., its causal potential is zero).
2. Since it is not effective, all stable and real differences before and after the therapy must be due to other causal factors than the therapy itself.

Conclusion:

1. The contingency between the therapy and the change in the symptoms must therefore be purely accidental.
2. The insurance company will neither pay for the costs invested in a zero-effect intervention, nor for purely accidental changes that occur as a consequence of other causal factors than the therapy. The claim of client P is declined.

Here's the likely reasoning in the second highly ineffective CBT case.

Premises:

1. There is strong scientific evidence that CBT is an effective treatment for this particular population of clients and this particular disorder. That is, the intrinsic positive causal-potential of CBT for disorder A is evidence-based.
2. Empirical evidence demonstrates that the actual effect of the therapy is probabilistic; this means that the causal potential of the therapy is the extent to which it is capable of increasing the probability that clients will be cured.

Conclusion:

1. Given the probabilistic nature of the effectiveness, one must reckon with the fact that this effective therapy might sometimes result in zero or even negative effects. However, since CBT has a scientifically proven effectiveness, zero or negative effects must be due to factors other than the therapy itself.
2. As the insurance company has the policy of reimbursing the costs of evidence-based treatments for clients complying with the properties of a particular target group, client N's claim for reimbursement will be awarded.

It is clear that, along these lines of reasoning, a typical substance-ontology approach has been adopted. The therapy is treated as a *secondary substance* or universal: the therapy is treated as a *kind* (i.e., CBT) (for a description of properties assigned to *substance*, see Chapter 4). This is in contrast with treating the therapy as therapy-as-process (i.e., a particular sequence of events with a particular client and therapist). In the reasoning of the insurance company, the therapy-as-kind has intrinsic causal properties that significantly reduce the frequency of symptoms in a population characterized by a specific diagnosis-as-kind (e.g., depression, as a secondary substance). Although the literature shows that effectiveness is partly due to non-specific therapy factors, such as the empathy of the therapist (i.e., highlighting the processual and individual nature of psychotherapy itself; Wampold & Imel, 2015; Schiepek, 2009; Budd & Hughes, 2009; De Felice et al., 2019), the standard psychotherapy praxis and the associated effectiveness research enact a substance ontology.

This illustration should not be used to defend a no-cure-no-pay view, nor does it encourage an everything-goes approach where all scientific knowledge about the effectiveness of various therapies is set aside. What it aims at demonstrating is the attribution of causal power to psychological interventions, such as therapies, in the standard substance-oriented praxis of sample-based average effect research, and to compare this with causality attribution in a process-oriented praxis (for a theory of causality as powers, see Mumford & Anjum, 2011; Anjum & Mumford, 2018). In a processual praxis, attribution of causal power takes place in the context of a therapeutic process for which the cause of improvement is a concrete, contextually situated network of causally or conditionally connected events, which, in view of its complexity and dynamic nature, is likely to be highly idiosyncratic (for a discussion of causal attribution in intervention effect studies, and the limits of the manipulationist or interventionist approach, see Eronen, 2020).

Schiepek et al. (2019a) characterize 'psychotherapy as dynamic support of clients' self-organizing processes' (p. 56). But as we shall explain in Chapter 8, self-organization and emergence cannot be accounted for in terms of classical uni-directional cause-effect relationships and require a different conceptualization of causality from that more commonly adopted. In the standard approach, a single psychotherapy process is viewed as a concrete, particular instantiation of a secondary substance (i.e., a universal, such as CBT-as-kind), in which, on the level of an individual, the intrinsic causal power of CBT-as-kind is contaminated by a host of accidental individual factors. By averaging over a great number of independent error-laden cases these accidental factors are cancelled out, revealing the true intrinsic causal power of CBT as a secondary substance or universal. This practice of averaging over actual cases to arrive at the essence of a secondary substance is a typical enactment of a substance ontology.

7.2 Causality and the Wish to Make a Difference

The quote at the beginning of this chapter, associating the law of causality with the monarchy in terms of the potential harm both could inflict, comes from an article written in 1912 by the famous British philosopher, peace activist, and (obviously) anti-monarchist Bertrand Russell. In the opening sentence of the article, he says 'In the following paper I wish, first, to maintain that "cause" is so inextricably bound up with misleading associations as to make its complete extrusion from the philosophical vocabulary desirable' (Russell, 1912–1913, p. 1; see also Price & Corry, 2007 for a recent recapitulation). According to philosopher Nancy Cartwright, there is no such a thing as a single concept of causality (Cartwright, 2007b). Instead, there are a variety of conceptualizations of causality that work for particular types of explanation. This leads to the assumption that the conception of causality that 'works' for the behavioural and social sciences is grounded in our everyday attempts to control some or other aspect of the world that is of direct interest to us, and to understand the world through the structure of our success in doing so.

7.2.1 Causality Is Grounded in 'Doing'

The standard model of causality typical of the social and behavioural sciences is explicitly determined by the intention to change, control, or predict a particular feature of the world (e.g., mental health, low self-esteem, children's reasoning). These intentions, and their resulting activities are typically defined at a high level of aggregation. In the case of the health insurance company, for instance, the causal factor will be the therapy as something that is the common factor in the actual therapies given by all its health contractors. The effect will be the group averages of therapeutic effects in the population of clients, in terms of the company's standard effectiveness measures inferred from the financial profits associated with them. The timescale involved in the standard causal model is typically that of immediate or short-term effects, for instance, the effects noticeable during the therapy and shortly thereafter, which is coherent with the notion of control and manipulation. Finally, the standard model focusses on causes that can be isolated from other factors. For instance, the insurance company has an interest in shielding off the therapy-as-cause from all other possible causal influences on its intended psychological health effects. What it wishes to claim in its insurance policies are the costs of the therapies given, and nothing else.

From the viewpoint of enacting ontologies, one might say that the overwhelming majority of psychological research enacts an ontology of manipulation and intervention through isolable and independent causes, that is, essences with an inherent specific causal capacity (Cartwright, 2007a, 2007b) or causal power (Mumford & Anjum, 2011). The theory of causality that corresponds with this particular perspective is aptly called the *Interventionist* or *Manipulationist Theory of Causality* (Reutlinger, 2013; Woodward, 2005, 2016; Baumgartner, 2009).

According to the Scottish philosopher David Hume (1711–1776) 'efficacy, agency, power, force, energy, necessity, connexion ... are all nearly synonymous' (Hume, 1960, p. 157, first published in 1739). Hume defined a cause as 'an object precedent and contiguous to another, and so united with it, that the idea of the one determines the mind to form the idea of the other' (p. 170). That is, causality is a direct feature of the way we perceive events. The Belgian experimental psychologist, Baron Albert Michotte (1881–1965; elevated to Baron for his contributions to psychology) showed that the 'causal' impression arising in perceiving contiguous events depends on the timing of their succession. For instance, if one black dot, appearing on a screen, approaches another dot, most people see this as a causal event (Michotte, 1946). In the 1940s, Fritz Heider and Marianne Simmel, Michotte's German contemporaries, made a little movie showing the movements of simple geometric figures that viewers perceived as intentional, causal activities (copies of the movie are freely available online, e.g., via YouTube).

Our impression of causality is rooted in perception, but also in our wish to control our environments for our own purposes. First, as autonomous agents, already from a very early age on, we focus on actions with reliable effects, that is, on the contiguity of actions and results, and on meaningful magnitudes of effect, proportional to our invested effort (see also Chapter 6). An example is a toddler opening the fridge to get some apple juice. This focus on action effectiveness generalizes to antecedent-consequent relationships beyond our own wilful activities that are of direct interest to our concerns. This will allow us to reliably predict and actively anticipate future events, and to discover properties of the world that make sense in terms of our goals and intentions. This combination of control, prediction, and discovery (Glymour, 2001, p. 39) is an essential feature of autonomous agency, and represents the standard view on causality.

The second characteristic of autonomous agents is that they combine, categorize, or generalize, which directly follows from the wish to *reliably* control, predict, and discover, which in practice often implies that a perceived antecedent-consequent relationship occurs with a big enough probability to warrant its being stored as useful information. This practical requirement complies with how Hausman and Woodward (2004) specify the relation between causality and probability: 'If some intervention with respect to Xi changes the probability distribution of some other variable Xj, then Xi causes Xj' (Hausman & Woodward, 2004, p. 848).

A third feature is that autonomous agents focus on effects that occur on the timescale of their direct needs, which are, to a considerable extent, short term (if you're thirsty, the possibility of finding something to drink in the fridge the day after tomorrow is of little direct interest).

The ability to explore covariation of events through intervention (doing or leaving something) and by so doing discovering conditional, probabilistic causal relationships is already present in young children, which is consistent with the claim that this is a fundamental feature of autonomous agents in a complicated world (Cannon & Woodward, 2012; Gopnik, Schulz & Schulz, 2007; but for a processual approach, see De Bordes et al., 2013 and Ganglmayer et al., 2019).

The general, causal format of practical, activity-based conditional relationships with the three characteristics described above, also applies to the most advanced forms of causal reasoning and discovery, namely scientific research (Pearl & MacKenzie, 2018; Glymour, 2001; Spirtes et al., 2000; Sloman, 2005). This causal format represents causal relationships in the form of *directed causal structures*, represented in the form of networks or nets. These networks consist of events or conditions (the nodes in the network) connected by resulting probabilistic effect relationships (the arrows or vertices; see Figure 7.1). Causal networks with probabilistic relationships are also called Bayesian nets. These causal nets are represented in the form of *Directed Acyclic Graphs*, that is, effects go from a cause to an effect (directedness) and effects do not affect causes (acyclicity).

Structural causal-models, or Bayesian nets, should comply with the requirements of *modularity, intervention,* and the *causal Markov condition*. Modularity means that 'it is possible to intervene at one place in a system without altering causal relationships elsewhere'. The opposite of a modular system would be a completely holistic one in which 'any

7.2 Causality and the Wish to Make a Difference

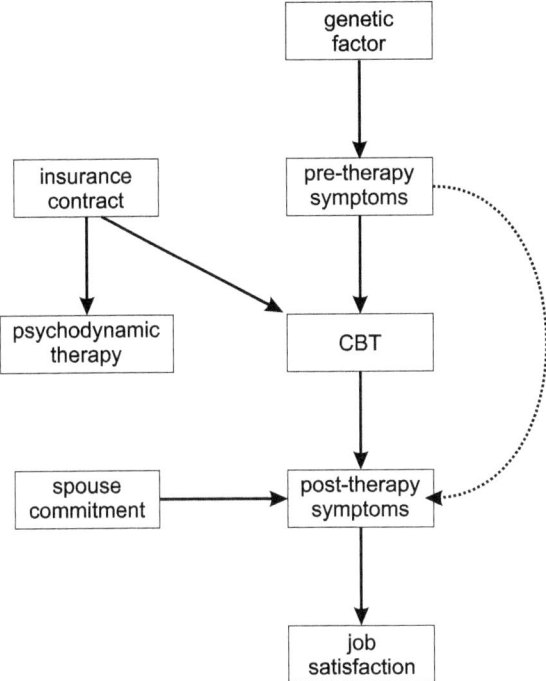

Figure 7.1 An imaginary causal graph focussing on a core node, namely post-therapy symptoms (which should be a reduced version of pre-therapy symptoms). This core node has two direct causal parents namely Cognitive Behavioural Therapy and Spouse Commitment with a possible third causal factor, Pre-therapy Symptoms. The statistical parameters of these graphs (strengths of the conditional relationships) can be found by means of structural equation modelling, which is based on an analysis of the covariation of variables in a population of interest.

intervention in one place reconfigures the causal mechanisms everywhere else' (Steel, 2010, p. 81). For instance, in the causal network above it should be possible to replace CBT with psychodynamic therapy without altering the (assumed) causal relationship between genes and symptoms, or any other additional causal relationship in the graph, for that matter. Modular systems are of course considerably easier to manipulate or control than non-modular ones, in that an agent can fix and alter the components one at a time, without fear that turning on the knobs of one component would also, unpredictably, change some other component, probably jeopardizing the effect one wishes to obtain by manipulating a particular component of choice.

Modularity relates to *transferability*: that is, if we have found a causal factor or simply a cause, doing something (i.e., having a certain causal capacity), we wish to 'transfer' or export that cause to other situations than the one in which it occurred originally. This requirement is related to the methodological principle of generalizability to the population (e.g., the population of people with depression). The causal factor can be transferred to another context if it is not determined by the context in which it originally featured, and if it exists independently of that context (for a critical account, see Cartwright, 2001, 2002, 2006). This implies that a cause-effect relationship is independent of the structural context in which it features (e.g., the structure shown in Figure 7.1). This requirement is known as the *Causal Markov Condition* (see for instance Hausman & Woodward, 1999, 2004), which implies that an effect is 'screened off' from all other causal nodes in the causal graph, except for its 'parents' and its own direct effects (the 'parents' of the post-therapy effect in Figure 7.1 are CBT and commitment of the spouse, the direct effect is increased job satisfaction).

The idea behind this form of causal modelling is that causal understanding implies the possibility of *intervention*. This intervention can be a human intervention, such as giving a particular kind of therapy, or a natural intervention, such as genes that cause a particular disease. Natural interventions can be empirically discovered, and then be avoided or counteracted by human interventions (e.g., Bollen & Pearl, 2013). The causal Markov condition is a more technical way of stating the principle of the intervention condition, or the principle of manipulability of causal factors (Hausman & Woodward, 2004). 'Among other things, causal hypotheses predict how the world will respond to an intervention' (Spirtes & Scheines, 2004, p. 833). All this implies that the importance of causal models is that they allow us to act in a more efficient way than if we did not know the cause of some event that we wish to change.

There is no doubt that considerable parts of the world can be assimilated to Bayesian nets of conditional probabilities, to such an extent that probabilistically successful intervention is possible, which is generalizable to a wide range of contexts. If the goal of scientific understanding is to make the world more controllable and predictable, Bayesian nets or causal nets are formidable tools, the probabilistic structures of which can be empirically studied and statistically specified. The pragmatic success of these Bayesian tools – allowing us to make successful interventions – however, does in itself not imply that they exhaustively reflect the objective causal structure of the world (see for instance Cartwright, 2007a, for a critique of the causal claims of these models; see also Spirtes et al., 2000).

Put differently, Bayesian or causal nets reflect the causal structure of the world from a particular perspective or human interest, namely the wish to intervene, *to make a difference* by manipulating some specific feature of reality.

7.2.2 Type-Causality Statements and the Standard Praxis of Psychological Research

To arrive at a better understanding of how causality assignment typically works in mainstream, substance-oriented psychological research, we shall refer to the distinction between *type-causality* and *token-causality* statements. Token-causal claims typically apply to particulars, that is, to primary substances in the form of individual persons or individual cases; for example, 'My uncle Pierre's smoking caused his lung cancer', or the Angel-Therapy discussion provided earlier.

Type-causality statements, in contrast, are more typical of the natural and social sciences (Menzies, 2005). They refer to general, category- or kind-related claims; that is, to the cause in the form of the powers or causal potential of a universal (i.e., secondary) substance. Examples are statements like 'smoking causes lung cancer'. Smoking and lung cancer are properties defining a particular class of individuals; for instance, those who smoke, or those who developed lung cancer (this also relates to the discussion of extensional and intensional definitions, see Chapter 6). It is important to note that the meaning of a statement like this depends on a whole range of presuppositions that are believed to be shared by all those who communicate such statements (e.g., researchers, journalists reporting on research findings, or policy makers). For instance, the presuppositions contained in 'smoking causes lung cancer' are represented by the more explicit but complicated statement 'prolonged (1) and frequent (2) smoking of [tobacco containing carcinogens] (3) [statistically significantly increases] (4) the [probability of lung cancer] (5) [relative to the frequency and duration of the smoking and relative to the occurrence of lung cancer in non-smokers] (6), [given a statistically reliable and representative sample of smokers] (7)'.

Type-causality statements take the perspective of ensembles, that is to say, they pertain to collections of individuals (i.e., particulars, in the philosophical sense of the word), and these individuals are independent of one another, being just members of a sample or ensemble. The ensemble-based nature of type-causality statements makes it possible to make a whole range of additional statements that are in fact very rarely made, because they use different but equally defendable presuppositions. In the 'smoking causes lung cancer' example, it is presupposed that lung cancer is a disease captured by someone who has smoked *for a long time*. An additional statement like 'lung cancer reduces smoking' is equally true or valid, under the presupposition that if long-time smokers have lung cancer, the majority of them will quit smoking, or maybe the lung cancer of some smokers helps other smokers to quit smoking or prevents potential smokers from developing the habit of smoking (one might even correctly say that 'smoking causes smoking', meaning that past smoking causes future smoking, in that smoking creates addiction, a physical dependence motivating further smoking).

In the social and behavioural sciences, type-causality statements are typically probabilistic. They pertain to the sample or population and express a difference in effect frequencies between the population or sample to which the intervening causal event does apply, and the population or sample to which the causal event does not apply (the 'control group'). The latter instantiates the *counterfactual* condition: if the cause does not apply, the effect does not occur. These frequencies are properties of a group of individuals (a sample or population, i.e., an ensemble of individuals). These ensembles are chosen such that they correspond with a natural kind (i.e., a universal or secondary substance). Typical examples of natural kinds are depression, male gender, five-year-olds (see also the section on extensional and intensional definitions in Chapter 6). In the standard practice of causal attribution, ensemble properties such as frequencies are customarily transformed into a property of the individual members of that ensemble. This practice is legitimated by the fact that the individual is a specific case of a natural kind (the individual is a primary substance, as opposed to the secondary substance represented by the ensemble). For example, an individual smoker is a specific case of smoking. This latter is a secondary substance, which has an important property, namely a frequency f of developing lung cancer. This ensemble property – a frequency – is taken to be caused by a property of its individual members, namely the individual smoker's probability p of developing lung cancer. It is of course a question of simple math to transform the frequency of occurrence of some event in a group of individuals into a probability that an individual member of that group will experience that event. For instance, you are a smoker, which means you are an instance of the secondary substance 'smoking'; therefore, you as an individual have a typical property of this secondary substance, which is the probability p to develop lung cancer. That is, the causal capacity of smoking is assumed to have *contextual unanimity* (Steel,

2008, p. 28): If smoking or any other causal factor has an intrinsic causal capacity that has been demonstrated on the level of a set or ensemble (i.e., a population), it must have that causal capacity for every subset, down to the smallest possible subset, namely an arbitrarily chosen individual from that population.

However, contextual unanimity (i.e., interpreting an ensemble-based probability as an intrinsic property of every individual member of that ensemble) is most often an incorrect or unwarranted assumption (for an analysis of the meaning of probability applied to individual processes, see Chapter 10). This wrong assumption is an example of the *ensemble-to-individual fallacy* (which is also known under the somewhat misleading term of *ecological fallacy*). If the fallacy applies to generalizing from ensemble properties to processes, which occur in individuals, it is known as the *ergodicity problem*, sometimes called the homology problem (Molenaar, 2004, 2008; Molenaar & Campbell, 2009; Mangalam & Kelty-Stephen, 2021). Ergodicity is discussed in Chapter 9, in the section on *ergodicity and the enactment of substance-entity ontology*). If the fallacy applies to generalizations from population to subpopulation (e.g., from 'students' to 'female students', it is termed *Simpson's paradox* Wagner, 1982). In short, an ensemble property cannot be automatically individualized, that is to say, there is no intrinsic or automatic relationship between the truth of an ensemble property and a property of every individual member that is derived from the ensemble property. Take the group-frequency-to-individual-probability transformation, which transforms an ensemble property (the frequency of lung cancer cases in a population of regular smokers) into a property of every member of that ensemble (the probability that a particular smoker will develop lung cancer): it is easy to assume that this ensemble-based probability is indeed an intrinsically individual property. In fact, this alleged individual property of a probability – which is supposed to be common to all the individual members of the ensemble – can be used to tautologically 'explain' the ensemble property of frequency, namely the number of people developing lung cancer in that particular ensemble. Because every individual has probability p for event E, the observed frequency of E in an ensemble is between f_1 and f_2, dependent on the size of the ensemble and the assumed individual probability; see Chapter 10 for a discussion on probability).

Concluding, in the majority of cases, type-causality statements are *not to be confused with general statements* (i.e., statements that apply to every specific case); they are statements about ensembles (i.e., populations or samples of individuals).

7.2.3 Causality, Experiments, and Randomized Control Trials

Randomized control trial methodology is known as the 'gold standard' of research into the causal effect of interventions. In this section, we will show that randomized control trials (RCTs) explicitly favour a substantialist ontology of causality, in terms of a universal, independent relationship between essences (universals, secondary substances, natural kinds).

We have seen that the notion of cause is deeply entrenched in the structure of human action, in our concerns and interests, and in our desire to manipulate or control the world in such a way that it suits our purposes in the best possible manner. In clinical, educational, or professional interventions, both the cause and the effect are defined on a high level of aggregation, which is the level of aggregation of secondary substances (i.e., *types, kinds,* or *universals* as discussed in the previous section). The notions of 'therapy' or 'genetic cause' are like summary concepts, where one word is used to denote what, in reality, is an often idiosyncratic web of connected events, such as the successive therapist-client meetings or the micro-events in a therapist-client discussion during a single session. If the causes are associated with something like a genetic factor, 'genetic cause' is a sort of shorthand notation for a range of processes nested on a variety of timescales, such as the steps in the short-term gene-based production of proteins, the short-term activity of proteins in tissues and organs, the functioning of organs in an organism, and the long-term organism-environment interaction and its epigenetic effects. That is, in the standard praxis, researchers are used to speaking about causes by taking a *high-level perspective* (i.e., *upscaling*), both on the level of the aggregated wholes (therapy, intervention, or genetic basis) as on the level of the timescales involved (for instance, by considering a therapy as one macroscopic event (i.e., pre-intervention) and the results of the therapy as another (i.e., post-intervention)). Researchers thus talk about cause and effect as a two-event connection, similar to a stone hitting a window and the glass breaking.

The quintessential example of an 'intervention' is experimental manipulation as it occurs in experimental behavioural research, which is customarily treated as the best way to reveal causality. The assignment of causal power is done by *downscaling the timescale* of the manipulation and of the effect (i.e., reducing the effect to immediate short-term events). This downscaling occurs in combination with *upscaling* the level of aggregation, as described in the context of RCTs. An intrinsic causal power is assigned to an experimental manipulation. For instance, you show your experimental subjects a couple of pictures of red meat and show your control subjects pictures of 'neutral' things.[1] Immediately after doing this, you let your subjects play a computer game where they can show various levels of altruistic behaviour toward (virtual) peers. The causal effects of the pictures shown are expressed in the form of averages of tokens (i.e., concrete cases) of 'altruistic' behaviour in the experimental versus the control group. Note that experimenters are usually *not* interested in the question of what would happen if they were to frequently and recursively repeat the experimental manipulation, in the observation of the effects over a long period, in how long the effects of their manipulations last, in what participants experience before they click a button on the computer screen on which the experiment is presented, or in individual fluctuations in response time. In the next chapter, we will discuss the consequences for experimental practices if researchers focus on these neglected issues, for instance, if researchers are interested in individual temporal properties of such response series (e.g., Van Orden, Holden & Turvey, 2003; Holden, Van Orden & Turvey, 2009).

In the standard praxis, experimental studies claim type-causality, but just like in the case of intervention effects, the type-causality pertains to ensembles (samples, populations). The claimed general causal-effect is operationally defined in the form of a probabilistic relationship between a sample of causal events (e.g., experimental manipulations in every single, participating subject) and a sample of effects (e.g., average reaction times or average levels of altruistic behaviour). These samples are believed to represent universals (natural kinds, secondary substances), and thus they are believed to represent general truths that apply to all specific cases in a probabilistic manner (see Chapter 6 for a discussion of *generic statements*). However, as we saw in Section 2.2, this general-to-specific reasoning may amount to an ensemble-to-individual fallacy.

In experimental or intervention studies alike, the effects are customarily expressed by calculating the statistical significance of differences between groups. If the groups are big enough, even very small differences might achieve statistical significance (there is extensive literature on the problematic nature of p-values; for example, Amrhein, Greenland & McShane, 2019; Wasserstein & Lazar, 2016). But these small differences are still interpreted as referring to meaningful property distinctions on the level of natural kinds (i.e., upscaling). For example, very small but statistically significant group differences between men and women are interpreted as

---

[1] See www.ad.nl/nieuws/vleeseters-egoistischer-en-minder-sociaal-dan-vegetariers-a986fa64/ and www.mcgill.ca/newsroom/channels/news/caveman-behavioural-traits-might-kick-dinner-table-eating-169419

meaningful differences between the sexes in general, or very small effects of day-care on aggressive behaviour are interpreted as general facts about the nature of day-care and of aggression (e.g., Belsky, 2001).

By randomly (i.e., a-selectively or blindly) assigning individuals to the experimental and control group, every causal factor that eventually affects the outcome is believed to be equally present in both groups except for the causal factor introduced by the experimental manipulation. By randomizing, the causal factor of interest is isolated from all others, and this is a necessary condition for the applicability of modularity (one can intervene at one place in a system without altering causal relationships elsewhere) and the causal Markov condition (the causal factor is 'shielded off' from others). Both are necessary requirements for a type-causal, general interpretation of experimental results. However, real randomization, which implies the equal distribution of *all* potentially relevant, causal factors across both the experimental and control group, is a hardly realizable ideal. In fact, most experiments or intervention studies simply take real randomization for granted, without actually checking it. For instance, randomization into control and experimental groups was used in Sweden in order to study the effectiveness of multisystemic therapy. Cartwright and Munro (2010) describe this case and show how the effectiveness of multisystemic therapy differed among countries with different social and cultural background conditions. The randomization in the original Swedish study could of course not randomize the background support of the Swedish social system and the socio-economic conditions of living in Sweden. These background conditions are likely to affect the outcome of the experimental factor, the multisystemic therapy. Put differently, RCTs function against the backdrop of complex causal networks, cultural and social-support systems, and educational institutions and practices. If an RCT shows that therapy works or does not work, it has shown that it has worked or not worked in a particular context of causal conditions. It has *not* shown that the effect of the therapy is a consequence of an inherent causal capacity of this therapeutic intervention (the intervention-as-kind, universal or secondary substance). And neither has the RCT demonstrated the *transferability* of the intervention (i.e., that it will work in other contexts) (Cartwright, 2011; Cartwright & Hardie, 2012; Cartwright & Munro, 2010; Deaton & Cartwright, 2018). In order to demonstrate that a particular kind of intervention has a causal capacity that is transferable to other contexts, it is necessary to go beyond the confinements of a single RCT and to integrate all available data and all relevant theory about how a particular intervention, or aspects thereof, affect all phenomena of interest, such as a therapy's effect or the willingness of practitioners and clients to follow or even understand the therapy's protocols (see also Pearl, 2018; Bareinboim & Pearl, 2016, for a similar criticism of the limited interpretation of the RCT's causal claims).

With regard to evidence-based policies, it should be noted that for many complex social and psychological interventions, it is not at all clear what exactly in the intervention (if anything in particular at all) is the primary isolable, transferable causal factor (Kazdin, 2007, 2009; Cartwright 2007b). Since such relevant factors may be highly context-dependent and interwoven, it will never be really clear to which extent they will indeed be transferred to the variety of new contexts in which a particular intervention will be applied (see also Morgan & Winship, 2012). In a new context, the relevant factor may just as well disappear or be significantly reduced. Cartwright (2007a, 2011) notes that researchers pay very little attention to the conditions under which the evidence-based intervention or the experiment was evaluated, and to the new contexts and conditions to which it will be applied. Instead, in evidence-based work, attention goes to the *methodological* conditions of the RCT approach in which the evidence was obtained: was the study properly controlled, are there enough subjects, do other studies corroborate the finding?

In short, RCTs typically enact a substance-oriented ontology: the intervention is treated as a secondary substance endowed with an inherent causal power (e.g., the power to significantly reduce depressive symptoms). RCTs are often described as the gold standard for evaluating the effectiveness of interventions, but this qualification reflects their status as a prime iconic example of a substantialist ontology of causation.

7.3 Causality and the Wish to Explain

7.3.1 Aristotle's Four Forms of Causal Explanation

If the first side of the causality coin is the wish to change something (i.e., to make a difference by doing something (see Section 7,2)), the other side is the wish to scientifically understand or scientifically *explain* a particular phenomenon or observed property of the world. Aristotle's theory of causality provides an influential framework for forms of explanation. Aristotle made a distinction between explanations in the form of a) *material causes* (i.e., what something is made of); b) *formal causes* (i.e., the particular form that explains why something is an instance of X); c) *efficient causes* (i.e., some event that preceded that which we are interested in and that produced it); and d) *final causes* (i.e., the function or goal of something). This is also called *teleological explanation*.

Take for instance the question 'why does this particular child have autism spectrum disorder?'. One answer to this question would be something like 'because this child has a typical autistic brain' or, 'because this child's amygdala is characterized by abnormal connectivity' (e.g., Ha et al., 2015). This sort of answer refers to Aristotle's *material cause*, that what the autistic child 'is made of', which is commonly sought in the brain.

Another answer to this question could be a typical sort of DSM-V-assessment answer: 'Because the child shows deficits in nonverbal communicative behaviours used for social interaction, stereotyped or repetitive motor movements, use of objects, or speech and inflexible adherence to routines'. This answer would typically count as a *formal cause* answer in the Aristotelian scheme, specifying the properties that 'make' the child 'be autistic'.

The third type of answer could be something like 'because this child has a mutation in the CACNA1C gene'(Abrahams & Geschwind, 2008; Jason et al., 2015). Comparable answers could be 'because this child has been vaccinated (and vaccines cause autism)', or 'because a wicked witch put a spell on the child when it was left unattended in its cradle' (Davidson, 2017; Joseph, 2018 and Gona et al., 2015, have analysed these beliefs). This is the sort of answer we would categorize under the *efficient-cause* answers. They typically comply with the interventionist or manipulationist theory of causality, and for this reason, efficient-cause answers are often considered the only really *causal* explanation. Without the mutation, vaccination, or the wicked witch, the child would not be autistic, all other things being equal. That is, they imply counterfactualism, which is an important feature of the interventionist or manipulationist forms of causality.

However, counterfactualism as such is not a unique feature of the efficient cause explanation, as it also applies to the first and second Aristotelian type of 'because' (i.e., material and formal causes). If the child would not have abnormal connectivity in the brain, or would not show these symptoms, it would not be autistic. Or, similarly, if the child would not have had the above-described symptoms, the child would not be autistic. Importantly, in the material and formal-causal cases, these counterfactual possibilities do not involve actual events that precede and are believed to bring forth autism. This is what distinguishes them from efficient causality, which the standard praxis views as 'real' causal explanations. Material and formal causality may be subsumed under *constitutive explanations*, which means explaining by mentioning what constitutes a particular phenomenon, such as autism (Ylikoski, 2013). For instance, repetitive movements are *properties* – not causes – of autism, and so is abnormal connectivity in the amygdala (e.g., Shen et al., 2016). However, an abnormal amygdala is easily interpreted as an efficient cause of autism. Needless to say, material, formal and efficient causes are often hard to distinguish, which makes the focus on efficient causation as the only form of 'true' causation somewhat dubious. Finally, the fourth type of explanation invokes a *final cause* or function, that is, the cause of a particular event is the goal it tries to realize. This form of teleological explanation has been seen as incompatible with scientific causal-explanation, as a future event (a goal) can never explain an earlier event (a current property of autism). In addition, it is difficult to see what goal would be pursued by autism (but see section 7.4). On the other hand, final causes, or teleological explanation, make perfect sense in the context of living systems, or self-organizing systems in general. The goal of living systems is to maintain themselves, and much of their properties can be explained in terms of their self-reproduction (Ellis, 2005; Maturana & Varela, 2012). Functional – and in a sense teleological – explanations feature prominently in the sciences of living systems, without contradicting the basic tenets of scientific explanation.

In summary, Aristotle's scheme shows that causal explanations can be given from various perspectives, none of which can claim exclusivity, in spite of the widespread belief that only efficient causes represent 'real' causality. Perspectives can be shifted, sometimes even gradually, thus allowing rich and multifaceted explanations. However, Aristotle's four causes do not exhaust the possibilities of causal explanation, as we shall see in the next section

7.3.2 Contrastive versus Processual Explanations

According to Van Fraassen's (1980) influential theory, explanation is a matter of asking a why-question, and of giving an answer that complies with a specific *relevance-criterion*, that is to say, a criterion on the basis of which the questioner determines whether the answer given is relevant to the questioner's interests. If the questioner is a researcher in psychology, the relevance criteria refer to what, in psychology, counts as a scientifically relevant explanation. However, what counts as 'scientifically relevant explanation' depends on whether one takes the road of intervention causality and the associated model of acyclic (unidirectional) graphs (explained earlier in this chapter), or whether one takes the road of complex dynamic systems and processual approaches (as we shall explain in Chapter 8).

In this regard, Botterill (2010) introduces a useful distinction between contrastive and process explanations. A *contrastive explanation* focusses on specifying the conditions that make a difference, for instance, the genes that make a (probabilistic) difference between becoming autistic or not, or neural structures necessary for developing a number concept or not. Contrastive explanations are usually given in answer to a *why-question*. A *process explanation* on the other hand 'aims to account for the process by which one gets from an initial state to some outcome or terminal condition' (Botterill, 2010, p. 288). It is typically given in answer to a *how-question*. Both questions are causal questions, and the answers are forms of causal explanation. In a typical intervention-oriented view on causality, only the why-question invoking a contrastive – and preferably manipulable – condition without which the effect would not have occurred, is seen as a true causal question and causal explanation. In a process-oriented view on causality, it is the *process answer* that is seen as the 'real' causal explanation. What counts as a causal explanation depends on the questioner's purpose or intention, which can be oriented toward the possibility of intervention, or to the identification of a causal history (and if one understands a causal history, one can possibly better understand the possibilities and constraints on interventions).

For instance, one might explain fingers and toes by invoking genes that code for them, implying that the absence of those genes, or defects in them, will result in absence of, or serious defects in, fingers and toes. This genetic explanation is based on intervention causality, with the genes in question featuring as a (natural) intervention, with a counterfactual opposite (absence of those genes). Smith (1999) contrasts this with a processual explanation: 'The real-time mechanisms which create fingers and toes, however, are general, probabilistic, emergent and distributed across several levels of analyses' (p. 133). 'The roles played by any part process of a relational developmental system … is a function of all co-acting parts and processes of the system' (Lickliter, 2018, p. 3; for an application to psychological development, see Anderson et al., 2000; Cohen, 2010).

From a typical interventionist causal approach, processual answers to 'why' questions are considered to offer little more than a *description* of the time course of a particular process, such as the growth of vocabulary in a child (see Chapter 8). Such criticism is based on the *premise* that a real causal explanation must imply the identification of a particular event (or a few such events or conditions) that literally *makes* a difference, but in most processes, basically any part or component could make a difference.

7.4 Toward Processual Explanations: Tinbergen's Framework

Which kinds of explanation are expected when we move from contrastive to processual explanations? In a famous article, published more than fifty years ago, Nobel prize-winning biologist Nico Tinbergen described the basic kinds of explanation in ethology (Tinbergen, 1963; Hogan & Bolhuis, 2008; MacDougall-Shackleton, 2011). They are to a certain extent comparable to Aristotle's causes (Hladký & Havlíček, 2013), but Tinbergen's scheme adds elements that are of considerable importance to fields where processual explanations are all-important, namely ethology (the study of behaviour) and, by implication, psychology.

The first of Tinbergen's forms of explanation is what he – for our purposes somewhat confusingly – calls the *causal explanation*, which is an explanation in the form of the underlying physiological mechanism that produces the behaviour, which includes the mechanism's interactions with environmental information. In the case of autism, causal explanation consists of specifying its underlying mechanism, namely the motor, physiological, neurocognitive mechanisms of processing and eliciting of information that produces autistic behaviour in response to environmental conditions, such as contact avoidance or ritualized, repetitive actions (see section 7.3.1). Tinbergen emphasizes the complexity and circularity of these processes, against the assumption of simple unidirectional cause-effect schemes. The brain- and gene-based explanations of autism that we discussed in the preceding section are examples of what Tinbergen calls causal explanations, which are in fact similar to Aristotle's material cause, which is not considered truly 'causal' from the standard interventionist perspective, favouring effective causes only.

The second form is *functional explanation*, that is, to the *function* that a particular behaviour has with respect to enhancing the individual's fitness (and in psychology, this may be extended to aspects such as success, efficacy, wellbeing, and so forth). By way of example, an evolutionary functional explanation of autistic behaviour might entail that it facilitates behavioural features that contribute to the fitness of the individuals belonging to a particular population. For instance, certain aspects of autism facilitate the invention and production of technical tools, skills, and goods that increase the survival value of conspecifics that also serve the interests of autistic persons by providing care and protection. Examples are scientific and technological innovations, which are facilitated by the 'systemizing' ability, which depends on brain properties that are typical of people with autism (Baron-Cohen, 2009; Greenberg et al.,

2018; Ruzich et al., 2015).[2] Pathological, dysfunctional autism might be the price the species pays for the benefits of 'mild' autism.

The third form is *ontogenetic explanation* (i.e., the development of the individual in question). The question of why a particular person has been diagnosed with autism must be answered by tracing the person's ontogeny, that is, the process that began at conception, and via embryogenesis led to a particular human organism that developed – in interaction with a social, cultural, and material environment – up to the point of its current social and behavioural functioning that gave rise to the diagnosis. A typical genetic explanation is only a small part of the entire ontogenetic explanation (see also Smith, 1999).

Ontogenetic explanations make sense only if we see the explanandum (what we wish to explain) in processual terms (i.e., as a state or moment in an ongoing process). For instance, we can view a child's or an adult's autism, as a current state in a process with the person's life span as its temporal extension (a state which can be either transient, or relatively stable in that its dynamics are conservative, i.e., self-maintaining). The standard praxis of dealing with autism enacts a substantialist or essentialist ontology, by treating autism not as a developmental process in itself, but rather as a persistent, non-temporal property of the person, that underlies instead of follows from a person's development. A similar substance-oriented view, applies to all nativist explanations of development (Simpson et al., 2005).

The fourth of Tinbergen's forms concerns *evolutionary explanation*, namely explaining a behaviour, trait, or physiological mechanism by tracing its evolution. For instance, how did autism evolve in the phylogeny of Homo Sapiens? In evolutionary psychology, personality traits and individual differences are explained on the basis of their assumed fitness-enhancing or fitness-reducing properties during the evolutionary history of the human species (Buss, 2009). Proceeding with our autism example, a possible evolutionary explanation is that genes involved in the development of autism are also involved in the development of intelligence, and intelligence can be conceived of as a fitness-enhancing property of individuals (Ploeger & Galis, 2011). A comparable evolutionary explanation relates to the systemizing ability that facilitates technological innovation and production, which have a fitness-enhancing value for the members of societies in which such innovations can take place.

---

[2] See the media coverage in www.independent.co.uk/life-style/health-and-families/health-news/autism-experiment-reveals-people-in-technical-professions-are-more-likely-to-have-autistic-traits-a6719956.html

7.4 Toward Processual Explanations

Like ontogenetic explanations, evolutionary explanations are *process explanations*. First, they refer to short-term processes (i.e., properties of individual organisms contributing to sustenance and reproduction). Second, they refer to long-term processes (e.g., selection and genetic changes on the level of the populations or the species). The process of evolution itself explains why species are 'fluent', process-dependent categories instead of 'essences', in spite of long periods of stasis in some species (Mallet, 2013). Mathematical models illustrate the processual nature of this type of explanation by employing coupled differential-equations, network dynamics, or agent-based systems, in line with a fundamental process approach (Puga-Gonzalez, Hildenbrandt & Hemelrijk, 2009; Wolf & Weissing, 2012; Proulx, Promislow & Phillips, 2005; Delmas, Besson & Brice., 2019; see Chapters 2 and 8).Ontogenetic and evolutionary processes are *mutually dependent:* development depends on evolution, and evolution depends on development (e.g., Evolutionary Developmental Biology; Hall, 2012). In contrast, typical nativist accounts of development often rely on a unidirectional influence of evolution on development to explain why a particular trait became an innate feature of the human species (e.g., Nowak, Komarova & Niyogi, 2001, on Universal Grammar).

Because Tinbergen's scheme typically addressed animal behaviour, what is missing is the fifth form of explanation that is typical of the human species, namely the *historical or sociogenetic explanation*, focussing on historical changes in their environmental conditions due to their own cognitive, technological, and productive activities. This sort of explanation is typically associated with Lev Vygotsky (e.g., Wertsch, 2010; Van der Veer & Valsiner, 1991), and is consistent with a Marxist interpretation, which formed the intellectual and social context in which Vygotsky developed his theories (Sawyer & Stetsenko, 2018). A comparable, but theoretically quite different attempt at integrating sociogenetic and ontogenetic processes is Piaget's Genetic Epistemology (Piaget, 1997).

In summary, Tinbergen's scheme leads to a basically processual form of explanation. It complies with an ontology of a complex universe characterized by *intrinsic interactions* between processes on all possible scales of aggregation, from quantum physical processes to processes in biological and human ecologies. In this universe, the nature of causality depends on the *organization* of the world (Bickhard, 2009a, 2009b; Witherington, 2011). As a result, causality must be reinterpreted as *complex process causality,* and explanations can be given on the levels described by Tinbergen's scheme. Complex process explanation is the topic of the next chapter.

CHAPTER 8

(Compl)explanation and King Alfonso's Lament
Complex Dynamic Systems and Causal Explanation

> Si hubiera estado presente en la Creación, habría dado algunas indicaciones útiles.
>
> (Had I been present at the Creation, I would have given some useful hints for the better ordering of the universe.)
> King Alfonso X of Castile, also known as 'El Sabio' (The Wise), around 1250; original source: Thomas Carlyle, *History of Friedrich the Second Called Frederick the Great* (1858–1865), Vol. 1, page 98

King Alfonso of Castile, Galicia and Leon, 'El Sabio' or 'The Wise' (1221–1284), was not particularly happy with the way the Creator had organized the heavens, and he would have gladly given 'some useful hints for the better ordering of the universe' (Bartlett, 2014, p. 128). In Alfonso's time, the ordering of the universe was described by the Ptolemaic, geocentric system.

In fact, the Ptolemaic system is far from simplistic, primitive or wrong (depending on how one wishes to understand 'wrong', of course). The Ptolemaic system is intuitively and conceptually clear and it complies with the major empirical facts (i.e., the major facts of observation of the visible celestial bodies). Its predictive power has been very strong and depends on the prediction of empirically testable facts about the observable sky (i.e., about the sky as it reveals itself to the relatively unaided eye, including relatively simple telescopes). The Ptolemaic model was thus sophisticated, and empirically correct as long as you take the Earth – our perspective – as the reference point. For these reasons, it has withstood objections for about 1,500 years, and as a model of the sky, it is still used in modern planetarium projectors.

But once we get into the realm of stars, galaxies, and other remote objects – in other words, once we want to describe or explain the entire cosmos, the Ptolemaic system completely loses its significance or meaningfulness. The standard model of causality (*interventionist causality*;

discussed in depth in Chapter 7) is a bit Ptolemaic. It functions quite well as a model of causal explanation for a specific set of human-centred questions: how can we do something (or avoid something) that makes a difference for something (or someone) else? But this cause–effect model of causality falls short when we want to explain how this difference comes about. While the standard model of causality suffices for particular kinds of question, it does not function well as a general frame of reference encompassing processes and complexity. Therefore, just as the Ptolemaic model can be seen as a special case of the general cosmological model (by taking the earth as its reference point), interventionist causality is a special case of causality that exists within a larger, more comprehensive, frame of reference for causality: complex causality. The aim of this chapter is to discuss the notion of causality in the context of a process-oriented approach to psychological phenomena, which we ground in the (meta-) theory of complex dynamic systems (Wagner, 1999).

8.1 Playing a Simple Tune

To concretely discuss how the principles and characteristics of complex systems provide an alternative perspective of causality, it is helpful to take a concrete example from human activity and learning: learning to play a simple guitar tune. Note that the general mechanisms in this example are the same as those in any complex system, such as physical systems – like laser light (Haken, 1992) or chemical reactions (Prigogine, 1980), ecological systems (Arumugam, Lutscher & Guichard, 2021), an economy (Barnett, Serletis & Serletis, 2015), or the brain (Tognoli & Kelso, 2014; Rabinovich, Friston & Varona, 2012; Damm et al., 2020). In short, psychological dynamics are complex, i.e., *interwoven* (Olthof et al., 2020c)

Let us imagine a guitar novice, Eric, who wants to play a simple tune with underlying chords. Playing a tune, including some chord strings, involves a lot of perception–action couplings: putting each finger on the right string and between the right frets, changing from one position to the other, plucking each string with each finger, listening to the sounds produced, correcting finger positions and so forth. Each of the micro-events, such as putting the index finger on the D-position of the sixth string, is in itself a complex coupling of even more microscopic sensory-motor processes with underlying neural and muscular changes. In the beginning, 'playing' is a series of single notes, resulting from an arduous process of getting each finger independently on the right string. A lot of mistakes are made, that is, the sound patterns produced vary quite significantly from what one intends to play, and the time intervals between the notes vary wildly. That is to say, the components of the intended tune are still relatively independent of one another, and they each have their own range of variation.

Technically speaking, the above process is a system with a very high degree of freedom (freedom of variation of each component). As the novice practises, some components start to function as a unit (e.g., a tune string with two underlying chord strings). This means that the level of variation within this unit is considerably reduced (that's what makes it a unit). That is, for this particular, small set of simultaneously plucked strings, all underlying sensorimotor microprocesses are now coordinated under a (simple) pattern. The variations in finger position and pressure on the strings are constrained or limited by the musical perception–action pattern, which is a coordinated organization of finger movements and perceived sounds. This pattern constrains the motor processes: they can vary only to the extent that they contribute to the pattern. With more practice, the sequence of musical perception–action units gets integrated into an overarching pattern, the tune and chords one wants to play. As Eric plays the tune, he hears the sounds he's producing, and he uses this ongoing sound perception to simultaneously control and correct the finger movements that produce the sounds.

When playing the tune the next day, mistakes will initially be played; Eric needs to find the right pattern again. Once Eric has the whole tune right, he may invite a friend, Charlie, who is a percussionist. Everything goes fine at first, but then Charlie starts increasing the beat, and although Eric can keep up with percussionist Charlie for a little while, Eric soon gets lost. Instead of playing the tune-plus-chord strings (the original pattern, let us call it Pattern 1), Eric switches to strumming chords only (Pattern 2 emerges), then starts omitting intermediary chords (Pattern 3), and finally, Eric quits playing (Pattern 4). After this, Eric and Charlie switch to an entirely different pattern of sensory-motor coordination – including language – by beginning a discussion about why the tempo was changed. These patterns each represent an emergent property of the system, i.e., Eric and Charlie playing the tune together, providing the descriptive space for the system.

In terms of causal explanation for the changing patterns, we could take a kind of Ptolemaic, anthropocentric approach, where we attribute the origin of all these processes to a single controller: the novice, where the novice's intentions, confusion, motivation, skill level cause the various processes

This may seem like a logical, and indeed common, way of explaining the outcome of the jam session. However, we could also explain the process of learning to play a tune on the guitar on the basis of process causality.

8.2 Process as Cause

What we will show in the current chapter is how a process approach is fundamentally different from the classical two-event scheme, where a causal event occurs as an antecedent for an effect event, and where 'time' (if considered) only relates to the order of the two, implying that a cause entails the effect, or predicates the effect (Rosen, 2000, p 38; Turvey, 2004). This standard cause–effect model is also known as the efficient-cause model from the Aristotelian scheme (see Chapter 7), which Van Orden and Holden (2002) call billiard-ball causality, and which Overton (2015) calls the mechanistic antecedent–consequent relationship. It is directly reflected in the causal theory of standard psychological praxis, which assumes that an internal entity, a secondary substance, is the causal ground of behavioural expressions of a variable. Researchers habitually call this type of internal entity a 'latent variable'. For instance, the latent variable 'depression' is conceived of as the cause of symptoms such as negative mood and sleeplessness, the latent variable 'object concept' causes particular search and retrieval behaviour. The latent variable 'theory-of-mind' is the cause of a child's reasoning about mental states, such as beliefs and desires (see Borsboom, Mellenbergh & Van Heerden, 2003, for a discussion of latent variables as causes of behaviour).

We will show how the basic process characteristics of complex systems result in the process being the cause, making 'cause' something that occurs across time (Anjum & Mumford, 2018), and making it distributed. This kind of causality stems from the view that understanding cause(s) starts with the system as a whole, and in relation to the processes that comprise the whole system (Overton, 1975; Witherington & Heying, 2015). Here, we can see how complex causality resembles the modern cosmological model – taking the entire system as a starting point.

In short, for complex systems, causes should be understood in terms of a reciprocity of affordances[1] and 'effectivities' (or abilities to make use of specific affordances) (Michaels, 2003; Withagen et al., 2012; Withagen,

---

[1] The affordance-effectivities scheme is a central component of ecological psychology, pioneered by J. J. Gibson. A much older dynamic theory of behaviour, Lewin's topological psychology (1936), referred to environmental affordances as dependent on an agent's psychological or physical state 'valences'.

Araújo & De Poel, 2017). A musical note provides a meaning affordance to the musician, but this is only the case for a person who can actually read musical notes and does so (a particular effectivity). This reciprocity dissolves, in a sense, the classical cause–effect divide (Turvey, 2004, focuses on the very similar issue of the perception–action divide).

8.3 Process Characteristics Relevant for Causality

Causal processes of complex systems rest upon a number of pivotal process characteristics (described in Chapter 2): First, iterativity, where any moment (i.e., state) of learning to play a guitar tune is a function of the preceding state. Second, multiple timescales, where iterative processes occur across various levels, from the sensory-motor micro-events of placing one's fingers, strumming strings, and hearing the produced sounds generate the tune to the macroscopic level of one practice session to the next (extended from weeks to months). Third, self-organization, where interacting processes coordinate (without external guidance) to form self-maintaining, temporarily stable, patterns or structures (i.e., organizations or coordinations of components). These structures occur on the above-mentioned multiple timescales. Fourth, the reciprocal coupling of processes occurring across different timescales: daily practice has an improving effect on one's long-term guitar playing skill, and that guitar-playing skill loosely determines the properties of each daily practice. The sensory-motor micro-events of placing one's fingers, strumming strings, and hearing the produced sounds generate the tune, while the properties of the perceived tune loosely determine and constrain the sensory-motor processes. All these processes – constraining, limiting, affording, determining – together create a crucial form of causality: cyclical (or circular) causality.

8.4 Features of Complex Process Causality

8.4.1 Self-Causation: Self-Organization, Emergence, and Circular Causality

In contrast to the mainstream framework of causality, complex process causality involves a kind of self-cause (i.e., *autopoiesis* (Maturana & Varela, 1980), or *final cause*, in the Aristotelian scheme): the cause of the process lies in the interactions between its components that are driven toward a stable state (Witherington, 2011; Wurzman & Giordano, 2009; Bechtel, 2017). In this way, the process is the effect of itself (Juarrero, 1999, 2000).

8.4 Features of Complex Process Causality

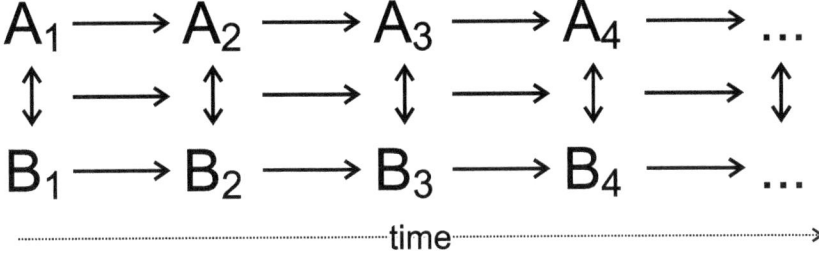

Figure 8.1 Circular causality between two parts of a system, A and B, over the course of time.

This feature is a direct result of *self-organization* (see Chapter 2 for our introduction to this concept). Self-organization implies that macroscopic properties originate out of the underlying, microscopic interactions, which is a form of upward causation (from a lower to a higher level, e.g., the tune originates out of pressing and plucking strings). This organization also constrains and canalizes the underlying interactions, a process called downward causation (the tune constrains the pressing and plucking strings; for a general introduction see Paoletti & Orilia, 2017). The unity of upward and downward causation is an example of *cyclical* (or *circular*) *causality* (Tschacher, Dauwalder & Haken, 2003; Bechtel, 2017; Van Orden & Holden, 2002) – shown in Figure 8.1, where A may be the tune that is created, and B is the pressing and plucking of the guitar strings. In many ways, this circular causality is a fundamental feature of complex systems and life in general (Rosen, 2000; Turvey, 2004; Richardson, 2006). Here we show circular causality between lower and higher levels of a system, but it is also characteristic of interactions between horizontal components (i.e., at the same level of a system – *horizontal causality*). The latter describes the strumming of guitar strings and the perception of the rhythm, or two individuals playing the tune together.

The notion of causality as operating through self-organization comes close to the original meaning of *cause* as 'bringing into being', and to 'work', according to Heidegger's interpretation of Aristotle's scheme (Stasiulis, 2019). The relative stability of a self-organized structure or pattern (an activity pattern, a belief, a family structure) is thus not passive, but active. It is a particular way of doing something or interacting with the world in the form of consuming resources. For instance, the living human body is a stable structure of organs, muscles, and limbs, but its stability results from its constant exchange of matter and energy (food, oxygen, heat), and this means that the internal state of the system is in constant change, it is an ongoing process (e.g., breathing or digesting). In this complex system that is the body, resources are consumed and turned into waste materials that are no longer usable as resources (e.g., oxygen is turned into carbon dioxide), and this process of consumption is what keeps the consuming system intact. The human body, as all complex systems, is a *dissipative* system, wasting useful energy and matter in such a way that the body's structure is conserved over time. Dissipative systems obey specific causal rules, which we will explain later in this chapter (for an introduction to dissipative systems, see Prigogine & Stengers, 1979; see also Friston, 2003; Friston, Kilner & Harrison, 2006; Swenson & Turvey, 1991 for related views in the context of brain and behaviour).

In a dissipative system, there is an intricate relationship between the incessant processes of energy and matter consumption and the stability or structure of the system: one constrains and shapes the other. Christensen and Bickhard (2002, p. 3) write that 'autonomous (or "self-governed") systems … possess a process organization that, in interaction with the environment, performs work to guide energy into the processes of the system itself'. This 'guiding' can thus be thought of as a process of conservation over time, through its interactions with its environment, and it often involves actively selecting, exploiting, and modifying their environments to achieve self-preservation.

The process of self-organization thus 'consumes' energy and also 'minimizes' the energy required for self-preservation (the patterns will optimize energy dissipation; e.g., Swenson & Turvey, 1991; Prigogine, 1980). This minimization of energy was described in Chapter 1, as a pivotal characteristic of attractor landscapes and their explanation of a system's behaviour. What this implies is that any *change* in the underlying pattern will require more energy, effort or work than maintaining the current pattern (irrespective of when the underlying pattern is pleasant or aversive, such as a dysfunctional family structure or a person's eating disorder (for further explanation see Section 8.5.5.2).

8.4.2 *Normativity and Intentions*

When studying autonomous agents that actively maintain their own integrity over time (as is the case for people), the time series of behaviours, actions, events and so forth must also be seen in light of what 'potential states' can be. That is to say, the evolution term must incorporate information about the types of states that are 'successful' for a certain kind of system and which are not (e.g., De Jesus, 2018; Allen & Bickhard, 2011). This refers to the norms (i.e., *normativity*) relevant for the system. Normative potential states can also be framed as intentions (much like goals), and thus constrain and canalize the components of the activity (Juarrero, 1999,

2000; Riley & Turvey, 2001; Van Orden & Holden, 2002; Spivey, 2013). For example, an adolescent strives for autonomy during an argument with their parents. Thus, coming out of the argument with a sense of autonomy would resemble a 'successful' potential state for the interactive process. Gaining this sense of autonomy was the adolescent's intention or goal, and thus guided (i.e., constrained and canalized) their actions and interactions with the parents. These norms vary from being generic and relevant to all concrete instances of a certain type of system (e.g., all adolescents) to being entirely idiosyncratic (i.e., unique to this specific adolescent).

Furthermore, given this potential state (i.e., sense of autonomy), we can say that the conflict discussion with the parents had the 'function' of affording and creating autonomy. In this way, we come close to the Aristotelian *final-cause* concept of explanation (i.e., the function or goal of something as causal). The cause of the interaction between the adolescent and the parents was the *function* that it had; namely, to afford the potential state of gaining a sense of autonomy.

Importantly, these norms are not fixed determiners of behaviour, as is the case in the common praxis. For example, it is not the case that a goal to have a sense of autonomy determines autonomy in a fixed way. This interpretation of intentions is of a preceding mental cause bringing about a particular activity as its effect – a *mentalist* approach (Van Orden & Holden, 2002; Spivey, 2013; Juarrero, 1999, 2000; Schlicht & Starzak, 2019). Alternatively, another common explanation may be a *physicalist* approach, where all events, including an agent's seemingly autonomous intentions and free will, are 'caused' by physical event chains in the brain (e.g., Libet's (1985) study showing that neurological brain events precede conscious intentions, and see Radder & Meynen, 2013, for a critical evaluation). Both of these reify intentions, treating them as functional antecedents of behaviour (Witherington & Heying, 2015).

In contrast to these mentalist or physicalist notions of intentions as antecedents, we are referring to intentions (or norms) as emergent properties of coherent activity (at the individual level, or the collective level depending on which level of normativity we are referring to) (Witherington & Heying, 2015). Let us take another example that is commonly discussed in developmental psychology: an infant reaching for an object. The infant's reaching for the object is not the 'result' of a static internal drive for the need to explore: It 'results' from the ongoing action–perception loops between situated physical (e.g., motor movements), material (the floor, the object in front of the infant), and social (e.g., a parent's encouragement) components. These interactions emerge into an intention. This emergent intention then constrains the activities that the infant is likely to undergo.

These upward and downward relationships are a particular case of circular causality that is driven by a so-called *gradient process* (i.e., a process of solving or reducing a disequilibrium, tension, or dissonance) (Tschacher & Haken, 2007). As an infant engages in the action–perception loop, tensions in the form of competing potentials (i.e., directions to move in or actions to do) are reduced. For example, an infant is offered many affordances in a setting in which there is an object that can be grasped. Aside from the object (which affords grasping), other adults present, or other spaces further away from the object offer affordances. Each of these corresponds with a different potential: the infant could ignore the object and make funny faces at the adult, or they could turn away from the object and explore the shadow on the ground made by their body blocking the light, for example. Should the infant engage with the object with an initial action (i.e., looking at the object), the resulting action–perception loop (e.g., the infant moves closer to the object, revealing its form, inviting the infant to grasp it, etc.) increases the likelihood that the infant will continue down this road of object exploration, rather than shadow exploration or social interaction. Thus, the 'competing potentials' fall away, and the intention to explore the object becomes a driving force in the next steps that will be taken. The intention (to grasp the object) thus emerged as the infant acted within the constraints of the environment, and this emergent intention subsequently constrained the infant's actions.

8.4.3 *External Causal Forces: Perturbations*

The fact that a complex system 'self-causes' does not imply that it is *not* influenced by external forces. Indeed, an important part of the learning-to-play-a-guitar-tune example was the friend, who joined the jamming session and increased the tempo. The influence that an external influence has on a system is called a *perturbation*. For instance, let us take our illustrative case of Eric learning to play a guitar tune – where the current skill level is our self-sustaining pattern. When Charlie comes to join the jam session and introduces a change in tempo, this results in a perturbation, such that Eric's guitar playing is interrupted. In many cases, the effect of a perturbation will only be transient, in the sense that the system will move back to its original state when the perturbation has been removed or has stopped. If drummer Charlie stops, or adjusts his tempo to that of our guitar-playing musician, the latter can then relatively easily return to the initial state of playing guitar.

The 'moving back' to an original state can be both a positive or negative thing for psychological systems. It is positive when it pertains to *resilience*, the capacity to overcome negative influences (Grimm & Calabrese, 2011 present various forms and definitions; and Martin, Deffuant & Calabrese, 2011 provide a mathematical treatment in the context of attractors). In contrast, bouncing back may also be something negative, like when pathological states (e.g., addiction), return after therapeutic interventions (e.g., rehabilitation), i.e., relapse.

In other cases, perturbations can result in a change in developmental trajectory of the system, changing the direction or quality of patterns. For instance, in the case of the person learning to play a guitar tune, the perturbation from the friend joining the jam session drives our musician to a state of *self-organized criticality* (Bak, 2013; see Chapter 2), where any seemingly small and insignificant event (such as the introduction of a slight variation in rhythm) can have a whole range of possible consequences. For instance, the musician may successfully adapt to the perturbations, moving them to a higher skill level in which both are able to improvise. Alternatively, the musician may stop and give up, resulting in a resistance to playing at all. The specific outcome is unpredictable, and the result of the self-organized criticality. As such, it cannot be predicted by, for example, the musician's level of motivation.

8.4.4 *Distributed Causality*

The dynamic systems feature of self-organization across multiple levels of a system make causality a *distributed* property. Causality does not occur, or can not be reduced to, any one specific level of the system (Overton, 1975). Causality is distributed across hierarchical levels of organization (from neural and muscular levels to the level of coordinated activity, e.g., playing a guitar tune; see Tognoli et al., 2020 on social behaviour), and within each level, causality is distributed across interacting processes (e.g., the guitar player, the guitar, and the jam partner).

Because of this distributed causality, the four Aristotelian causal explanations (described in Chapter 7) 'collapse' into a unity: processes within the system (and between the system and environment) causally depend on the structure of the whole (i.e., *formal causation*), and processes contribute to other processes or make them possible (i.e., *efficient causation*). And this then brings us back to autopoiesis, as the function of the processes is to maintain the integrity of the whole. A part of the integrity (that is to be maintained) is the collection of maintaining processes themselves (i.e., *final causality*). For all of this, exchanges of energy with the environment are necessary to produce and maintain the whole structure (i.e., *material causation*). Under a process approach, these various forms of causality are inseparable from each other, together creating and maintaining the whole system and its activity.

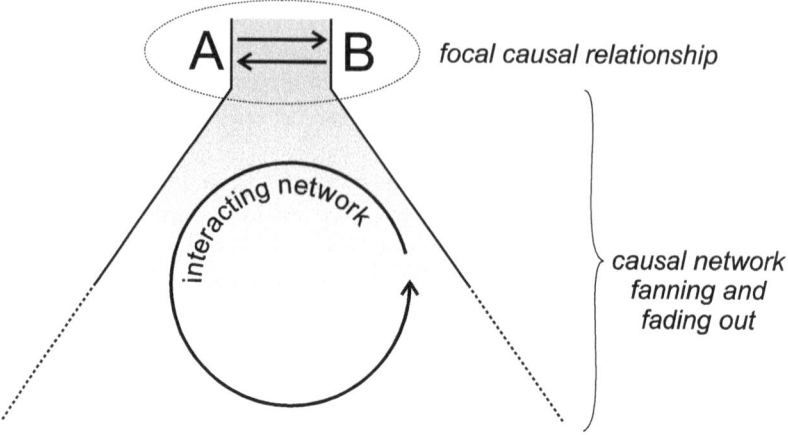

Figure 8.2 The causal fan, that is, the totality of interactions contributing to the current interaction between two components (A and B).

With distributed causality, it is difficult (if not impossible) to say where exactly the causal processes end that underlie a phenomenon such as playing a tune. This is known as the *problem of limitation* and was specified by J. S. Mill in 1843 (for this reason, it is also sometimes called *Mill's problem*). The 'problem' is that 'The real Cause, is the whole of these antecedents; and we have, philosophically speaking, no right to give the name of cause to one of them, exclusively of the others' (as quoted in Botterill, 2010, p. 289). The *interventionist approach* (described in Chapter 7) solves this 'problem' by isolating causes from their antecedents ('shielding off'), which is a pragmatic solution, rather than a description of real finite causal chains. In a process approach, however, the aim is to conceptualize the distributed process of causality as accurately as possible. One way of doing this is to conceptualize causality as fanning out and fading out (Figure 8.2). Specifically, macroscopic processes and their interactions (e.g., such as a tune played by two individuals jamming, A and B in Figure 8.2) rest on a causal network that is increasingly large as we move down, and where these numerous causal processes become increasingly *less* pivotal – on their own – in maintaining the system's highest-order processes. As shown in Figure 8.2, there are no intrinsic boundaries or limitations with regards to where the causal influence stops, but they become increasingly distributed as we move down to the supportive processes enabling the focal process.

8.4.5 Causality as Probabilistic and Processual

An important part of the above 'distributed causality' characteristic is that causality is then necessarily *probabilistic*, referring to something increasing the probability of an effect occurring (Hitchcock, 2021; Schaffer, 2001). Causality is distributed across moving parts, and thus cannot be deterministic. While probabilistic causality is in some ways typical for social sciences, the standard approach to probabilistic causality is fixed, where individual cause-and-effect associates are added together. A typical cause-and-effect association may be something like the effect of a causal intervention like psychotherapy, and the effect could then be the reduction in depression symptoms. Probability then refers to a fixed property (e.g., the average reduction of depression symptoms in a large sample of individuals; e.g., Williamson, 2009). Based on an implicit (but unfounded) ergodicity assumption, this probability is assigned to every individual in the sample or the population it represents (e.g., the probability that a particular therapy reduces the symptoms in an individual; see also Chapter 10). This fixed probabilistic property, therefore, can most likely not contribute to a causal explanation for individual outcomes at all.

In complex systems, causal forces like intrinsic dynamics, constraints, or perturbations are – firstly – not deterministic. We cannot say with certainty that a certain force will actually perturb a system, nor how an eventual perturbation will play out (see *self-organized criticality* above), for example. Instead, certain causal forces increase the *likelihood* of certain iterative outcomes. Secondly, this probability is not fixed. It is dynamic, and thus a processual property. Probability depends on the current state of the system, which thus changes with each iteration. Whether a system will be perturbed or not thus depends on whether it is currently in a deeply entrenched attractor (where it will probably not be perturbed) or in a state of self-organized criticality (where it will almost certainly be perturbed even if the perturbation is arbitrarily small), for example.

In the following subsections, we provide an overview of some ways in which the above features are applied in order to specify complex process causality in dynamic systems.

8.5 From Abstract to Concrete: Specifying Causality in Complex Systems through Models

Recall from Chapter 2 that a common definition of a dynamic system is a specific 'rule' (i.e., *evolution rule*) for how a system changes across a state space (Meiss, 2007). In this way, a pivotal part of complex process causality is the transmission of causal influence from one state to the next (i.e., the iterative characteristic of dynamic systems) (Salmon, 1998; Dowe, 2000, 2009, 2012). If the iterative nature of a dynamic system can be described as $x_{t+1} = f(x_t)$; $x_{t+2} = f(x_{t+1})$; $x_{t+3} = f(x_{t+2})$; $x_{t+4} = f(x_{t+3})$, then the operator f (which is the system's *evolution rule*) specifies the *causal* processes (Érdi, 2008, p. 109). This is the function that transforms the current state into its next state. Defining this function is a way of specifying the *causal power* (Mumford & Anjum, 2011).

For a dynamic model to be a *causal* dynamic model, it is crucial that the mathematical functions express a plausible causal mechanism of change. For instance, in the case of a child learning to use determiners in speech, the underlying mechanism consists of a plausible theory of language learning in a child based on information the child can get from a caretaker's child-directed speech, and a plausible theory of child-directed speech as an adaptation of the caretaker's speech based on their perception of the child's current language. For example, Bassano et al. (2011) and Van Dijk et al. (2013) present an empirically verified dynamic model based on a general theory of adaptive child–parent interaction and demonstrate how it generates time series of determiner use, mean length of utterance and vocabulary in child speech and child-directed speech.

The aim of such modelling is generalization through theory building and replication, rather than the estimation of population parameters (which is more typical in the standard praxis) – more on this in Chapter 11. To this end, the focus of such models are *individual* trajectories. Individual cases differ in the values of the model control parameters (e.g., the parameters specifying a parent's tendency to adapt to the child's speech) – described below. The totality of parameter values forms a *parameter space*, and this parameter space corresponds with a particular population (the population for which these parameter values are plausible possibilities). By simulating many such individual trajectories for a particular parameter space, a population may be simulated and its statistical properties may be compared with empirical data (e.g., Steenbeek & Van Geert, 2007, 2008). A dynamic model may thus provide a causal explanation of individual processes as well as group distributions.

With the extensive consideration of a parameter space, models provide ways of studying the complexity hidden in apparently simple conceptual models. For example, Van Geert (1998, 2000) and Van Geert & Steenbeek (2005b) transformed the Vygotskian and Piagetian models (which are conceptual) into dynamic models, and showed the extent to which those models indeed generate the theories' typical developmental phenomena. Examples are stages and discontinuities in the case of Piaget's stage model of cognitive development and self-maintaining optimal versus sub-optimal learning-teaching trajectories in the case of a scaffolding for Vygotsky's theory. A dynamic model of Vygotsky's theory of the zone of proximal development, involving two coupled equations, demonstrated surprisingly complex dynamics (Merlone, Panchuk & Van Geert, 2019).

By studying causality via models, causality is treated as a temporal chain, where the roles of cause and effect are continuously shifting over the steps (or flow) in the process. In psychology, the possibility of such mathematical specifications of processual causes of change is limited, but certainly not negligible, as examples from language, cognitive, social and personality development demonstrate (e.g., Van Geert, 1991; Kunnen, 2012; Van der Maas et al., 2006; see also Chapters 9 and 10 on Measurement).

8.5.1 Wiener–Granger Causality

The notion of intervention causality (see Chapter 7) can be applied to dynamic systems (e.g., in coordination dynamics) if it remains a specification of causality *across a process*, as opposed to a static 'intervening variable' being manipulated to produce a certain outcome (which corresponds with the specification of causality in mainstream psychology). For this, Wiener–Granger statistical models have been widely and successfully used, for example in neurobiology (Bressler & Seth, 2011; Friston, Moran & Seth, 2013; Friston et al., 2017).

These models are named after mathematician and originator of cybernetics Norbert Wiener, and Clive Granger, econometrist and winner of the 2003 Nobel Prize in economics. Seth (2007) defines Granger causality, as it is customarily named, in the following way: 'if a signal X_1 "Granger-causes" (or "G-causes") a signal X_2, then past values of X_1 should contain information that helps predict X_2 above and beyond the information contained in past values of X_2 alone'. This type of model can thus be used to specify which (if any) of the coordinated processes is actually taking the lead in a dynamic coupling or an interaction, examining causal relationships over a non-trivially long period of time (e.g., Jeronimus et al., 2014; Ma, Aihara & Chen, 2014).

A Wiener–Granger model allows researchers to estimate the extent to which each step in a process helps predict the following step in another process. This may reveal that one process is consistently influencing the other, for instance a staff member is taking the lead in the interaction with a client with mild intellectual disabilities (Reuzel et al., 2013). On the other hand, it may also reveal that the direction of influence shifts from one process to the other; for instance, a young child is gradually taking over the lead from a teacher in a conversation about a science problem as the child's understanding increases (Van Der Steen et al., 2014). Although one process is taking the lead, the processes are still interdependent.

With the above specifications, time may be treated as discrete, where change occurs in steps (t, t+1, t+2; etc.), where the 'step' (i.e., +1) represents any duration of time of choice. In a simple exponential growth process, such as the spread of infections across a population, the evolution rule can be as simple as a multiplication. For instance, the next number of infected people equals the preceding number multiplied by 1.1 (for instance the (in) famous R number used during the COVID-19 pandemic) A more complex evolution rule might add a negative number; namely, the number of people leaving the population of infected persons, either by death or by recovery.

8.5.2 *Interacting Causal Agents: Agent-Based Models*

A form of causal dynamic modelling that is of particular relevance to behavioural and social sciences is agent-based modelling, although it is still rarely used in psychological research (Axelrod, 2006; Schlesinger & Parisi, 2001; Sawyer, 2004; Smith & Conrey, 2007). The processes that these models try to explain are sequences of activities of agents, including internal activities such as thinking, expressive activities such as emotional expressions, the adoption of beliefs and so forth. Examples include dyadic play over the course of minutes (Steenbeek & Van Geert, 2008; Steenbeek, Van der Aalsvoort & Van Geert, 2014; Hesp, Steenbeek, & Van Geert, 2019), the formation of friendship groups related to risk versus socially conventional behaviour in adolescents over months (Schuhmacher, Ballato & Van Geert, 2014) or ideological polarization of global economic behaviour in a population over the course of years (Banisch & Olbrich, 2021; Boero et al., 2015).

The underlying causal model is that of an autonomous agent interacting with other autonomous agents and with an environment, containing objects or resources that are relevant for the agents at issue. 'Relevance' can be described in the form of an agent's concerns, interests, needs and so forth, which are basically aimed at maintaining the agent's integrity (e.g., its survival or well-being). Agent-based models typically bestow agents with individual intentions or interests, with perceptual and motor means, and with the ability to adapt or change on the basis of their experiences (Steenbeek & Van Geert, 2007, 2008). These agent properties are conceived of as emergent properties of underlying processes (see Section 8.4.2 for more on this).

For agent-based models, agency (in relation to the maintenance of integrity) is a pivotal underlying theoretical assumption, much like it is for ecological and Gibsonian psychology or for theories of enactment and autopoiesis (for a discussion of the fundamental nature of agency, see Bickhard, 2009a, 2011b; Campbell, 2010). This contrasts the standard praxis of psychological explanation, where agency is often downplayed in favour of statistical relations between independent variables and dependent behaviour across samples of subjects.

In agent-based models, the cause of a phenomenon of interest is the totality of adaptive actions and interactions performed by agents over time, highlighting the distributed characteristic of causality. This distribution can also be described as fading out and spreading out. Take, for example, an agent-based model between two individuals. The cause of their interactive phenomenon (e.g., socially conventional behaviour) is distributed between them and their ongoing interactions, but it is also distributed (in a faded way) across their proximal and distal environments. A specific culture among their group of extended friends is co-created by, and emergent from, the activities of each individual agent as it interacts with other agents. Even further out, cultural agency (i.e., manipulation of cultural objects) is also part of the causal explanation (e.g., Malafouris, 2013). This could be a typical aspect of causal explanations based on theories of affordances and constraints presented by material objects and environments (Rietveld & Kiverstein, 2014; Tillas et al., 2017; Withagen, Araújo & De Poel, 2017).

Practically speaking, agent-based models can be created with a variety of tools. The *Netlogo* software for instance, is a widely used and well-known tool for agent-based simulation. The number of currently available software platforms is rapidly expanding, however (Abar et al., 2017). The easily accessible *InsightMaker* platform provides tools for agent-based modelling, as well as system dynamics.

8.5.3 Continuous Processes

Time need not be treated as discrete though. In continuous time, change occurs as a *flow*:

$$\dot{x} = f(x) \text{ or } \frac{dx}{dt} = f(x)$$

An evolution function that features in a wide range of psychological and biological (ecological) models is the logistic function (e.g., Van Geert, 1991). It is a way of coupling a state in a system (e.g., a child's current lexicon L) with a relevant state in the environment (e.g., the lexicon presented in the child's family environment, C).

$$L_{t+1} = L_t + L_t * r * (1 - L_t/C)$$

In this equation, r is a rate of increase, the effect of which depends on the available resource C, becoming zero (0) if Lt = C, implying that L approaches a stable level.

In a dynamic system, the evolution term is a way of specifying the dispositional property, or equivalently, the *causal power* (Mumford & Anjum, 2011; Hüttemann, 2013) or causal propensity, of every possible state in a process. It specifies what every possible state of the system will bring forth in the form of the next state. In this sense, a dynamic system is a model of efficient causality in the form of a temporal chain, where the roles of cause and effect are continuously shifting over the steps in the process (or the flow).

For every step in the temporal sequence (or moment in the flow) we can apply the classical causal criteria of contingency (a particular step or moment precedes the next step or moment), of counterfactual reasoning (if the preceding step would have been different, the next step would have been different), and of generalizable connection (the connection is an expression of a general, plausible mechanism or function; e.g., a logistic function, or a mechanism of damped exponential growth, as in epidemiology).

Specifying the evolution term of a dynamic system places the focus on the system's behaviour at the level of *collective variables* or *order parameters* (Kelso, 1995; Haken, 1992; Willems, 2007). These are parameters or variables that describe the ordered, coordinated or organized nature of patterns. In this way, it can be thought of as a *collective causal term* that represents a simplified higher-order representation of the macroscopic system behaviour (e.g., the *skill* of playing a tune), which necessarily includes the myriad underlying processes, involving social and material interactions, perceptions, actions, object properties and so forth (e.g., Pereira, Smith & Yu, 2014). The collective causal term represented by the evolution function is therefore, in a sense, distributed across the myriad underlying processes.

8.5 From Abstract to Concrete

8.5.4 Provocations of Development: Control Parameters

Aside from the core feature of self-cause (by means of self-organization), there will also be properties or forces (i.e., control parameters) that provoke transitions from one state to another, or from one pattern to another in multi-stable systems (i.e., perturbations, see earlier). The term *control parameters* is somewhat misleading, as these parameters do not literally 'control' activity, but rather lead it through instabilities or perturbations (De Greene, 1993, p. 112). Examples from physical systems can be intensity of light pumped into a laser, or heat transmitted to a liquid. Control parameters can be external or self-imposed. For example, during the process of writing (where a self-maintaining flow-like process takes place), external control parameters may be someone downstairs calling up, while a self-imposed control parameter may be an increasing need for food. When either of these exceeds a certain threshold (in time, or in ability to ignore a craving for food or the person calling from downstairs), a rapid reorganization from one activity pattern (i.e., writing) to another (i.e., not writing) will occur. The craving and the calling from downstairs thus refer to the control parameter, which then causes the system's behaviour (i.e., a state of writing) to change in some way or another.

8.5.5 Qualitative Process Dynamics as Specifications of Causality

The application of order parameters and control parameters to specify evolution functions typically involves the *mathematical* specification of causal power. While this can be a useful way to specify temporal causality, it is also possible to express causality in the form of a *qualitative model*. Such a model may describe how a process changes and is governed by specific constraints, such as autonomy and relationship concerns, in the case of parent-adolescent communication dynamics (e.g., Lichtwarck-Aschoff, Kunnen & Van Geert, 2009; Hollenstein, Lichtwarck-Aschoff & Potworowski, 2013; Lichtwarck-Aschoff, Kunnen & Van Geert, 2010). The qualitative model applies these constraints in an iterative fashion, where each successive state is a function of the constraints on the previous state.

A qualitative model of process causality can be theoretical or empirical. A qualitative model based on empirical data can be derived by means of *observation-oriented modelling*, for example. This is an approach developed by Grice and colleagues (Grice, 2011, 2015; Grice et al., 2012) that 'relies primarily upon techniques of visual examination to detect and explain

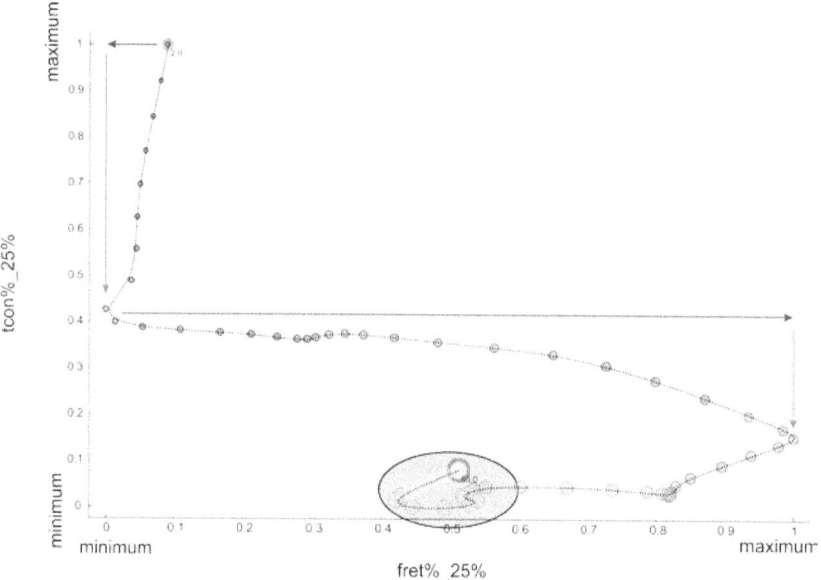

Figure 8.3 A two-dimensional state space based on locally smoothed trends in physical contact (vertical dimension) and fretting (horizontal dimension) during the first year of life in one child. The dimensions vary between the minimum and maximum values of each variable. Every point represents the average of several hours of observation during one day a week, with a total of 64 weeks.

dominant patterns within a set of observations' (Grice, 2015, p. 2). Models are represented in visual or iconic formats that are very similar to the network models of complex dynamic systems theory.

Figure 8.3 illustrates such a qualitative model based on empirical data (from De Weerth & Van Geert, 2001). This example is based on data from observations of parent-infant interactions. The physical contact between infant and parent and the infant's fretting behaviour (i.e., signs of distress without crying) were mapped across the span of the infant's second week of life and sixty-fifth week of life (the data-point size is proportional to age in weeks). Here we can see that the relationship between physical contact and fretting changed considerably over time. In the first months there was a significant decrease in physical contact with minor decrease in fretting, afterwards we can see a transition to a completely opposite relationship, with a significant increase in fretting and a minor decrease in physical contact. Finally, a (temporarily) stable relationship between physical distance and fretting can be observed (i.e., the grey ellipse) which signifies a final

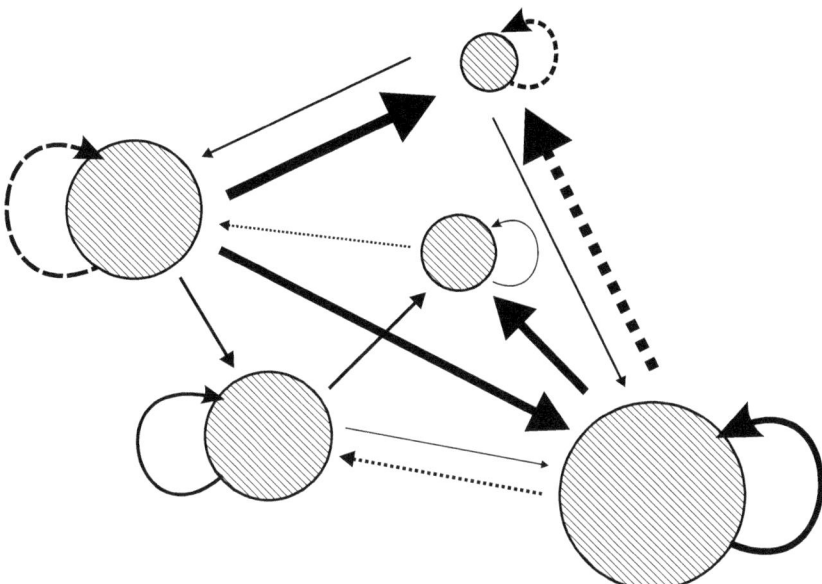

Figure 8.4 A simple and generic network representation of coupled dynamics between components. Arrows represent causal relationships; dashed arrows represent negative relationships, solid arrows represent positive relationships. The size of the arrows corresponds with the coupling strength; and the size of the circles corresponds with the value of each variable at the current time.

attractor region. This example illustrates the modelling of an individual trajectory, providing theoretically relevant information about processes of fretting in infants.

8.5.5.1 System Dynamics, Network Models, and Dynamic Fields
System dynamics originated in the context of industrial production processes as early as the 1950s, but has now far exceeded its highly limited origin. System dynamics are represented in the form of network models: components (nodes) that are dynamically coupled through relationships (vertices) (Figure 8.4). In this way, they involve the qualitative modelling of complex systems.

Dynamic networks are used to model a wide variety of phenomena, such as the relationship between depressive symptoms in individual clients (Schmittmann et al., 2013); excellent performance over the life span (Den Hartigh et al., 2016), or the g-factor in intelligence (Van der Maas et al., 2006). These dynamic networks are highly idiosyncratic and person-specific

(Fried et al., 2016). For the great majority of phenomena (e.g. a particular disorder, such as depression), there is no single etiology and no single underlying cause or property that is common to all individuals to which this phenomenon applies (Fried et al., 2017; Nuijten et al. 2016; McNally et al., 2015); Woods et al., 2020; Fisher, Medaglia & Jeronimus, 2018; Schiepek et al. 2020; for a discussion see among others Pilgrim, 2019, pp. 131 ff).

Despite the inherently idiosyncratic nature of such network models, it is possible to cluster them into categories based on partially overlapping properties, so-called *semantic family resemblances*. Using person-specific network models as a starting point for determining semantic family resemblances indicates an important turn toward personalized models and personalized treatment that can, nevertheless, be used for larger populations (Dotterer et al., 2019).

While the above description of networks stems from the current turn toward network thinking, the originator of system dynamics, Jay W. Forrester, introduced this form of modelling in a much broader way than they are currently used:

> The system dynamics process starts from a problem to be solved – a situation that needs to be better understood, or an undesirable behavior that is to be corrected or avoided. The first step is to tap the wealth of information that people possess in their heads ... The management and social sciences have in the past unduly restricted themselves to measured data and have neglected the far richer and more informative body of information that exists in the knowledge and experience of those in the active, working world. (Forrester, 1993, p. 199)[2]

Researchers in psychology possess a 'wealth of information'. For example, concluding sections of empirical research papers often entail theoretical speculations that are far richer than the data they are based on, and often reflect knowledge based on a body of research and theoretical argumentation (see Grice, 2011, 2014, 2015, for a similar argument). These argumentative models of processes can be modelled in the form of system dynamics as well. In this way, system dynamics can include whole networks of components of different kinds. Moreover, these models are primarily visual schemes (to which equations are added). With this more pluralistic and holistic approach to networks, these models can allow researchers

---

[2] The quote still bears the mark of industrial production processes, which is where System Dynamics originated in the 1950s.

8.5 From Abstract to Concrete

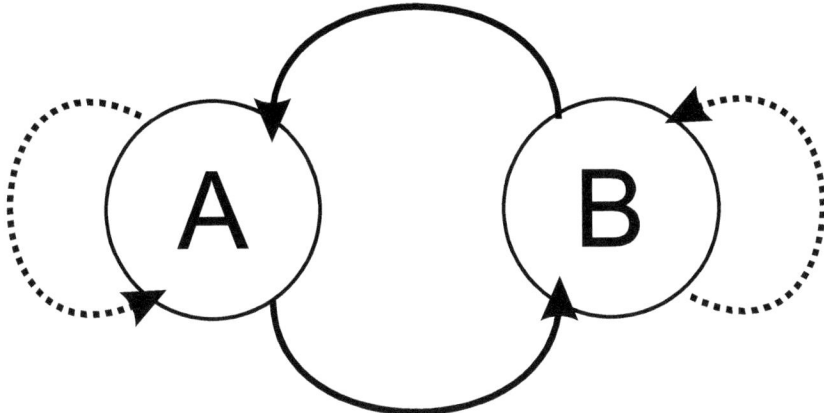

Figure 8.5 A basic and generic causal-loop graph, showing how components cause each other and themselves. Dashed arrows represent negative relationships, solid arrows represent positive relationships. Causal loop graphs are network representations of dynamic systems (see Chapter 2, Figure 2.2).

to theoretically investigate the possibilities, limitations and consequences of their argumentative models, making them a method for 'experimental theoretical psychology' (Van Geert, 1994; Kunnen, 2017; Gräbner, 2018).

Currently, there is a wide variety in commercial as well as free software that greatly simplifies the building of such dynamic models and in some cases its empirical validation based on process data.[3]

System dynamics represent complex causality in the form of cyclical graphs (i.e., negative and positive feedback coupling), as opposed to the acyclical graphs of intervention or manipulationist causality (see Menzies, 2007; Byrne & Uprichard, 2012). Causal influences and effects take the form of time evolutions (i.e., processes of change or flows), but can also entail single intervention events, in the form of perturbations or 'shocks'. *Causal-loop graphs* (Figure 8.5) can be used for this, showing interactions between components as basic qualitatively formulated negative and positive feedback loops.

Causal-replace looping by loop graphs are entirely visually specified models. For the interested reader, a very nice implementation is Loopy (http:/ncase.me), and another is IModeler (www.consideo.com/software-imodeler.html).

---

[3] See https://en.wikipedia.org/wiki/Comparison_of_system_dynamics_software.

In principle, the state of a dynamic system is represented by a single point in its state space. An example is the current level of help given by the teacher combined with the current number of maths problems made by a student, which are like coordinates on two dimensions, specifying one point in the two-dimensional space. However, at any point in time, there's in fact a probability distribution of possible levels of help given by the teacher, and a probability distribution of numbers of problems solved (see also Chapter 10). Instead of a point in the state space, we thus have a field of states, one of which will be actualized in a real lesson. This is the topic of *dynamic field theory* (Schöner & Spencer, 2016). Continuous perceptual, motor, and cognitive dimensions, such as spatial location or degree of similarity between objects, are represented in the brain in the form of changeable fields of possible states. They incorporate the input from the environment (e.g., in the form of a perception) and the effects of memory and learning. They can be used to simulate and explain a wide variety of developmental phenomena (Spencer, 2017; Samuelson, Kucker & Spencer, 2017; Samuelson, Jenkins & Spencer, 2015; Buss & Spencer, 2014). They can also be used to simulate macro-developmental phenomena that depend on more or less continuous 'inputs' (e.g., a continuous stream of experiences, Van Geert, 1998).

8.5.5.2   Visualizing Complex Causality: Changing Attractor Landscapes
Visualization is an important way of specifying the form and properties of complex dynamic systems (Abraham, Abraham, & Shaw, 1990; Van der Sluis et al., 2019; Xu et al., 2020). A helpful way of understanding causal processes in complex systems in particular, is through *attractor landscapes* (introduced in Chapter 2). This framework of attractors and attractor landscapes provides a general, visual scheme for causal reasoning.

To understand how such a landscape can help explain change and development, and how this differs from how change or development is explained in the standard praxis, let us start with a very simple one-dimensional state space of a person's well-being (Figure 8.6). Assuming that we can order every person's well-being, and changes of that feeling of well-being over time, on a simple descriptive dimension, we can start with the representation of well-being as a straight line, let us say from very low to very high. In the standard linear model, we can explain a person's level of well-being as the additive result of contributions of independent variables, which we can write down as a standard linear regression model. Let us say we confine ourselves to three independent variables, A, B, and C, which for person i implies that his level of

8.5 From Abstract to Concrete

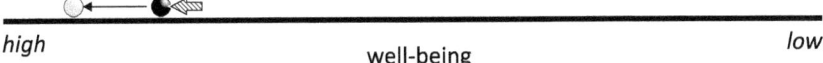

high   well-being   low

Figure 8.6 The variable well-being, represented by a straight line, ranging from high to low. The ball represents the current position of an individual on the well-being dimension, which corresponds with the magnitude of causal factors A, B and C, plus random influences. A causal intervention, e.g., in increase in the causal A factor (hatched arrow) causes a shift in well-being (to the left) proportional to the 'strength' (quality, duration, dose) of the intervention.

well-being $W_i = A_i + B_i + C_i + e$ (for e the error or noise component). For every specific value of A, B, C, and e, we obtain a specific value for well-being, W.

The variables $[A_i, B_i, C_i]$ are forces acting on the person's well-being, corresponding with a specific state or value of well-being. If these forces work in an additive way (irrespective of whether this occurs in a deterministic or a probabilistic fashion) the corresponding changes in W_i are proportional to the changes in the forces exerted by each of the independent variables. This is a simple metaphorical representation of classical intervention causality.

If the person is a complex system, his well-being is a collective variable, or order parameter, resulting from a self-organized and self-maintaining pattern of activities, emotions and interactions, which implies that the general principles of transitions will be applicable to well-being, and by implication, to clinical problems and psychotherapy (Hayes & Andrews, 2020; Hofmann, Curtiss & McNally, 2016; Tschacher & Haken, 2019, 2020). Recall the definition of a self-organized, stable pattern as the specific way of optimizing resource consumption to form and maintain a pattern (i.e., the reduction of a gradient of dissonance or tension). That is, in order to represent a particular person's well-being, and the stability or evolution of this well-being over time, we need to add a second dimension: the *dimension of required energy or effort* (see the Y-axis in Figure 8.7). Hence, the particular state of a person's well-being is the *local minimum* of this required energy or effort dimension (as represented by the vertical line in Figure 8.7). Each of the points on the curved line represents a potential for the system's behaviour. Note that these attractor landscapes are idiosyncratic. So, for another person, the attractor landscape might be just the opposite, with a deep attractor of low well-being with a large basin of attraction and a shallow attractor of high well-being.

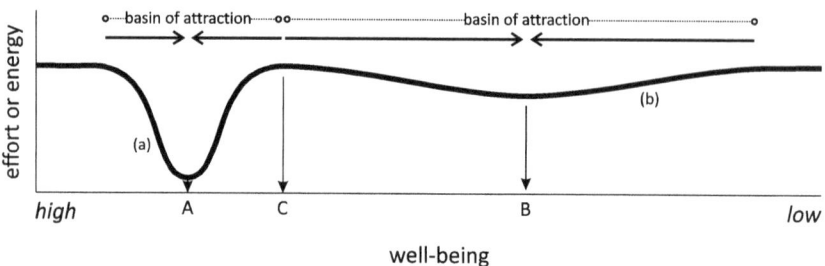

Figure 8.7 A system with two local minima, that is, stable states: A is a stable state of high- and B a state of low well-being. They each have a basin of attraction: this is the range of well-being-values that will draw the system to the nearest stable state, either A or B.

The form of the curve is a mathematical function of the control parameters acting on the system (Wagenmakers, Van der Maas & Molenaar, 2005; Tschacher & Haken, 2019). Interestingly, the form of the work or effort curve determines what we can expect if external or internal causes exert an influence on a person's wellbeing (i.e., perturbations) (Van Orden, Kloos & Wallot, 2009).

The slopes around each local minimum (Figure 8.7) can be broken down to their width and depth: the steeper the slope, the more effort or energy is needed to cause a specific amount of change and move the system toward another stable state. This brings us back to the notion of perturbations, described earlier. Modelling the attractor landscape like this allows us to visualize how perturbations can play out: In this particular system (shown in Figure 8.7), it is quite hard to affect a person's state of high-wellbeing, because high-wellbeing implies effective coping with negative experiences. Low well-being is easily affected by relatively minor experiences, represented by the slopes of the B-attractor, which are considerably less steep than those of the A-attractor (Figure 8.7).

A perturbation brings about a discontinuous change to the system (the position of the ball, representing the position on the well-being dimension) as soon as it moves to the new attractor state (e.g., Van der Maas & Molenaar, 1992 and Jansen, Raijmakers & Visser, 2007 in the context of cognitive development, and Van Dijk & Van Geert, in language development). A perturbation may bring the system (momentarily) to a *repellor* (point C in Figure 8.7), where the system is automatically drawn away from. Given the instability of the system at the repellor point, it is virtually impossible to predict what will happen at point C, as any virtually unnoticeable event might cause the system to move left (to high well-being) or

8.5 From Abstract to Concrete

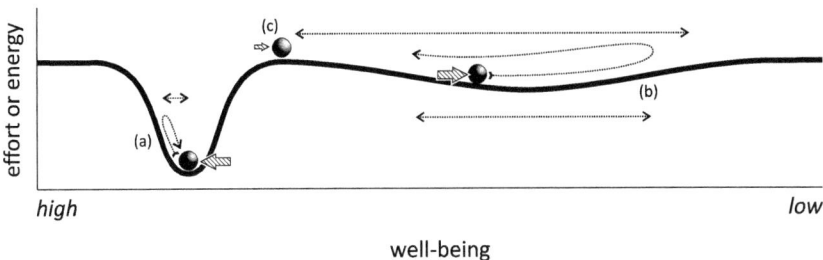

Figure 8.8 A visual representation of the effect of forces, that is to say of interventions, the strength or magnitude of which is represented by the size of the hatched arrow.

right (to low well-being) (this phenomenon resembles self-organized criticality, discussed earlier, in terms of the behaviour of the system, but the causal mechanism is different).

The slopes also specify the *spontaneous rate of change* of the system (i.e., the speed at which it will self-organize back to the point of stability). For instance, a negative experience may reduce a person's well-being from A to a level between A and C, but after that negative experience, the system will quickly rebound to its self-maintaining higher level. A similar experience taking place around level B will take much more time before its effect is undone (Figure 8.8).

Whereas perturbations (as visualized in Figure 8.8) concern the effects of temporary influences, shocks or disturbances of the system, larger or more sustained influences can change the control parameter. An attractor landscape model can help explain these changes, as a change in a control parameter corresponds with a change in the landscape itself (Figure 8.9), as the landscape is not static, but malleable.

Changes in control parameters, such as increasing the difficulty of the maths problems a child has to solve in a test, or increasing the distance between a team of rowers and their competitors in a rowing contest, result in changes in the attractor landscape (from motivated, correct math problem solving to frustration and incorrect solutions, or from positive to negative psychological momentum, e.g., Den Hartigh et al., 2014).

In Figure 8.9, we see (a) the original attractor landscape with two attractors. The system will predominantly occupy the attractor to the right, showing relatively stable behaviour (as perturbations will have small effects and the system will quickly move back to its 'preferred' level). As a continuous change in a control parameter occurs (b), we see the original attractor to the right 'filling up' while the attractor to the left deepens. During this developmental change period, the fluctuations of the system will become more

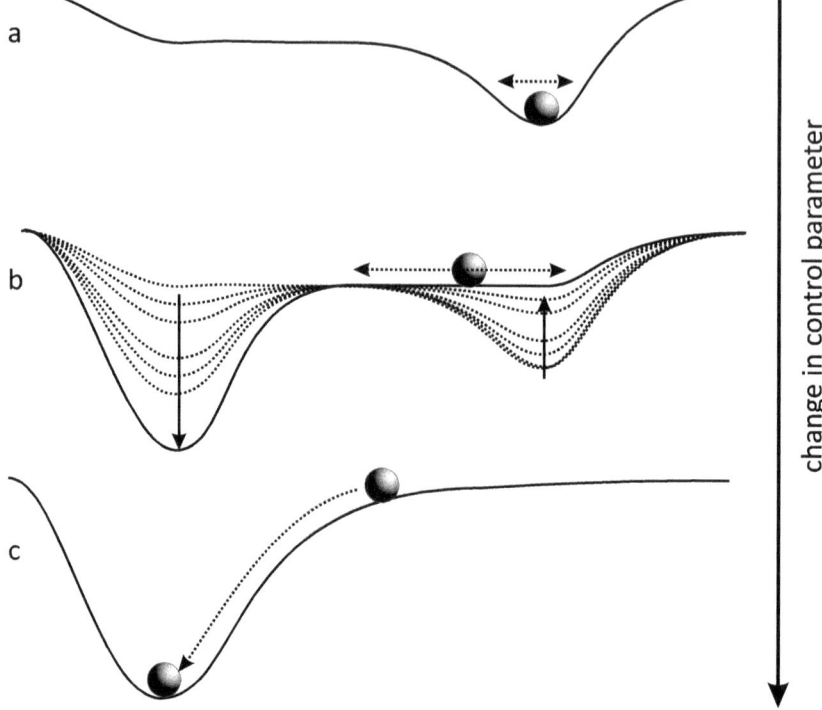

Figure 8.9 A change in the attractor landscape due to a change in a control parameter across time (top to bottom). First the attractor state to the right is deepest (a). As the control parameter changes, the attractor to the right is gradually vanishing, and an attractor to the left is emerging, i.e., increasingly gaining depth (b).

erratic: it shows critical fluctuations and critical slowing down respectively (Kelso, 2008; Gilmore, 1993). Gilmore (1993) distinguished a total of nine patterns of erratic variability typical of a transition stage, the 'catastrophe flags'. Spontaneous recovery becomes increasingly slow, as small perturbations may have considerable and relatively durable effects on the increasingly shallow attractor state that was once much deeper. At the end of this particular developmental phase (c), the system reaches a new point of stability, as only one attractor remains (to the left) and the system settles in the left attractor state. However, this results in typical phenomena of change and variability. The attractor landscape itself changes in a gradual fashion (i.e., one attractor is 'filled up', getting shallower, the other is deepened, or unaltered).

Note that this developmental change (in this case from two to one potential attractor states (from a to c)), can occur across any timescale.

An area where modelling of this nature has proven exceptionally useful is in transitions between clinically relevant states for clients suffering from forms of psychological distress who are undergoing psychotherapy, where change processes like that in Figure 8.9 represent developmental change from unhealthy to healthy psychological states (Schiepek & Perlitz, 2020; Schiepek, 2009; Schiepek & Aichhorn, 2013; Tschacher & Haken, 2019, 2020). Other examples are transitions in cognitive development (Van der Maas & Molenaar, 1992), or in attitudes (Van der Maas, Kolstein & Van der Pligt, 2003).

8.6 Conclusion: Causality Is Interaction and Interaction Is Causality

'What brings this phenomenon about?' This is the fundamental question of causation, and 'this phenomenon' can stand for anything that matters to psychology, such as reduction of depression symptoms to an increase in self-esteem. We have seen that this question can be answered in two different ways: either by referring to a natural or human intervention that makes the difference between the phenomenon occurring or not (i.e., see Chapter 7, the standard praxis of causal explanation), or by referring to the underlying complex system in which the phenomenon of interest is embedded.

In this chapter we have come to the conclusion that causality is interaction, and that interaction is causality (Ingthorsson, 2002). We discussed various features of complex causation: self-cause via self-organization, emergence, and circular causality, as well as normativity, perturbations, distributed causality, and probabilistic causality. Looking at this list of features that are central to complex causation, it can be concluded that they are all forms of interaction. It is evident that the standard vocabulary of cause–effect relationships used in mainstream psychology does not provide an adequate lexical and conceptual tool to speak about *complex* causality, a causality that is about 'being and becoming'. What we hoped to have shown is that causation in complex systems cannot be understood by artificially applying 'A-causes-B' on these systems. They simply do not function in this way, so any A-causes-B statement will not be valid. Instead, researchers must learn how to embrace being and becoming as a form of causal explanation, where processes, interaction, and multiple timescales are placed in the foreground, and where explanatory tools are broadened to include formal, empirical, and visual models, as discussed in this chapter.

The typical causality questions featuring in the social and behavioural sciences often amount to the effectiveness of interventions of various sorts (intervening variables or events), where researchers focus on *whether* these interventions are successful and to what *extent*. However, it is important to keep in mind that these phenomena of interest are not closed and static systems. While researchers may treat them as such, their true nature is processual: a parent's behaviour toward their child is part of an ongoing and bi-directional interaction, an intervention is context dependent and involves the breaking and reformation of patterns. Students' performance levels are but snapshots of an individual processes that is embedded in the collective action of the classroom and their personal history. To understand how any phenomenon that is of interest to psychologists is brought about or changed, researchers must formulate their questions in terms of *how*.

This is basically a matter of changing one's frame of reference. Just as the Ptolemaic system used the earth as the frame of reference for the structure of the heavens, one might use the efficient cause–effect scheme as reference frame for all forms of causality. This reference frame appeals to our daily, pragmatic view on causality and may work very well for a limited domain of questions. However, it runs into serious problems as soon as processes typical of complex systems must be described and explained. Therefore, we urge researchers to use 'being and becoming' as a standard frame of reference – one which allows us to answer a much wider array of questions, and to use efficient causality ('billiard-ball causality') as a special case. The typical intervention-causality statements that abound in psychological and educational research should thus always be embedded in a framework of complex causality in order to make them interpretable as explanatory causal claims (e.g., Koopmans, 2014).

CHAPTER 9

What's in a Name?
On the Ontology of Psychological Measurement*

'It is painful to me to see these creatures that are bred merely as pets,' said Dorothea, whose opinion was forming itself that very moment (as opinions will) under the heat of irritation.
George Eliot, Middlemarch, p. 32

Die Möwen sehen alle aus,
als ob sie Emma hiessen.
'The seagulls by their looks suggest that Emma is their name'.
From *Das Möwenlied, The seagulls' song,* by the German poet
Christian Morgenstern, Translation by K. F. Ross.[1])

Much that is routinely called 'psychological measurement' might not be measurement at all.
Michell (2021, p. 14)

In *Middlemarch*, George Eliot (1819–1880) describes how a certain Sir James Chettam offers Dorothea (a woman he adores) an irresistibly cute Maltese puppy, which Dorothea refuses to accept. But, says Eliot, '[her] opinion was forming itself that very moment (as opinions will) under the heat of irritation'. Opinions are emergent, temporally assembled properties. But in standard parlance, opinions are relatively fixed things that people *have*, residing in some internal repository. Such opinions can be measured, just like a whole lot of other properties of persons such as their intelligence, personality, or conservatism. However, is the set of practices that we call *measurement* in psychology, such as measurement of intelligence or of self-esteem, rightly called so?

Names are very often assigned with the aim of achieving something. The name *George Eliot* suggests a somewhat posh Victorian gentleman. In fact, it was the pen name of Mary Anne Evans, a female, English novelist,

---

* This is a single-authored chapter written by Paul Van Geert. For this reason, the chapter makes use of first-person singular pronouns.
[1] The German version and English translation can be found at www.alb-neckar-schwarzwald.de/morgenstern/morgenstern_poems.html

poet, journalist, critic, and translator, who called herself George, among other names, with the aim of avoiding gender-biased, and therefore negative, reception of her literary work. Are we calling certain kinds of activities *measurement* because we wish to avoid the negative bias that they are not truly scientific (see also Chapter 4, section on *Natural-science envy*)? And isn't it so that, paraphrasing the German, absurdist poet Morgenstern's Emma-quote, psychology has the tendency to dress up a considerable range of its practices and activities, so that they, primarily by their looks, suggest that *measurement* is their name?

9.1 Understanding (Psychological) Measurement

9.1.1 The Standard View

The dominant, representational view of measurement is based on the idea of a homomorphism (a similarity in terms of form) between an empirical system, and a formal system of concepts and their relationships. The open collection of all possible, concrete manifestations of emotions in individual persons is an example of an empirical system. The system of concepts and their relationships consists of a limited, exhaustive set of emotion terms (e.g., happy, angry, sad). The homomorphism implies that, in principle, every empirical manifestation of emotion can be mapped onto one of these emotion terms. In practice, this categorical assignment can be difficult or uncertain, but that does not affect the principle of homomorphism. Another example of a formal conceptual system is the number system, with numbers as its fundamental concepts, defined by their mathematical relationships (e.g., of additivity). For instance, all possible empirical manifestations of intelligence can be mapped onto a number, the intelligence quotient. This view complies with Stevens' (1946) classical distinction between nominal, ordinal, interval, and ratio levels of measurement, each implying different types of formal conceptual systems. Stevens (1946) reserved 'true' or ideal measurement for 'the assignment of numerals to objects or events according to rules' (p. 1). The notion of a homomorphism between empirical and formal systems is also a characteristic feature of positivism (see Chapter 5).

If measurement implies this homomorphism, we should ask ourselves whether, or to what extent, the form of the measured phenomenon is indeed similar to the form of the measurement. For instance, if intelligence is measured by means of a numerical quotient, we should ask ourselves whether or not intelligence *is* indeed a quantitative entity. In this regard, Michell (1997) makes a distinction between 'the scientific (task) of showing that the relevant attribute is quantitative; and the instrumental (task) of constructing procedures for numerically estimating magnitudes' (p. 355). Michell (1997) claims that psychology has strongly neglected the scientific task, taking for granted that the scientific task is appropriately covered by the success of the instrumental task (for a recent summary of the discussion, see Hohn, 2020; Lamiell & Slaney, 2020). However, according to Trendler (2019), it is principally impossible for psychology to empirically demonstrate the quantitative nature of the properties,[2] as psychological properties cannot be subjected to the sort of controlled experimental and instrumental manipulations that would be necessary to show that such properties are indeed quantitative in nature (or categorical, for that matter, if we deal with nominal scales).

The actual praxis of psychological measurement demonstrates the ease with which protocoled procedures called 'measurements', are developed for assigning numbers and categories to virtually any observable psychological phenomenon. In an arbitrary selected set of psychological research papers (the first series of papers in *Frontiers in Psychology* of 21 February 2019) researchers stated that they measured: beliefs, in-group satisfaction, self-esteem, sense of personal control, and so forth, with a total of at least fifty variables that the articles claim have been measured. In this plethora of articles measuring all sorts of things, only one (the ninth article of this issue of *Frontiers*), does not mention the word 'measurement' at all (except in a quote from an interviewed person who said 'she felt measured').

In short, in standard research praxis, the word *measurement* is omnipresent. It is used to refer to the application of procedures following prescriptions for correct use of a dedicated instrument. This instrument must ideally have passed through procedures of reliability and validity checking. However, the meaning of reliability and validity are totally dependent on the underlying ontology of measurement, and, as we shall argue, are entirely different for a typical substance/entity versus a typical process ontology.

---

[2] Although Michell, as well as Trendler, focus on quantitative measurement, I am inclined to think that much of their reasoning also applies to strong forms of the other levels of measurement as distinguished by Stevens; for instance, when nominal measurement scales are applied to emotions, the implication that emotions can be divided into various natural kinds corresponding with the nominal categories remains unproven.

9.1.2 A Processual View on Measurement

In contrast with the standard view of measurement based on assumed homomorphisms between empirical and formal systems, we shall conceive of measurement in a much broader and more fundamental sense, namely measurement as activity. More precisely, we define measurement *as any interaction between systems that provides information* (which is consistent with a fundamentally processual view, in particular, interactivism; Bickhard, 2009a). The systems can be two billiard balls and the interaction is their hitting one another. A more down-to-earth example concerns systems in the form of two persons talking to each other. In this very broad sense of measurement, which we have extracted from the discussion of measurement in quantum mechanics,[3] the interaction provides information for the systems involved. This information can be defined as anything that covaries with a system's subsequent actions. This view is basically similar to the view on information in ecological or Gibsonian psychology; namely, information as a direct affordance for a specific action, dependent on an organism's effectivities (what the organism can do). For instance, I talk to my colleague – one system interacting with another – and this provides information, the content of which is entirely defined by the actions that it elicits. My action might consist of subsequently sending my colleague an email, her action might be an emerging expectation that makes her check her mailbox. According to the fundamental, 'first principles' definition, our interaction is a form of mutual measurement, resulting in specific information, the content of which is defined by the specific activity that we perform as a consequence of the interaction. The question is of course how this very broad definition of measurement can lead us to the standard view of measurement in psychology.

The most important feature of this fundamental definition is that it conceives of measurement as a process or, eventually, as a particular component or event in a stream of events that we characterize as activities of measuring. There are many such activities of measuring, each implying their own specific meaning of measuring and measurement. There's the activity of a carpenter measuring the width of an opening in a wall, or of the researcher in quantum mechanics who has to reckon with weird quantum phenomena that make his notion of measurement very different from that of his colleagues in macroscopic physics. And then there's a measurement in psychology.

---

[3] See www.askamathematician.com/2011/06/q-what-is-a-measurement-in-quantum-mechanics/

9.1 Understanding (Psychological) Measurement

As far as psychology is concerned, the lion's share of measurement activities implies interactions between one human activity (e.g., a psychologist administering a test), with another human activity (e.g., a person taking a test). The measurement activity is defined asymmetrically: the psychologist obtains the measure of the tested person. The information provided by this interaction – a measurement in the broadest sense of the word – is defined by the activity or activities resulting from it. For instance, one possible activity resulting from the test interaction is the extraction of a single number (the IQ) and to register it in a file or written report. Another possible activity is using observations made during the test interaction to help decide about which school a particular child should be sent to. Yet another activity is the tested persons changing their idea about their mental capacities following their experiences during the testing. Together these habitual activities – totally obvious for the practitioners – constitute an intelligence *measurement praxis*, which, as any other praxis, enacts a particular ontology (i.e., a set of connected beliefs about the world in which these activities are embedded). For instance, in the way that psychologists standardly use the information provided by the interaction they call an intelligence test, they enact the belief that it measures a pervasive internal factor, differing among individuals, causally underlying all forms of intellectual performance. Consequently, the test information can be used to rank individuals, classify them or assign them to specific educational contexts.

If the measurement is conceived of as an interaction between two systems, we must reckon with the fact that interactions affect none of the participants, or only one, or both, with the eventual effects possibly pertaining to the information about a measured property. The first possibility is that the act of measuring as such is a trivial fact relative to the information obtained, not interfering with or affecting the measured property (let us call it the *independence condition*). This is more or less the standard case with macroscopic physical properties being measured through a microscopic event. For instance, measuring the wavelength of light from a distant star does not alter the light emitted from the star, or tasting soup does not change the taste. The independence condition is taken for granted in standard intelligence measurement: testing a person's intelligence does not change or otherwise affect that person's intelligence.

The second possibility is that the causal or conditional sequence of events of performing a measurement actively interferes with the processes that determine the measured property, in which case the independence condition no longer holds. In such a case, the measured property is basically *created* by the measurement activity itself and its interaction with the measured property. For instance, if physicists measure the level of the quantum physical processes, they should reckon with the major effect their measurement has on the measured properties (Hilgevoord & Uffink, 2016). Or, if you measure the speed of a turkey by chasing it, the animal will either run faster, hide under a bush or turn around to peck you. From a typical process-oriented view on the nature of human performance, we expect this *dependence condition* to be the rule in psychological measurement (of course, for very different reasons than those that apply to quantum physics or turkeys). Psychological measurement is a process where performer and context dynamically interact and are mutually dependent. For instance, in typical dynamic systems and ecological psychology-oriented view, any performance is a local, time-bound process of self-organization and emergence (or as it is sometimes called, of *soft assembly*). A test and the procedures of test administration generate a specific, time-varying context of performance. The test performance emerges in interaction with the time-varying context: what a person does or answers in an intelligence or personality test, is local, time-bound, self-organized, and soft assembled. In that sense, the activity of measurement creates what is measured in a nontrivial way; or the measurement of self-esteem creates self-esteem (see Chapter 4).

9.2 The Ontology Enacted in Standard Psychological Measurement

Psychologists, habitually using tests or many other forms of measurement in their daily research or applied activities, are in principle not concerned with metaphysical discussions on issues of ontology. Nevertheless, any praxis of measurement in psychology can be interpreted as the enactment of a specific ontology, which in the case of the standard psychometric praxis is that of a substance-entity ontology. In Section 1.1 we discussed the major properties of this praxis and the associated ontology, and in Section 1.2 we briefly referred to the measurement of intelligence. As the latter is quite generally viewed as the jewel in the psychometric crown, we shall use it as a case study in the properties of psychological measurement, in particular with regard to how measurement practices enact specific ontologies.

The notion of psychometric intelligence or intelligence tests such as the WISC are examples of what Latour (1987) has called 'black boxes'. Black boxes are highly established inscription devices or the concepts that they are assumed to capture. Note that Latour's black box concept

9.2 Ontology Enacted in Standard Psychological Measurement 195

differs from the black box typically referred to in psychology, where it denotes an object or phenomenon the inner workings of which are totally unknown and where we can see only an 'input' followed by an 'output'. Latour's black box is more like a consolidated agent in the network of science, that is, a generally accepted fact, model, theory concept, or measurement instrument that is used without the necessity of a constant defence and justification. They are 'low maintenance' agents (Harman, 2009, p. 3), backed up by a vast, 'hinterland' of related tools and practices (Law, 2004).

The history, knowledge, and assumptions associated with black boxes (in Latour's sense) are very well documented, but this information remains hidden under the automaticity of the frequent and self-evident use of the black box in question. Such a black box is seen as a whole or unit with specific properties, which is used in scientific activities of various kinds (for instance, in research on the relationship between socioeconomic status and intelligence, to name just a very trivial example).

9.2.1 Intelligence: An Example of a Thriving Praxis of Measurement

On Tuesday 13 December 1994, the *Wall Street Journal* published an article, endorsed by fifty-two experts, on mainstream views on intelligence,[4] to correct for what the article called the 'pervasive misstatements of the scientific evidence in the media'. Although the article appeared twenty-five years ago (from the time of writing this), nothing much has changed with regard to three fundamental points that we shall briefly discuss here (for an overview of the historical attempts at defining intelligence, see Danziger, 1990, and Richardson, 2002).

The first fundamental point concerns a definition: 'Intelligence is a very general mental capability that, among other things, involves the ability to reason, plan, solve problems, think abstractly, comprehend complex ideas, learn quickly and learn from experience'. An imaginary physicist might compare this definition with a definition of temperature as a very general physical capability that among other things, makes water boil, people sweat, smelt iron, allows people to skate and to bake an egg. A later survey of definitions of intelligence (Legg & Hutter, 2007) came up with an impressive list of seventy-one definitions, to which the authors added their own: 'Intelligence measures an agent's ability to achieve goals in a wide range of environments' (what I am missing here is 'on a wide range

---

[4] In 1997 the article was reprinted as an editorial of the journal *Intelligence* (24, p. 13–23).

of timescales, including future generations'). And then there is the (in)famous quote from Edwin Boring (1923), which, if put in a little more context says 'intelligence as a measurable capacity must at the start be defined as the capacity to do well in an intelligence test. Intelligence is what the tests test. This is a narrow definition, but it is the only point of departure for a rigorous discussion of the tests'. (p. 35; and see Van der Maas et al., 2014, for a discussion of why Boring was right in this respect).

The second and the third general statement in the *Wall Street Journal* have lost none of their topicality: 'Intelligence, so defined, can be measured, and intelligence tests measure it well. They are among the most accurate … of all psychological tests and assessments' (p. 13 of the 1997 Intelligence version) and 'While there are different types of intelligence tests, they all measure the same intelligence'.

In spite of underlying theoretical differences regarding the structure of intelligence (Gardner, 2013), the psychometric theory is the most widely used, which is based on a very specific praxis of intelligence measurement through typical performance contexts in the form of tests in the use of inter-individual differences.

9.2.2 *The Ontology of Measured Intelligence in the Standard Praxis*

If a researcher measures a person's intelligence by means of an intelligence test, they basically enact the belief that a fundamental distinction exists between the 'real thing', which is the underlying intelligence with its specific quantitative property, and a transient set of events, the person's answering the test items. The latter are specific manifestations caused by the subject's intelligence. The real thing can only be accessed via its accidental manifestations, and this limitation is the origin of the typical measurement problems of psychology. This ontology is clearly reflected in classical measurement theory, which makes a distinction between latent and manifest variables. The standard theory of latent variables views the latter as fundamental but not exhaustive causes of the observable manifestations (e.g., Borsboom, Mellenbergh & Van Heerden, 2003).

9.2.2.1 *Abilities as Pervasive Entities with Independent Existence*

The praxis of separating sources of (typically inter-individual) variance of transient manifestations such as test scores into contributions from several latent variables is an enactment of the belief that such latent variables have an independent existence. Paul E. Meehl (1993, p. 4) stated:

9.2 Ontology Enacted in Standard Psychological Measurement 197

For a scientific realist, a factor is presumably a physical entity possessing a quantitative property. (I exclude metaphysical dualism, held by hardly any psychologists.) The physical entity exists in the person, hence, in the brain. (Where else? Cognitive, affective, and motivational states, events, and dispositions are not located in the kidney!) The general intelligence factor g is 'in' the CNS. (see also Stedman et al., 2016, for further discussion).

If we apply this view of psychological factors to intelligence, the existence and fundamental properties of intelligence as such are assumed to be independent of the existence and fundamental properties of motivation, socioeconomic status, and so forth. Intelligence would still be conceived as a real existing entity even if motivation or socioeconomic status did not exist. In Meehl's definition, psychological factors are variables that, in spite of having an independent existence of their own, are nevertheless connected. Psychological factors or variables may affect each other's properties (e.g., intelligence affects the ability to learn, or socioeconomic status affects intelligence). The habit of speaking about independent variables and the associated statistical practices point in that same ontological direction.

As the measured property is assumed to have an independent existence, it follows that it must exist totally independently of any measurement or observation. In practice, we know that observed scores are to a certain, often trivial extent, sensitive to measurement activities, for instance in the form of learning effects eventually resulting from taking a test, test motivation, or the effect of 'incentives' (rewards following good test performance; Duckworth et al., 2011). However, in such cases, researchers are supposed to do everything they can to avoid such accidental effects because they obscure their access to the 'true' property (which is yet another way of enacting the belief that this true property is independent of the measurement).

The assumption of an ability being an independent mental entity is further corroborated by the praxis of using a highly constrained and specific context– in this particular case the typical intelligence test – as a window, a peephole, that provides an unconstrained view on this internal substance or entity (this is also discussed and illustrated in Chapter 4 on self-esteem).

Independent entities are thought to be context-free, although they can be combined with specific contexts. For instance, intelligence as a context-free entity permeates all its context-specific manifestations (i.e., all instances of intelligent performance in specific contexts).

Another feature of the principle of independent existence is the substance's (i.e., intelligence's) independence from its particular bearers, which implies that intelligence-qua-substance is independent of the intelligence of concrete individuals. The ubiquitous praxis of investigating a particular psychological construct in the form of inter-individual variability in a large sample of independent (i.e., non-interacting) individuals forms the concrete enactment of this ontological belief. The substance in question – intelligence – is defined as that which is common across specific manifestations in particular cases (i.e., a *universal or secondary substance*). These cases are specific individuals who are treated as representatives of a particular class or natural kind (e.g., adult women). The *particular* case (an individual person, i.e., a *primary substance*) is viewed as a specific case of the general property, and thus typically 'inherits' the properties of the general or universal category. This underlying belief is enacted by the praxis of applying models based on inter-individual variability in large samples, such as factor-analytic models, to individual cases. The inter-individual model is interpreted as a *general* model, for instance of the structure of the intellect, which is applied to *specific* cases (i.e., individual persons). This is an instance of reasoning from the general rule to the specific case. However, this general-to-specific reasoning is not allowed here, as the inter-individual big-sample model cannot be conceived of as a general model of intelligence per se. In fact, the model (e.g., a factor-analytic model of intelligence test scores for a great number of individuals) is a *specific* model itself, namely a model of intelligence distributions across a population. This population model is generalizable to other populations to the extent that the population on which the model is based is representative of other populations.

In summary, the standard practices of intelligence measurement enact an ontology of intelligence as a secondary substance, an enduring entity that exists independent of other such substances. It is explicitly assumed that the properties of intelligence, as a secondary substance, can be discovered by analysing the variability in test scores among many individual persons, and that the properties, inferred in this way, constitute a general model, of which individuals are specific cases. However, as we shall explain in the next section, the implicit identification of population models, such as factor-analytic models of intelligence, as general models pertaining to specific cases (i.e., individuals), is not warranted, unless ergodicity applies.

9.2.2.2   The Identity of the Ability Is Conserved Across Occasion and Time
The typical intelligence measurement context operates on the principle that by taking a little piece of some substance, in the form of the highly specific and narrowly defined context of intelligence testing – at a specific time or occasion – one obtains a fairly objective image of the whole. Think

about the Alkmaar or Gouda cheese masters who use a cheese drill to take a small piece from a big cheese to determine the quality of the cheese on the basis of this small sample. They base this practice on the – as far as cheese is concerned – correct assumption that the sample they take is (sufficiently) identical to the rest of the cheese, and the correctness of this assumption is justified by their knowledge of how cheese is produced. For a psychologist, this corresponds to the foundational belief that the information provided by the small sample of micro-performances requiring intelligence – answering the items of an intelligence test – is representative of the person's intelligence as a whole (give-and-take some practical limitations). That is, the intelligence that is manifested in a person taking an intelligence test is conceived of as the same as the intelligence manifested in that person's solving professional or daily problems. An intelligence test for children samples the same ability as an intelligence test for adults. That is, the standard measurement praxis operates under the principle of identity of the measured ability across occasions.

The standard praxis of intelligence measurement conceives of intelligence as an enduring entity. That is, the nature of such an entity is self-identical ('similar to itself') across the whole duration of its existence in a particular case (e.g., a specific person). Put differently, the entity as such does not consist of temporally distinct parts: there is neither short-term nor long-term change in the nature of a person's intelligence. As to short-term change: one test item answered by a person is supposed to sample the same intelligence as the next test item, and one test administration samples the same intelligence as a repeated administration. The *observed* variability in answers or scores is commonly interpreted as measurement error, due to interference of factors external to the measured ability, not to intrinsic changes in the measured ability – intelligence – itself. Self-identity of intelligence across the long-term timescale (i.e., the human lifespan) is achieved by defining IQ scores relative to the performance of individuals of the same age. In this way, all properties concerning developmental evolution or qualitative changes in intelligence are actively removed. There is evidence of real, long-term changes in IQ scores of individuals across the life span (e.g., Breslau et al., 2001; Ramsden et al., 2011), and there is also the well-known phenomenon of declining fluent and increasing crystallized intelligence over the life span. These changes concern the quantitative aspect of a person's intelligence and do not concern the qualitative nature of intelligence. To illustrate the difference with a processual view of intelligence as consisting of qualitatively different temporal parts on the long-term timescale we refer to Piaget's theory (Piaget, 1976). Piaget's stage model describes a succession of qualitatively different forms of intelligence. These qualitative shifts, however, are not assumed in the standard praxis of intelligence measurement, which acts under the assumption that intelligence is an ability that is self-identical across time.

9.2.2.3 Ergodicity and the Enactment of a Substance Ontology

A very common practice in standard psychological measurement is to apply models based on statistical information about large representative samples of individuals to individual cases (group-based information is used as information about individuals). Examples are the application of factorial intelligence models to the structure of intelligence of individual persons, or the Big Five of personality traits to individual personalities. Each time researchers do this, they are enacting the principle of *ergodicity*, without actually testing whether or not the principle applies.

What does ergodicity of processes mean? Take for instance the following examples of processes: a person's schooling history, the person's life span, a person's solving practical problems as part of their ongoing professional activity, or a family visiting theme parks over the course of several years. Such processes are *ergodic* if they are stationary over time (their long-term averages are fixed) and if their long-term statistical properties (averages and distributions) are similar to corresponding properties of samples of many independent cases (i.e., persons forming a representative sample) (so-called 'ensembles'; Molenaar et al., 2009; Mangalam & Kelty-Stephen, 2021; Lowie & Verspoor, 2019; Medaglia et al., 2011).

Models based on inter-individual variability in big, representative samples of individuals, can be correctly applied to individual cases if the individual cases are ergodic processes. However, it is easy to find examples of individual processes that are not ergodic: there is virtually no individual person's life history that is similar to the averages taken from the life histories of the person's contemporaries. A person's voting behaviour over the years is almost never similar to the average of votes over all political parties in the person's country. So why is ergodicity so easily or automatically assumed? We can give three reasons for explaining this ubiquitous practice.

The first reason is that assuming ergodicity is very convenient for psychometric practice. In psychology, it is considerably easier to sample many people once[5] than to sample one person over a very long time, with a very

---

[5] Only once, or even twice or three times as in research that claims to measure longitudinal processes, and by sampling individuals on very few occasions implicitly limits longitudinal processes to very simple patterns.

9.2 Ontology Enacted in Standard Psychological Measurement

high sampling density. Such intensive sampling would probably seriously disrupt a person's life. This is different from physics, where intensive sampling of a single process (e.g., variations in electrical conductivity) is often easier than sampling only once over many independent instances of the process. However, convenience is not a sufficient reason in itself.

The second reason for assuming the ergodicity assumption is that researchers are strongly occupied with obtaining *general models* or general knowledge, which pertain to individuals as specific cases. General models are models that apply to natural kinds, that is, secondary substances (gender, psychopathologies, see Haslam, 2014). These general models are extracted from groups or samples representing these natural kinds (see also the section on extensional definitions, Chapter 6, Section 6.1.2). Because they are general models, they apply, by definition, to specific cases (i.e., individuals; see Section 9.2.2.1 in this chapter). However, this reasoning from-general-truths-to-specific-cases is correct only if ergodicity applies. Hence, before a model assumed to be general can be correctly applied to individual cases, the truth of the ergodicity assumption must be explicitly tested. In standard practice, the latter is almost never done, because the outcome of this test might be rather devastating for the generalizability claims of the great majority of psychological research. In cases where long-term, frequent, and intensive process measurements in individuals are actually done, the evidence clearly shows that ergodicity basically never applies; that is, that the structure and statistical properties of individual processes are not reducible to the structure and statistical processes of inter-individual variability in typical independent samples (samples representative of a population; Molenaar, 2004, 2008, 2015). In the case of the Big Five personality traits, for instance, individual processes' structures may differ quite considerably from the group-based Big Five structure (e.g., Molenaar & Campbell, 2009). Developmental trajectories are person-specific and idiosyncratic, they do not equal the average population trajectory with individual random variation added (Molenaar et al., 2009). In short, researchers often commit the ensemble-to-individual fallacy (or ecological fallacy, see also Chapter 7, Section 7.2.2) because of the need to arrive at general models as quickly as possible (e.g., in the course of a single empirical investigation; see also Chapter 10, Section 10. 3.2).

The third reason that ergodicity is easily and automatically assumed is that it assimilates smoothly into the mainstream, substance ontology, where substances such as abilities are conceived of as temporally self-identical things. Assuming ergodicity is a way of avoiding 'cognitive dissonance' caused by practices that are, at least at first sight, experienced as contradictory (e.g., universalist, generalizing substance-oriented research practices versus particularist, idiosyncratic process-oriented ones). The ensemble-to-individual assumption – which requires ergodicity – is deeply entrenched in psychological thinking and research. For instance, if the average verbal IQ is higher in a representative sample of women than in a representative sample of men, it is easily assumed that an arbitrarily selected woman, or a 'typical woman', is likely to have a higher verbal IQ than an arbitrarily selected man. The assumption that aggregation over individuals reveals the essential property of the population to which they belong goes back to the work of a Belgian nineteenth-century statistician, Lambert Adolphe Jacques Quetelet (1796–1874), who coined the term 'l'homme moyen', the average man (Quetelet, 1869). Other examples of the ensemble-to-individual assumption, which implies ecological fallacy, concern correlations in groups that are applied to correlations in individuals (or subgroups of individuals, the so-called *Simpson's paradox*; Robinson, 1950; Simpson, 1951). For instance, if IQ correlates with academic success in a representative sample of Dutch boys, it is assumed that this correlation will also apply to, or be highly likely, in any subgroup of the boys or in any Dutch boy. However, correlations apply to individuals only if the individual is represented by a large enough sample of time-dependent observations, in which case non-ergodicity most likely applies. That is to say, homology of ensemble and individual is taken for granted, because the population-individual distinction is seen as an application of the general-to-specific principle.

9.3 Psychological Measurement and the Enactment of a Process Ontology

9.3.1 *A Thought Experiment on Running*

9.3.1.1 *A Substance Ontology of 'Currence'*
In the preceding sections, we focused on the ability of persons to act intelligently (i.e., to do things in a 'smart' way, with some people being able to do certain things in smarter ways than others). This ability is called intelligence, a noun that suggests that this ability is 'something', a substance. By turning the ability to act in a specific way (smart, intelligent) into a 'thing', a secondary substance, we are actually assigning a whole lot of properties to it. In the standard approach, these properties, such as identity across time and occasions (see Section 9.2.2.2), are taken for granted, but, from a processual point of view, they are actually quite strange or mystifying. In

order to analyse this process of 'mystification', we shall perform a thought experiment, where we shall deal with the human ability to run as we deal with the ability to act in intelligent ways in the standard psychometric measurement model.

We shall call the ability-to-run *currence*, after the Latin word *curro*, meaning *to run*. We will define *currence* as a very general somatic-psychological capability that, among other things, involves the ability to win athletic contests, escape from looming figures in a park late at night, or be the first in an unexpected sell-off or a bread line. *Currence*, so defined, can be measured, and *currence*-tests measure it well and accurately. While there are different types of *currence* tests, they all measure the same *currence*.

Clearly, I have just copied the definition and principles mentioned by experts on intelligence in the *Wall Street Journal* article discussed earlier (see this chapter, Section 9.2.1). Suppose we now design a *currence test*, the items of which are various short runs on a standard smooth and flat surface. They are to be performed by a single individual, who does not have information about how others are doing and generally has no information about how they themselves are doing). The test result consists of an average-speed score, which is turned into a running quotient by dividing an individual's score by the average score of the individual's age group. This running quotient can be interpreted as a stable, person-specific internal trait. Actual running *performance* can be expressed as the sum of the person's true *currence* plus the effect of independent variables such as motivation, and context influences such as the slope and irregularity of the terrain, plus unexplained influences (error).[6] The *currence* ability – which is a latent variable – is the internal cause of actual running (see the discussion on latent variables as causes, this chapter, Section 9.2.2). With sufficient variation in the items of the test (e.g., runs of different durations) the pattern of inter-individual differences in the item scores can be used in factor analytic techniques that are likely to reveal factors such as *currence-*G, short-duration *currence,* and long-duration *currence*. This factor analytic model of *currence* could then be used to predict running in real life (e.g., in athletics or sports), and I assume that correlations in the order of 0.4 (i.e., 16 per cent of shared variance) would be very well possible. In general, reliability and various forms of validity, such as predictive validity, should not be an issue for *currence* tests.

---

[6] In line with item response theory, we can also interpret the person's running ability as the probability that the person will run with a particular speed during a particular running item from our test.

9.3.1.2 A Process Ontology of Running

The previous view on running ability is clearly a bit odd. Why this is so might become clear if we focus on running as a process. Running is a sequence of coordinated events over time. Running implies that the runner coordinates forces applying to the runner's body – limbs, bones, joints, muscles, etc. – as they interact with the changing properties of the context (the terrain over which the running takes place). Running is an *ongoing* process of coordination of motor actions and perceptions of the terrain that change as the runner moves across the terrain. These changes in the perceived terrain provide changing affordances for the actual running movements (e.g., if the runner sees an obstacle). Running is a process that evolves over the time course of an actual run, and that is deeply intertwined with the properties of the terrain (e.g., running on an athletics course vs running through a wood or on a stoney slope). Running also changes over the long term in the form of practice, improving one's running skills and endurance, learning to adapt to various terrains and contexts of running (e.g., to the context of competitive athletics). Or it may deteriorate if a runner no longer practices. Running is intentional, it has meaning for the runner. One may frequently run on athletic courses as part of one's ambition to become an athlete with the support of a professional coach, or run to escape from a bear in some dense Canadian forest, or run to catch a train.

With this description of running as a process, I intend to illustrate that it is virtually impossible to understand running without explicitly invoking principles of its dynamics, that is to say, changes over time. That is, running is a complex dynamic system with properties of complex dynamic systems (see Chapter 2). To understand a particular process of running (i.e., to understand the causal structure of a running process), one must take the coupled runner-environment system as the unit of analysis (a basic principle of dynamic ecological psychology, Richardson et al., 2008). Running is an iterative, ongoing process: the next step follows from the preceding one and requires iterative coordination of actions resulting from perceptions, and perceptions resulting from actions. Perception and action occur in continuous loops. They are reciprocal and mutually constraining: running movements bring about information about the running surface which is directly perceived by the runner in terms of how to continue the movement pattern of running (e.g., in how to adapt to the particular coarseness of the running surface).

The actual running, on a particular terrain, for a particular duration and purpose, is a self-organizing process, not some sort of deployment of an internally stored movement pattern. This self-organizing process takes place on a variety of coupled timescales, from the short-term timescale of actual running to the long-term timescale of improving or losing one's running skills. The long-term processes causally and conditionally depend on short-term processes, such as actual running, training, coaching, and so forth, and short-term processes depend on the long-term changes.

To understand running as a process, one must understand it as an activity of an intentional organism, driven by concerns, interests, or goals, defined in the form of result-oriented activities, which take place in a variety of contexts that are characteristic of the organism's or person's life space, or ecological niche (running for your life or running for a train). These activities are subject to intentional and effortful learning in the form of personal practice and external support (e.g., from teachers or coaches) and often involve comparisons of one's own performance to that of others. A typical feature of running-qua-activity is the high degree of interindividual specialization: the overwhelming majority of people are running only very occasionally or in a slow and clumsy manner. For a minority of individuals – athletes – it is a skill that branches into a virtually infinite number of specializations: sprints, middle- and long-distance running of various lengths, hurdling, steeplechase, marathons, running to prepare for various kinds of jumps, and so forth. Each of these is a specific skill, requiring specific running patterns and practice, each with their rank ordering of performers in terms of excellent and often exceptional performance (e.g., Olympic medals, records, and so forth). It makes little sense to rank order all the performers of these specialized forms of running on a single, similar dimension of running ability.

This 'diversification' of skills into a wide range of specialisms each requiring their own practice and forms of excellence is not just typical of running, but of virtually every broad domain of human performance: artistic, intellectual, technical, commercial, entrepreneurial, political, and whatever else one can think of. Human abilities are extremely domain-specific, and to view them as based on underlying abilities of a very general nature does not particularly contribute to understanding their nature and how they develop in individuals. The difference between domain-specific performance in all fields of human activity on the one hand, and general abilities such as intelligence, on the other hand, becomes clear if one inspects their distribution across the population. A general ability such as intelligence shows a typical symmetric distribution, the great majority of individuals located in the middle. Virtually all domain-specific forms of performance show very asymmetric distributions, with the overwhelming majority of persons located on the left of the distribution, and a very long tail of increasing performance levels achieved by fewer and fewer performances. Whereas the symmetrical distributions result from the addition of many independent sources of random influences (as explained by the central limit theorem), strongly asymmetric distributions result from cyclical, iterative interactions between person-specific components and environments (Den Hartigh et al., 2016).

In short, the 'real' thing is the performance of running itself, in various environments by various runners in various action contexts. It is not a monolithic ability: it has diversified into ever more specific forms of running performance, skill, and ranks of excellence. Running ability is not an internal, time- and context-independent latent variable. Measurement of running must imply the context-, person-, and time-specific measurement of actual running performance in a highly diverse range of contexts, not the measurement of an assumed, general ability that I have called *currence* for the occasion. For a process theorist, the concept of *currence* is as odd as the concept of *intelligence*.

9.3.2 A Process Ontology for the Measurement of Psychological Abilities

9.3.2.1 The Concept of Ability in Relation to Measurement

When people use the word *ability*, they are referring to the sort of things they believe a particular person (or object or system in general) *can do*, the sort of activity and performance you can expect from this person, that is, a particular potentiality. The notion of ability is closely related to the Aristotelian distinction of *actuality* versus *potentiality*, which is also a very important feature of dynamic systems (Cohen & Reeve, 2020; see Chapter 2 and Chapter 10). From a substance-oriented view, an ability is a time-independent, internal entity, the cause of various manifestations of the ability in the form of concrete action. It is there all the time, from the beginning to the end of a person's lifetime. However, from a processual point of view, the notion of ability and the associated actuality-potentiality distinction implies the distinction between the past and present, on the one hand, that is, what a person does and has done, and the future, that is, what the person *will* do, which depends on what the person *can* do, which is constrained by what the person has done. For instance, a person has learned a new skill (past and present), which means the person has the ability, or potentiality, to practise that skill in the future. A young soccer player performs above the level of his peers and is assigned a 'talent' that sets expectations for future excellence.

9.3 Psychological Measurement and Enactment

The fundamental principle of assessing a person's ability (i.e., their potentiality for the future) is no different from the principle of time series analysis: an existing time series, covering what happened in the past, is used to extract general trends and systematic seasonal fluctuations in order to forecast future events. Likewise, a dynamic systems analysis uses a system's past trajectory through its state space to extract the system's evolution rules, which can be used to determine future trajectories, given the present state of the system. General trends, seasonal variations, and evolution rules are in fact compressed or condensed descriptions of the system's history. They result from applying formal, statistical, and mathematical procedures to data. In the same vein, a person's ability (e.g., intellectual ability) is a compressed or condensed description of a person's past, up to a particular, present point, that is used to generate expectations about the person's future performance. In time series or state-space analysis, the histories from which information to predict future events is extracted are specific and explicitly given. This is different from the assignment of abilities to persons, as their relevant histories are mostly not available, explicitly recorded, or specific. If, at a particular moment in time, we wish to assign a particular ability to a person, we must try to reconstruct the person's history of the activities (relevant to the ability in question, e.g., intellectual, artistic, linguistic, etc.), based on vague and incomplete information. This reconstructed history is compressed or condensed into a sort of 'abbreviated' description we call the person's potentiality (i.e., the person's ability) with the aim of predicting or foreseeing the person's future.

The reconstruction and condensation of a person's history into a specification of that person's ability depends on the nature of the ability we focus on. In case of highly domain- and context-specific abilities, such as the ability to calculate differential equations, defining the history of how this ability emerged in a specific person is usually quite straightforward, because it mostly consists of a specific, formalized trajectory of schooling and training. Whether or not, or to what extent, a person masters this very specific ability at the end of the training trajectory is established by means of an exam (a form of test). The exam provides, in all likelihood, a reliable representation of the training trajectory, checking the math skills the students should have learned. Passing the exam results in a diploma or certificate, which serves as a condensed or compressed representation of the history of the ability in question (the capacity to work with differential equations). Employers who wish to hire persons who can calculate differential equations can use the diploma or certificate as adequate predictors of their employees' required skills.

However, to assess very broadly defined abilities such as 'intelligence' (i.e., a person's intellectual potentiality), the relevant personal history of intelligent performance, from which predictive information can be extracted, is very hard to specify. It is basically the person's entire's life span, covering all the person's activities where 'intelligence' has played a role, which is virtually everything. Hence, it is very difficult to make specific predictions about a person's intellectual performance, unless those predictions are limited to domains where the history of intellectual performance is well known and specific (e.g., the domain of the person's past professional activities).

In the standard praxis, the long and tedious road toward assessing an 'ability' via the description of histories of activity is avoided by taking the shortcut of a test (e.g., an intelligence test). In the standard psychometric approach, an intelligence test is customarily viewed as a highly compressed, yet valid representation of a person's intellectual history covering all aspects and domains of intellectual activities (performal, verbal, over a variety of content domains). However, it is highly questionable whether a typical intelligence test does indeed provide a valid compressed representation of a person's history of intelligent performance. An intelligence test taken at a particular moment in time by a particular person is just one of the many context-specific and variable events that together constitute the person's history of intellectual performance, and which thus define his intellectual ability – intelligence – up to the current moment. If one knows nothing about a particular person's past, a very small sample of intellectual performance taken in the form of an IQ-test administration may indeed provide just enough information to allow for relatively crude predictions on a population level (which, in the standard praxis of intelligence testing, is hailed as a major accomplishment). However, the information extracted from a short-term process such as taking an intelligence test is mostly far too crude or imprecise to make processual predictions (i.e., predictions on the level of individual processes).

In summary, the discussion on assessing ability from a processual point of view, which focused on the example of intellectual ability, never used – or needed – the term 'measurement'. Assessing ability is all about optimizing one's expectations with regard to a particular person's future performance on a particular domain, by extracting information from the person's history. The usability of the extracted information heavily depends on how much *specific* knowledge we have about the person's relevant history, which, in the case of very broad abilities such as intelligence, is usually very little.

9.3.2.2 Toward a Processual and Complexity-Oriented Reconceptualization of Intelligence

9.3.2.2.1 Intelligence as an Ability of Living Systems
The aim of this section is to work toward a broad, processual definition of intelligence that focuses on intelligence as a basic feature of living systems, more precisely, organisms, even up to the level of the living cell (Richardson, 2017).

Living systems – human beings, organs of the body, ants and ant colonies, amoeba – are characterized by their internal organization, and their interactions in the form of exchanges of matter and energy with their environments, serve to maintain this internal organization for as long as possible (usually until the living system has produced a copy of itself, i.e., until procreation). Rephrased in the jargon of complexity theory, living systems are *autopoetic* (self-reproducing) *dissipative* systems, 'consuming' energy to maintain their internal structure (Maturana & Varela, 2012; Prigogine & Stengers, 1979). The (re)production or maintenance of internal structure (autopoiesis) is the basic goal or concern of a living system. The system's internal structure is in fact the tool by means of which the internal structure is maintained. For instance, a cell has an intricate internal structure, governing exchanges of matter and energy with the cell's environment, and these exchanges serve to keep the structure of the cell intact, at least for a while (Christensen & Bickhard, 2002 speak about the living system's normative functional organization).

The basic goal of maintaining one's internal structure ('surviving') requires effort (processing of matter and energy, for instance in the form of acquiring and processing food or information). Living systems are under constant pressure to maximize their basic goal achievement and minimize the use of energy and resources required to do that, as the latter are limited commodities. For instance, if survival requires more resources than the environment can provide for, or that an organism can extract from it, the organism will die (i.e., it cannot maintain its internal structure and will disintegrate). Living systems optimize goal achievement – effort investment functions through action, by exploring and exploiting the possibilities or potentials of their own organization (their possibilities for action) and of the environments in which these activities are deployed. All these processes take place on a variety of coupled timescales and coupled levels of organization (between short- and long-term, between body parts and the whole organism, between the organism and the environment). This coupling of timescales is important: any short-term activity optimizing goal achievement should be sufficiently consistent with optimizing goal achievement over ecologically relevant future timescales (a very successful fishing method that in the long term completely depletes your fishing grounds is not particularly optimal).

I propose to use the term *intelligence* as an *overarching term for all these optimization processes of achievement-versus-investment through exploring and exploiting the organism-environment system and interacting timescales, and anticipating and withstanding threats to and perturbations of the organism's structural integrity*.

Optimization varies: a particular activity can be more or less optimal than another. An activity is more intelligent to the extent that it makes better use (e.g., less resource-demanding or risky) of the given opportunities. For instance, one organism may achieve a particular goal at a considerably greater cost than another organism (e.g., because the other organism has learned from past experience). Therefore, in the long run, if resources are scarce, which they often are, learning is favoured over not-learning. The optimality also depends on the timescale chosen (e.g., one activity can have a better or worse short-term over long-term balance than another activity, e.g., using cheap fossil fuel that provides short-term benefits but causes serious long-term harm). That is, we define a more intelligent activity or performance, *relative to timescales relevant to the organisms' long- and short-term goals*, as one that presents a better optimization of goal-achievement-versus-resource-investment than another, alternative activity.

If we focus on typical biological organisms such as animals, the active optimization and the exploring and exploiting of the organism-environment system is done through action-perception loops of the organism operating on its environment (e.g., by changing its position, perceiving its effect, and the resulting properties of the environment leading to the next action). These loops require tools and organs for action and perception (limbs, brains, muscles). Optimization of these tools is part of the general problem of optimizing invested effort versus acquired results. The activity patterns are self-organizing or emergent (Koutroufinis, 2017). They result from the organism-environment interactions and are not pre-defined as internally stored action scenarios. Action aimed at optimization requires information. In principle, information is given in the organism-environment interaction itself and consists of the relationship between this information and resulting activities (see De Carvalho & Rolla, 2020; Polani, Sporns & Lungarella, 2006).

9.3.2.2.2 Properties of Intelligence in a Processual, Complexity-Oriented Framework
First, *intelligence is defined as a basic feature of the living* on all levels of organization, from cells to organisms, including human beings. It can even be applied to non-living systems to which processes of energy optimization for the maintenance of internal structure apply (e.g., Turvey & Carello 1981; Richardson, 2000, 2017). The generality of this definition implies that the standard, psychometric definition – as something that can be measured by an intelligence test – can only be an extremely limited specification of the concept of intelligence, even if we confine ourselves to intelligence in human beings. The reason is that a standard test provides only an extremely impoverished instance of the above-mentioned optimization problem. That is, it is not particularly representative of the wide variety of problems of optimizing the balance between goal achievement and resource investment that a person is confronted with during their lifetime.

Second, relevant properties of intelligence can in principle be formally specified and quantified, as long as 'intelligence' is specified as a property of a specific activity in a specific context, by a specific person or community of persons. For example, a person can achieve the goal of catching a ball thrown to them by optimizing the information available in a perceptual flow by means of adaptive movements of head and body).[7] The quantification of these optimality problems in real action-perception contexts is one of the aims of ecological psychology (e.g., Reed, 1996, Shaw & Bransford, 2017). The ecological approach is not limited to physical activity, governed by physical, computable parameters. It also extends to using symbols and symbolic tools, for instance in education or language development (e.g., Lobo, Heras-Escribano & Travieso, 2018; Allen, Otto & Hoffman, 2004; Rączaszek-Leonardi et al., 2018).

Third, intelligence *is a property of a dynamically coupled (interacting) organism-environment system, on particular timescales*. It is not an internal and isolable property of an individual organism as such (an internal substance or entity). In the case of human beings, the causal networks that represent coupled organism-environment systems are in all likelihood deeply individual, idiosyncratic, embodied, biological, historical, cultural, economic, material, and political. These idiosyncratic causal networks provide specific affordances for the individual human being. They will change as a result of the activities of the organism or person (i.e., they

---

[7] See, for instance, http://psychsciencenotes.blogspot.com/2011/10/prospective-control-i-outfielder.html

change during learning on development). They are typically interaction-dominant, which implies that their dynamics primarily depend on the way components interact, rather than on isolable and additive contributions of separate components (Van Orden, Holden & Turvey, 2003; Ihlen & Vereijken, 2010; Wallot & Kelty-Stephen, 2018).

As to the importance of specifying the timescale of activity, we have already noticed that efficient activity on the short-term timescale can be detrimental at the long-term timescale. This timescale dependence of what 'intelligent' action entails provides additional support for our view that intelligence as such cannot be quantified in any absolute sense, and therefore that it cannot ever be 'measured well' (see this chapter, Section 9.2.1).

Fourth, intelligence *is an emerging property in real-time, contextual processes*. That is, every intelligent activity (as defined above) is a soft-assembled, transient, and more or less successful solution to a local and temporal problem, given the affordances and difficulties of a particular temporary context (Thelen & Smith, 1994). Soft assembled, contextual activities typically vary in individuals, across occasions and time. The theory of multiple intelligences (Gardner, 2011) is consonant with this contextual, domain-specific view on the nature of intelligent performance: the notion of 'different intelligences' implies that people resonate differently with different contexts (i.e., that a context offers different affordances to different people).

The implication of a given intelligence as an emergent processual feature is that variability, in the sense of fluctuation over time, is a fundamental feature of processually defined intelligence, not a sign of measurement error or noise added by independent factors. This means that the empirical study of the temporal structure of this variability is a fundamental aspect of studying intelligence in general. This temporal structure is quantifiable, measurable, and based on valid mathematical theories (e.g., as 1/f noise, Van Orden, Holden & Turvey, 2003; or patterns of recurrence in problem solving and in syntactic coordination, e.g., Guevara et al., 2017; Dale & Spivey, 2006).

Since the goal-resource optimization problem, on the basis of which we defined the concept of intelligence, entirely depends on the idiosyncratic causal network in which its solutions have to be found, intelligence as such is as idiosyncratic as the causal network on which it depends. The idea of a universal intellectual power measured by IQ tests is typically enacted in the practice of correlating achievements with IQ, with high correlations being used as evidence that such correspondences are universal (not person-specific) and objective proof of how much intelligence, as a pervasive substance, goes into an achievement such as a particular college degree, or health and longevity (e.g., Ritchie, 2015).

The emergent nature of intelligence also applies to the long-term dynamics of activity. In a dynamic-network model of intelligence, consisting of iterative, relatively weak interactions between components of many different kinds (neural, perceptual, performance-related, experiential), those interactions may produce long-term correlations between various forms of intelligent activity. Van der Maas et al. (2006) have shown that the general intelligence factor g is a self-organized, emergent product of long-term interactions between lower-order components of intelligence. This stands in stark contrast with the standard view, where g or *general intelligence* is seen as an enduring entity, a component that causes long-term correlations between different manifestations of intelligence (verbal, performal, spatial, or whatever).

Intelligence is deeply rooted in the bodily properties of the acting organism (i.e., it is *embodied*), and in the typical environments in which organisms function (i.e., it is *embedded*). The organism-environment coupling is typically species-specific (it's quite different for a sparrow than for a human being). A typical species-specific feature of the human-environment coupling is the historical building of societies and cultures in the development of material and materially grounded symbolic tools, shaping human activity in terms of goals and opportunities (this was a characteristic feature of Vygotsky's theory of higher-intellectual activity). Given the long-term process of developing intelligent tools and social structures, human intelligence is deeply cultural. However, individuals and social groups differ considerably in their possibility of – or actual choices for – participating in these cultural and social structures, and using these culturally and socially evolved tools and opportunities, to achieve health, wealth, and well-being. That is, their possibilities for optimizing goal-achievement/resource-environment problems differ, and for some, these possibilities will be greatly reduced in comparison with others, profiting from more favourable person-environment couplings. If intelligence is viewed as a person-specific, internal ability, it follows that, since their intelligent solutions to the aforementioned optimization problems are hampered, 'their intelligence is lower' than that of better-placed individuals. If this conclusion is drawn on the level of individual abilities, a fallacy is committed, namely of moving a dynamic property of activity of an organism-environment system to the level of an intrinsic, personal property. This fallacy entails 'the abstraction of intelligence as a single entity, its location within the brain, its quantification as one number for each individual, and the use of these numbers to rank people in a single series of worthiness' (Gould, 1996, p. 21). That is, intelligence cannot be compared (in terms of a single underlying magnitude or scale), between groups or individuals that have very different environments (see also Sternberg, 2003).

9.3.2.3 Measuring Abilities?

Measurement is a ubiquitous term, which psychologists use in all possible (and eventually also impossible) contexts. Although serious doubt has been raised as to whether psychologists can 'measure' all the things they claim to measure (e.g., Section 9.1.1), measurement of psychological abilities is still the jewel in the crown of psychology's achievements. In this chapter, I have discussed the measurement of intelligence as the brightest jewel of all, and have tried to demonstrate how common measurement practices enact a specific, substance-oriented ontology about the nature of psychological abilities – by means of intelligence as an example. As an alternative to the psychometric view on abilities as measurable substances, I presented the beginnings of a processual, complexity-oriented view, again with intelligence as an example. This leads to a view on abilities as properties of organism-environment couplings, in the form of real activities, on various, coupled timescales. The properties of these abilities, in the form of actual processes and open potentialities, can be objectively studied and eventually quantified without invoking the problematic notion of measurement of internal psychological properties. If the aim of psychological research is to contribute to better understanding the potentialities of individuals and to predict their future activities and life trajectories, further exploration of a processual and complexity-oriented approach is probably more fruitful than continuing with ever further refining the standard measurement-approach.

CHAPTER 10

(Un)Certainties
*Epistemological Issues of Psychological Measurement**

> It's difficult to make predictions, especially about the future.
> The origin of the quote is uncertain, attributed respectively to Niels Bohr, Samuel Goldwyn, K. K. Steincke, Robert Storm Petersen, Yogi Berra, Mark Twain, Nostradamus and probably many others: https://quoteinvestigator.com/2013/10/20/no-predict/#note-7474-2

> The question Zadeh always insists upon asking is, 'To what degree is something true or false?'
> From 'what is fuzzy logic?', www.azer.com/aiweb/categories/magazine/24_folder/24_articles/24_fuzzywhat.html; Lotfi Zadeh (1921–2017) is the creator of fuzzy logic

10.1 The Colours of Uncertainty

To be uncertain, or not to be uncertain, that is the question. If Hamlet were a researcher, that might be the quote for which he would become famous. In the preceding chapter, we discussed the praxis of measurement, and (un)certainty of measurement was highlighted as a very serious issue. If I measure something, how can I know I haven't made an error, and how can I know how big or small my measurement errors are? Can I be sure about the predictions I make about a person's future academic trajectory? Can I be sure that the knowledge I attribute to a person is correct, and to what extent do I know that it is correct? From all the possible forms of (un)certainty, measurement error has drawn the most attention, in particular in the context of the standard measurement praxis discussed in the preceding chapter. I shall begin the discussion about uncertainty in psychological research with this specific problem and will do so with a somewhat irreverent example,

---

* This is a single-authored chapter written by Paul Van Geert. For this reason, the chapter makes use of first-person singular pronouns.

namely measuring the colour of my socks. It is meant to demonstrate that in an arguably simple case – of someone trying to determine the colour of the socks that I am wearing if only scant evidence is available – a range of problems regarding uncertainty, including ambiguity and indeterminacy will arise. These problems are even more pregnant and complicated in the considerably less simple cases that we typically care about in psychology. I will then proceed with a processual alternative to measurement error, followed by a discussion of uncertainty in the form of vagueness and ambiguity in the context of a processual, complexity-oriented research praxis.

10.1.1 *A Universe of Plain-Colour Socks: On Classical Measurement Error*

Let us first assume that (my) socks are monochromatic (i.e., that they are always of plain uniform colour), which corresponds with a drawer containing only plain colour socks from which I choose every day (i.e., there is some sort of repository from which items can be retrieved). The measurement space is the standard Red-Green-Blue (RGB) colour space, with numerical dimensions for red, green, and blue. The three-dimensional colour space is like a metaphor for a structural theory of a psychological variable (e.g., intelligence with general, performance, and verbal factors). This colour space can be used as a state space, which allows any observer to specify the trajectory of the plain colour of the socks I am wearing every day over an arbitrary long period of time. The colour of the socks I am wearing today (or any day before) is a *determinate property* (it is an existing state-of-the-world, with precise and specific properties, for example, the colour occupies a precise and specific position in the colour space; Wilson, 2021).

Today, I am wearing powder-blue socks, and this colour is perfectly and objectively measurable: it corresponds with a single point in the RGB colour space with coordinates (204,204,255). The colour of the socks that I am wearing today is a fundamentally *determinable* property, that is, it can be objectively determined by applying a suitable measurement procedure. The colour of my socks is practically determinable to the extent that an observer is capable of scanning the socks that I am wearing with a validated colourimeter device to measure the RGB values. This colour measurement might show some measurement error (e.g., the true colour value is (203,204,255), the measurement is (202,204,255), and the measurement error is (1,0,0)).

However, the gist of the example about the colour of my socks is that the possibility of measuring it, say by an observer O, is highly limited. As I am reluctant to show my socks to other people, observers must rely on casual visual inspection of the part between the rim of my shoe and the bottom of my trousers. That is, the measurement must rely on a casually accessible test window that is highly limited in time and space. The casual inspection can be further hampered by the fact that I ran through the mud and stained my socks, or by poor lighting conditions. This constraint consisting of a highly limited window of access is what the sock example has in common with measuring psychological variables.

To measure the colour of my socks after casual and brief observation, observer O could pick a colour swatch from a colour panel that matches the briefly observed colour as closely as possible. As the colour impression is brief and casual, O is more or less obliged to pick a range of swatches that is likely to comprise the real colour. All colour swatches have of course exact RGB values.

The swatches that the observer has selected form a *confidence interval* in the colour space, for instance, between RGB(190,190,200) and RGB(224,227,255). Instead of selecting a confidence *interval,* O could also pick a *point value* in the form of a colour swatch that O thinks is the best approximation of the colour of my socks, let us say desert blue (51,102,153). In the latter case, there is a *determinate and specific measurement error* (true colour minus estimated colour which equals RGB (124,122,67). Since the true colour is not known, the measurement error is also not known. Yet, the observer knows the error is a *determinate,* that is specific, existing value – but hardly determinable – value.

The reason I am bothering the reader with the colour of my socks is that they provide a simplification of the range of problems that we encounter in the standard psychological measurement of abilities (e.g., intelligence). The ability is assumed to be a determinate property: it is an existing and enduring property of a person and has a specific – though eventually unknown – point value in a quantitative measurement space. Its actual manifestations (performance) are drawn from the content of some internal repository (e.g., the brain or 'the mind') like my socks are taken from my drawer. Measurement comes with a certain level of uncertainty, which is due to measurement error, due to contaminating and limiting factors. But this uncertainty, measurement error, has a determinate, specific, but unknown value. All these assumptions, which apply to psychological abilities, apply directly to the current example of measuring the colour of my socks, and to the uncertainty of the measurement, given the very limited opportunities for observation. As far as the socks that I am wearing today are concerned (selected from this universe of monchromatic socks), the conclusion regarding the nature of uncertainty is correct, because the underlying ontological assumptions correctly apply to the universe of monochromatic socks taken from a drawer with limited content. The question is of course whether this notion of uncertainty as determinate measurement error also applies to abilities studied in psychology. We shall argue that it does not. But let us first see what happens with uncertainty in another universe, namely that of polychromatic socks.

10.1.2 *A Universe of Patterned Socks: On Qualitative or Categorical Error*

Let us imagine a sock universe corresponding with a drawer containing socks with a large variety of colour patterns. They range from simple two-colour stripes to detailed prints of the Mandelbrot fractal (which befits the complex dynamic systems orientation of the wearer), and from highly regular geometric patterns to random splatters. What is the colour of my socks if my socks show a variety of colour patterns? 'The color of my socks' has become an ambiguous term, and the uncertainty problem now concerns how it should be defined properly, such that the colour of my socks can be measured. The colour of the socks that I am wearing today is a complex distribution of points in the colour space (it is a pattern of colours), which is no longer specifiable in the form of a single point value in the colour space. Is the colour of my socks the distribution of all colours on the pattern? Is it the dispersion of the colours on the pattern? Is it the average colour, that is, the weighted average of the RGB values of all the colour patches on my socks? Is it the colour that occurs most frequently in the pattern? Solving this uncertainty is likely based on ontological assumptions (remember we are discussing the rather special case of sock ontology), which are enacted in the form of practices. Remember that in the imaginary case we are discussing here the answer to this question must be given on the basis of rather scant evidence, based on casual observation of just a small piece of my socks as I walk past the person who intends to measure its colour.

Observers assuming a universe of plainly coloured socks (as in Section 10.1.1) are likely to assume that the *real* colour of socks is plain and uniform. It is likely for them to interpret the variation in the very briefly observed colour patches between my shoe and trousers as accidental, perceptual error. An observer may act in accordance with this ontological assumption by squinting, which is a perfect way of reducing a colour pattern to a single colour shade as it averages the various patches to a single, often rather murky colour. The observer can select this murky colour from the colour panel, or select a range of murky colour swatches that represent a confidence interval, and for each of these swatches, the RGB measures can be objectively measured. This interval corresponds with the likely measurement error, which has a specific value in the RGB measurement space. But in fact, the observer is just plain wrong: the single colour is not the 'real' colour. In fact, it is a colour created by the observational procedure (the measurement procedure of squinting, then selecting matching swatches). This entire praxis is self-confirming: it complies with the observer's basic assumptions about the nature of reality (of the colour of socks), the praxis is empirical (it consists of observation and measurement practices). Since meticulous observation of the complete sock is excluded under the current constraints of observation, there is virtually no possibility to correct this wrong assumption about the true colour of my socks. In fact, it is even possible to empirically validate this (nevertheless incorrect) colour assumption: it is likely that for a large enough sample of observations, the murky colour of the socks correlates with the equally murky 'average' colours of the trousers that I am wearing.

Given the limited opportunities for an observer to measure the colour of my patterned socks, the observer must reckon with a considerable amount of uncertainty about the colour of the socks I am wearing on a particular day. An observer might reduce this uncertainty by making the bold assumption that the entire content of my drawer of socks represents the 'true' colour of my socks, which remains constant as long as the content of my drawer remains unchanged of course. In order to arrive at this true colour, an observer combines a number of error-laden daily observations or measurements of the colour of my daily socks, which are based on the approved procedure of squinting and colour swatch selection. If this number of observations is big enough to cover a substantial number of socks from my drawer, the measurement error is considerably reduced. That is, the difference in RGB values between the average of all the socks in the drawer and the average of the sample of socks, is smaller than the difference between the average of all the socks and the observed colour of the socks I am wearing on a particular day. Given the procedures of observation and averaging, all the colours concerned are artificially constructed, murky shades. In spite of this strong reduction in measurement error, the resulting representation of the colour of my socks, as I am wearing them on a particular day, is still completely wrong. That is, this averaging of observations has no effect whatsoever on the *real* uncertainty of the observer with regard to the *real* colour of my socks. In spite of all the measurement procedures followed, the observer – without knowing it – is still totally uncertain about the colours and patterns of my socks.

10.1.3 The Socks of Tomorrow: Determinacy and Indeterminacy

When psychologists measure a person's abilities such as intelligence, they not only want to represent actuality (i.e., how the ability has manifested itself in the present and past performance of the person) but also they are even more interested in the person's potentiality (i.e., in what the person is likely to be doing, how they will be performing, in the future). Let us move this intention, of knowing about the future, to our example of the colour of socks. For simplicity, let us again focus on the universe of monochromatic socks, and ask the questions about (un)certainty regarding the socks I will be wearing tomorrow. If I were Bertie Wooster, this question would be of utter importance to my Butler Mr Jeeves, whose professional prestige depends on his ability to predict the socks that I will pick from my drawer tomorrow morning, so that he can iron a matching shirt today. *Today*, the colour of the socks that I will be wearing *tomorrow* is an *indeterminate* property (for a discussion of determinable and (in)determinate properties, see Wilson, 2021). That is, it is a property that does not actually exist yet (today is not yet tomorrow), or more precisely, it exists only in the form of a possibility or potentiality. Indeterminate properties can be transformed into determinate properties by performing specific activities, which in this case consist of the actual selection of a pair of socks from my drawer and putting them on. This activity collapses a distribution of possibilities into one single actual state. As indeterminate properties are only possibilities, they come with a great deal of uncertainty. This uncertainty can be reduced in the form of predictions or expectations. They can be tested once the future state (tomorrow) becomes the present state (today), which will further reduce the uncertainty. However, uncertainty, even of determinate, actualized properties cannot be reduced beyond some limit, which I discussed in the preceding section.

Note that the distinction between determinate and indeterminate properties is a typical characteristic of a processual approach. Under a substance ontology, a future event (e.g., choosing a pair of socks) is unspecified in the present, but the *potentiality* as such is a determinate (specific, existing, enduring) property. It is conceived of as a fixed internal condition, which can be measured and known with relative certainty. For instance, my drawer contains ten blue, ten red, five pink, three green and two lilac socks. Hence, my drawer constrains or fixates my colour selection in terms of a distribution according to the ratio 10:10:5:3:2 of possible colours. It is assumed that, for a long enough sequence of days and of selected socks, the frequencies will approximate those of the drawer (i.e., of the 'internal repository'). However, given likely limitations on the number of possible observations by an external observer of my selecting a pair of socks, the observed frequencies will deviate from the frequencies based on the drawer's content. This deviation is a form of uncertainty, more precisely of measurement or observation error, due to the lack of precision of observations, which is, in principle, a repairable problem (with more effort, more observations could have been made).

This substance-oriented representation of a fixed, determinate and enduring potentiality – in this case of the selection of differently coloured socks – is most likely wrong, for a variety of reasons. To begin with, I tend to wear out my socks rather quickly, and this of course applies in particular to the socks with the colours that I favour most. I buy new pairs, often rather impulsively, for instance because they are cheap, not because I particularly like the colour. Some socks I virtually never wear, but when all the others have holes in them, I will have to wear these socks – that I don't like – every day. I could go on explaining my sock-wearing habits, but what matters is that it illustrates that my sock wearing is in fact a complex, adaptive, variable, open-ended, sometimes erratic, dynamic system. It is not a fixed, determinate property that can be known or measured with arbitrarily great certainty. What applies to the case of my sock selection potentiality, applies even more clearly to the complex adaptive systems that psychological research is interested in (Juarrero, 2000; Di Paolo, Cuffari & De Jaegher, 2018; Birhane, 2021).

Irrespective of the underlying ontology – substance or processual – a person's psychological potentials, such as dispositions or abilities, must be represented or stored in something we might loosely call a sort of repository or storage space. This repository may be the brain, or the human body as a whole, or the person and their environment, including affordances and tools. But this repository is not fixed or determinate, like an ordinary storage room of a shop, or like the fixed collection of socks in a drawer. This repository of psychological potentials is likely to be an indeterminate property itself: it will change in the form of adaptive and creative actions, it is open-ended. These actions are entangled and autocatalytic processes. That is, they are processes where the determinate 'products', e.g., events, choices, or performances, enter into the process dynamics, creating and maintaining the contexts, conditions, and material, bodily and physical substrates under which these processes unfold their 'repositories'.

The implication is that these potentials, dispositions or abilities are not measurable in the classical sense, as they are constantly changing. In the long run, these changes may be constrained, occur within certain limits, they may show long-term recurrent (repetitive) patterns (i.e., attractors). That is, relative uncertainty about concrete future events – the socks I will wear tomorrow – coexists with relative certainty about overall patterns. However, this balance between certainty and uncertainty itself can change. For instance, on the basis of my history of selecting socks, it is possible for an external observer to detect *constraints* on my future actions, in the form of expectations about which socks I will select. These constraints will change as a consequence of long- and short-term activities, such as wear, loss, damage, buying or a sock donation to the local thrift store. However, given the process represents a complex dynamic system, new features of the process may eventually emerge that will cause surprise in the observer. For instance, one day I decide not to wear socks anymore, which turns the existing potentiality of sock selection into an entirely new one.

We have seen that actually selecting a pair of socks in the morning is an act of determination: I turn an indeterminate property (possible socks) into a determinate one (actual socks). An act of measurement often amounts to an act of determination (i.e., a procedure of turning an indeterminate into a determinate property, i.e., of collapsing a range of possible futures into a single present). Taking a test is a way of collapsing a range of possible test scores – which together form a numerical representation of my intellectual potentiality – into an actual test score.[1]

10.1.4 Back to Psychological Capabilities

The properties that we discussed in the preceding sections have direct repercussions for measurement models formulated in the context of processually defined phenomena. First, processes consist of events occurring on the short and long-term timescales, from selecting a pair of socks in the morning, to enacting self-esteem in adolescent–parent interactions (Chapter 5) to intelligent activity (as defined in Chapter 9). Second, these processes show typical variability – including differences as well as recurrences of similar states – over their own proper timescale (i.e., they have temporal or processual structure). This structure may vary in terms of its stability or instability over the timescales involved. Third, for each moment in time, there is a division between a determinate past, consisting of the actual events that have taken place, which is known

---

[1] Readers with some knowledge of measurement in quantum physics will see a certain similarity here, although the underlying explanation for this collapsing of possible states is of course entirely different (e.g., Hilgevoord & Uffink, 2016).

to a limited extent, and an indeterminate but typically constrained (as well as open-ended) future, describable as an arbitrarily complex distribution over the chosen state space (or measurement space). Fourth, at the demarcation point between past and future, we have actual events or actual activities. These activities – actually selecting a pair of socks, actually having a parent–adolescent discussion enacting self-esteem, a person taking a test – consist of short-term or real-time person–environment interactions, which turn indeterminacy (the potential future before the action took place) into determinacy (the actual state of affairs after the action has taken place). Fifth, this environment is, to a considerable but variable extent, dependent on, and a creation of, the particular history of person–environment interactions (think about the changing content of the drawer in the case of the socks, or the ecological niche in which a particular person deploys their more or less intelligent activities or a particular adolescent–parent relationship).

We have seen that actually selecting a pair of socks in the morning is an act of determination: I turn an indeterminate property (possible socks, with its characteristic uncertainty) into a determinate one (actual socks, with its characteristic certainty). An act of measurement of a psychological ability is also an act of determination (i.e., a procedure of turning an indeterminate into a determinate property). That is, it collapses a range of possible futures into a single present, or, put differently, it collapses a range of potentialities into a single actuality. Taking an intelligence test, for instance, is a way of collapsing a range of possible test scores into an actual test score. This means that my IQ, which is considered a measure of my intellectual potentiality, is in fact a range of possible test scores, with some scores more probable than others, given a range of possible contexts. Some of these scores are more likely than others, and so are some of the possible contexts. In short, my intellectual potential is expressed by a range of test scores, and this range of scores represents the intrinsic uncertainty associated with the property of intellectual potential. It is an open (i.e., changeable) range of possibilities, not a fixed 'true' score.

The distinction between determinate and indeterminate properties is closely related to the Aristotelian distinction between potentiality and actuality, which amounts to the distinction between *Energeia* and *Dunamis* (Cohen & Reeve, 2020; Stedman, et al., 2016). *Energeia* refers to 'doing' or activity, that is, the process through which a potential state becomes an actual state (e.g., choosing a pair of socks, or answering a particular item in a test). *Dunamis*, on the other hand, refers to the power to do something, a potentiality. *Dunamis* is of course recognizable in 'dynamic systems', which implies that dynamic systems theory is literally the theory of specific potentialities of change.

The distinction between energeia and dunamis is relevant for the philosophical domain of *dispositions*. In the standard philosophical definition, a person has a disposition I (e.g., for intelligent action), if the person acts in a highly intelligent way, given a condition C, e.g., a condition that demands non-routine problem solving in a particular problem domain without support from others (many other such possible conditions are thinkable). The notion of disposition is fundamental for psychological science and for its attempts to measure psychological abilities, which are basically forms of dispositions (Choi & Fara, 2021). In complex systems, dispositions are indeterminate, they are possibilities. Indeterminate properties are not measurable (for measurement, you need a determinate, i.e., specific property). Yet they are quantifiable as ranges of possibilities and expectancy values, given a specific timescale (e.g., short- versus long-term).

This distribution of potential or of possibilities is *not a confidence interval*, which is a strength-of-beliefs interval, specifying uncertainty over where exactly in this interval the true score or true value of something is located. The following example illustrates the difference between the distribution of possibilities and the confidence interval. Suppose I have put my phone somewhere in my study, but don't remember where. For each place in my study, I have a weak or strong belief that my phone will be there. However, the truth value of the phone's position is maximal (1) for one specific place – that's where the phone actually is – and minimal (0) for all other places. The confidence interval defines my uncertainty regarding the true position of my phone, but my phone is in only one place. The same reasoning holds for a confidence interval (e.g., for an intelligence test score). The observer is uncertain about what the tested person's true score is, but this uncertainty is limited to the confidence interval. But only one score is the person's true score. However, if you ask me where I *habitually* put my phone when I'm in my study, I can answer by specifying a distribution or range of possibilities. That is, for every place in my study there is a potential or likelihood that I will put my phone there, which depends, among others, on my habits (strict versus sloppy) and my intentions (e.g., put my phone in plain sight or hide it). Each of these possible places is as true as any other within the range of possibilities. This distribution of potential properties – places, scores, activities – is a dynamic, time-dependent field of possibilities or likelihoods distributed over a space that can be material (as in the case of my study), or that can be abstract, or a combination. Examples of abstract spaces are the RGB colour space, illustrated in

10.2 Observation and Measurement as Processes of Uncertainty Management

10.2.1 Measurement, Information Exchange, and Coordinated Interaction

I have argued that abilities that psychologists routinely study are in fact ranges of uncertainties, or stated in more positive terms, ranges of potentialities. Ranges of potentialities consist of person-specific distributions of possibilities for action (some more likely than others) given person-specific distributions of typical contexts (Van Geert, 2002). To measure an ability, in this sense, is to chart this distribution of potentialities in a person on a relevant timescale (e.g., that of a few repeated actions versus that of developmental change) for personally relevant contexts. In Chapter 9, I defined measurement in the broadest possible sense as 'interaction between systems that provides information' (Section *9.1.2*). Hence, measurement of an ability implies a particular interaction between a measuring observer and a measured person, on a long enough timescale to capture the distributional and dynamic properties of the ability of interest. 'A distinctive feature of interactions is mutual information exchange: One member of a pair changes in response to the other while simultaneously producing actions that alter the other.' (Dumas et al., 2014, p. 1). Information implies the reduction of uncertainty, and information about what one person is doing allows the other person to adapt their action to that of the first. Mutual information allows both persons to act adaptively, or, put differently, to coordinate their activities.[2] Smooth, long-term coordination of interaction implies that the participants have greatly reduced their uncertainties about each other's action potentialities (i.e., that both are continuously accomplishing an adequate measurement of each other's potentialities, i.e., of each other's abilities). In a coordinated interaction, uncertainty is continuously reduced (in the form of a present 'step' in the coordinated activity) and continuously created (in anticipation of the next 'step' in the activity).

If interaction, mutual information exchange and coordination across a timescale relevant for the ability in question constitute the archetype of

---

[2] See, for instance, the notion of the Human Dynamic Clamp, involving coordination between an artificial system and a human system, where the artificial system then serves as a measurement of the ability underlying the coordinated action; (Dumas et al., 2014).

ability measurement, most measurement processes will be totally informal. They consist of natural interactions between people, such as child–parent conversations, play, teaching–learning interactions and so forth. In this case, the measurement is enacted, and there is no inscription device that turns the activities into numbers. What distinguishes informal, implicit measurement in social interactions from formal measurement in the context of psychological research or assessment is not the short-or long-term coordinated interaction as such. What distinguishes scientific from informal measurement is the introduction and use of formal inscription devices and activities where the products of those devices are processed. Examples of inscription devices are coding systems and coding activities, checklists, observation schemes, and so forth.

10.2.2 Measuring Vocabulary as Participation in Child–Parent Conversations

Let us take the measurement of a child's vocabulary as an example of how a processual approach to measurement can be shaped, and how it defines forms of uncertainty about the measured – or observed – properties. In the standard praxis, the size of a child's vocabulary is a latent variable that can be measured indirectly through observable phenomena, such as the number of word types a child uses in conversations or egocentric speech. It can be measured by means of a vocabulary test (which is a brief observation of a particular linguistic activity), or by means of a systematic parental report format, such as the DLPF (Développement du Langage de Production en Français) (Labrell et al., 2014). In all these cases, a child's vocabulary is presented as a single, determinate state, with typical problems of uncertainty and determinability (i.e., measurement error, and reliability).

However, the child's vocabulary is an aspect of an ongoing coordinated interaction, mostly between the young child and a parent. It can be registered by means of dedicated inscription devices such as recording equipment and transcription methods. The interaction takes place on the short-term timescale of a conversation, and the long-term timescale of early language development. The coordinated interaction forms a typical example of a dynamics of ongoing mutual information exchange, of co-adaptation, resulting in usually very smooth interactions (Van Dijk et al., 2013). A child–parent conversation is an example of an ongoing creating and solving of uncertainty, of potentialities turned into actualities. Children and parents ask each other questions, comment on what happens, tell what they think or feel, and so forth. Vocabulary is just one of the many dimensions of this coordinated activity. Measuring a child's vocabulary in the form of an evolving ability can take the form of repeated recording of observations of child–parent interactions and processing them through the mill of a particular inscription device, vocabulary coding. The use of these coding devices introduces particular forms of uncertainty; for instance, with regard to interpretability and ambiguity of what is said during a conversation (Van Dijk & Van Geert, 2005; Van Geert & Van Dijk, 2003). These forms of uncertainty will be discussed in the next major section. Vocabulary – as a specific ability of a child – is what emerges in a process of coordinated activity, of mutual information exchange that forms the condition under which a child's vocabulary, as a property of a dynamic, adaptive process can grow and develop. Knowledge of words is dynamic, emerging each time anew in concrete activities (Samuelson, Schutte & Horst, 2009). The notion of an internal word repository (vocabulary) from which words are retrieved and the properties of which can be measured, does not cover the ongoing dynamics of word use and word learning (for a comparable, dynamic approach, see Adolph, 2019; Fischer & Van Geert, 2014).

In an ongoing, coordinated interaction, much if not all of the exchanged information remains implicit: it guides the coordination of action, but is not given in the form of explicit numbers or descriptions. This lack of explicit representation can also be viewed as a form of uncertainty. The use of inscription devices such as recordings, coding, response formats such as questionnaires, etc., can therefore be interpreted as forms of uncertainty reduction, more precisely of making explicit what is nevertheless implicitly present in the form of information driving the coordinated interaction. In natural interactions based on mutual information exchange, much of the processes and mechanisms that serve as the causes of smooth – or erratic – interaction remain implicit as well. That is, the mechanisms are uncertain in the sense of not being explicitly described. The mechanisms themselves are open-ended causal networks for specified timescales, for instance, a particular conversation that unfolds in real-time in real contexts with real children and parents (see Chapters 7 and 8). Some of these mechanisms can be made explicit by participating in those open-ended causal networks (e.g., by manipulating aspects of an ongoing interaction provided the coordinated interaction as such is not disturbed). That is, by interacting with an interaction between an adult and a child, researchers have found that changes in focussing attention while acting with objects turn out to be important features of interaction dynamics involving word use, creating a context of learning (Smith et al., 2002).

10.2.3 Measuring Psychopathology as Participation in Symptom-Generating Processes

Following dynamic systems and processual approach to psychopathology has consequences for the interpretation of the measurement problem: it no longer refers to the problem of reducing uncertainty about a person's psychopathology by assigning a measure or magnitude to an underlying entity or substance that takes the form of a latent variable such as depression. Instead, the measurement problem boils down to qualitatively and quantitatively identifying the complex dynamics of a particular person's stream of activities, defined in terms of activities related to or interpretable as mental health-related symptoms.

Advances in repeated, high-frequency measurement in the form of experience sampling by means of widely used devices such as smartphones open up new possibilities for getting a grip on dynamic clinical phenomena, which clients themselves can observe and report relatively effortlessly (Schiepek, Aichhorn & Schöller, 2017; Schiepek et al., 2016; Schiepek et al., 2019b). The experience sampling is part of the complex, coordinated activities that constitute a particular psychopathology: it serves as a form of mutual information exchange that allows the suffering person to communicate with another person who tries to understand the dynamics of the process. The other person may be a researcher or a clinician, or both.

The processes that are revealed by experience sampling are often far from the gradual and smooth changes based on averages over many individuals. Some changes take place in the form of sudden gains, which are typical examples of nonlinear clinical change (Olthof et al., 2020b; Helmich et al., 2020). Other examples are discontinuities and patterns of variability in the form of critical instabilities (Schiepek, 2009; Heinzel, Tominschek & Schiepek, 2014), and of rapid early responses preceding therapy and temporary spikes in symptom severity (Hayes et al., 2007a). Anomalies in short-term variability of indicators of the severity of psychopathology, another example of non-linear aspects of change, have been shown to predict sudden shifts, for better or for worse, during clinical treatment (Wichers et al. 2016., Helmich et al., 2020; Wichers et al., 2016; Olthof, et al., 2020b; Van de Leemput et al., 2014).

In the standard approach, major depression, or any other psychopathological category for that matter, is conceived of as an underlying substance or entity (i.e., a latent variable that is the cause of the observable symptoms). This basically essentialist view is supported by a biogenetic explanation, identifying a material substrate as a cause of psychopathology, which increasingly dominates professional as well as public views (Haslam & Kvaale, 2015; Racine et al., 2010). An example is the chemical imbalance explanation of depression that affects clients' and clinicians coping with the symptoms (Kemp, Lickel & Deacon, 2014; Lebowitz & Ahn, 2014; but see Ahn et al., 2006). In principle, a chemical imbalance can be measured (i.e., specified as a point value on a quantitative dimension, e.g., degree of imbalance). The processual alternative is to treat psychopathology such as depression as a dynamic system of causally or conditionally connected symptoms that affect one another over time (Cramer et al., 2016; Nuijten et al., 2016; Fried et al., 2017). This view has direct consequences for the measurement of depression, namely as a process of time-serial, quantitative and qualitative monitoring of the changes in symptoms and symptom relationships. Examples of relevant symptoms are sleep problems, fatigue, concentration problems, self-reproach, loss of interest, problems at work, thoughts of suicide, irritability and so forth (Fried et al., 2016). The properties of symptoms, such as characteristic fluctuations, bandwidths or discontinuities, are to a considerable extent open to direct observation. They tend to fluctuate on the level of short- and long-term timescales (e.g., in the form of changing associations between symptoms in individual persons; e.g., Cramer et al., 2016). That is, the certainty provided by measured properties is continuously broken down in the dynamics of the measured process and measurements must be constantly renewed.

10.3 Vagueness and Ambiguity as Forms of Uncertainty

In the preceding sections I focussed on 'classical' uncertainty, that is, lack of knowledge about determinate, specific properties (such as a 'true' score). However, not all properties of interest – in particular those pertaining to abilities or potentialities, concern determinate properties. They entail their own forms of uncertainty in the form of 'openness' (i.e., in the form of ranges of possible realizations, ranges of possible futures). In the current section, I shall focus on two other forms of uncertainty, vagueness, and ambiguity. Vagueness implies the lack of clarity or distinction, fuzziness. Ambiguity refers to the multiplicity of interpretations, inconsistency or incoherence. With regard to these forms of uncertainty, there are two opposing ontological stances (Hyde, 2016; Morawski, 2021). The first is that although the world is very complicated, in essence, it is intrinsically specific, determinate, fixed and unambiguous. This is a stance associated with a substance ontology. Vagueness, ambiguity and the like are 'weaknesses' or 'limits' in our knowledge and are therefore fundamentally – but not necessarily pragmatically – solvable. The second stance is that the world is not so much complicated, as it is *complex* (Den Hartigh, Cox & Van Geert, 2017). Vagueness and ambiguity are intrinsic, irreducible properties of the world. For instance, things or events are often in a state of becoming, they turn from A into B, and in that process of becoming they are both A and B, or neither A nor B. Change and becoming are fundamental features of the world, implying that states of affairs, or categories of being are often intrinsically ambiguous, intrinsically transient or equivocal, or intrinsically fuzzy (McDaniel & Driebe, 2005). How can vagueness and ambiguity be systematically treated in scientific, psychological research?

10.3.1 Vagueness and Ambiguity and the Praxis of Psychiatric Categorization

A typical feature of vagueness is the existence of borderline cases, that is cases at or around the border between two different kinds or categories. The problem of 'borderline cases' is basically a problem of in-between cases (i.e., those that fall in between categories, e.g., separating normality from disorder). It's hard to tell whether the borderline cases have the disorder, or do not have it. Vagueness involves the often difficult problem of determining a boundary or demarcation line between things of different kinds or belonging to different categories, for example, clinical diagnostic categories (Sorensen, 2018). Problems of vagueness and ambiguity typically occur in cases where categorization is based on combinations of criteria that are gradual. Psychiatric diagnosis, for instance, based on the categorical distinctions in DSM-V, provides a typical example. It is based on the principle of assigning a categorical description to a phenomenon if the latter satisfies the 'm-out-of-n criteria' principle, where each of the criteria represents properties or symptoms that can vary in magnitude or severity. For instance, borderline personality disorder is diagnosed on the basis of at least five out of nine criteria each of which is a matter of degree (American Psychiatric Association, 2013, p. 663). This means that each criterion implies borderline cases (borderline now meaning being at or close to borderline distinguishing categories). For instance, how disturbed should identity be to comply with the criterion 'Identity disturbance: markedly and persistently unstable self-image or sense of self' (APA, 2013, p. 663)? Although this problem of borderline cases (i.e., cases around the demarcation line separating two categories) is acknowledged in DSM-V (APA, 2013, p. 6), the resulting realization that psychiatric disorders are fundamentally fuzzy and vague classifications has little more than the status of a footnote in the theoretical foundation of the praxis of assessment.

The problem of continuous or gradual dimensions defining discontinuous categorical distinctions gives rise to what is known as the *Sorites paradox*, which we owe to the Greek philosopher Eubulides of Milete (fourth century BCE). If you have a heap of sand and remove one grain of sand at a time, there will never be a particular grain that transforms the heap into a non-heap. This leads to the paradoxical conclusion that a single grain of sand is still a heap. The paradox concerns the question of which small difference – if any such difference exists – marks a categorical difference. Which small difference corresponds with the demarcation line between two categories, a heap and a non-heap, depression or no depression? For instance, which infinitesimally little bit of social-emotional reciprocity marks the difference between – or the transition from – 'normal' to 'deficit', in the case of autism, for example? Sorites paradox tells us that, although the difference between categories is big (e.g., between being auistic or not), there is no small difference that marks the demarcation line. Categorical differences that are based on continuous dimensions are commonplace in psychological research, which means that the Sorites paradox should be a pervasive problem in psychological research.

A typical solution to the problem posed by this paradox consists of deciding on an arbitrary but reasonable demarcation line. For instance, if the value of some diagnostic dimension is two population standard deviations below the population average, we call it a deficit or disorder. This arbitrary difference is an exact demarcation line that separates people with a particular disorder from people without it, for instance dyslexia. Such sharp separations are pragmatically acceptable on the level of populations, where subpopulations are dealt with in terms of their averages, which are not affected by small differences in the position of the demarcation line. But for the individual person, these sharp demarcation lines may have serious consequences, for instance in terms of whether or not a particular child is given a particular treatment and whether or not the health insurance is reimbursing it. The problem with those arbitrary demarcation points is that they very easily lead to almost ineradicable practices of reification and essentialism, where the arbitrary boundary on a continuous dimension becomes a point of alleged qualitative discontinuity, with very serious practical and methodological consequences. This is an example of how a particular praxis is transformed into an explicit belief in classifications as the expression of strictly separated categories (instead of the other way around, where a belief is transformed into a praxis).

The problem of in-between cases, those that fall in between two categories, can in principle be solved by creating a new category. This is entirely consistent with a substance-oriented view, where all forms of psychopathology correspond with a specific underlying entity (i.e., a latent variable that causes the symptoms, clearly distinct from other latent variables). For instance, children are either diagnosed as having a specific pervasive developmental disorder in the form of autism or not. But many children are in-between cases, they do have a pervasive developmental disorder, but not sufficiently so to be diagnosed with Autism Spectrum Disorder. As in-between cases, they can be grouped under a new category, namely PDD-NOS (pervasive developmental disorder, not otherwise specified). However, introducing such additional in-between categories basically doubles the problem of in-between cases. If you have categories A and B, you have the problem of A-B (in-between) cases. If you classify them under a new category C, you'll have in-between cases A–C and B–C. Hence, adding in-between categories does not solve the vagueness problem (i.e., the problem of unclear distinctions).

Adding categories not only occurs if there is a problem with in-between cases, but it also occurs if a category is felt to be ambiguous (i.e., if it covers multiple qualities and qualitatively different individuals). For instance, the category personality disorder covers a wide range of qualitatively different forms and has been split up into as many as ten different categories. One of those categories, borderline personality disorder, was introduced in the literature as a class in between psychotic and neurotic types, and has been further divided into different subtypes (e.g., Smits et al., 2017).

The praxis of adding sub- and in-between categories easily results in a so-called *categorical proliferation* or *categorical explosion*, that is, the unbridled generation of new categories in answer to the fact that every new category introduces its own problems of vagueness and ambiguity. According to Allen Frances,[3] this categorical proliferation is one of the main problems of DSM-V (e.g., Frances, 2013). Proliferation is a solution that maintains the underlying substance ontology of psychiatric classifications, which assumes that the classes represent natural kinds (Kincaid & Sullivan, 2014). However, it is a pseudo-solution in that it denies the problem of intrinsic vagueness of psychiatric disorders – or most other psychological categorical distinctions, for that matter – that directly follows from their complex and processual nature.

---

[3] Frances contributed to DSM-4, but became an outspoken critic of DSM-V.

However, the problem of vagueness and ambiguity extends far beyond the problem of gradual versus discontinuous distinctions. With a minimum of five out of nine criteria, combinatorial maths leads to 256 different forms of Borderline Personality Disorder (Van Heugten–Van der Kloet & Van Heugten, 2015). With posttraumatic stress disorder, the number of different combinations amounts to 636,120 ways a person can have posttraumatic stress disorder (Galatzer-Levy & Bryant, 2013). That is, there will be subgroups – up to the level of single individuals – of people with BPD or PTSD that have nothing in common with other subgroups of people with BPD or PTSD. This lack of even a single common property in members of a class or category (BPD, PTSD) raises serious doubts and worry about the underlying assumption that the class represents a secondary substance or universal (i.e., something that is common to all particulars (individuals) that are members of this class). However, the standard scientific praxis of psychiatric assessment does not show any signs of significant worry. This lack of worry is one of the many ways of enacting the view that categories of psychiatric disorder are common underlying entities causing various particular (i.e., person-specific) collections of symptoms. This view might be warranted if all these symptoms had a similar biological etiology, but at present, there is little evidence that this is indeed the case (e.g., Borsboom, Cramer & Kalis, 2019; Pilgrim 2019, pp. 131 ff).

The third form of vagueness and ambiguity is that a single person shows symptoms of multiple disorders, or, in general, falls under multiple, often mutually exhaustive categories. In psychopathology, this is known as the *comorbidity problem*. Comorbidity, which is the co-occurrence of two or more psychopathological conditions, is a phenomenon that occurs surprisingly more frequently than is often assumed (Plana-Ripoll et al., 2019; Marshall, 2020). For instance, '96% of patients with BPD have a mood disorder during their life, and lifetime depression is reported at 71% to 83% ... Anxiety disorders are also extremely common: 88% of patients have an anxiety disorder, 34% to 48% have panic disorder, and 47% to 56% have PTSD. Alcohol and substance abuse or dependence are reported by 50% to 65%; eating disorders affect 7% to 26% over a lifetime'[4] (see also Shen, Hu & Hu, 2017). That is, from the perspective of a particular person there is an amalgam of – often causally and conditionally related – symptoms, and there is no guarantee that such amalgams will be conceptually consistent from the viewpoint of an underlying system of categorical distinctions.

---

[4] www.psychiatrictimes.com/view/comorbidities-borderline-personality-disorder

From the perspective of a primarily substance-oriented ontology, a person is like a container for various, fundamentally distinct and independent, coexisting disorders. From this perspective, the chances for this co-occurrence of these disorders can be interpreted as a consequence of yet another independent entity, namely a personality factor corresponding with a general susceptibility to psychopathology (e.g., Revelle & Wilt, 2013), or a single psychopathology factor (the *p-factor*, which is based on the analysis of inter-individual variability in a great number of cases; Caspi et al., 2014; Allegrini et al., 2020; Smith et al., 2020). This general p-factor is comparable to the general g-factor in intelligence, namely as a factor common to specific manifestations of psychopathologies or of intellectual performance.

The substance-oriented approach to comorbidity is fundamentally different from a dynamic systems perspective, which explains comorbidity as well as an eventual general factor as the emergent *result* of person-specific dynamic relationships between various kinds of symptoms that form dynamic networks (Cramer et al., 2010). The relationships between the components of these networks – symptoms – can be causal or conditional, and the effect of one symptom on another can strengthen or weaken another symptom. As with many such processes in variable, complex systems, the processes occurring in these person-specific symptom networks are idiosyncratic and non-ergodic. The latter excludes the possibility that a general p-factor based on inter-individual variability serves as a component of the individual networks. Instead of being a factor causing, and thus preceding, effects on symptoms and susceptibility, the general p-factor itself is most likely the emergent result of the dynamic interactions on the level of emerging and changing symptoms. Van der Maas and coworkers (Van der Maas et al., 2006; Van der Maas et al., 2017) have convincingly demonstrated that in networks of dynamically coupled components, a general factor emerges from network processes if the connections between the components of the network are predominantly positive (i.e., if the effect of one component on another is mostly positive (strengthening, supportive)). Although the demonstration focussed on the general factor of intelligence, g, it is likely to apply to the abovementioned *p*-factor, or susceptibility factor, as the nature of the dynamic networks is similar in both cases.

10.3.2 *Complementarity and Superposition*

Vagueness, in the sense of gradual transitions between categories, or ambiguity, in the sense of multiplicity and superposition of seemingly mutually exclusive properties are problems for an ontology that views the world as

10.3 Vagueness and Ambiguity as Forms of Uncertainty

basically uniquely defined, consisting of clearly separated essences or substances. However, for a processual ontology that views becoming and complexity as fundamental features of reality, gradual transitions, multiplicity and apparent contradictions are not signs of our lack of knowledge, but are in fact the fundamental features of reality itself. An example of this intrinsic vagueness and ambiguity comes from complex dynamic systems theory of how the brain works, but it extends to complex dynamic systems in general. It is related to the property of *complementarity* and *meta-stability* (Kelso, 2001, 2005; Tognoli & Kelso, 2014; Kelso & Engström, 2006). Complementarity implies the unity of seemingly opposite properties. A complex system, for instance, is defined as a dynamic unity of order and disorder: one property emerges from the other in a mutual or cyclical relationship (see Chapter 8, Section 4). Meta-stability implies that a system such as the brain is stable in the sense that it covers a whole range of attractor states, none of which it ever fully or uniquely occupies. One attractor state of the brain, for instance, corresponding to what a person experiences as a specific belief, already incorporates other possible attractor states, potentialities (i.e., other possible beliefs). The brain shows 'multiple tendencies coexisting at the same time' (Kelso, 2005, p. 78). It may tend toward a particular attractor state and yet at the same time be in a multiple state of dispositions toward other possible attractors (e.g., Tognoli & Kelso, 2014). Although it should be kept in mind that the brain virtually never operates in an independent fashion as it is always immersed in specific perception-action loops in specific environments, it can nevertheless be stated that if the brain explores the properties and possibilities of a particular, specific attractor state, it also explores the properties and possibilities of states in-between possible attractor states. That is, the brain is characterized by states of *meta-stability*. Meta-stability generates complementarity, in that the dynamics governing meta-stability integrate apparently opposing tendencies. Meta-stability of brain activity means that it is simultaneously integrating and differentiating information, creating distinctions and undoing them, that it simultaneously produces order and disorder (Kelso & Engstrom, 2006). In short, what counts as unwanted vagueness and ambiguity in a substance-oriented ontology, are intrinsic features of reality, namely complementarity and meta-stability, in a processual complexity approach.

According to Kelso and co-authors (Tognoli & Kelso, 2014; Kelso & Engström, 2006) this complementarity is a direct consequence of the coordination dynamics of a complex system such as a brain, a human being or a society, where processes take place on a variety of interacting levels, each characterized by their own components and typical dynamics.

Complementarity between order and disorder, of regularity and stability on the one hand, and novelty and surprise in the form of emergent features, on the other hand, is one of the most characteristic features of complex systems. The study of their dynamics shows how such seemingly opposing tendencies can co-exist, and how one aspect creates the other and vice versa (Nicolis & Rouvas-Nicolis, 2007).

A clinically relevant example of complementarity is the kinds-versus-continua discussion in psychopathological assessment: are psychopathological categories qualitatively different natural kinds, or are they arbitrary cut-offs on continuous, descriptive dimensions (Kamphuis & Noordhof, 2009; Borsboom et al, 2016)? The question focusses on the question of whether, in accordance with DSM-V, psychological conditions are of a categorical nature, which are assumed to correspond with natural kinds (real, not artificial categories; Kincaid & Sullivan, 2014). However, according to the dimensional alternative, psychopathology depends on continuous inter–individual differences on a variety of dimensions (Trull & Durrett, 2005; Krueger & Piasecki, 2002). Borsboom et al., 2016 argue that this is not an either-or question. Psychopathologies may tend toward categorical distinctions in some persons or at some moments in time, and toward dimensional variation in other persons or during later stages of the evolution of symptom constellations. That is, categorical and dimensional features of psychopathology are examples of intrinsic complementarity. In a totally different field, language development, Van Dijk & Van Geert (2007) demonstrated that individual developmental time series show a complementarity, in the sense of co-existence, of continuous and discontinuous change.

10.3.3 Emergence and the Boundary Problem

In the preceding sections, I suggested that problems of apparent vagueness and ambiguity result from the inability to account for the nature of transformations, change and emergence in complex systems. The field of language development provides an opportunity to further clarify this point. For an observer of a child's language development, basic linguistic categories such as nouns or prepositions, emerge diachronically from the contextual processes of language use over the course of weeks or months or years.

For instance, in the developmental trajectory of a particular child, there is an initial state which is clearly 'non-prepositional', and a final state where prepositions have emerged. But this implies a long-term transitional stage that is neither prepositional nor non-prepositional, or maybe non-prepositional and prepositional at the same time (Van Dijk & Van Geert,

2005). The question of where or when exactly in a particular child's language development a non-prepositional state becomes prepositional poses a near unsolvable boundary problem if one sticks to a substance ontology where such categories amount to distinct either or entities. In a processual or dynamic framework, a preposition, or any other linguistic category for that matter, is basically a way in which a particular word (e.g., 'in' or 'on'- relates to other words and word forms in a concrete context of use). This network of relationships is a soft-assembled property of a specific usage event, and the pattern of this network changes over the course of developmental time. There is no need to subsume the changes in these patterns under a sharp categorical distinction of being a preposition or not.

Having said that, however, it is clear that early patterns of usage are clearly distinct from later, stabilized ones, to which we assign the category 'preposition'. A similar reasoning applies to stages of cognitive development. Stages, such as different levels of cognitive complexity, or different cognitive strategies to solve a balance scale problem, may co-exist in the form of overlapping frequencies. For instance, children may show a 'scalloping' pattern of alternating levels of cognitive complexity while they are solving a particular problem (e.g., Fischer, 2008; Van Geert & Fischer, 2009; Fischer & Van Geert, 2014; see also the overlapping waves model, Siegler, 1996; Boom, 2015). In principle, these models still assume that there are distinct, clearly separable levels or cognitive strategies, which alternate, albeit on the short-term timescale of real activity. But in a complex system, we should reckon with the possibility that seemingly opposite or distinct states are simultaneously present, which is a typical feature of meta-stability (Kelso & Engström, 2006). On the long-term timescale, the composition and dynamics of such stabilities and superpositions of properties will change. For instance, one dynamic pattern, representing a particular and 'high' level of functioning will become dominant.

In summary, instead of reducing all forms of observed ambiguity or multiplicity to insufficient knowledge, they should be dealt with as intrinsic features of emerging properties (i.e., properties that are in a process of becoming).

10.3.4 Vagueness, Ambiguity, and the Distributed Nature of Psychological Processes

If a psychological phenomenon such as a thought, emotion, ability or personality dimension is conceived of as a strictly internal feature of a person, the main question is to which extent a particular assignment of a particular property, such as having a particular thought, or a particular IQ, is correct and specific. That is, the main question is about the extent of uncertainty, vagueness and ambiguity of a particular psychological feature of a person. However, what does this question mean if such psychological properties are not properties of the person alone? According to the 4E cognition approach, cognition, which is traditionally viewed as something that takes places 'inside' the individual person, is in fact embodied, enacted, embedded in, and extended across environments (Newen, De Bruin & Gallagher, 2018). This view is consistent with a basic axiom of ecological psychology, namely that psychology's unit of analysis is the organism–environment system (Richardson et al., 2008; see also Thelen & Smith, 1994, with regard to development). That is to say that psychological abilities and properties are typically distributed across various levels of organization, including the levels of the organism or person and that of the environment with which the person interacts. Elements of the context itself are crucial and fundamental aspects of the causal processes that constitute a particular cognitive activity. This *causal distributivity* is a typical feature of dynamic field theory (Schneegans & Schöner, 2008) and of dynamic network models (e.g., of psychopathology) (Cramer et al., 2016; Contreras et al., 2019) or of expertise and excellence (Den Hartigh et al., 2016).

Psychological properties such as abilities and dispositions emerge in the form of processes (i.e., concrete activities), which are person–environment interactions. During this process, environment and person are co-dependent. Hence, if one takes a processual stance, there is no way to separate the contributions of organism and environment as independent, additive components. This has implications for the assignment of personal properties, such as intelligence, personality, or self-esteem: they become properties of the coupled person–environment system (see also Chapter 6 for the case of self-esteem). In this sense, a person's characteristic environments, the person's 'ecological niches', are a property of that person, just as the person's characteristic activities and levels of performance are properties of the environments in which a person is functioning. Intelligence, for instance, becomes a dynamic property of a coupled person–environment system, which means that it is domain-specific (context-or environment specific), variable and multiple (as there are multiple kinds of contexts that are characteristic of a particular person).

From a processual view, the boundaries between persons and their environments are not fixed and to a great extent also indeterminate, open-ended and variable, as they change across a particular activity and over the course of many, iterative activities. Methodologically, one can of course

10.3 Vagueness and Ambiguity as Forms of Uncertainty

refrain from a processual and person-oriented approach and focus on sources of independent, additive variance of persons and environments, particularly in samples of interindividual variation (i.e., the typical samples of independent subjects). In this sense, one can separate statistical information about persons from information about environments, and assign properties to persons, such as an IQ, that are fixed and determinate properties of the person and the person only (see also Chapter 4, on a substance-oriented approach to self-esteem). Uncertainty applies to whether such assignments are correct or not. However, if properties are not properties of persons alone, but of their interactions with environments that vary within person-specific, yet very broad limits, the psychological property as such becomes an intrinsically indeterminate, open-ended, and fuzzy feature (see, for instance, the discussion on the complex and dynamic nature of intelligence, Chapter 9).

10.3.5 Probability and Uncertainty

Probability statements are ways of turning uncertainty into something determinate and determinable (i.e., something that is specific, set in the language of mathematics, and objectively determinable, as always within certain limits of preciseness). For instance, for a particular US population, in 2003, the probabilities for graduate school attendance were 0.36 for low SES and 0.52 for high SES students, (Walpole, 2003). The probabilities specify a particular uncertainty, for instance about any particular low-SES student attending graduate school in the future (there is a 36 per cent chance that they will). Probability is of course a basic tool for dealing with the expected future, with the possibilities of what can happen or possibilities of what one can find in a sample of subjects (for an authoritative overview, see Hájek, 2019). In spite of the fact that the statistical procedures that researchers habitually follow when they calculate probabilities are very specifically described, the concept of probability itself is far from clear. The resulting probabilities suggest a high level of precision, but the probability values themselves are often indeterminate, imprecise, or ambiguous. Various purely technical solutions have been suggested to account for this (Cozman, 2013). However, the conceptual problems regarding the intrinsic vagueness or ambiguity of the probability concept as it is commonly used in standard psychological research praxis are not solved by technical solutions. In order to understand these conceptual problems a bit more, I shall very briefly discuss some important conceptualizations of probability in psychology, namely the *frequentist*, the *propensity* and the *subjective* view (Talbott, 2016).

10.3.5.1 The Frequentist Interpretation

The standard, though mostly tacit, interpretation of probability in psychological research is that it is a generalization of observed relative *frequencies*, for instance, the frequency of low SES students attending graduate school in a specific group or sample of low SES students. Frequencies are properties of specific groups or samples of cases or individuals. Probabilities on the other hand are, in the first place, properties of natural kinds (e.g., SES students). To make a reliable, error-free switch from an actual frequency to a probability typical of a particular natural kind such as low SES, the number of observed cases must ideally be infinite, but an approximation in the form of a big enough random sample of cases will mostly pragmatically suffice. The probabilities are mathematical properties, expressing the ratio of cases of interest (SES students going to graduate school) over all cases (all SES students). The probability represents a general truth about SES students (the contextual limitations in terms of geography and time are very often neglected). Based on the principle that general truths apply to specific cases, the standard practice is to assign this probability to the individual representatives of the natural kind. For instance, a specific low SES student has a 32 per cent probability of later attending graduate school. This probability allows us to further specify the region of uncertainty in the form of a confidence interval. In random samples of twenty low SES children with 32 per cent probability of attending high school, we know that the actual number of students attending high school, we know that in 95 per cent of the samples, the actual numbers are between three and eleven (15 per cent and 55 per cent). So it seems that a frequentist probability concept elegantly solves the problems of uncertainty, expectation or belief about the future.

The application of the frequentist probability interpretation to solve problems of uncertainty with regard to potentialities of individuals suffers from the same problems we already have encountered several times. First, it almost certainly commits the ensemble-to-individual fallacy, by assuming that an ensemble property (a big sample of low SES students) is a general property of a natural kind that applies to individuals. A similar sample property (frequency) allows for a large, basically indeterminate range of possible individual histories, corresponding with very different probabilities (e.g., of attending high school). Second, frequentist probability is based on sampling independent cases: any systematic relationship between those cases, other than a class or set property such as SES, must be avoided, in order to arrive at an unbiased estimation of the ensemble property, in this case, a frequency turned into a probability. An individual person, on the other hand, is a process, a sequence of connected, interdependent events. This sequence is likely to be non-ergodic: frequencies of particular events, e.g., conflicts with parents, tend to vary over time, and they are likely to be highly idiosyncratic. Hence applying an ensemble property such as a probability to an individual is an example of the non-ergodicity fallacy. To make this issue more clear, take for instance the question of the difficulty of a particular IQ-test item for ten year olds, which is a typical question for Item Response Theory (IRT). The difficulty of the item is the probability that the item will be correctly answered by a ten year old, which is estimated by counting the number of correct answers in a large sample (e.g., 1,000, of ten year olds). Now take another typical IRT question, namely how difficult this IQ-test item is for a particular ten-year-old Jan. This difficulty is the probability that Jan will give a correct answer to this item. To estimate that probability, you can ask Jan to answer that item 1,000 times in a row, which is obviously a rather bizarre proposal. The process of 1,000 answers will lead to Jan's increasing boredom or unwillingness to invest effort or showing resistance by giving mock answers. So, this sequence of repeated answers to a particular test item will yield anything but the hypothetical point probability that Jan will give a correct answer. The process consists of interdependent, idiosyncratic events. For instance, after twenty-seven repeated answers given with increasing irritation, Jan will throw the test form through the window and run away. In the long run, Jan will show an irreparable disgust for and resistance to intelligence tests, making it virtually impossible to measure his IQ in the future. One may respond by saying that Jan is only a single case. However, the question we asked was a standard assessment or measurement question, which almost by definition applies to single cases. The problem we encountered is an example of the *single-case problem*, i.e., the application of a frequentist probability interpretation to a single case (Gillies, 2016; Hájek, 2019; for a discussion of the many problems related to the frequency interpretation, see Hájek, 1997, 2009).

10.3.5.2 The Single-Case Problem and the Propensity Interpretation
According to various authors (Gillies, 2016; Hájek, 2019), the frequency interpretation of probability is meaningless in statements about single cases (the single-case problem). In order to make sense, single-case statements require a shift toward the so-called *propensity interpretation* of probability, which has been introduced by Popper (1990; Hájek, 2019; Galavotti, 2017). That is, a probability is in fact a propensity to act in a particular way, or show a particular property. The notion of propensity, used in

the context of probability, is virtually similar to the notion of disposition that we discussed earlier (e.g., Gillies, 2016). The propensity interpretation is consistent with the psychological concept of an ability or capability, a potentiality to act, which we discussed extensively in Chapter 9. However, the notion of propensity, interpreted as ability, poses very serious problems that cast doubt on the claim that it solves or avoids the single-case problem (i.e., the assignment of a probability to an individual person). First, if a person's potential or ability is shown only very infrequently, or maybe never, its probabilistic interpretation becomes very difficult if not impossible to demonstrate, and, consequently, virtually meaningless. For instance, although Bill had the capacity to successfully finish high school (a propensity interpretable as a probability that he would have done so), he never actually attended high school. Second, human propensities or abilities are subject to change, adaptation, learning and development, which may range from linear and gradual to discontinuous and erratic. The notion of a propensity in terms of a typical frequency of often repeated behaviours or performances makes sense only under quite specific conditions, namely of short- and long-term stability (i.e., statistical stationarity). An example of a relatively stationary ability to which the notions of probability and frequency apply is the ability of a particular person to speak English as a foreign language, after a sufficiently long period of training and practice. If the person speaks English very often, probability features such as fluency, vocabulary, grammatical errors and so forth can be reliably established as characteristics of this individual's linguistic propensity. In summary, the propensity interpretation does not allow us to solve the problems raised by the specification of uncertainty in terms of probability.

10.3.5.3 *The Subjective Interpretation of Probability*

The frequency and propensity interpretations view probability as a property of the world (e.g., of natural kinds), or of individual persons. Bayesian statistics, on the other hand, is based on a subjectivist interpretation of probability, namely as a quantification of a subjective degree of belief. For instance, my statement that Bill has a 32 per cent chance of successfully finishing high school reflects my belief that Bill can accomplish this. My uncertainty whether he will succeed is expressed in the form of a probability (i.e., a number that assigns an exact value to the degree in which I hold that belief) (for a discussion of historical roots, see Jackman, 2009; epistemological problems are concisely discussed in Talbott, 2016 and Romeijn, 2017).

How can a precise numerical value (a probability) be assigned to a subjective state, namely a particular person's belief? The answer to this question is that we can do so by asking the believer to make a bet on the belief (e.g., to put a certain amount of money on whether or not a prediction will come true, e.g., Bill will finish high school; or that in general children of low SES will finish high school). The idea is that, in the long run, bets will be profitable only if they correspond with the logic of conditional probabilities, that is, if the beliefs are expressed in terms of specific probability values that statistical gamblers assign to their bets. A collection of bets that are based on wrongly assigned probabilities, i.e., bets that make the gambler lose in the long run, is described in a so-called Dutch Book (yet another example, in addition to Dutch treats, Dutch Uncles and Dutch widows, that bears witness of the somewhat dubitable nature of the Dutch image). As the bets are probabilistic, many such repeated bets would be needed to establish the truth of a particular subjective probability (e.g., the degree of confidence of my belief that Bill will finish high school, expressed as a 32 per cent probability). These bets would need to go unnoticed by Bill, as his mere observation of the fact that such bets are made could change his efforts to go to high school and finish it successfully. These requirements would be hard to satisfy in cases pertaining to individuals.

However, in spite of this difficulty, applying the logic of Bayesian inference to processes is remarkably successful (see Chapter 7, Section 2.2.1 for a discussion of Bayesian nets). In addition, Bayesian reasoning is easy, as it can be successfully done by children as young as seven to ten years (Gigerenzer et al., 2020). Children's learning is based on informal Bayesian reasoning (Gopnik et al., 2001; Gopnik et al., 2004). Bayesian models can be used to control and predict processes in an iterative fashion, as they predict future states of a process and update their parameters based on the information that the predictions provide (e.g., Deventer, Denzler & Niemann, 2002). That is, Bayesian procedures provide a way of managing uncertainty about the parameters and determinants of a process by allowing an observer to participate in it, in the form of predictions and adaptations (see also Sections 10.2.2 and 10.2.3 in this chapter, for a similar processual approach to how uncertainty can be managed in the form of smooth process participation).

10.3.6 Iterative Reduction of Uncertainty: Dynamic Systems

In the preceding sections we saw how an iterative updating of parameters and determinants of a process can take place by using formal (e.g., as in coordination dynamics or Bayesian statistics) and informal ways (as in natural interaction, e.g., in child–parent conversations) to enable smooth participation in an ongoing process. This iterative updating of a state of a system is a fundamental characteristic of dynamic systems. A dynamic system accomplishes this task by iteratively applying evolution rules that take a present state to generate a new state (see Chapter 2). A dynamic systems model of a process (e.g., of child–parent interaction; Van Dijk et al., 2013) does not participate in it, but attempts to understand the process by reconstructing it in the form of a simulation of sequences of states in a state space. Simulations of natural processes are confined to reconstructing major qualitative and quantitative features of processes (e.g., the general qualitative time evolution of an interacting parent and child, or friendship and group formation among adolescents) (e.g., Schuhmacher, Ballato & Van Geert, 2014). Dynamic systems models can contribute to our understanding of seemingly chaotic or erratic phenomena, where uncertainty about future steps in a process is very high, and prediction seems virtually impossible. Examples of such phenomena explained by relatively simple models are critical sensitivity to initial conditions (e.g., Betz, 2007), strange attractors, such as the Lorenz model of the weather system (e.g., Cook, 2020), unexpected, discontinuous changes as in catastrophe theoretical models (Thom, 1989), meta-stability (Tognoli & Kelso, 2014) or self-organized criticality (Bak, 1996/2013). These models contribute to our qualitative understanding of virtually unpredictable processes by explaining their underlying principles.

10.3.7 *Fuzzy Logic*

If vagueness and ambiguity are intrinsic properties of the real, changing world, we need tools to specify this vagueness beyond viewing it as an expression of lack of knowledge. In normal parlance, we might say 'It's a little chilly in here' (or 'very chilly'), and we might intuitively categorize children as being 'very autistic', or only 'mildly' so, or say that a person has a hint of autism. Fuzzy logic is a formal system for dealing with this kind of vagueness and ambiguity of classifications that are based on, mostly, continuous criteria (Zadeh, 1975, 1978, 2006; Nguyen, Walker & Walker, 2018). Classifying or categorizing a state of affairs, objects, or persons is the same as assigning a class membership. For instance, I classify the current temperature – a continuous dimension – in this room as a member of the class 'chilly', and I can use linguistic modifiers such as 'very', 'a little' or 'quite'. Fuzzy logic makes these vague qualifications specific by assigning *degrees of membership* to object properties. For instance, the current temperature has a degree of membership of 0.7 to the class 'chilly', and 0.3 to the temperature class 'moderate'. These memberships correspond with the modifier 'a little (chilly)'. If the temperature had a degree of membership of 1 to the class 'chilly', we would call it 'quite (chilly)'.

A similar logic can be applied to the classification 'autism' (more specifically ASD). For instance, instead of saying that a child has ASD or not, fuzzy logic specifies a degree of membership which is in the interval between 0 (definitely not a member) and 1 (definitely a member). For instance, Hans' degree of membership to the set 'people with autism' is 0.6, which implies that his degree of membership to the complementary set, 'people without autism' is 0.4. Hans is both autistic and not autistic, and the extent to which he is both is expressed by the membership degrees.

The applicability of degrees of membership to psychiatric disorders follows from the fact that the classification into a particular disorder category is based on sets of criteria, a minimum number of which must apply, and which occur in variable degrees (e.g., degrees of deficit in non-verbal communicative behaviours). The term 'autistic' can be modified by linguistic variables such as 'typical', 'atypical', 'strongly', 'moderately', and these linguistic modifiers can be linked to degrees of membership.

Prototype diagnosis of psychiatric disorders provides a graded assessment of the extent to which individuals are similar to a prototype description or 'ideal case' description of a syndrome (DeFife et al., 2013; Jablensky, 2005; Westen, Shedler & Bradley, 2006; Westen, 2012; Nakash, Nagar & Westen, 2019). In this sense, it is a form of fuzzy classification, which can, in principle, be treated by means of the formal framework of fuzzy logic.

Although fuzzy logic could serve as a formal tool for dealing with the inherent uncertainty, vagueness and ambiguity of DSM-V disorder classifications, the literature offers only very scant consideration of this possibility (exceptions are Jablensky, 2005; and Kwiatkowska & Kielan, 2013 with an application to depression; Van Geert, 2002; Carvalho, 2013, for a dynamic interpretation). This is surprising as fuzzy logic has been successfully applied in engineering contexts, including image recognition, where differences of degree must be translated into control decisions in the form of yes–no decisions and of gradual interventions and control systems (Kosko, 1993; Arfi, 2010, Nguyen, Walker & Walker, 2018, Ragin, 2009; Siler & Buckley, 2005). Notwithstanding, the fact that decision and intervention based on fuzzy categories and properties are also of central concern in clinical applications (e.g., assigning a particular therapy to a client or not) the link with the latter still needs to be established.

The main reason why fuzzy logic has never been seriously embraced by research psychology is most likely the belief that vagueness and ambiguity result from the lack of knowledge about a world of essential 'crisp' and clear distinctions and classifications. This lack of knowledge, expressed in the form of vagueness and ambiguity, must be solved by obtaining more information (e.g., about the properties of a particular person's psychiatric disorder). However, in a world based on dynamics and complexity, human attempts toward crisp classification and distinction are doomed to fail, as phenomena are intrinsically transient and fluctuating, within certain limits or constraints that are themselves changeable. Hence, vagueness and ambiguity are intrinsic properties of the way human agents relate to the world. Instead of denying their existence, it is better to use tools, such as fuzzy logic, that can make this vagueness and ambiguity manageable.

Variability and fluctuations over time form the natural basis for a degree of membership description of psychological propensities, dispositions or abilities. For instance, young children show typical day-to-day fluctuations in mean length of utterance (MLU). In the standard praxis, we can view these fluctuations as random variations around a true MLU value that we can approximate by taking the average of those fluctuations. If we view the child's MLU as a 'fingerprint' or indicator of an underlying, complex dynamic network, we must consider all actual MLU's as information about this underlying system. However, some MLU values occur more often than others, that is, they are more typical or characteristic of this child, during this developmental period, than MLU values that occur considerably less often. For instance, we can take the 60 per cent most often occurring MLU's as the typical levels, with the remaining levels corresponding with decreasing typicality or distinctiveness (Van Geert, 2002; Van Dijk & Van Geert, 2005, 2007). These MLU values form a region (e.g., between MLU's of 1.2 to 1.7) to which we can assign a degree of membership of 1 to the class 'this child's MLU' (see Figure 10.1). The range with the degree of membership equal to 1 can be characterized as the child's (current) *typical* MLU region. MLU's of 2, for instance, are assigned a degree of membership of 0 (i.e., they are very atypical for this child at this moment, for the simple reason that they haven't been observed in the current corpus of child utterances). These values will of course shift as a consequence of the child's language development.

The idea of a region of typicality can of course be easily extended to any number of such underlying dimensions (i.e., to state spaces of arbitrary complexity). It can just as well be extended to categorical distinctions or categorical state spaces (for each categorically defined state of the system, there is a level of typicality or likelihood, at any time point). In fact, a typical state space grid with its representation of frequencies and dispersion

10.3 Vagueness and Ambiguity as Forms of Uncertainty 247

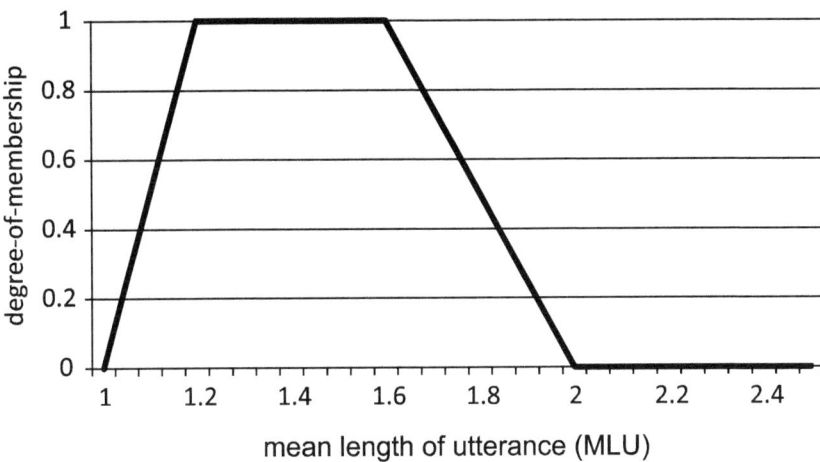

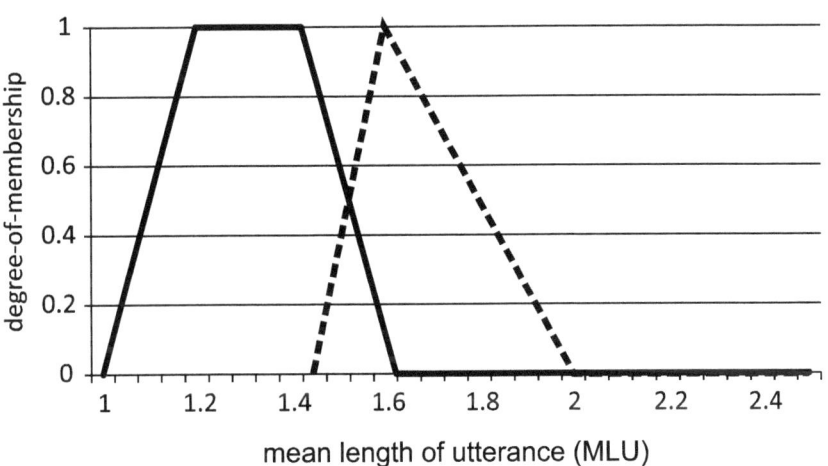

— egocentric speech context

- - - - - - conversation context

Figure 10.1 Instead of specifying a child's current MLU as an estimated, true point value (e.g., 1.5, which is the average of the observed MLU's), a fuzzy representation assigns MLU as a degree of membership. The graph above specifies a child as a member of an MLU class between 1.2 and 1.6, and as a non-member of the MLU class of 2, and as a 0.5-degree member of the MLU class 1.8. Fuzzy graphs can be assigned in a contextual way, e.g., in the context of egocentric speech or the context of conversation with an adult.

of states can be interpreted as a representation of the fuzzy and dynamic nature of the state of a system, such as a language learning child, over a particular period of time (e.g., Van Dijk & Van Geert, 2011). In fact, any measure of dispersion of performance levels or frequencies and magnitudes of symptoms may be used as a basis for a fuzzy logic specification of degrees of membership of the category 'typical of this particular person'.

Note that fuzzy regions can have a variety of forms (Van Geert, 2002). Assume for instance that the child's typical mean length of utterance is considerably bigger in a conversation with a parent than in a solitary speech activity, for instance, when a child accompanies its play activity with descriptive utterances. In this case, the child's MLU potential could be represented by a bimodal distribution (see Figure 10.1, bottom). Both the solitary speech activity and the conversation with a parent are highly characteristic contexts for this particular child's language production. The fuzzy description of the person-specific typicality of particular MLU levels combines with the typicality of the contexts in which these MLU levels are produced. We could of course bring the child to a very scary environment and observe that its MLU is basically reduced to 1. But this scary environment is – hopefully – highly uncharacteristic or atypical for this particular child's ecological condition. Let us say its typicality, expressed as the degree of membership, is virtually zero, which, if applied to the observed MLU value of 1, provides a degree of membership typicality of virtually 0 to this MLU value). In fact, by subsuming contexts under the same dimension of typicality or distinctiveness as the observed activities or performances, fuzzy logic representations may solve the contextual proliferation objection against the view that abilities or capacities are intrinsically context-dependent. This objection holds that a person's ability should be defined by measurements in all possible contexts, which is virtually impossible. However, the overwhelming majority of these possible contexts are likely to be highly uncharacteristic or atypical of the person in question, they hardly ever occur (e.g., because the person actively avoids them). This implies that any performance in such contexts would be equally uncharacteristic, and be absent from the specification of this person's typical performance levels. If applied to the case of intelligence, one might wonder to what extent the standard intelligence test is a typical or distinctive context for every person whose intelligence it pretends to measure.

In summary, a fuzzy function (e.g., Figure 10.1) provides a formal representation of our often vague and ambiguous beliefs or expectations with regard to the potential of a particular person in typical, person-specific, ecologically relevant contexts. Fuzzy logic offers a variety of technical tools for explicitly dealing with uncertainty in the form of vagueness and ambiguity, for instance, in the form of decisions with regard to interventions. Examples are the intensity of therapeutic intervention, or the level of financial family support for a child with a psychiatric disorder, which is assigned with a particular degree of membership. These tools can also be used for optimal 'defuzzifying', that is, for transforming degrees of membership into yes–no decisions (e.g., assigning therapy or not, sending a child to special education or not).

10.3.8 Working with Uncertainty

In this chapter, I compared two different views on uncertainty, including vagueness and ambiguity, that are relevant for psychological research and applications in the form of assessment, diagnosis and intervention.

The first, which stems from a substance-oriented ontology, views the world as consisting of intrinsically distinct substances (i.e., things, properties, psychological abilities and so forth) with properties endowed with specific true values. Our knowledge of the world is always limited: measurements for instance are always of limited precision, and what we measure is contaminated by accidental influences we cannot totally control and avoid. The difference between the true properties of the world and our knowledge of these properties expresses our uncertainty. The standard praxis of measurement and classification (e.g., psychiatric diagnosis) enacts these ontological assumptions, in the form of actual practices of measurement and concepts such as measurement error. In this chapter, I analysed these assumptions and concluded that practices of measurement and classification act like self-fulfilling procedures: they implicitly confirm the assumptions of clearly distinguished categories (e.g., natural kinds) and specific properties (e.g., true IQs).

The second, which stems from a processual, dynamic and complexity-oriented ontology, views the world as a place where things and properties are constantly changing, becoming rather than being, gradually or suddenly transformed into different things and properties. Our knowledge about this complex, dynamic world is given in the form of our continuous interaction with it, in a variety of activities that, among others, involve the use of inscription devices, models, formal procedures and so forth. Measurement and classification are in themselves processes of participating, intervening in and interacting with the world. Our human impressions of vagueness and ambiguity are in fact the direct reflections of the fundamental properties of a complex world that is in constant change and flux, yet governed by constraints and limitations, boundaries within which the changes occur. They are not only, or not by definition signs of our incomplete knowledge. They must be understood as expressions of emergence and of the complementarity of properties. Probability, the standard way of solving the problems of uncertainty, is not a unitary concept with a clearly defined meaning, and it must be treated with caution if it is used to describe the properties of the phenomena that psychologists are interested in. Dynamic systems theory, models and simulations on the one hand, and fuzzy logic on the other hand have been discussed as methods for dealing with the intrinsic vagueness and ambiguity of the world that we interact with as researchers in psychology.

CHAPTER II

Troubled Waters of Heraclitus' River?
A Process View on Reproducibility and Generalization in Psychological Research

> You could not step twice into the same river.
> Heraclitus, as quoted in Plato, Cratylus, 402a
>
> Everything happens only once, and at one place.
> Bruno Latour, *The Pasteurization of France* (1988, p. 162)

With his river metaphor (see opening quote above, described in Chapter 1), Heraclitus tells us that nothing stays the same, and nothing can be repeated exactly. The notion of 'repetition' is central in the mainstream praxis of psychological research, forming a main concern for many. But what do we mean when we demand replicability? How exactly do we want scientific studies to be repeated? Exact and full replication, or just the major properties? The methodology? The general results and the conclusions? If the world is a sort of river that you cannot step into twice, are we then not expecting something that is impossible when we demand the replicability and reproducibility of psychological studies and phenomena?

These questions are pertinent, given that an estimated number of 52 per cent of researchers in a broad range of sciences – including psychology – currently consider their science to be in a state of *crisis* (Baker, 2016; Sturm & Mülberger, 2012). They consider this crisis to be one of *reproducibility*, where only 40 per cent of scientific findings have been replicated (Open Science Collaboration, 2015). A frequently quoted article by John Ioannidis (2005), ominously entitled 'Why most published research findings are false', demonstrates this nicely. This article questions whether research findings actually represent general truths, such as *true* relationships between variables. For many, the future credibility of the field of psychology depends largely on the alleviation of this crisis.

11.1 The Reproducibility Crisis

The reproducibility discussion focusses on two different terms, namely *replicability* and *reproducibility*. The Latin roots of these words refer to different meanings. Replicability literally means something like 'fold back' or fold over something on something else, with the implication that something that you can fold back on something else has the same form or shape as the latter (as in the concept of a replica). Reproducibility, in contrast, means 'to bring forth again', with an intended meaning of bringing into being again.

According to the authors of the widely discussed replication study in psychology (Open Science Collaboration, 2015), replication studies should replicate the results of the original study. This begs the question, however: what is supposed to be the 'result'? Indeed, generating results involves the complex transformation of a stream of concrete sample-specific outcomes into decontextualized findings (this stream of transformations, or translations, will be explored below). For example, on its Digest webpage,[1] the British Psychological Society (BPS) published a list of '10 famous psychology findings that it's been difficult to replicate'[2]:

1. Power posing will make you act bolder
2. Smiling will make you feel happier
3. Self-control is a limited resource
4. Revising after your exams can improve your earlier performance
5. Exposure to words pertaining to ageing will make you walk more slowly
6. Cleaning your hands will wash away your guilt
7. Babies are born with the power to imitate
8. Big brother eyes make us behave more honestly
9. Sniffing the 'cuddle hormone' will make you more trusting
10. Being reminded of money makes us selfish

These statements are examples of 'results': they are the findings from psychological research that were thought to equate *facts*, and thus *truths* (Haig & Borsboom, 2012; Assay, 2018; Haig & Borsboom, 2018).

However, 'being true' is not an *intrinsic* property of the above statements. There is something that *makes* them true (or not), which means that 'truth' is the result of a specific process, namely *truthmaking* (MacBride, 2020). What is it that makes it true or not that smiling will make you feel

---

[1] https://digest.bps.org.uk/2016/09/16/ten-famous-psychology-findings-that-its-been-difficult-to-replicate
[2] Admittedly, these findings are rather mediagenic, but as befits a respectable society such as the BPS, the webpage refers to the original papers, to the research that did not reproduce the findings and to eventual rebuttals of the authors of the original studies.

happier? What is its *truthmaker*? According to Assay (2021), 'truthmaker theory is the branch of metaphysics that explores the relationships between what is true and what exists'. MacBride (2020) says that 'a truth-maker is that in virtue of which something is true' (p. 4). Thus, the truthmaker of the statement 'smiling will make you feel happier' is the fact that smiling makes people feel happier.

However, this fact is not openly and explicitly available. To demonstrate that this is indeed a *truth*, one needs research, done in accordance with approved procedures, and made publicly available in the form of publications. The problem is that there is a rather complicated relationship between the various steps that this process of truth making consists of. The collection of actual findings of the research, which we will probably find in the article's Results section, is not actually the same as the statement 'smiling makes you feel happier' that we find in the conclusion section of the research article. Each step requires a transformation to arrive at the next step, and these transformations are necessary steps of the process of truthmaking of the statement 'smiling makes you happier'. These transformations are virtually always left totally implicit. It is as if the specificity of the truthmaker of the general fact 'smiling makes you happier', namely the actual conditions, methodological procedures, manipulations and activities of the research, does not matter.

However, the large number of studies for which the outcomes cannot be replicated suggest that the process of truthmaking is all but unproblematic. If the process of truthmaking was unproblematic, a lack of replication would be rare: if a study carried out according to the standard methodological rules[3] has led to a truth, a similar study (i.e., a replication, should lead to the same truth. Many of the recommendations surrounding the reproducibility debate make a plea for a meticulous following of the original procedures, and for being explicit about all the variables that need to be controlled, in order for replication studies to be successful in terms of reproducibility of the original results (see for instance Zwaan et al., 2018; Baumeister & Vohs, 2016; Sripada, Kessler & Jonides, 2016). That is, the truth of a general statement 'smiling makes you happier' is 'made' by the very specific conditions that the research has realized.

It is also possible, however, that the requirement of exact methodological replication is indicative that the truth made by the research activity in

---

[3] As the studies that have been replicated have virtually all been properly reviewed, we can assume that lack of replicability is not due to insufficient methodological quality.

question is deeply context-specific (for a discussion of the implications for psychological theory, see Gollwitzer & Schwabe, 2021). From a complex dynamic systems view, this context-specificity holds for a great number of empirical findings in the social sciences, and thus, relatively poor replicability is not surprising at all (Wallot & Kelty-Stephen, 2018; Gernigon et al., 2021). Put differently, the failure of exact replication does not follow from psychology's lack of methodological rigour, but rather from psychology's failure to account for the nature and complexity of the human subject (Maiers, 2021).

11.2 Picking Apart the 'Crisis'

11.2.1 Heraclitus Wouldn't Be Bothered: A Culture of Expectations

So why does the general psychological community mind so terribly that results such as those above are so difficult to replicate? Heraclitus wouldn't mind, but then Heraclitus is long gone. It all begins with the specific beliefs we hold about what 'general facts' and 'generalizability' are. In mainstream psychology, these beliefs have resulted in an overly specific and limited praxis (see also Arocha, 2020; Lee & Baskerville, 2003; Van Geert, 2011, 2014; Salvatore & Valsiner, 2010; Lamiell, 2003).

For mainstream psychology, the commonly held belief is that having carefully followed specific procedures, in terms of composing the sample of subjects, applying specific research procedures and measurement instruments, leads to certain reliable and *general* conclusions. General conclusions are assumed to pertain to objective and invariant truths about general categories, such as 'babies' or 'honesty'. These categories are assumed to correspond with meaningful distinctions or divisions of nature; natural kinds.

This implies that any honest replica of your study that does not reproduce your results confronts you with a serious problem; namely, that the true fact that you hoped to demonstrate does not exist. For this reason, divergent conclusions must be mutually incompatible. If the results of two or more studies do not match, it must be concluded that at least one of the studies must have been done in a sloppy way (for instance, not having controlled the important variables, or having committed some other methodological sin). It is for this reason that the lack of reproducibility has led to a crisis. If it turns out that, not just an occasional study, but the majority of studies cannot be reproduced, then the credibility of the larger body of knowledge is at stake.

In addition, generic statements commonly used in academic articles tend to employ unclear extensional definitions of constructs. Articles often refer to categories using bare nouns, such as 'women' or 'autism', which implicitly creates extensional definitions that refer to indeterminate sets (i.e., *all* women, in all contexts, and at all moments in the past, present, and future, or at least some intermediate version of this)(see Chapter 6, where this practice is discussed in depth). Hence, general statements are statements about a whole set, or a whole population.

There are two issues here. First, it is (virtually) impossible to investigate a population in its entirety. Second, this is complicated even more because a population will almost always be an open set, for instance because its members come and go (by birth or death). If researchers thus believe in objective and invariant truths about natural kinds, and if they believe that it is possible to measure these truths via objective means, we can see why a crisis is inevitable. The leap between what researchers can realistically do with any given study (i.e., investigate a specific sample) and what they hope that this study will provide (i.e., an invariant truth that is the same as an invariant truth found in another similar study) is thus tremendous. Researchers are in fact expecting something of their studies that these studies will never be able to achieve.

As an intermediate compromise, generalization is thus often defined as the extent to which a statement about a representative sample is similar to a comparable statement about another representative sample, or to a more representative (i.e., bigger) sample of which the first is a subset. Here too, researchers are faced with a very real limitation, namely the samples that are available to them in the first place. Most samples consist of the WEIRD population (Western, Educated, Industrialized, Rich, and Democratic) (Rad, Martingano, & Ginges, 2018; Hruschka, 2018). The common concern is therefore that, even a very large sample (or a replication across samples) will not be able to realistically produce general statements that can conceivably represent an entire natural kind. Most problems of reproducibility relate to this particular form of generalizability, as other samples cannot reproduce the finding from the sample of the original study. As generalizability relates to the truth of a statement about a natural kind or natural kind relationships, absence of reproducibility implies that the original study must be wrong.

A companion assumption of generalizability as defined above is that results are explained by a superposition of variables (e.g., an observed difference in a dependent variable between two natural groups is explained by the additive superposition of all common independent variables that affect it plus the independent variable on which the two groups differ). That is, theories explaining psychological phenomena are *component-dominant*, meaning that the outcome is determined by the components (i.e., variables) themselves. The additivity or component-dominance assumption has direct implications for the reproducibility question: if variables make independent contributions, then controlling them (e.g., keeping them constant) should control the outcome. For example, manipulating whether someone smiles or not should have a meaningful effect on the happiness outcome. With this assumption, a *failure* to control an outcome via a predetermined variable implies that the universal law we thought exists does not exist (e.g., a causal relationship between smiling and happiness).

The above beliefs ultimately pertain to larger beliefs about the nature of reality (i.e., ontological beliefs) and about the ways in which reality can be known (i.e., epistemological beliefs). These are closely related: what we believe to be the basic properties of reality, such as the belief that there are independent and invariant underlying psychological variables or 'constructs', is closely connected with what we believe about how such features of reality can be known; for example, by measuring them by means of typical psychological tests that should be replicable. If researchers believe in a substance-oriented reality, they will indeed expect that underlying substances (universal entities in the form of natural kinds and universal truths) *should* be reliably discovered across contexts, across time, across activity. As we will describe in Section 11.3 an alternative is to *expect* and *focus* on the context-, time-, and activity-specific emergence of facts.

11.2.2 *A Restricted Account of What Constitutes 'Results'*

Part of the current replication crisis is that 'results' that are expected to be reproduced are in fact the generic statements (e.g., power posing makes people act bolder). These statements, however, are based on the study's concrete results, which are based on the analysis of the raw data, which have been treated for analysis, which are thus versions of the raw data, which were collected with very specific measurements (thus relating to the question of what counts as scientific data; Leonelli, 2015).

Given the layers of results implied in any empirical study, perhaps the purest result is the raw data itself. These can be conceived of as the primary facts. Etymologically, a 'fact' is something that has been done, has been made (in French 'fact' and 'made' are the same words, 'fait'). In that sense, the raw data are what results from applying certain research procedures to the real world (and applying such procedures is an effortful and laborious sort of work, requiring highly specific skills). Raw data are not regularly presented in the results section of research publications. However, there is increasing pressure to include raw data in the publication process, for instance, in the form of web-based materials. Furthermore, in some sub-disciplines of psychology the lines between data and analysis, and indeed results, are by nature quite blurred. For example, in Conversation Analysis a transcript is the data, but it is also where the analysis takes place, and where the results are displayed to the readers in publications. With this practice, there is thus a high degree of transparency with regard to where the results came from.

The collection of raw data and what we do with this data is not a trivial part of the generalization procedure, and perhaps raw data should therefore have a more central role in the discussion of generalizability. With the same set of raw data you can do an almost infinite number of different interpretive things. Reaction times provide an interesting example for this. Reaction times can be processed on the basis of the associations between variables, but they can also be processed as within-individual time series of decision-making events. We have seen that, if one does the latter, the raw data of reaction time experiments may reveal interesting hidden results, such as the existence of scale invariance of reaction times, or the fact that the variation in reaction times reveals so-called 1/f noise (see Gilden, 2001; Kello et al., 2010). These data, which have always been present in the raw data of reaction time experiments, were typically discarded in favour of group aggregated statistics.

Next, every psychological research activity generates an array of facts – events, behaviours, feelings, interpretations, hesitations and so forth of the subjects – that are in fact not even recorded. However, these events are a result of the research activity, and could just as well be used as the focus of the study (for an example, see the section on *A qualitative account* in Chapter 5 on processual self-esteem research). Not only are these events interesting as results on their own, these 'irrelevant' actions can also dramatically change both the outcome of the process *and* the interpretation of the underlying mechanisms of the outcome (this is clearly demonstrated in the process approach to the A-not-B error, as described in Chapter 6).

Next, we have the statistical outcomes. Suppose we have a study in which we found a correlation of 0.4 between two variables A and B. Our research finding could be any of the following: a) there is a correlation of 0.4 in this particular sample, in this particular context and time of testing and with this particular sample; b) there is a correlation of 0.4 between A and B in the population that this particular sample represents;

c) there is an enormous amount of difference between the individuals with regard to how their individual values of variables A and B interact (with a correlation of 0.4, there is indeed a very considerable amount of inter-individual variability, since only 16 per cent variability is shared by the A and B variables); or d) the association between A and B is considerably weaker (or stronger) than we expected. There are thus various interpretations about what is meaningful with regard to a concrete outcome.

The trivial conclusion is that what counts as facts or results depends on the nature of one's orientation to research, one's research question, and ultimately, the ontology that the particular research praxis enacts. As described in the previous sections, the substance-oriented praxis privileges the final stages of this generalization process as 'results', but there are many previous steps in the research process that are informative, meaningful, and interesting, and which can contribute to the generalization process in their own way.

11.2.3 *Underdeterminacy: One of Many Roads*

Above, we described the various steps in the research process that may, in fact, be conceptualized as results. The reproducibility requirement that most researchers hope to achieve refers to a very specific series (both in content and order) of these results: standard reproducibility requires a particular kind of research activity (e.g., a specific scale must be used, or a specific experiment), a specific transformation of a specific selection of the data generated (e.g., averages of particular variables), a specific analysis of this data (e.g., inferential statistics), and a specific type of conclusion (e.g., a generic statement about a social or conceptual category, or about a universal law, such as autism, honesty, or the relationship between X and Y, respectively).

Given the etymology of 'fact' (a thing made or done) and 'data' (a thing given), the results of research demonstrate a tension between being made and being given. Specifically, the objectivist assumption that characterises much of mainstream psychology suggests that data will speak for themselves, revealing the underlying truth that they instantiate. What we hoped to have demonstrated above, however, is that facts are indeed *created* (which is not the same as 'made up' or 'invented'), and that this constructive process can take many more directions than the standard praxis would suggest.

The specific series of results that the standard reproducibility requirement expects is what the science-and-technology-studies approach calls the 'hinterland' of a particular research activity (Law, 2004). It is a description of the prescribed set of related activities and theoretical orientations that researchers are expected to enact. The hinterland of the replication process in mainstream psychological science enacts an important substance-oriented belief. The dominant practice of using central tendencies (e.g., averages) and inferential statistics (e.g., regressions) as the expected series of results enacts the belief that *persons or individuals are random instantiations of a specific variable (or specific variables, for that matter)*, and moreover, that *variables are invariant universals* (i.e., they are universal properties common to a particular natural kind).

Hence, it is assumed that by aggregating over individuals, the 'real' (underlying) universal property (and its 'real' relationship with other real universal variables) can be reconstructed. This set of beliefs typically leads to a reproducibility-of-results requirement that is fulfilled by a particular study (i.e., it is the task of *a replication study* to reproduce a result). Reproducing a truth is thus something that is done within one study, via a restricted set of research steps. This belief, and the resulting praxis (of a restricted route that must be taken to achieve reproducibility) has become so ubiquitous and pervasive that, for many researchers, an alternative is simply unimaginable.

It is important to realize that these beliefs – and associated research norms – are *underdetermined* by the available empirical evidence, i.e. the facts. That is, they do not logically or compellingly follow from these facts. This is referred to as the underdeterminacy or Duhem-Quine thesis. The beliefs and research norms that have led to (and maintain) the replication crisis are held together by, what Quine referred to as the *web of belief* (Quine & Ullian, 1978; Resnik, 2007). Scientific knowledge, and knowledge in general, forms a network of beliefs, experiences, facts, and practices, which stand in supportive or competitive relationships with one another. The beliefs and practices described above, therefore, support each other, and keep each other active (this notion is explored more globally in Chapter 12). Moreover, the facts themselves (that researchers try to reproduce) are part of this web. They too cannot be verified or falsified in isolation. A particular failure to reproduce a finding (a particular fact), therefore, does not necessarily mean that that fact is false, or that the beliefs or the theory built upon that fact is incorrect (e.g., Haig, 2021).

Furthermore, it is not the responsibility of one study – or its exact replication(s) – to create, prove, or reproduce a fact. Instead, evidence is something that is gathered across time, contexts, and with a variety of different research actions and results. This is what the process approach to generalization supports, which we will describe below.

11.3 A Process Approach to Generalization and Reproducibility

11.3.1 Expecting Variability

The dominant discourse regarding the necessary solutions to the reproducibility or replication crisis is one of ever refined and stricter methodological recommendations (Open Science Collaboration, 2015; Nelson, Simmons & Simonsohn, 2018; Nosek, Spies & Motyl, 2012; Klein et al., 2012; Ferguson & Heene, 2012; Curran & Hussong, 2009; Flora, 2020; Wagenmakers et al., 2012; Shrout & Rodgers, 2018; Zwaan et al., 2018; Nosek et al., 2021). While these kinds of refinement may be valuable, we believe that they overlook the real theoretical issue; namely, what should (and can) we expect of psychological phenomena? Is it reasonable to expect phenomena to behave similarly (or indeed the *same*) across separate studies (reproducibility) and across separate individuals (generalizability)? As we have discussed in the previous sections, clearly, mainstream psychology-researchers believe that these expectations are reasonable, and necessary conditions for demonstrating *real* truths. As we showed, these expectations enact a larger belief in the nature of reality as substance-oriented.

The main departure that a process-oriented approach takes is that we can (and should) *not* expect phenomena to replicate across contexts and to generalize across individuals, at least not in the way that standard psychology expects. Instead, any result (i.e., from the stage of data to the final conclusion drawn) is inherently context- and time-dependent. Moreover, a particular psychological study is also a context- and time-dependent event. It is therefore impossible to 'replicate' studies, as it is simply impossible to *step twice into the same river*. There may be explicitly intended and realized similarities between a replication study and the original study, but the inevitable differences afford their own context-dependent research activities, participant experiences, data collection and treatment practices. A lack of reproducibility is then to be expected for every, and any, sample and experiment.

In this way, a variable is not conceived as an independent and invariant entity. It must be seen as intrinsically connected to *the context of particular persons* engaging with other particular persons, in a particular point in time and in a particular context. Variability in how a variable emerges in a particular study (and how it relates to another variable) is thus to be expected (Arocha, 2020; Van Geert & Van Dijk, 2002).

The notion of controlling variables in order to unravel how variables (which are usually in fact *processes*) interact is another assumption that

11.3 A Process Approach to Generalization and Reproducibility 261

cannot be realistically held. In standard psychological practice, the 'control' of variables is a statistical operation on data stemming from independent subjects (the traditional representative samples). The universal law (i.e., association between variables) that the process-oriented researcher is interested in, however, is *not* one of between-individual differences. For example, questions of what happens when we clean our hands, are exposed to certain words, or adopt certain physical positions, are all *individual process*-questions. The idea that the standard between-person control pertains to underlying processes that take place within individuals is an example of an unproven ergodicity assumption (see Chapter 9). Phenomena that researchers claim to control are therefore, in reality, actually entangled processes interacting within persons, in the context of materials, context, and time (e.g., Wallot & Kelty-Stephen, 2018; Gernigon et al., 2021); they cannot be manipulated independently of one another.

Instead of seeing this as threatening or a lost cause, however, we can see the *inherently variable* and *context-dependent* nature of phenomena as an opportunity to understand the phenomena. If a result (i.e., the behaviour of a system or phenomenon) is situated and emergent, this provides an opportunity to understand the context-specific activities on the short-term timescale of the research project itself, and the long-term timescale of the scientific histories into which this particular result is embedded (Law, 2004). It is an opportunity to map and follow the behaviour of this phenomenon as a complex dynamic systems, or as an an actor in a larger actor network (from Latour's perspective, see Chapter 1; Latour, 1987; Latour & Woolgar, 1979; Law, 2004; Harman, 2009).

11.3.2 Patterns as the Aim of Generalization

Crucially then, a process-oriented approach to research does not require or presuppose reproducibility of specific results, in the sense of 're-producing' the numbers, events, and actions observed during the study. These smaller 'results' *underdetermine* outcomes, and thus, true properties of the population. This does not mean that process researchers are unconcerned with reproducibility or generalizability, however. Instead, *what* we aim to reproduce across contexts or individuals refers to theoretically relevant *features* of the *processes* involved. For example, in Chapter 5 we showed how extremely different contexts for valenced self-experience (including dyadic interaction, isolated self-reflection, and situated daily-experiences; in De Ruiter et al., 2015; Wong, 2014; and Fortes et al., 2004, respectively) and diverging operationalizations of self-esteem (i.e., concrete behavioural or affective performances or expressions of self-experience, narratives, self-reports) all demonstrated patterns of self-maintaining intrinsic dynamics. This process characteristic is crucial for understanding the nature of self-esteem as a process, and works to re-conceptualize self-esteem from the previous baseline conceptualization (e.g., Kernis et al., 1993).

Moreover, a particular case is not intended to 'represent' a specific population in the common sense of that word. Instead, a single case (or collection of cases) 'stand for' other cases. 'Standing-for' does not mean 'being similar to all others', but instead, representing a possibility. A single case shows that a particular property is possible, and that it is *likely* – to some extent – to occur for others. As single-case studies are repeated, that possibility becomes more and more likely, and perhaps more and more concrete with regard to its specific manifestation. Patterns can thus be identified across cases, increasing the likelihood that the finding is a possibility for a larger population (Holden & Lynch, 2004). This assumption is foundational for many fields that primarily adopt qualitative approaches, where it is common and accepted practice to generalize about highly complex and processual phenomena when a small number of cases is collected that demonstrate this phenomenon. In line with this, any divergent outcomes between case studies must be turned into potentially interesting information that can shed further light on possible affordances or constraints that stem from the different contexts, for example.

11.3.3 *Generalization and Reproducibility as a Reflective and Long-Term Process*

Generalization (e.g., across contexts or samples) is not something that we as researchers can expect as a single-study outcome. But we can expect generalization to emerge from a long-term process of accumulating, reflecting upon, and theorizing about concrete and situated findings. We must then shift our expectations from findings as *absolute* and *revealing of invariant truths* to *contextually explanatory* and *revealing of possible characteristics* (Gordon, 1991). Studies of processes, e.g. of individual persons, are idiographic, they refer to specific cases (Piccirillo & Rodebaugh, 2019; Picione, 2015; Van Geert & Fischer, 2009). Yet, every study, in its similarity or dissimilarity to previous studies sharing some goal, method, or design, adds to our understanding of the phenomenon in question and helps guide our reflections and hypotheses about relevant dynamics or processes.

As such, a process view of generalization views it as a process of *inference to the best generalization*. Generalization is not a fact, but a process. It emerges from the connections and resonance between empirical, methodological and theoretical studies, which are necessarily conducted by many researchers across time. All of the relevant information is then gathered in an attempt to arrive at the *best possible explanation* for a *relatively broadly defined* phenomenon.

Generalization, in this sense, is an approach that is similar to the principle of *inference to the best explanation* (Vogel, 1998; Lipton, 2000; Douven, 2021): the best explanation is based on criteria such as depth, comprehensiveness, simplicity, and unifying power (Vogel, 1998). Abduction is a specific form of this type of reasoning, developed by the philosopher Charles Sanders Peirce, to provide an alternative to deduction and induction, which are both limited forms of inference in terms of coming to overarching explanations. Although Peirce's treatment of abduction is far from consistent (Douven, 2021), Salvatore (2020) provides a quote from Peirce that helps to clarify what it means: 'abduction is the form of reasoning that infers the cause from the effect, through the reconstruction of the dynamics mediating between the former and the latter' (Salvatore, 2020, p. 191, referring to work Peirce published in 1897 and 1902). Abduction thus stresses the need to examine actual within-individual processes (as these are where the dynamics occur that mediate the cause and effect), and the need to *follow* this process as closely as possible in order to understand it (something that we described in Chapter 1 as characteristic of the process approach).

The long-term process of inference to the best generalization (which includes the process of abduction or inference to the best explanation) thus implies many different sorts of generalization activities, such as doing creative and exploratory original empirical work as well as replication studies, large-scale as well as case-study work, theory building and simulation models, and relying on cross-disciplinary explanations (e.g., Valsiner, 2019). This proposal therefore supervenes the dominant proposals for how to remedy the current crisis, and simply makes room for a broader approach that will ultimately improve the quality of research. All information counts, therefore; at least in principle. From this perspective, even fraudulent research may teach us important lessons about our tacit prejudices regarding valuable research facts and publication-acceptance culture, as the famous case of one Dutch social psychologist has very clearly revealed (Abma, 2012; Crocker & Cooper, 2011; Markowitz & Hancock, 2014).

The view on scientific generalization as a long-term process of abduction and inference to the best explanation, given all available data and theory, corresponds with our critical realist stance on research. This stance conceives of the cyclical, dynamic relationship between reflection, facts, instruments, procedures, theories, models and technologies as the driving force of science (Pilgrim, 2019).

11.4 Conclusion: Stepping into the River

We began this chapter with our feet in Heraclitus' fleeting river. We then asked ourselves what this metaphor might imply for the future of the science of psychology. Does psychology have a future, qua science, if the phenomena it studies are changing all the time, for instance if they depend on fleeting contexts or historical conditions? The question is urgent in light of what is currently seen as a serious crisis in psychology – one of the many that psychology seems to have been struggling with Sturm & Mülberger, 2012) – and which is known as the crisis of reproducibility or replicability. Results that cannot be reproduced are typical cases of Heraclitian fluidity. Full of hope you step into the same river, that is, you reproduce the research activities someone else performed earlier. But then, to your dismay, you find that the river is not the same or that 'other waters flow around your feet'. If that occurs too often – and it indeed seems to do so – psychology has indeed a dim future in store.

The answer presented by the majority of contributors to the current discussion of the crisis is that our only hopes for a brighter future are to change our habits of doing research: explicitly specifying and controlling all the variables that contribute to our results, make the raw data accessible to other researchers, specify and publish the predictions and methods in advance and so forth. In order to promote a cumulative science of psychology, some researchers hold that the future lies in the accumulation of small effects, as small effects is what we should expect to find given the complexity of psychological phenomena (Götz, Gosling & Rentfrow, 2021). Others call for large effect sizes as the stepping stones toward a more reliable psychological science (e.g., Fanelli, Costas, & Ioannidis, 2017).

But we believe any methodologically driven solution (or collection thereof) is both impossible and insufficient. First, it is impossible to achieve what many researchers want to achieve; namely, the controlled reproduction of outcomes that are actually inherently variable and context-dependent within-individual processes (see Section 11.3.1 for our argumentation).

Second, the introduction of more specific or rigorous methods or analyses is an insufficient response to the crisis, as such a crisis requires a deeper ontological and epistemological reflection about the nature of reality and the expectations we can realistically place on the behaviour of systems (Gernigon, Den Hartigh, Vallacher & Van Geert, 2021). Indeed, the majority of recommendations to placate the crisis are further enactments of a substance ontology (Morawski, 2021), and thus work to further entrench expectations of reproducibility, which we argue will exacerbate (rather than alleviate) the crisis.

Crises in psychology seem to be recurrent phenomena for our discipline (Sturm & Mülberger, 2012). From Vygotsky's description of a lack of coherence of psychology as a science in the late 1920s (Vygotsky, 1997), to the crises that emerged in social psychology in the 1970s (Dafermos, 2015), to the general crisis of psychology and its problematic relationship with practice (Teo, 1998) and theory (Eronen & Bringmann, 2021), to our current replication crisis, our field abounds with crises. Rather than responding to these waves of concern with a tightening of empirical approaches, such crises invite more serious reflection upon internal contradictions that need to be solved.

We must therefore begin by acknowledging the implicit and underlit, yet clearly evident, 'contest over the nature of psychology's objects' (Morawski, 2021, p. 12). If we can then come to embrace psychology's objects as fundamentally dynamic and time- and context-dependent, this ontological shift will then have implications for our approach to fundamental issues such as measurement, explanation, generalization and so forth (e.g., Dale & Duran, 2013). As such, we believe that the only true solution to the current 'crisis' is a general shift in meta-physical assumptions and the corresponding shift in praxis, which we will explore in the following chapter (Chapter 12).

CHAPTER 12

Psychological Science as a Complex Dynamic System
From an Entrenched Substance-Oriented Praxis to the Emergence of a Process-Oriented Praxis

> Working together 'may take place between parts of a system, between systems or even between scientific disciplines'.
> Haken, 'Synergetics', *Scholarpedia*, 2(1), p. 1400

Psychological science is a constructive process. We construct knowledge, ontologies, and by virtue of this, realities. These constructive processes are centred around a particular 'object' of study that is, unlike physical objects, malleable, variable, and intrinsically dynamic and interconnected: people. What we aim to reveal in this book is that our field demonstrates a fundamental disconnect between this obvious fact (i.e., the evident processual nature of people), and the knowledge we are constructing about how people function. This book lays bare the multitude of ways in which psychological science enacts an ontology of fixed, enduring, and isolable 'things', rather than processes. We hope that, for readers, the obvious conclusion of this disconnect is to embrace the processual nature of people, and to adapt our constructive processes to it. While we can carry on tightening the reins on our current methodological practices in an attempt to eliminate variability, uncertainty, and 'noise' in our data, we ask: is it not more obvious to adapt our methodologies to the nature of people, so that we are able to truly understand human functioning?

While the sheer number of ways in which knowledge construction diverges from the processual nature of real people may seem unnavigable, what we also wish to stress is that psychological science is a system of activity. Our current entrenchment in a substance orientation is not a static property of psychological science, nor is it immutable. Psychological science is a praxis, emerging from our actions and interactions with each other. Actions and interactions are variable and dynamic, they are changeable. Recognition of the underlying and implicit ontologies that our practices enact is necessary to lay bare the limits and constraints that they put on our field and on the 'object' of our study, namely individual people. Making this explicit allows us to then reflect on the ways in which our praxis may be redirected, so that practices may enact a more appropriate ontology of processes.

In this final chapter, we concretely demonstrate what this proposed shift might look like and how it may come about by conceiving of psychological science itself as a complex dynamic system. In doing so, this chapter takes what we have attempted to convey throughout the book about praxes and action, about entrenchment of enacted ontologies, and complex dynamic systems, and applies it to psychological science as an active system. We describe how the current state of psychological science can be characterized as an entrenched attractor state, and how the emergence of a new attractor state – marked by a process approach – may come about.

This chapter functions as our concluding chapter, drawing on the themes that we have discussed in various chapters and tying them together to demonstrate a praxis shift in psychological science. It uses concepts from complex dynamic systems theory (Chapter 2) to concretely discuss how a shift can be made in a praxis via enacted ontologies (Chapters 4 and 5, and Chapters 6–11 by extension), specifically a shift toward a praxis that enacts a process ontology (Chapter 1) and is value-laden and action based (Chapter 3).

12.1 Mechanisms of Praxis Development

12.1.1 The Formation of Actant Networks

Key to the notion of psychological science as a complex dynamic system is the concept of agents. As we described in Chapter 3, Latour referred to all components within a praxis as 'actants' (which we refer to as 'agents'). This conceptualization emphasizes the constructivist nature of our everyday doings. When we do psychological science (discuss findings with or suggest readings to students or colleagues, or select a methodological framework for our next empirical study) our actions affect others. Thus, each action is not isolated in the here and now, but acts upon other agents. As agents interact over time, they become linked, forming networks of agents spread across communities of psychological scientists and the public.

In network theory, the agents within the network are the network's nodes, and the interactions between them are the connections between the nodes, also called vertices (see Figure 12.1).

The conceptualization of nodes as 'agents' stresses the dynamic nature of the network, where the interactions (demonstrated by the connections in

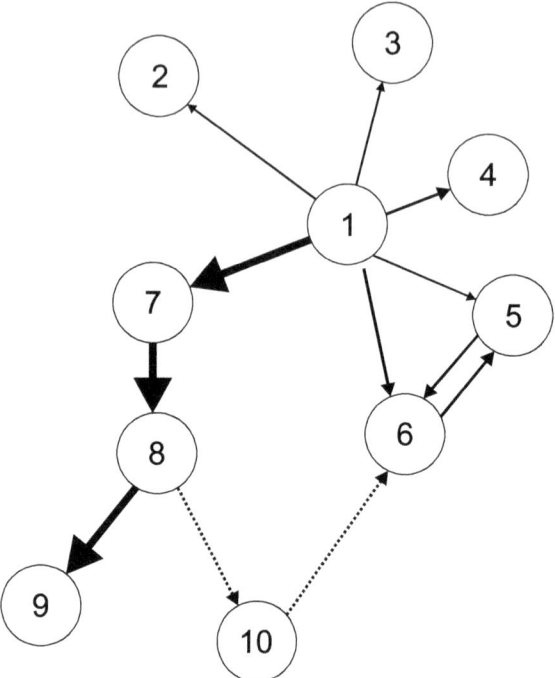

Figure 12.1 A simple and generic network representation of coupled dynamics between components. Arrows are the vertices, which are the causal relationships between nodes; dashed arrows represent negative relationships, solid arrows represent positive relationships. The size of the arrows corresponds with the coupling strength; and the size of the circles corresponds with the value of each variable at the current time (see also Chapter 8, and the discussion of Figure 8.4).

the network) are forces. One node thus acts upon another, by virtue of the other node's susceptibility to or cooperation with the first. These connections have a direction (which can also be bi-directional) and a strength. For example, when one of us (Paul or Naomi; node 1) reads a particular article (node 2), our reading of it may have a small positive impact on the article (for instance, we add one download to the list of downloads of the article, or we add one citation to the long list of citations the article already has). Next to this, our reading of the article might have a small to moderate positive impact on a handful of students to whom we recommend the article (nodes 3, 4, 5, and 6; student 5 and 6 have a mutual moderate positive effect on each other's appreciation of the article). Our reading of the article has a great positive impact on the aim of our next study (node 7), and thus on the article that we will be publishing next (node 8), which then has a high positive impact on one reader (node 9) and a moderate negative impact on another reader, a colleague of ours, who dislikes our article (node 10), and who has a small negative impact on student 6's appreciation of the article, and so forth.

Not only do our everyday actions function as agents that influence other actions (making the network dynamic), but the nature of the influence itself may also change over time. For example, our enthusiasm for the article (node 1) may gradually diminish, such that the connections between node 1 and the other nodes become weaker – potentially disappearing in the future. The vertices between nodes are thus not immutable and static descriptions of relationships, but real-time processes between activities, which will strengthen or weaken depending on what else emerges (or does not emerge) in the larger network.

12.1.2 Emergence of a Higher-Order Praxis

Importantly, the nature of agents within a network will demonstrate some kind of unity or coherence. In the case of psychological science as a network, this coherency might be a certain orientation toward a specific ontology – a worldview (Overton, 2015) and a corresponding approach. With coherence, we refer to the notion of *resonance*, as defined in ecological, Gibsonian psychology, where organisms are tuned to the properties of environments or other organisms, and vice versa (Gibson, 1966, 1979). Resonance allows organisms to synchronize with, and easily adapt to those properties, without requiring explicit representations of the assumptions that make this resonance possible.

The notion of resonating with the properties of our environment highlights how our everyday actions as researchers become aligned with larger values and norms that characterize the academic (and larger societal) culture in which we act. Researchers, and practices in general, begin to resonate with a mainstream commitment to a substance ontology without this being their intentional focus. This is not to say that the nature or the particular resonance must remain implicit. Of course, researchers can critically reflect on their underlying assumptions, and adapt their practices to what these critical reflections tell them. And indeed, according to critical realism they should regularly do so. However, such reflections are easily suppressed by the flow of daily, habitual research activities.

Aligning our practices with the mainstream ontological orientation is therefore a natural course of action, and does not require us to reflect on it.

In this way, any choices that we make (a choice to read or not read a certain article, to use one article over another one as the theoretical foundation for a study, a choice for one method over another) is an implicit enactment of underlying philosophical assumptions. In this way, mainstream philosophical assumptions have an 'orienting effect on one's scientific work' (Herbert & Padovani, 2015, p. 225). Researchers will thus naturally be inclined to align their practices with these deep-seated philosophical assumptions; drawn to methods, theoretical frameworks, conferences, and collaborations that resonate with them.

12.1.2.1 A Self-Maintaining Praxis via Self-Organization

The notions of resonance, alignment, and potential coherence bring us to the complex dynamic systems concept of *self-organization* (see Chapter 2). When agents in a network interact, the ongoing reinforcing and reciprocal effects that they have on each other results in the formation and transformation of patterns. We can think of these patterns as being the resonance, alignment, and coherence between researchers, practices, and their environment. What is stressed here though, is that while the larger environment (including widespread ontological assumptions) may 'orient' agents in a particular direction (Herbert & Padovani, 2015), this does not imply a rigidly or unidirectional causal process. These patterns emerge through the interaction between agents, while situated in an environment that affords certain interactions. The principle of self-organization also highlights how the patterns that emerge are both self-maintaining and adaptive. These two characteristics (i.e., self-maintaining and adaptive) are crucial for understanding the behaviour of a system such as psychological science, and we will return to them in more depth later.

The patterns that arise from this self-organizational process are typically referred to as *emergent* properties. They are higher-order properties that cannot be reduced to the sum of their parts (see Chapter 2). A praxis can be conceptualized as an emergent property. It is self-maintaining, yet adaptive, and the nature of this praxis cannot be reduced to any specific agents. As such, the praxis that characterizes psychology is itself not a static property, but an emergent property. It is a property that self-maintains itself while potentially adapting through the process of self-organization. Conceiving of our psychological praxis in these dynamic terms is useful, as it provides a way to concretely think about our research practices as emerging through the interconnections between individual, social, and cultural processes (Raeff, 2016). Moreover, this conceptualization allows us to reflect on how these interconnections give rise to the emergence of a substance-oriented praxis specifically, and how we may self-organize in a new direction; toward a process approach.

12.1.2.1.1 Self-Organization of a Substance Orientation As we argued throughout this book, the higher-order norms, values, worldviews, and praxis of psychological science are currently characterized by a general and persistent orientation toward phenomena as quantifiable and static entities, entities that produce and generate certain outcomes and are themselves predicted by static antecedents. This is an orientation which we refer to in this book as a *substance orientation* (see Chapter 1), and which corresponds with what Overton (2015) describes as a mechanistic and Cartesian-split worldview.

This substance orientation can be seen at all levels of the dominant research praxis (illustrated in Chapters 4 and 5), which is what we aimed to lay bare in the various chapters of our book. At a broad level, science demonstrates a culture of competition and production (Chapter 3). At the level of shared scientific aims, psychological science is primarily driven by the need to predict static outcomes, and to do this in such a way that they can be replicated across contexts and generalized across individuals (Chapter 11). At the level of how findings are shared and communicated with others, psychology focusses on categorization and generic statements (Chapter 6). At the level of how research aims are specifically realized, our discipline is fraught with the application of manipulationist cause–effect models of causation (Chapters 7 and 8) and the measurement of phenomena as static and independent entities (Chapters 9 and 10).

12.1.2.1.2 Emergent Substance-Orientation with Causal Power Higher-order properties are not epiphenomenal. That is to say, they are not simply produced without further consequences for the behaviour of the system. Here we return to the core characteristic of 'self-maintenance' introduced in Section 1.2.1: The emergent properties (i.e., general practices) of the psychological-science system have causal power over the behaviour of the system, allowing the system to maintain itself through its own dynamic interactions. We will break this down below.

First, higher-order properties of psychological science are not epiphenomenal because they also take part in *horizontal causality* (described in Chapter 8), where interaction occurs between practices on the same level. This horizontal causality then gives way to yet higher-order properties. An emergent property is both an outcome and the input for further 'horizontal' causal processes. Because of this constant horizontal causation between emergent practices, each level becomes nested in yet larger emergent properties. No emergent property is the 'final' outcome.

At the lowest level of our psychological-science system, we have the concrete acts, inscription devices, and interactions that psychologists take part in and rely on to conduct research. The interaction between these (horizontal) concrete acts gives way to shared practices of linguistic communication-norms, causal-explanation models, measurement norms, and shared scientific aims. These (horizontal) practices then give way to yet higher-level practices, such as an academic culture of competition and production. The emergent academic culture most certainly interacts with other horizontal properties, such that they are nested within a general societal culture of capitalism, for example.

Second, higher-order properties are not epiphenomenal because of the constraining effect that these properties have on lower-order interactions (Haken, 2007). This is *downward causation* or *constraint*; see Chapters 2 and 8, and Witherington & Heying, 2015). Downward causation brings us back to the 'self-reinforcing' characteristic of emergent properties that we referred to earlier: a particular praxis becomes robust through its constant 'orienting' effect on individuals' behaviour. Once emergent practices emerge, they therefore do not simply exist as a static description of psychological science. These properties then 'act' on the system's behaviour and have causal power over those very interactions that gave way to their emergence. This is true for each level of the system, where every emergent property or practice loosely constrains the interactions between lower-level practices, all the way down to our choices for concrete inter(actions) and materials.

This downward causation (or 'orienting' effect) makes it more likely that lower-level practices will resonate, or be in line with, the higher-level properties. Filip Vostal (2016) described this in 'Accelerating Academia: The Changing Structure of Academic Time', where he described how ideologies of acceleration in academia normalize and encourage pressure for more publications in less time, increased competition, and increased standards of excellence. In a similar vein, Vostal (Vostal, 2016; Vostal, Benda & Virtová, 2019) describes how these ideologies function like self-fulfilling prophecies that shape the lived experiences of temporality in academic work. 'Temporality' here refers to the standard timing of research activities, for instance the time one is expected to write and publish an article (and thus the number of articles one is expected to publish within one academic year), to complete a PhD, or to start and finish a research grant. These ideologies are similar to those we described in Chapter 3 (in our discussion of Aristotle and Arendt), relating to doing research for the sake of production (*poiesis* of *episteme*) rather than for the act of research itself (*phronesis*), and engaging in research as 'work' rather than 'action'.

Accelerated temporality also relates to the issue of replicability and reproducibility of scientific results (discussed in Chapter 11). These pressures reduce the chances of deliberate, extensive checks on research results, including self-replication, or of the publication of negative results. It also hampers the accumulation of person-specific research, required for the population-generalization of processual data on psychological phenomena.

A capitalist-based society clearly orients academia toward the acceleration of production and the 'dog-eat-dog world' that academia has become. Research practices that have more 'market value' will thus be more competitive in such a world (Vostal, 2016). Specific practices that have more market value in psychology are those that communicate sellable outcomes of prediction and categorization (discussed in Chapters 4, 6, and 7), which are based on large-sample studies and inferential statistics. Highly marketable practices are thus prioritized and chosen over 'slow' methods that involve the meticulous observation of how processes function in individuals and in contexts (Schiff, 2017).

Similarly, the pressure to treat scholarly work as the production of sellable 'products' constrains the work of researchers by orienting them toward specific types of research. Types of research that lend themselves more readily to generalizable and generic statements will be privileged, as these kinds of facts can be neatly packaged and communicated. Think back to statements such as 'Power posing will make you act bolder' or 'Sniffing the "cuddle hormone" will make you more trusting' described in Chapter 11. Here the lack of replication is not what is relevant, but the popularity of these kinds of statements. These are the kinds of statements that spread through networks of users of psychological knowledge. Indeed, few people will not have heard of 'power posing' and the 'cuddle hormone'.

To generate research facts that lend themselves to these kinds of statements, researchers will be encouraged to pursue variable-oriented approaches. Studying variables, like 'boldness' or 'oxytocin', means that these constructs must be 'measured' in the standard sense. They must be as 'objective' as possible. When drafting a proposal for a prestigious curiosity-driven grant, for example, researchers are technically free to pursue any topic and to propose any methodological approach. However, the competitive nature of these grants incentivises applicants to choose more mainstream, accepted – indeed objective – types of research (Alberts et al., 2014), often resulting in an inclination toward sub-disciplines that have a more natural-science orientation (Madsen & Aagaard, 2020) – like the case of oxytocin. Topic choice, while seemingly free, is thus highly constrained. Little room is given to pursue interpretive, conceptual, and small-scale research approaches – those approaches that generally demonstrate a commitment to a process ontology.

The above ideologies all enact a substance ontology in their focus on, or need for, universal and fixed truths. In this way, they all constrain the autonomy and the degrees of freedom of individual agents in the same way. The temporality, methodological approaches, and the content of academic activities in psychological science are all oriented toward a substance approach. This is not to say that academic activity is *determined*. The process of downward causation still affords a (often very) small degree of freedom to counter this constraint (but we will explore this more in Section 12.3.1).

12.1.2.1.3 The Role of Feedback Loops in Maintaining an Entrenched Attractor State An important explanatory concept for understanding downward causation is the emergence of entrenched *attractor states* (Chapter 2). This is a specific property that the system is 'attracted' (or drawn) to, such that this specific property is actively maintained or reproduced by the system via interactions between its components, making it a state to which the system repetitively returns. The system either maintains or frequently returns to it because maintaining it requires less energy relative to alternative states (see our description of attractor landscapes in Chapter 2; Thelen & Smith, 1994; Friston & Ao, 2012).

'Maintaining or frequently returning' to a particular property is something that the agents in the system do in their interactions with each other. The substance-ontology praxis (as a higher-order property) of psychological science repeatedly re-emerges when researchers (and their actions) act in accordance with a substance ontology. It is not something that 'happens to' them, but something that they 'do'. This is indeed at the heart of 'enaction'.

Each action is involved in feedback loops (see Chapter 2). A *positive* feedback loop is self-amplifying, magnifying changes and moving the system away from its equilibrium state. Positive feedback loops can result in the further entrenchment of a system, reinforcing certain properties. Positive feedback loops are evident in both horizontal and downward causation whenever the causation is recursive and bi-directional. For example, reading an article about traits being isolable entities increases the likelihood of the reader adopting a questionnaire and large-scale approach, which increases the chances that the next papers the reader reads are about the isolable traits. Likewise, an increased temporality of writing articles may increase the competitive nature of scholarly work, which then further increases the temporality of writing articles, and so forth. These are examples of horizontal feedback loops, working at different levels of the praxis.

The system's stability is also produced by means of *negative* feedback loops between other sets of agents. These are inhibitory and typically reduce the effect of perturbations or deviations from a particular equilibrium state. For instance, take a researcher studying self-esteem from a typical substance-oriented framework who relies on the standard questionnaire methodology and is interested in cause–effect causal models (see Chapter 4). This researcher submits their manuscript to a journal and receives a suggestion from a processual reviewer to include a body of scholarship about self-as-process in their manuscript. Imagine that the substance-oriented researcher reads the suggestion with a general degree of interest, but upon reading the recommended processual literature itself, they are primarily turned off. This negative response thus works to inhibit any further pursuit of processual literature. Rather than incorporating the self-as-process literature into the manuscript, the substance-oriented researcher might then describe to the editor why this literature is irrelevant for the manuscript. The processual-reviewer's interaction with the substance-oriented researcher (and their work) will have worked to inhibit change.

The principle of negative feedback loops between agents is thus helpful in explaining how a mainstream commitment to a substance ontology can occur at the same time as a (more fringe) commitment to a process ontology. Process-oriented agents exist within the larger network of psychological science, but they likely act within a sub-network within this larger network. This sub-network may be characterized by positive feedback loops amongst itself but may demonstrate negative feedback loops with the mainstream network. Clearly, psychological science also includes agents that act in a process-oriented way. There are numerous researchers (e.g., ourselves, the many scholars cited in this book, and more), journals (e.g., *New Ideas in Psychology, Nonlinear Dynamics, Psychology, and Life Sciences, Journal of Person-Oriented Research, Human Development, Ecological Psychology, Qualitative Research, Theory & Psychology*, to name a few), conferences and associations (e.g., Jean Piaget Society), and resulting scholarship that maintain process-oriented values, aims, and norms, and use corresponding methods and theories (see also Chapters 2, 5, 8, 10, which explicitly illustrate processual scholarship).

The vertices connecting substance-oriented agents and process-oriented agents will most likely also be weak in strength (thinner arrows in Figure 12.1) and there will be fewer connections to the tighter network of substance-oriented nodes. For instance, the finding that individual time series (from motor movement; Kelso et al., 1981, to cognitive control; Amon, Pavlov, & Holden, 2018; to self-esteem; see Chapter 4) are characterized by self-similarity and fractal patterns is a major finding for researchers working within the framework of complex dynamic systems theory. For them, such empirical findings defy the general linear models that form the inspiration for the overwhelming majority of studies within psychological science, and are evidence for the validity of a complex dynamic systems explanation of human behaviour. These studies, however, are rarely cited in mainstream articles that investigate the temporal nature of the same phenomena (e.g., Hutteman et al., 2015; Wagner, Lüdtke & Trautwein, 2016, in the case of self-esteem processes).

Another example is the finding that the so-called Big Five personality structure does not apply to individuals (where personality structure might be described by 'big three' or 'big seven' depending on the underlying structure of the individual complex system). This finding does not seem to elicit the kind of concern in mainstream psychology that one would expect (see, for instance, Molenaar & Campbell, 2009).

Similarly, the use of p-values and statistical significance testing demonstrates a far-reaching resistance to accumulating concerns. Although many statisticians have criticized this practice for many years now, providing strong arguments against it (Amrhein, Greenland & McShane, 2019, with special reference to the illustration by David Parkins; Halsey, 2019; Pike, 2019), it still continues to be a dominant, virtually ineradicable practice in psychological research.

Findings that directly contradict the underlying assumptions of some research lines and theories in mainstream research do not seem to impede the momentum of substantialist knowledge-construction, where notions of stable and universal latent traits remain the norm.

The conceptualization of the process approach having predominantly vertices connecting them to the larger, and more dominant praxis is nicely underlined by Eagly and Riger (2014), who note: 'In Kuhn's view, when a scientific paradigm is widely accepted, its basic assumptions are shared among scientists and often go untested. Nonfitting data generally do not seriously threaten such paradigms until a major shift in understanding occurs' (p. 686). For a process orientation to enter into the mainstream network of interacting agents, a major shift (or *perturbation* in complex

12.1 Mechanisms of Praxis Development

dynamic systems terms, see Chapter 2) is needed. We will discuss what this may look like in Section 12.3 later on.

12.1.2.2 Supportive and Oppressive Structures as Central Nodes

The activities that we – as individual agents – engage in are encouraged or discouraged by the structures in place that have a normative role in psychological science. We conceive of these 'structures' as agents that have a relatively large impact on the way that we as academics interact with the world of academia (referring back to Figure 12.1, these structures may be the large circles that are connected to other nodes via thick arrows (i.e., they are strongly coupled)). Some agents thus demonstrate a high degree of centrality in the network.

These structures may be supportive tools, such as introductory textbooks (Bickhard, 2009a), that perpetuate certain scientific values and norms. Supportive tools constrain what budding psychologists come to see as 'correct' or 'good' science (i.e., an important part of the process of *natality*, as described in our discussion of Arendt in Chapter 3). Individuals follow guidelines laid out by the textbooks, but the textbooks can only continue to claim certain methods and scientific values as being superior if these methods and values are indeed perpetuated by common practices. The individual actions and the more cemented supportive tools thus depend on, and reinforce, each other.

Other kinds of dominant structures in psychological science are the hierarchical structures and the employment systems of universities that erode job security. These systems of hierarchy and job insecurity are likely to discourage the kinds of research practices that would allow for innovation of psychological science, such as explorative research, collaborations with junior researchers (again, see Arendt's *natality* concept in Chapter 3), or boundary crossing into disciplines lower in the prestige ranking of 'scientificness' (Fish, 2000). It is these kinds of curiosity driven, creative, and risk-taking practices that a process approach thrives on. These kinds of activities, however, are high risk and low prestige, thus harming one's chance of climbing the academic ladder and attaining job stability.

Similarly, systems of selection such as audit practices are highly central in the psychological praxis. They act to stifle creativity, exploration, and boundary crossing, and to encourage working within established and popular research frameworks (e.g., Sparkes, 2007). Dominant systems of selection use quantitative measures to determine and rank quality. As such, methodologies and collaborations that boost these quantitative measures are thus privileged, while others are rejected, discouraged, and under-funded. Processual, case-study, time-intensive observational, qualitative, and theoretical studies (which are ideal for illuminating the process-relational nature and dynamics of social-science phenomena) belong to the latter, while questionnaires and inferential statistics – that enact a substance ontology (see Chapters 5 and 7) – belong to the former.

12.1.3 Historicity: A Discipline with Memory

A crucial part of a *non-static* conceptualization of psychological science is the fact that temporal patterns or properties typically demonstrate 'memory'. What this means is that the current state encases the history of the preceding properties. The praxis of science is thus deeply history-dependent, and scientific activities are co-determined by those that took place before them. This is true even if that history is implicit in current activities.

Recall that a dynamic system can be defined as 'a means of describing how one state develops into another state over the course of time' (Weisstein, 2020, p. 501; see Chapter 2). This characteristic of history-dependence highlights how our research choices should not be seen as occurring only in the here and now (together with current agents), but also as being nested in our past choices and those of (potentially) many generations of psychological scientists. For example, it is obvious that a choice we make for a particular method will envelop past choices about who we chose to work with, or articles we enjoyed reading.

The notion of 'memory' in a system is closely connected to the distribution of events across time. If we assume that psychological science indeed behaves as a complex dynamic system, then we would expect that changes in a praxis orientation will follow a *power-law distribution*. That is to say, the magnitude of changes in a praxis will be variable, with only very few being of considerable magnitude and affecting the discipline as a whole (see Chapter 2 for a discussion of power-law distributions). The overwhelming majority of changes across time will be relatively minor, demonstrating relative continuity with the past (as observed by Elgaard Jensen, 2019). This implies strong historicity or memory.

We see this strong continuity in the very narrative of psychology, and in substance-ontology beliefs repeatedly carried forward to the agents at play. Introductory textbooks, as pivotal support structures (described earlier), carry forward philosophical underpinnings of positivism when they privilege large-scale research methods over case studies, and quantitative methods over qualitative ones (Rennie, 2012). The values communicated in these instrumental texts may shift ever so slightly from year to year, with a paragraph or two added about the value of systems perspectives, for example. However, the general narrative remains largely substance-oriented, and only very rarely can we expect to see large changes in ontological enactment in these texts.

The same kind of history dependence and slow process of change can be observed in psychological-research output too. Topical innovations occur slowly, with a few large innovations in the form of *topic bursts*. These are the relatively rapid growth of numbers of studies and researchers focussing on a particular new topic (Mane & Börner, 2004; Chen, 2004). Examples in developmental psychology are the burst of studies on theory of mind and bullying around the 1990s.

On an even larger scale, we see changes in paradigms or approaches that are largely resurrections of historical positions, now slightly adapted. This is the case when scholars revert to historical positions that, up to that moment, were considered obsolete. This recurrence of earlier topics can be seen in the current surge of research on embodied cognition, which was inspired by Merleau-Ponty's phenomenology of the 1950s and 1960s, in Cartesian innovations in linguistics (Chomsky, 1966) that were inspired by Chomsky's discussion of seventeenth century Port-Royal grammar, in the reference that evolutionary psychology makes to Darwin (see, for instance, a series of articles in the *Psychological Science Agenda* of May 2009 on the influence of Darwin on evolutionary psychology (APA, 2009), or our own references to philosophical developments since the Greek pre-Socratic philosophers in defense of a process-oriented praxis of psychology (see Chapter 1).

12.2 Created Ontologies Accepted as Realities

An important process that bars a shift in the mainstream praxis of psychological science is the fact that the iterative generation of substance-oriented knowledge creates a particular lived reality (or way of construing reality) within and outside of academia. As explored in Chapters 4 on self-esteem, and Chapter 6 on the communication of research results, findings from academic studies trickle down to the object of their study – to lay people, and their everyday behaviour, interpretations, and attributions. Scientific facts do not simply reflect reality, but they construct ontologies, and in doing so can then change reality itself. The creation of reality by means of studying reality is called the *looping effect* (Hacking, 1995a, 1995b; Strle, 2018). Looping effects are examples of iterated, reciprocal dynamic interactions between the nature of the researched reality and the form and

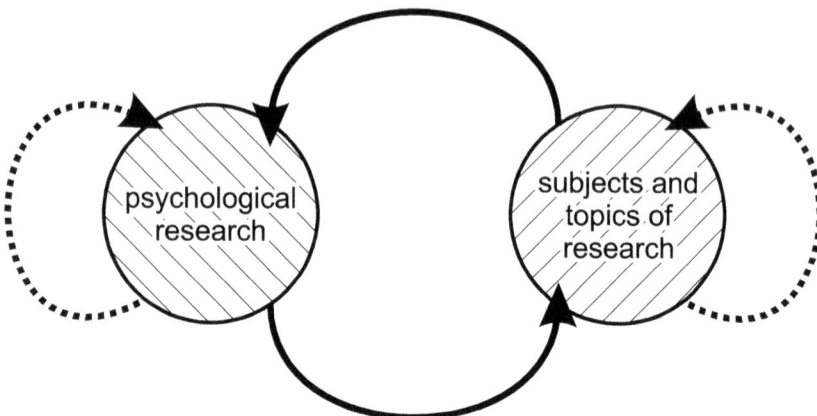

Figure 12.2 Basic continuous causal loops between two high-level interacting components (psychological research and the subjects and topic of research). The causal loops are reflexive (self-causation, see Chapter 8; represented by dotted arrows) and mutual (solid lines).

content of the knowledge resulting from this research (see Figure 12.2), embedded in institutional and behavioural frameworks of social mechanisms (Kuorikoski & Pöyhönen, 2012). The looping effect is a form of horizontal causality characterized by positive feedback loops.

Looping effects are common in psychological science. A prime example concerns psychiatric disorders, where communication of scientific findings via public media (Bessière et al., 2010) and institutionalized care and health-insurance policies (where specific care is provided and reimbursed based on diagnostic labels) leads to narrative shifts in people's perception of the nature of their mental problems (e.g., Markowitz, Angell & Greenberg, 2011; Link & Phelan, 2013; Valentine, 2010). These narratives are of deterministic, stable, and categorical disorders as 'kinds'. As these narratives are situated in institutionalized care, there is a public-induced case proliferation, where individuals have an interest in acquiring a particular diagnosis because it allows them to obtain treatment or financial compensation (Tellings, 2020). The importance of obtaining a diagnosis then exacerbates diagnostic inflation (Batstra & Frances, 2012a, 2012b), which in turn leads to further shifts in the public experience and perception of these disorders. The process of studying and treating disorders thus results in a shift in the public perception and phenomenology of those disorders, which will of course be manifest in subsequent studies of these disorders.

The continuous and bidirectional interaction between psychological research and the topics and subjects that are studied corresponds with the way that a complex dynamic systems approach conceptualizes the relationship between a person and their environment. A person is not 'affected by' an independent environmental variable. Instead, the two are mutually interconnected across time in a history-dependent way (see also Chapter 8 on complex causality). The environment then also becomes person-dependent (in the sense that the person acts on the context, thereby changing it), and aspects of the person become deeply context-dependent (such that the person acts on particular affordances in the context; Thelen & Smith, 1994).

The process of reification – which was central in the analysis of mainstream self-esteem research in Chapters 4 – is an important mechanism of the looping effect. Reification is typical of the variable-oriented focus adopted in mainstream psychology, where concepts are transformed into objects that have a 'life of their own', that do things as abstract entities (Schiff, 2017). While many psychological scientists working in mainstream research may not wish to contribute to the reification of the phenomena they study, it is a common consequence of these studies (Barclay, 1997). The standardized methods of assessment for phenomena such as self-esteem or depression communicate to participants or clients that these properties are tangible entities that define them (Hyman, 2010). In short, the constructive process of psychological science is not only carried out by psychological researchers, but also – and interactively – by the 'object' of psychological science, namely the people to which the discoveries of psychological science apply.

12.3 Bringing about Change to the Mainstream Praxis

With the above subsections, we used complex dynamic systems concepts to explain why it is that the mainstream praxis of psychological science is so entrenched and robust, despite frequent critiques about this praxis (e.g., Braun & Gavey, 2008; Schiff, 2017; Schraube, 2015). In Latour's view, standard models and practices have many allies, functioning as heavily armed troops protecting the status quo. We showed that these allies take the form of dominant structures such as institutions, narratives, communication norms, textbooks, and as higher-order properties such as a culture of capitalism, and an ideology of acceleration. All these structures are emergent properties, and they all enact a worldview of phenomena as substances. Together, these allies continuously reinforce and further entrench the attractor state of a general substance-oriented praxis.

The *emergent* nature of complex dynamic systems, however, is of course such that adaptation is possible, which we noted at the beginning of this chapter. This potential for adaptation is where novelty and self-sustained change comes into play. What is required to bring about such an adaptive response, is perturbations, which we will discuss in the next section.

12.3.1 Perturbations Wanted

In keeping with Latour's imagery, what is necessary to 'battle' the heavily armed allies of the mainstream praxis? As we alluded to earlier in this chapter, forces (of sufficient strength or duration) are necessary to perturb a system's self-maintaining dynamics and start the processes of changing the control parameters of psychological science. As we described in Chapter 2, perturbations are brought about by forces acting on the system in such a way that they counter the intrinsic dynamics of the attractor state.

For perturbations to have an influence on the control parameter of psychological science, they need to come from many sustained or accumulated forces (i.e., micro-level or meso-level perturbations, occurring across relatively small timescales) or a few substantial forces (i.e., macro-level perturbations occurring across larger timescales). While the former can be characterized as a system temporarily reacting to a force (i.e., *dynamic or reactive flexibility*, for micro- and meso-level perturbations respectively), the latter is a change that is larger in scale and duration, resulting in *developmental flexibility* (Hollenstein, Lichtwarck-Aschoff & Potworowski, 2013). The psychological praxis will thus likely experience only dynamic or reactive flexibility if temporary and small-scale perturbations take place, leaving the praxis to re-stabilize on the standard substance-praxis. With a larger scale perturbation, however, the praxis may exhibit developmental flexibility, allowing it to re-organize (Hollenstein et al., 2013). Integrating this notion with that of a network of agents, micro-level perturbation may be conceived of as affecting a small number of agents, while macro-level perturbations may impact a large portion of the network's agents.

12.3.1.1 Micro- and Meso-Level Perturbations: Individual (Inter)Actions and Events

Micro- and meso-level perturbations to the psychological-science system can be conceptualized as counter forces to the mainstream substance-oriented praxis that occur within or across contexts; these are actions that individuals do as they interact with materials or others and events that take place.

12.3 Bringing about Change to the Mainstream Praxis 283

At this level, a researcher's own inclination to conduct large-scale studies focussed on predicting central tendencies might be swayed by a paper they read, or an inspiring conversation they had with a new process-oriented colleague. The extent to which a micro-level event such as this successfully perturbs the individual's methodological habits is directly related to the extent to which their original substance-oriented attractor is entrenched. Highly entrenched attractors result in a high *spontaneous rate of change* (see Chapter 8), such that the system quickly rebounds to its original point of local minimum. In the case of a researcher inspired by a process-oriented interaction, if they are tightly connected to the mainstream substance-oriented praxis, micro-level perturbations would need to be sustained and repeated across the long term for a shift in their attractor to occur. This would effectively mean that they are repeatedly pushed out of their comfortable substance orientation before change can take place. With this change, positive vertices would be created between this researcher and processual nodes in the praxis network.

This process of accumulated micro-level perturbations is likely already at play. For example, the finding that statistical structure based on interindividual variability has no logical relationship with that of intraindividual variability or processes (i.e., non-ergodicity; Molenaar, 2004, 2008) may not have had an immediate effect on the praxis of psychological science as a whole (for a discussion, see Chapters 7 and 9). However, over the years the importance of non-ergodicity seems to be having an influence on the way that statisticians are thinking about statistical models (Bringmann et al., 2018, 2015; Hamaker, 2012). While there is of course a long road between the development of innovative statistical models and the mainstream praxis, one might say that the network composition is changing.

Another example of a praxis shift with regards to methods could be the number of researchers adopting accessible and intuitive methods for describing the structure and properties of processes, such as the State Space Grid technique, pioneered by Marc Lewis and Tom Hollenstein (e.g., Hollenstein, 2007, 2012, 2013; for a graph of its temporal development, we recommend Google NGram 'state space grid').

In contrast with micro-level perturbations, those at the meso level can be conceptualized as changes from context to context, spanning a relatively large amount of time (compared to the concrete (inter)actions of micro-level events that occur within a context). An example of such a meso-level perturbation to the mainstream substance-orientation may be a conference itself. For example, the forty-eighth annual meeting of the Jean Piaget Society (Amsterdam, 31 May–2 June 2018) was dedicated to *The Dynamics of Development: Process, (Inter-)Action, & Complexity.* This event involved a large number of attendees and presenters, all of whom engaged with a process approach for a number of days. This relatively sustained contextual move toward a process approach imposed demands on the various agents involved, encouraging them to communicate and create process-oriented knowledge. Such a meso-level force will have perturbed the psychological-science system, slightly at least, as the presentations and collaborations that took place during the conference (and the publications or studies that they led to) will have entered the knowledge-construction process in developmental psychology. This meso-level event illustrates how meso-level perturbations encompass lower-level perturbations (Hollenstein et al., 2013). The event as a whole acted on the individuals that partook in it, their interactions with each other and their research, thus activating many individual agents in the network to change their orientation (for the duration of the event at least, if not longer for some).

Finally, macro-level perturbations to the mainstream substance-orientation of psychological science refer to the strong forces against the self-maintaining dynamics of the attractor state, forces that impact many agents simultaneously and for a longer duration of time. These are the perturbations that are most likely to change the control parameter of the system (i.e., the ontological orientation of our system).

12.3.1.2   Macro-Level Perturbations: Replacing Structures of Support
As we discussed in the section *Emergent substance-orientation with causal power*, dominant structures (of education, employment, assessment) act as pivotal nodes in the psychological-science praxis. Replacing the current structures of support with process-oriented structures of education, employment, and assessment, may result in a macro-level perturbation to the larger network of agents in psychological science, and thus a widespread and sustained shift in the properties of the psychological-science system.

Research excellence, for example, is currently assessed by means of quantitative criteria such as journal impact-factors or citation rates and is based primarily on a productivity mindset. As we discussed in earlier sections, this mindset encourages researchers to conduct the highly specific kind of research that is normally published in top-tier journals, namely, large-scale studies demonstrating high levels of statistical significance, as these will be the ones cited the most (despite the fact that many statisticians view this practice as obsolete).

If standards of excellence were to shift toward more qualitative assessments, such as the creativity and innovation of articles or their theoretical

12.3 Bringing about Change to the Mainstream Praxis

and methodological rigour (see also our discussion on reproducibility and generalization in Chapter 11), we expect that the landscape of publications would shift quite remarkably. This kind of change would make room for studies that employ methods such as rigorous case-studies, intensive observations and time-series analyses, theoretical work, and qualitative studies. These approaches are often concerned with theoretical development and would thus provide space for processual research to enter into the arenas.

There are currently initiatives under way to bring about such a shift in assessment norms. In the Netherlands, for example, Dutch public knowledge institutions and research funders (VSNU, NFU, KNAW, NWO, and ZonMw[1]) have declared their commitment to modernising the system of recognition and rewards, including 'a reduced emphasis on quantitative results (such as number of publications) and a greater emphasis on quality, content, scientific integrity, creativity, contribution to science, academia and/or society, and acknowledgement of the academic's specific profile and domain(s) in which the academic is active' (VSNU, NFU, KNAW, NWO and ZonMw, 2019, p. 5). These institutions and funders acknowledge that bringing about the necessary change will involve 'a culture change as well as national and international coordination between all parties involved. Moreover, it requires the academics themselves, including academic leaders, to give shape to this modernisation and to embrace it' (p. 3). This last statement acknowledges that even a change to a central node can only instigate large-scale transformations if other agents in the network allow themselves to be changed. Perhaps large-scale forces such as a change in assessment need to be timed strategically; for example, at a moment in which the network is already sensitive to change, or in which an accumulation of micro-level perturbations has already taken place. Indeed, it is now a number of years down the road since the Dutch public knowledge institutions and research funders made this statement of commitment, and it is apparent that the parties involved (or the connected agents) have not yet been perturbed. Nevertheless, the effort made by these institutions and funders illustrates the type of macro-level forces that may, in the future, act as a successful macro-level perturbation.

---

[1] VSNU (Vereniging van Samenwerkende Nederlandse Universiteiten; Association of Universities in the Netherlands); NFU (Nederlandse Federatie van Universitaire Medische Centra; Netherlands Association of academic medical centres); KNAW (Koninkijke Nederlandse Academie voor Wetenschappen, Royal Netherlands Academy of Arts and Sciences); NWO (Nederlandse Organisatie voor Wetenschappelijk Onderzoek, Dutch Research Council); ZonMw (ZorgOnderzoek Nederland & Medische Wetenschappen, Netherlands Organisation for Health Research and Development).

12.4 A Multi-Stable Praxis: A Tug of War

What might developmental flexibility, or the reorganization of the system, look like for our praxis? As we described in Chapter 8, attractor landscapes can be a useful tool for visualizing changes in the form and properties of complex dynamic systems. On the x-axis of the landscape is the specific *order parameter* (i.e., the macroscopic properties of the system) that we are theorizing or examine. Here, this order parameter is the orientation of the psychological praxis, which we show in Figure 12.3 as ranging from a substance to a process orientation. In the top scenario, a, we see the current situation, where the deepest attractor in the landscape is that of a substance orientation. With this landscape, we see how the psychological-science praxis will quickly move back to its preferred substance-oriented state after it is perturbed. This is represented by the position of a ball, which will roll downhill and come to rest at the bottom of the valley to which it rolls (i.e., the *local minimum*). This is the preferred state for the system of our praxis, and the one that can be maintained with the least amount of 'energy' or resistance.

If the control parameter begins to shift, however, due to sufficiently long-lasting or large perturbations e.g. representing a control parameter of increased organizational pressure on qualitative publications, away from pressure on as-much-as-possible), this landscape will adapt in a self-sustained way. This is scenario b in Figure 12.3. Here we see the original substance-oriented attractor (to the right) 'filling up' while a new attractor (to the left, i.e., a process-oriented praxis) deepens. A gradual shift in a control parameter (e.g. professional pressure on a particular publication praxis) would then allow the system to stabilize more frequently in a new attractor state. During this developmental shift, our praxis would be characterized by two local minima: the previously dominant attractor state (i.e., substance-oriented praxis) and the newly emergent attractor state (i.e., process-oriented praxis).

During such a developmental change period, our discipline would be marked by erratic fluctuations. This is illustrated in Figure 12.3 by the increased width of variability (i.e., degrees of freedom) in the system's development from *a* to *b* (see the lengthened horizontal arrow in *a* compared to *b*). During this developmental phase, it would take longer for the psychological system to recover to a stable point in one of the two attractor states when momentarily perturbed. Moreover, a small perturbation would have considerably larger effects on the system's behaviour as both attractor states are relatively shallow.

This high degree of variability and sensitivity to perturbations thus characterizes a system in unrest. For individuals, this kind of multi-stable and highly variable system characterizes those suffering from an unclear

12.4 A Multi-Stable Praxis: A Tug of War

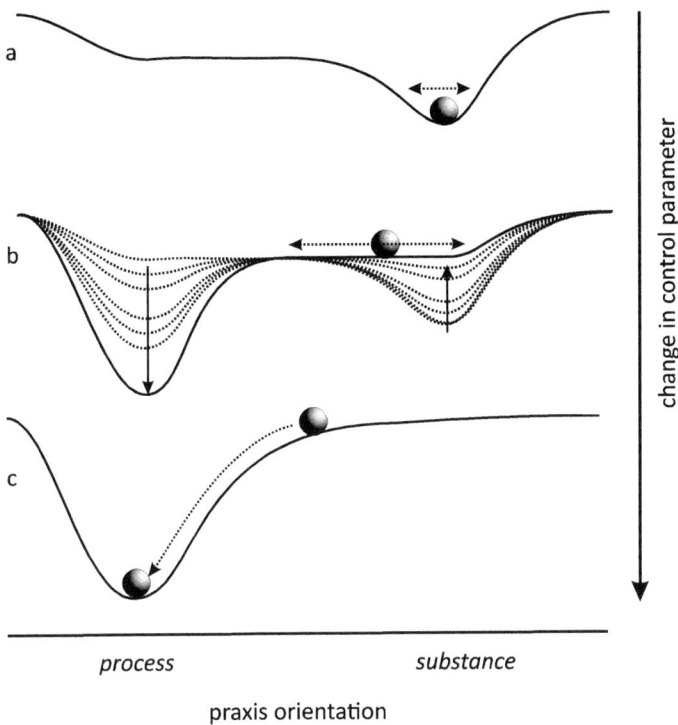

Figure 12.3 A change in the attractor landscape due to a change in a control parameter across time (top to bottom), adapted from Chapter 8. Figure 8.9. A change in the attractor landscape due to a change in a control parameter across time (top to bottom). First the substance-oriented attractor state is deepest (to the right), see a. As the control parameter for the praxis orientation changes, the attractor to the right gradually vanishes, and a process-oriented praxis emerges and increasingly gains depth (to the left), see b.

self-concept (Wong, Vallacher & Nowak, 2016). For individuals, this is experienced as 'suffering' because a clear and coherent self-concept is important for a sense of well-being (Erikson, 1968; Marcia, 1980). In the same way, an unstable psychological-science system would lack a consistent and coherent self-concept, where researchers' actions, choices, collaborations would be pulled between two disparate praxes.

The current state of psychology may in fact resemble something like an intermediate phase between *a* and *b* in Figure 12.3, where there is clearly a dominant mainstream praxis, but there is another small but clearly present attractor state that adopts a separate space in the psychological science landscape. Schraube (2015), for example, noted that 'Since the 1970s … a variety of alternative approaches have emerged parallel to conventional psychology (a process actually ongoing throughout the history of academic psychology). These approaches range from phenomenology (Giorgi, 2009), feminist psychology (Wilkinson, 1986) and cultural-historical activity theory (Wertsch, 1991) to cultural psychology (Valsiner, 2007), discursive psychology (Harré, 1979) and social-constructionism (Gergen, 2009)' (pp. 535–536). Perhaps these approaches, including others such as the complex dynamic systems approach, already belong to a competing attractor state – with criticism of mainstream psychology as their anchoring property.

As described in the case of self-esteem research in Chapter 5, the coexistence of two separate sets of ontological assumptions, aims, methodological and linguistic norms may – for the time being – work sufficiently well. Such a situation would be manageable if researchers were aware of the entire praxis – from philosophical and metaphysical assumptions to methods – that they are enacting (see the critical realist approach that we described in Chapters 1 and 4). This would prevent the kind of misattributions and mismatches between aims and methods that occur far too often at present (e.g., generalizing group-based findings to individual processes).

Such a multi-stable system can be characterized by two separate processes of self-reinforcing trends occurring in isolated parts of the academic community (i.e., two separate sub-networks within the larger network of psychological-science agents). However, recall that the landscape itself is not static, but a dynamic whole that changes when the attractor states within it change. The multi-stable nature of the landscape may further develop in a number of different ways, which we will sketch below.

Imagine that both attractors are almost exclusively enacted by two distinctly separate networks of agents, such that researchers from a substance approach and process approach do not interact and they maintain distinct practices. This is a scenario in which the larger psychological praxis encompasses two separate networks that are minimally connected via vertices. In this picture, we would see a further polarization between the two praxes, and a larger chasm between the two. When a space on an attractor landscape is virtually never visited and actively avoided, a hill emerges in the landscape (i.e., a *repellor*, see Chapter 8). With the emergence of a repellor, it becomes nearly impossible for the system (at any level) to inhabit such an in-between space. A polarized psychological science is surely not something that would be conducive to the quality of psychological research as a whole, nor to the wellbeing of the individuals that make up the discipline and are caught in the middle of the tug of war.

Perhaps a more harmonious scenario is one in which the interaction between the two opposing attractor states becomes that of mutual interest, such that collaborations begin to flourish, and the two become integrated. Indeed, Salatino, Osborne, and Motta (2017) provide extensive empirical evidence that suggests that 'a significant increase in the rate of collaboration between existing topics provides a strong indicator for predicting the emergence of new research areas' (p. 22). Perhaps such a new research area could be one that is broad with regards to topic and methods, but united by a common processual acknowledgement. What we have attempted to describe throughout this book is that, from a processual perspective, there is nothing inherently wrong with methods commonly used in substance-oriented research. Indeed, questionnaires, large-scale studies, experiments, and group comparisons are, and should remain, an important part of psychological science. The issue we wish to address is when these practices are used to make generic statements and generalizations about processes, when group-based facts are applied to the level of the individual, and when interventionist cause-and-effect models become the only model of causality. For example, it will always remain relevant to ask whether a particular clinical or educational intervention is more effective than some alternative intervention for a given population. These differences, however, can more meaningfully be studied in terms of distribution of effects, rather than aggregated effects (see Chapter 7). Moreover, to fully understand these differences, we should not stop at determining differences. It is also important to understand the ways in which individual trajectories differ, where researchers may examine clusters of effective and ineffective pathways. Likewise, we can only truly understand the effectiveness of clinical or educational interventions if we also zoom in on the context-specificity of different processual outcomes.

What we wish to emphasize is that a more critical reflection on the specific phenomenon in question, its ontology, causal processes, and relevance to society, will allow for a more suitable selection of research practices and a broader use of methodology. These need not compete with each other, as long as we acknowledge that they each serve a unique and distinct purpose for understanding phenomena.

12.5 Conclusion

With this chapter, we have described the many reinforcing and inhibitory interactions that take place within the psychological-science network that work to maintain a dominant substance-orientation. This orientation is pervasive at all levels of the network, such that it emerges via the interactions between concrete agents, while also constraining the degrees of freedom of those agents. We also described the kinds of micro-, meso-, and macro-level perturbations that may result in a developmental shift in the landscape of the psychological-science system. Many counterforces are already at play, from the development of new process-oriented methods to large-scale commitments to changing the way that academic excellence is assessed. These forces have yet to effectively *perturb* the current substance orientation, but they do demonstrate that this process is likely under way.

We firmly believe that changing the landscape of psychological science's praxis is something that would benefit the field as a whole, as well as the object of our collective study (i.e., individual people). Creativity and innovation are central to the core aim of science, namely, to push the boundaries of knowledge, to create new and successful theories, methodological models, and instruments. This emphasis on the emergence of novelty is something that is central to a process approach, stemming from the fact that complex dynamic systems are by definition open to novel forms of emergence (Thelen & Smith, 1994; Van Geert, 1994). Indeed, embracing a process approach means embracing and exploring the emergence of novelty and innovation.

With this innovation will come a more accurate and in-depth understanding of how people, as individuals, behave, interact, and experience their realities. In embracing the complexity, dynamics, and situated nature of the phenomena we study, we will be able to engage in knowledge construction that both reflects this ontology and protects it. It is important for us, as researchers, to engage in critical self-reflection concerning our practices and what they are doing. With this, perhaps we can work to resist the negative impact that the looping effect can have on the realities we are studying. Rather than slowly enforcing a world of categories, strict cause-and-effect relationships, and isolated properties onto people, we think that it is important to communicate to consumers of psychological knowledge that variability, fuzzy boundaries between categories, and uncertainty, are a natural and exciting part of our reality. They are properties that originate from the processual and emergent character of psychological phenomena. These are not things to be avoided and feared, neither by researchers nor lay people. These properties can be embraced and celebrated. Rather than hoping for them to go away, we as researchers can expose them and directly study them. The first step, therefore, is to stop and reflect on the deeply processual nature of our reality, and what this means for our epistemology.

A processual shift is in line with the developments seen in the broader field of science. Bickhard (2009a), for example, noted that psychological science is the only science that has not yet progressed from conceptualizing phenomena in substance terms to understanding them as being processes (where he refers to physics and biology as having made this transition already). Moreover, the humanities and arts have long embraced the value of understanding the subjectivity and context-embeddedness of persons, rejecting the study of populations to infer how individuals behave, experience, and learn (Sugarman & Martin, 2020; Teo, 2017). Following the examples set in these disciplines would thus represent a step forward in scientific innovation in psychological science.

As this chapter illustrated, renegotiating the praxis of psychological science will ultimately be done by the agents that make up the network and their collaboration with each other. While the grip that the mainstream praxis has on our actions is a tight one, we must remember that it is not a deterministic grip. We are ultimately free to act on the system, and indeed, as Arendt's work has shown us (discussed in Chapter 3), it may be our responsibility to do so. As Vostal (2016) pleaded, we can and should reclaim our autonomy with regard to our research activities. We hope that this book has sufficiently encouraged readers to (continue to) adopt process-oriented practices in their own work, ultimately contributing to an exciting and promising direction for psychology.

Glossary

In this Glossary, we define the fundamental concepts and terms used in this book that are not standard psychological concepts. The Glossary does not provide standard or general dictionary definitions of these terms but focusses on how they have been developed in this book.

Actuality: a term borrowed from Aristotle, as the complement of the term *Potentiality*. Actuality is that which an agent is currently doing (the agent's acting). Actuality also implies bringing about a particular *Potentiality*.

Affordances: an affordance is a property that allows an organism, equipped with adequate effectivities, to act in a particular way, and that invites, triggers, or suggests the organism to do so. It is a property of a specific organism-environment coupling. See also *Effectivities*. The notion of affordance features prominently in ecological psychology and is in line with *interactivism*.

Agent: a concrete instance of anything that is acting upon something or someone else, from a person to a tool or instrument that is used to transform observed phenomena to concrete inscriptions. Tools, instruments, and the resulting inscriptions, are concrete instantiations of a *Practice*.

Attractor: any specific region in the *State space* of a *Dynamic system*, to which that system will move (i.e., *evolve*), given (1) specific forms of interaction between the system's components governed by the system's *Evolution rules* (i.e., rules or regularities of the interaction between components) and (2) the attractor's possible starting points on the attractor's basin of attraction (see *Epigenetic Landscape*). Following from this definition, an attractor is a *Self-maintaining* state of a dynamic system, where the system will self-maintain unless it is affected by a strong enough *Perturbation*. The term attractor is often used to describe a system's typical behaviour, such as a family in which the members display typical forms of interpersonal activity. Attractors can have various forms, from stable states, to cycles between states, to complex *Recurrent* patterns.

Causality (Horizontal, Vertical, Up, and Downward, Circular): a *horizontal model* of causality refers to the cause–effect relationships that are on the same level of organization (see *Complexity/Complex system*). Horizontal models of causation describe causality within single levels of a complex system, but can also describe the mainstream and standard cause–effect model, such as a stone hitting a windowpane and breaking it, or psychotherapy reducing a person's depressive symptoms. *Vertical causality* contrasts horizontal models of causality and is typical in complex models. Vertical causality includes different levels of organization, which emerge when interactions between system components generate emergent properties that pertain to the system as a whole (the total system of interactions) – see *Emergence*. Vertical causality includes both *upward* and *downward* causation. Upward causation is the process of interactions between the components causing a higher-order emergent property (i.e., there is upward causation from lower to higher levels of organization). Downward causation is the process of the emergent property putting constraints on the interactions between the components of the system, such that they maintain or continue to produce the higher-order emergent property. In complex systems, upward and downward causation coexist and constitute forms of *Circular causality*.

Circular Causality: see **Causality, Circular**

Complexity/Complex System: a complex system is a *System* typically consisting of many components, the interactions of which are interwoven (e.g., one action brings about many other actions that have an effect on the action itself). The interactions between the components organize into collective activity on the level of the system as a whole (see *Emergence*). Complexity refers to the fact that the collective activity is such that novel properties emerge that cannot be reduced to the properties of the components or to the properties of the constituent interactions. Complex systems organize into interacting levels of organization, and action takes place on each of these levels across different, but interconnected, timescales. Complex systems typically show both variability and stability, depending on the level of organization that is observed.

Coordination Dynamics: studies the general principles of how the actions of components of a system become coordinated as a consequence of how these components interact. The coordinated behaviour of components of the system forms the collective system behaviour that cannot be reduced to the properties of the constituents (i.e., it is an emergent property; see *Complexity*). The major founder of coordination dynamics is J. S. Kelso. Coordination dynamics is related to the concept of *Synergetics*.

Critical Realism: see **Realism, Critical**

Criticality: criticality means that a system is in a 'critical state', which implies that any minor or otherwise insignificant *Perturbation* may have considerable (and typically highly unpredictable) effects on what the system will do. Criticality typically occurs in systems that undergo repetitive and minor perturbations. The totality of such effects has typical statistical properties, most notably a distribution that obeys a 'power law' (as opposed to a symmetric, e.g., Gaussian, distribution).

Downward Causality: see **Causality, Downward**

Dynamic System: is a *System* whose current state in its *State space* changes into its next state over the course of time (i.e., a system for which *Iterativity, Evolution rules, Trajectories*, and *Self-maintenance* can be observed).

Ecological Fallacy: occurs when group statistics are treated as general facts about a natural kind or grouping category that apply to any specific case from that group or category (e.g., a group-based correlation is treated as a fact about the way in which processes are correlated at the individual level). The fallacy occurs if *Ergodicity* is wrongly assumed and is related to *Simpson's Paradox*.

Effectivities: are possibilities (see *Potentials*) of an organism to act in a particular way, given the right *Affordances*. For example, a bird may fly in a particular direction, given that it is presented with a sufficiently open and large space in the air.

Embodiment/Embodied: implies that a particular phenomenon exists or occurs in the form of activities by concrete subjects (i.e., a specific being with a physical body in a physical environment), and that the phenomenon can only be truly understood if this embodiment is accounted for. The term features in the 4E approach, stating that every cognitive phenomenon is embodied, enacted, embedded, and extended, and is most commonly applied in the context of cognitive science.

Emergence/Emergent properties: *Emergence* is a process in which interactions between components of a system generate novel and higher-order properties of a *System* as a whole. *Emergent properties* cannot be reduced to properties of the constituents or components of the system (see *Complexity*), and they are not trivially inferable from simple aggregations of those components. In causal terms, emergence is the process of *Upward causation*, and it subsequently results in *Downward causation* on the processes through which it originated. The ontological status of emergent properties is a matter of debate. In this book, we use emergence and *self-organization* interchangeably, which reflects our position that most self-organizational processes involve the emergence of novelty and downward causality. Note that some literature distinguishes between emergence and self-organization, where the former is a specific case of the latter. In this literature, self-organization need not necessarily involve truly novel properties, nor downward causality.

Enactment/Enactive Approach: holds that phenomena that are typically seen as representational or cognitive are constituted by, representative of, and emergent from the activities of autonomous organisms. This approach emphasizes that an organism creates its specific, individual properties (i.e., its 'identity') as an emergent process out of activity (i.e., the interactions between concrete actions), and that the activity emanating from the organism itself is needed to keep that identity intact. An enactive approach treats organisms as *Complex systems*.

Entity or **Substance:** *entity* and *substance* both refer to 'something that is', with a thing- or object-like quality. An entity/substance is believed to be independent, stable, permanent, universal and enduring; it is believed to underlie any fleeting and non-enduring appearances of the entity/substance that we might observe (in the form of processes that the entity/substance undergoes or undertakes). Aristotle differentiated between types of *substance*: 'Primary substances' are individual entities (also called 'particulars', such as 'Bill's self-esteem'), and 'secondary substances' are *kinds* of entities with universal laws (also called 'universals', such as 'self-esteem'). In this book, we tend to use the term 'entity' to refer to primary substances, and 'substance' to refer to secondary substances.

Epigenetic Landscape: a graphical method of describing possible trajectories of a *Dynamic System* which, in its simplest form, consists of two dimensions: on the x-axis is a 'behavioural variable' describing the behaviour of a particular property (e.g., kind of behaviour, feeling, psychological quality); and on the y-axis is a variable describing 'potential energy'. Potential energy corresponds with the amount of energy (or effort) needed for a particular magnitude of change, ranging from low to high. A third dimension can be added: 'time', which would result in a 3D-representation of the landscape. Together, the dimensions form a 'landscape' of hills and valleys. The lowest point of a valley (i.e., 'local minimum') is the system's *Attractor*. A system will always spontaneously move from higher to lower levels of potential energy (from hilltops to the bottom of valleys, respectively) – and ultimately, to attractors. The entire trajectory of the system on the landscape is determined by the form of the landscape (hills and valleys) and by *Perturbations*. The landscape is malleable over time, such that hills and valleys can change in width and depth, disappear, and new ones can emerge. Epigenetic landscapes provide ways of describing stability, instability, change, variability, and the role of perturbations on system-level changes, in one single representational format.

Ergodicity: when statistical properties obtained from a group of independent subjects (i.e., based on inter-individual variability, such as correlations, averages, or distributions) are similar to the statistical properties obtained from an individual (process). A statistical property can be obtained by sampling either a set of single points taken from all cases in the ensemble set (e.g., all persons) or by sampling over the entire time trajectory of an individual case (e.g., a specific person). If both methods produce the same result, the process is ergodic. If not, the process is non-ergodic. Non-ergodicity is problematic when group statistics are treated as general facts applicable to specific cases (which is standard practice in substance-oriented research in psychology) because it denies the fact that individual subjects are idiosyncratic processes, and are in fact not representative of arbitrary points of an immutable or timeless feature. Ergodicity is associated with *Simpson's paradox* and the *Ecological fallacy*.

Evolution Term/Rule: is the specification of a mechanism or force that has the power to change the position of a system in its state space. In typical dynamic systems models, evolution terms are expressed in the form of differential or difference equations; in psychological models they can be represented by qualitative terms representing principles of change.

Extensional and Intensional Definitions: *Extensional definitions* refer to how a term is defined in terms of the collection of concrete instances to which a categorical definition applies. For instance, the extensional definition of "human being" is the set of all human beings. The extensional definition clarifies whether a term is used to refer to particular instances of a category ('this two-year-old'), most instances ('the majority of two-year-olds'), or all instances ('all two-year-olds'). *Intensional definitions* enumerate the properties or semantic content of the term being used and that distinguish it from other terms (e.g., the properties that define "human being").

Generic Term: used to refer to whole classes of things (i.e., all individual cases or instances that share a common property, called an *extensional set*). Generic terms tend to be used in the context of general (rather than specific) truths, but are also often ambiguous in this regard.

History Dependence: implies that changes depend, in part, on preceding changes. The term stresses the role of *Iterativity* in addition to how systems respond to external forces. History dependence is related to the property of *Hysteresis*.

Horizontal Causality: see **Causality, Horizontal**

Hysteresis: refers to asymmetries in how the occurrence of an event depends on the way a *Control parameter* (see *Parameter, Control*) has changed in the (immediate) past. Hysteresis is closely related to history dependence but stresses the non-linear relationship between an event and a control parameter.

Intensional Definition: see **Extensional and Intensional Definitions**

Intransitivity: the (aspects of the) world that exist independent of our thoughts and actions, such that we have no influence on it. See *Realism, Naive*.

Interactivism: a view on the nature of reality (an *Ontology*) that states that reality is integrated, such that there are no entities that exist independent of interactions (exchanges) with other entities. Interactivism suggests that reality consists of *Processes*, and that the interaction between processes gives way to (and is a necessary condition for) *Emergence*. Interactivism, in psychology, was developed by Piaget and, more broadly, by Marc Bickhard.

Intervention Causality: see **Manipulation or Intervention Causality**

Iterativity or Recursiveness: *Iterativity* means that an event at $t+1$ is dependent on the event at t. *Recursiveness* focusses on the fact that the current state (of the system or of the evolution rule) 'draws upon itself'.

Process Causality: a model for describing processes as primary causal mechanisms. Any identifiable state in a process (see *Actuality*) is a causal consequence of processes in the form of interactions: a) interactions across time, making the current state a consequence of its preceding state or states and, potentially; b) causal interactions taking place within a *network* (not limited by unidirectionality, see *Manipulation/Intervention causality*). Process causality implies a process *ontology*, and it can include *Horizontal, Vertical, Up- and Downward, Circular* Causality (see *Causality*).

Manipulation or Intervention Causality: a model for explaining phenomena of interest as effects of factors, where the factors are in principle isolable from, and independent of, other such causal factors. These factors 'intervene' in ongoing processes (including states of stability) or 'manipulate' ongoing processes. Counterfactualness is another property of this model, implying that the change would not have occurred if the manipulation or intervention had not occurred. The model implies unidirectionality, in that it only considers causal processes running from cause to effect, and implies modularity, in that causal factors are separate modules that can be altered without affecting others. Manipulation or intervention causality is one example of *Horizontal Causality* (see *Causality*).

Metaphysics: the philosophical study of foundational concepts that underlie our view on the nature of reality, and that often serve as axioms (i.e., premises or starting points) for how we deal with reality (e.g., in the form of empirical research). If metaphysics deals with the fundamental nature of reality (e.g., the question of whether the fundamental units are substances or processes) it is an *Ontology*.

Natural Kind: a 'kind' is a grouping or classification of things (e.g., individual people, concrete activities) that are believed to share a similar property or properties that justify membership in the classification. *Natural kinds* refer to classes that correspond with fundamental and meaningful distinctions. The question of how 'natural' the natural kinds are in psychology is a topic of debate. The notion of 'natural kind' is related to issues concerning *Extensional* and *Intensional Definitions*, including the practically important issue of 'representative samples'.

Network: a set of connected components (e.g., people, properties, processes, or variables). The connections represent relations between the components. If the network is a mathematical graph, the components are called 'nodes', and the connections are called 'vertices'. The connections between the nodes can be characterized in many ways (e.g., symmetrical or asymmetrical), making them useful tools for modelling or representing complex dynamic systems.

Ontology: literally speaking, a 'discourse, doctrine or theory' (-logy) about the nature and fundamental properties of 'being' (onto). The way people deal with reality in the form of actions, emotions, or beliefs is an *Enactment* of a particular ontology. Enacted ontologies often remain tacit, implicit, and somewhat ambiguous.

Parameter, Control, Order, Space: *Control Parameters* refer to the properties or forces that provoke transitions or *Perturbations* from one state to another, or from one pattern to another in multi-stable systems. *Order parameters* refers to a system's higher-order *emergent* behaviour that is necessarily ordered, coordinated, or organized (see *Emergence*). *Parameter Space* is the totality of parameter values that corresponds with a particular population for which these parameter values are plausible possibilities.

Perturbation: any mostly external and sudden force applied to a system that makes the system move out of the local minimum (i.e., the point on a state space that requires the least amount of energy to maintain; an attractor), and, if the perturbation is sufficiently strong, toward other local minima (if present); perturbations are often identified as "shocks" to the system.

Positivism: considers reality as fixed, with universal and permanent laws, where this reality is independent of changing contexts, and where our actions and interactions with reality are primarily a matter of discovering or confirming reality (rather than co-constructing it). Positivism rejects *Interactivism*.

Potential: see **Epigenetic Landscape**

Potentiality: the counterpart term of *Actuality*. Potentiality is the possibility of something to do a particular kind of thing, or to change in a particular way. The Greek word for potentiality is *dunamis*, which means power or force, thus stressing the *capacity* to do something. Potentiality should not be confused with *potential*, which features in epigenetic landscapes.

Practice: any concrete activity done by an embodied person that is in some way shared or common within a community. These activities are broadly construed, ranging from procedures, use and production of tools and products, communication norms, valorization norms, or justification norms. Practices are embedded in social and organizational power-structures that regulate these practices. A practice is a component of a *Praxis*.

Praxis: an open, *History-dependent*, *Self-maintaining Network* of interacting *Practices* that are *Embodied* and carried out by a community of *Agents*. A praxis *Enacts* a particular *Ontology*.

Process: any temporal sequence or flow of events that are causally or functionally linked to one another, such that the events showing temporal interdependence (see also *Iterativity*). A process occurs in concrete subjects (e.g., a brain, person, dyad, family, group, or society) and is thus 'circumstantially concrete'. Processes occur, and are ontologically intertwined with, their material, social, and cultural context, and are thus embodied and embedded. Processes involve change that is underpinned by *Activity* related to *Potentials* and *Potentialities*. Processes have temporal properties or structure that *Emerge* over the course of the process. A process occurs across multiple interconnected timescales, ranging from the micro-level to macro-level timescale (note that the units of time that characterize each level are phenomenon dependent). As we move up in timescales, from micro- to meso- to macro-level, the variability of smaller timescales becomes increasingly patterned and gains *Self-maintaining*, temporal stability.

Processualism: a stance that assumes process *Ontology*.

Process Ontology: an *Ontology* that assumes that fundamental properties of reality are time-dependent, fleeting *processes*.

Realism, Anti-, Naive, Scientific, Critical: *Realism* is the metaphysical or ontological position that there is a reality independent of our human presence, interaction, or understanding, with properties that can be known through interacting with that reality in specific ways. *Anti-realism*, in contrast, does not assume the existence of an external reality. Realism can take many forms, each of which has its own emphasis. *Naive realism* rests on positivism and on the empirical domain of reality to describe the totality of reality. *Scientific realism* is similar to naive realism in this emphasis, but focusses on the role of scientific investigation of the empirical domain of reality. *Critical realism*, adopted in this book, assumes the existence of a reality, but emphasizes the context dependency of how we *construe* reality. Critical realism therefore emphasizes that knowledge of reality is a human construct that is time and context dependent. With this core assumption, critical realism stresses the need for reflexivity concerning the ways in which our knowledge bears fundamental features of the constructive activities that have led to this knowledge. Critical realism endorses judgemental rationalism, which is the premise that some accounts about the world are more likely to be true than others, in a particular context and from a particular perspective or knowledge interest (pluralism). Finally, critical realism favors *Processualism*.

Recurrence: in the course of a particular process, certain events or properties occur repetitively, with variable intervals and with variable similarity (e.g., an event may occur repeatedly, but never in an exactly similar form). That is, these properties or events *recur*.

Reification: the construal of abstract psychological phenomena as concrete, tangible, objective, and internalized cognitive phenomena. Reification transforms phenomena into isolable 'things' that people 'have'.

Self-Maintenance: when a system's activities result in the reproduction of these activities, and hence, in the reproduction of the system's properties. A self-maintaining system is an *Attractor*. In a formal dynamic system, these 'activities' are specified in the form of (an) evolution term(s), applying to a particular state in the state space.

Self-Organization: see **Emergence**.

Self-Organized Criticality: see **Criticality** and **Self-organization**

Simpson's Paradox: is the erroneous assumption that statistical features that apply to a particular group (e.g., regression lines, trends or correlations) also apply to any subgroup; or that combining subgroups (e.g., female students and male students) that show similar properties (e.g., a negative correlation between variables A and B) into an overarching group (e.g., students) will show the same property as that observed in the two subgroups (e.g., the negative A-B correlation). It is an example of the *Ecological Fallacy*, and is related to the problem of (non-)*Ergodicity*.

Soft-Assembly: the characterization of properties or phenomena as emerging in interaction with the current context and its specific affordances. Soft-assembly contrasts the characterization of properties or phenomena as fixed and enduring structures. A specific kind of soft-assembled property or phenomenon that demonstrates *Recurrence* is called an *Attractor*. The process of soft-assembly occurs via *Self-organization*.

State Space: any set of descriptive dimensions that are used to describe the possible states (see *Potentiality*) of a particular *system*. The dimensions of the state space can take various forms: qualitative, in which case the dimension consists of a set of descriptive categories (e.g., angry, neutral, happy), or quantitative, in which case the dimension may refer to a continuous quantity represented by numbers.

Substance: see **Entity** or **Substance**.

Substantialism: a stance that assumes *Substance Ontology*.

Substance Ontology: An *Ontology* that assumes that fundamental properties of reality are independent, stable, and enduring *Entities* (see also *Entity or Substance*).

Synergetics: the study of the general principles of self-organization of complex *systems* irrespective of the nature of the individual components. The approach was pioneered by H. Haken. Synergetics shows many commonalities with *Coordination Dynamics*.

System: any set of components that are connected through their interactions. Components can be of any kind (e.g., processes, entities, or systems); directions can be direct (A influences B), bi-directional (A interacts with B), indirect (A is connected with C through the connections A-B and B-C), and dynamic (influences of A on B change over time), or static.

Time Evolution: see **Trajectory**

Trajectory: is a temporal sequence of states in a state space resulting from the *Iterative* activity of the system. The term is primarily used for sequences in which the next state differs from its preceding state, thus forming a path. A trajectory resulting from *Evolution Terms* is also called a *Time Evolution*.

Upward Causality: see **Causality, Horizontal**

Vertical Causality: see **Causality, Vertical**

References

Abar, S., Theodoropoulos, G. K., Lemarinier, P., & O'Hare, G. M. (2017). Agent-based modelling and simulation tools: a review of the state-of-art software. *Computer Science Review*, 24, 13–33. https://doi.org/10.1016/J.COSREV.2017.03.001

Abma, R. (2012). *Changes in publication culture and the Stapel fraud case*. In ESHHS meeting, Montreal, August (vol. 124). www.academia.edu/6769553

Abma, R. (2013). *De publicatiefabriek: Over de betekenis van de affaire Stapel*. Nijmegen: Vantilt.

Abraham, F. D., Abraham, R. H., & Shaw, C. D. (1990). *A visual introduction to dynamical systems theory for psychology*. Santa Cruz, CA: Aerial Press.

Abraham, R. (2014). Agent-based modeling of growth processes. *Mind, Brain, and Education*, 8(3), 115–131. https://doi.org/10.1111/MBE.12045

Abrahams, B. S., & Geschwind, D. H. (2008). Advances in autism genetics: on the threshold of a new neurobiology. *Nature Reviews Genetics*, 9(5), 341–355. https://doi.org/10.1038/nrg2346

Adamson, J., Ozenc, C., Baillie, C., & Tchanturia, K. (2019). Self-esteem group: useful intervention for inpatients with anorexia nervosa? *Brain Sciences*, 9(1), 1–11. https://doi.org/10.3390/brainsci9010012

Adolph, K. E. (2019). An ecological approach to learning in (not and) development. *Human Development*, 63(3–4), 180–201. https://doi.org/10.1159/000503823

Adolph, K. E., & Kretch, K. S. (2012). Infants on the edge. In A. M. Slater & P. C. Quinn (eds.), *Developmental psychology: revisiting the classic studies* (pp. 36–58). Los Angeles and London: SAGE Publications.

Adolph, K. E., Kretch, K. S., & LoBue, V. (2014). Fear of heights in infants? *Current Directions in Psychological Science*, 23(1), 60–66. https://doi.org/10.1177/0963721413498895

Ahn, W. K., Flanagan, E. H., Marsh, J. K., & Sanislow, C. A. (2006). Beliefs about essences and the reality of mental disorders. *Psychological Science*, 17(9), 759–766. https://doi.org/10.1111/j.1467-9280.2006.01779.x

Alberts, B., Kirschner, M. W., Tilghman, S., & Varmus, H. (2014). Rescuing US biomedical research from its systemic flaws. *Proceedings of the National Academy of Sciences*, 111(16), 5773–5777. https://doi.org/10.1073/pnas.1404402111

Alessandri, G., Zuffianò, A., Vecchione, M., Donnellan, B. M., & Zuffianò, A. (2016). Evaluating the temporal structure and correlates of daily self-esteem using a trait state error framework (TSE). *Self and Identity*, 15(4), 394–412. https://doi.org/10.1080/15298868.2015.1137223

Allegrini, A. G., Cheesman, R., Rimfeld, K., et al. (2020). The p factor: genetic analyses support a general dimension of psychopathology in childhood and adolescence. *Journal of Child Psychology and Psychiatry*, 61(1), 30–39. https://doi.org/10.1111/jcpp.13113

Allen, B. S., Otto, R. G., & Hoffman, B. (2004). Media as lived environments: the ecological psychology of educational technology. In D. H. Jonassen (ed.), *Handbook of research for educational communications and technology* (2nd ed.) (pp. 215–241). Mahwah, NJ: Lawrence Erlbaum Associates. https://doi.org/10.4324/9781410609519

Allen, J. W., & Bickhard, M. H. (2011). Normativity: a crucial kind of emergence. *Human Development*, 54(2), 106–112. https://doi.org/10.1159/000327096

APA (American Psychiatric Association) (2013). *Diagnostic and statistical manual of mental disorders* (5th ed.). Washington, DC: American Psychiatric Association. https://doi.org/10.1176/appi.books.9780890425596

APA (American Psychiatric Association (2009). *Evolutionary theory and psychology, science briefs*. www.apa.org/science/about/psa/2009/05/sci-brief.aspx

APA (American Psychiatric Association (2015). About APA: frequently asked questions about the American Psychological Association. American Psychological Association. www.apa.org/support/about-apa

Amon, M. J., Pavlov, O., & Holden, J. G. (2018). Synchronization and fractal scaling as resources for cognitive control. *Cognitive Systems Research*, 50, 155–179. https://doi.org/10.1016/j.cogsys.2018.04.010

Amrhein, V., Greenland, S., & McShane, B. (2019). Scientists rise up against statistical significance. *Nature*, 567(7748), 305–307. https://doi.org/10.1038/d41586-019-00857-9

Anderson, D. I., Hubbard, E. M., Campos, J. J., et al. (2000). Probabilistic epigenesis, experience, and psychological development in infancy. *Infancy*, 1(2), 245–251. https://doi.org/10.1207/S15327078IN0102_6

Anjum, R. L., & Mumford, S. (2018). Dispositionalism: a dynamic theory of causation. In D. J. Nicholson & J. Dupré (eds.), *Everything flows: towards a processual philosophy of biology* (pp. 61–75). Oxford: Oxford University Press. https://doi.org/10.1093/oso/9780198779636.001.0001

Antonietti, A. (2010). Emerging mental phenomena: implications for psychological explanation. In A. Corradini & T. O'Connor (eds.), *Emergence in science and philosophy* (vol. 6, pp. 266–288). Abingdon and New York: Routledge. https://doi.org/10.4324/9780203849408

Archer, M., Decoteau, C., Gorski, P., et al. (2016). What is critical realism? *Perspectives: a newsletter of the ASA theory section*, 23 December. www.asatheory.org/current-newsletter-online/what-is-critical-realism

Arendt, H. (1958). *The human condition*. Chicago, IL: University of Chicago Press.

Arfi, B. (2010). *Linguistic fuzzy logic methods in social sciences* (vol. 253). Heidelberg: Springer. https://doi.org/10.1007/978-3-642-13343-5

Arocha, J. F. (2020). Scientific realism and the issue of variability in behavior. *Theory and Psychology*, 31(3), 375–398. https://doi.org/10.1177/0959354320935972

Arumugam, R., Lutscher, F., & Guichard, F. (2021). Tracking unstable states: ecosystem dynamics in a changing world. *Oikos*, 130(4), 525–540. https://doi.org/10.1111/oik.08051

Assay, J. (2018). The role of truth in psychological science. *Theory & Psychology*, 28(3), 382–397. https://doi.org/10.1177/0959354317752875

Assay, J. (2021). Truthmaker theory. In *The internet encyclopedia of philosophy*. https://iep.utm.edu/truth-ma/

Axelrod, R. (2006). Agent-based modeling as a bridge between disciplines: handbook of computational economics. In K. L. Judd & L. Tesfatsion (eds.), *Agent-based computational economics: Vol. 2. Handbook of computational economics* (pp. 1565–1584). Amsterdam: North Holland.

Bak, P. (1996/2013). *How nature works: The science of self-organized criticality*. New York: Springer Science & Business Media. https://doi.org/10.1007/978-1-4757-5426-1

Baker, M. (2016). 1,500 scientists lift the lid on reproducibility. *Nature*, 533(26), 353–366. https://doi.org/10.1038/533452a

Baldwin, S., & Hoffmann, J. (2002). The dynamics of self-esteem: a growth-curve analysis. *Journal of Youth and Adolescence*, 31(2), 101–113.

Banisch, S., & Olbrich, E. (2021). 'An argument communication model of polarization and ideological alignment.' *Journal of Artificial Societies and Social Simulation*, 24(1), 1. http://jasss.soc.surrey.ac.uk/24/1/1.html

Barclay, M. W. (1997). The metaphoric foundation of literal language. *Theory & Psychology*, 7(3), 355–372. https://doi.org/10.1177/0959354397073004

Bareinboim, E., & Pearl, J. (2016). Causal inference and the data-fusion problem. *Proceedings of the National Academy of Sciences*, 113(27), 7345–7352. https://doi.org/10.1073/pnas.1510507113

Barnett, W. A., Serletis, A., & Serletis, D. (2015). Nonlinear and complex dynamics in economics. *Macroeconomic Dynamics*, 19(8), 1749.

Baron-Cohen, S. (2009). Autism: The empathizing-systemizing (ES) theory. *Annals of the New York Academy of Sciences*, 1156(1), 68–80. https://doi.org/10.1111/j.1749-6632.2009.04467.x

Bartlett, J. (2014). *Bartlett's familiar quotations* (17th ed., J. Kaplan (ed.)). Boston and New York: Little, Brown & Company.

Bartsch, L. A., King, K. A., Vidourek, R. A., & Merianos, A. L. (2017). Self-esteem and alcohol use among youths. *Journal of Child & Adolescent Substance Abuse*, 26(5), 414–424. https://doi.org/10.1080/1067828X.2017.1322018

Bassano, D., & Van Geert, P. (2007). Modeling continuity and discontinuity in utterance length: a quantitative approach to changes, transitions and intra-individual variability in early grammatical development. *Developmental Science*, 10(5), 588–612. https://psycnet.apa.org/record/2007-12306-010

Bassano, D., Maillochon, I., Korecky-Kröll, K., et al. (2011). A comparative and dynamic approach to the development of determiner use in three children acquiring different languages. *First Language*, 31(3), 253–279. https://doi.org/10.1177/0142723710393102

Batstra, L., & Frances, A. (2012a). Diagnostic inflation: Causes and a suggested cure. *The Journal of Nervous and Mental Disease*, 200(6), 474–479. https://doi.org/10.1097/NMD.0b013e318257c4a2

Batstra, L., & Frances, A. (2012b). DSM-5 further inflates attention deficit hyperactivity disorder. *The Journal of Nervous and Mental Disease*, 200(6), 486–488. https://doi.org/10.1097/NMD.0b013e318257c4b6

Baumeister, R. F., Campbell, J. D., Krueger, J. I., & Vohs, K. D. (2003). Does high self-esteem cause better performance, interpersonal success, happiness, or healthier lifestyles? *Psychological Science in the Public Interest*, 4(1), 1–44. https://doi.org/10.1111/1529-1006.01431

Baumeister, R. F., Campbell, J. D., Krueger, J. I., & Vohs, K. D. (2005). Exploding the self-esteem myth. *Scientific American*, 292(1), 84–91. https://doi.org/10.1038/scientificamerican0105-84

Baumeister, R. F., & Vohs, K. D. (2016). Misguided effort with elusive implications. *Perspectives on Psychological Science*, 11(4), 574–575. https://doi.org/10.1177/1745691616652878

Baumgartner, M. (2009). Interdefining causation and intervention. *Dialectica*, 63(2), 175–194. https://doi.org/10.1111/j.1746-8361.2009.01191.x

Bechtel, W. (2009). Looking down, around, and up: mechanistic explanation in psychology. *Philosophical Psychology*, 22(5), 543–564. https://doi.org/10.1080/09515080903238948

Bechtel, W. (2017). Explicating top-down causation using networks and dynamics. *Philosophy of Science*, 84(2), 253–274. https://doi.org/10.1086/690718

Bedau, M. A., & Humphreys, P. E. (2008). *Emergence: contemporary readings in philosophy and science*. Cambridge, MA: MIT Press. https://doi.org/10.7551/mitpress/9780262026215.001.0001

Beebee, H., & Sabbarton-Leary, N. (eds.). (2010). *The semantics and metaphysics of natural kinds*. Abingdon: Routledge. https://doi.org/10.4324/9780203852330

Belsky, J. (2001). Emanuel Miller Lecture: Developmental risks (still) associated with early child care. *The Journal of Child Psychology and Psychiatry and Allied Disciplines*, 42(7), 845–859. DOI: 10.1111/1469-7610.00782

Berezow, A. B. (2012). Why psychology isn't a science. Los Angeles Times. http://articles.latimes.com/2012/jul/13/news/la-ol-blowback-pscyhology-science-20120713

Bergman, L. R., & Wångby, M. (2014). The person-oriented approach: a short theoretical and practical guide. *Eesti Haridusteaduste Ajakiri. Estonian Journal of Education*, 2(1), 29–49. https://doi.org/10.12697/eha.2014.2.1.02b

Bessière, K., Pressman, S., Kiesler, S., & Kraut, R. (2010). Effects of internet use on health and depression: a longitudinal study. *Journal of Medical Internet Research*, 12(1), e6. https://doi.org/10.2196/jmir.1149

Betz, G. (2007). *Prediction or prophecy? The boundaries of economic foreknowledge and their socio-political consequences*. Springer Science & Business Media. https://doi.org/10.1007/978-3-8350-9053-8

Bickhard, M. H. (2003). Mind as process. In F. G. Riffert & M. Weber (eds.), *Searching for new contrasts* (pp. 294–303). Vienna: Peter Lang. https://doi.org/10.1080/09515080500169306

Bickhard, M. H. (2009a). The interactivist model. *Synthese*, 166(3), 547–591. https://doi.org/10.1007/s11229-008-9375-x

Bickhard, M. H. (2009b). Interactivism: a manifesto. *New Ideas in Psychology*, 27(1), 85–95. https://doi.org/10.1016/j.newideapsych.2008.05.001

Bickhard, M. H. (2011a). Some consequences (and enablings) of process metaphysics. *Axiomathes*, 21(1), 3–32. https://doi.org/10.1007/s10516-010-9130-z

Bickhard, M. H. (2011b). The dynamics of acting. *Humana Mente*, 4(15), 177–187.

Bickhard, M. H. (2011c). Systems and process metaphysics. In C. Hooker (ed.), *Handbook of the philosophy of science, vol. 10: philosophy of complex systems* (pp. 91–104). Amsterdam: North Holland. https://doi.org/10.1016/C2009-0-06625-2

Bickhard, M. H. (2016). Inter- and en-activism: some thoughts and comparisons. *New Ideas in Psychology*, 41, 23–32. https://doi.org/10.1016/j.newideapsych.2015.12.002

Bickhard, M. H & Campbell, D. (2000). Emergence. In P. B. Andersen, C. Emmeche, N. O. Finnemann, & P. V. Christiansen (eds.), *Downward causation* (pp. 322–348). Aarhus, Denmark: University of Aarhus Press.

Billig, M. (2013). *Learn to write badly: how to succeed in the social sciences*. Cambridge, UK: Cambridge University Press. https://doi.org/10.1017/CBO9781139208833

Billig, M. (2019). *More examples, less theory*. Cambridge, UK: Cambridge University Press. https://doi.org/10.1017/9781108696517

Bird, A. (2018). The metaphysics of natural kinds. *Synthese*, 195(4), 1397–1426. https://doi.org/10.1007/s11229-015-0833-y

Bird, A., & Tobin, E. (2018). Natural kinds. In E. N. Zalta (ed.), *The Stanford Encyclopedia of Philosophy* (Spring 2018 Edition). https://plato.stanford.edu/archives/spr2018/entries/natural-kinds/

Birhane, A. (2021). The impossibility of automating ambiguity. *Artificial Life*, 27(1), 1–18. https://doi.org/10.1162/artl_a_00336

Birkeland, M. S., Melkevik, O., Holsen, I., & Wold, B. (2012). Trajectories of global self-esteem development during adolescence. *Journal of Adolescence*, 35(1), 43–54. https://doi.org/10.1016/j.adolescence.2011.06.006

Blijd-Hoogewys, E., & Van Geert, P. L. (2017). Non-linearities in theory-of-mind development. *Frontiers in Psychology*, 7, 1970. https://doi.org/10.3389/fpsyg.2016.01970

Boero, R., Morini, M., Sonnessa, M., & Terna, P. (2015). *Agent-based models of the economy: from theories to applications*. Berlin and Heidelberg: Springer. https://doi.org/10.1057/9781137339812

Boker, S. M., & Laurenceau, J.-P. (2006). Dynamical systems modeling: an application to the regulation of intimacy and disclosure in marriage. In T. A. Walls & J. L. Schafer (eds.), *Models for intensive longitudinal data* (pp. 195–218). Oxford: Oxford University Press. https://doi.org/10.1093/acprof:oso/9780195173444.001.0001

Boker, S. M., & Martin, M. (2018). A conversation between theory, methods, and data. *Multivariate Behavioral Research*, 53(6), 1–14. https://doi.org/10.1080/00273171.2018.1437017

Bollen, K. A., & Pearl, J. (2013). Eight myths about causality and structural equation models. In S. L. Morgan (ed.), *Handbook of causal analysis for social research* (pp. 301–328). Berlin and Heidelberg: Springer. https://doi.org/10.1007/978-94-007-6094-3

Boom, J. (2015). A new visualization and conceptualization of categorical longitudinal development: measurement invariance and change. *Frontiers in Psychology*, 6, 289. https://doi.org/10.3389/fpsyg.2015.00289

Boring, E. G (1923). Intelligence as the tests test it. *New Republic*, 36, 35–37. https://doi.org/10.1037/11491-017

Borsboom, D., Cramer, A. O. J., & Kalis, A. (2019). Brain disorders? Not really: why network structures block reductionism in psychopathology research. *Behavioral and Brain Sciences*, 42(e2), 1–63. https://doi.org/10.1017/S0140525X17002266

Borsboom, D., Mellenbergh, G. J., & Van Heerden, J. (2003). The theoretical status of latent variables. *Psychological Review*, 110(2), 203. https://doi.org/10.1037/0033-295X.110.2.203

Borsboom, D., Rhemtulla, M., Cramer, A. O., Van der Maas, H. L., Scheffer, M., & Dolan, C. V. (2016). Kinds versus continua: a review of psychometric approaches to uncover the structure of psychiatric constructs. *Psychological Medicine*, 46(8), 1567–1579. DOI: 10.1017/S0033291715001944

Bortolan, A. (2018). Self-esteem and ethics: a phenomenological view. *Hypatia*, 33(1), 56–72. https://doi.org/10.1111/hypa.12388

Botterill, G. (2010). Two kinds of causal explanation. *Theoria*, 76(4), 287–313. DOI: 10.1111/j.1755-2567.2010.01079.x

Bourdieu, P. (1977). *Outline of a theory of practice* (R. Nice, Trans.). (Original work published 1972). Cambridge, UK: Cambridge University Press. https://doi.org/10.1017/CBO9780511812507

Boyd, R. N. (2003). Finite beings, finite goods: the semantics, metaphysics and ethics of naturalist consequentialism, part I. *Philosophy and Phenomenological Research*, LXVI, 505–553. https://doi.org/10.1111/j.1933-1592.2003.tb00278.x

Braun, V., & Gavey, N. (2008). Tribute to *Feminism & Psychology's* founding editor: 'imagining a space': Sue Wilkinson's contribution to feminist psychology. *Feminism & Psychology*, 18(1), 13–20. DOI: 10.1177/0959353507084949

Breslau, N., Chilcoat, H. D., Susser, E. S., et al. (2001). Stability and change in children's intelligence quotient scores: a comparison of two socioeconomically disparate communities. *American Journal of Epidemiology*, 154(8), 711–717. https://doi.org/10.1093/aje/154.8.711

Bressler, S. L., & Kelso, J. A. (2016). Coordination dynamics in cognitive neuroscience. *Frontiers in Neuroscience*, 10, 397. https://doi.org/10.3389/fnins.2016.00397

Bressler, S. L., & Seth, A. K. (2011). Wiener-Granger causality: a well established methodology. *NeuroImage*, 58(2), 323–329. http://doi.org/10.1016/j.neuroimage.2010.02.059

Brian Arthur, W. (2021). *Economics in Nouns and Verbs.* arXiv:2104.01868v2 [econ.GN].

Bringmann, L. F., Ferrer, E., Hamaker, E. L., Borsboom, D., & Tuerlinckx, F. (2018). Modeling nonstationary emotion dynamics in dyads using a time-varying vector-autoregressive model. *Multivariate Behavioral Research*, 53(3), 293–314. https://doi.org/10.1080/00273171.2018.1439722

Bringmann, L. F., Lemmens, L. H. J. M., Huibers, M. J. H., Borsboom, D., & Tuerlinckx, F. (2015). Revealing the dynamic network structure of the Beck Depression Inventory-II. *Psychological Medicine*, 45(4), 747–757. https://doi.org/10.1017/S0033291714001809

Brown, J. D., & Marshall, M. A. (2001). Self-esteem and emotion: some thoughts about feelings. *Personality and Social Psychology Bulletin*, 27(5), 575–584. https://doi.org/10.1177/0146167201275006

Budd, R., & Hughes, I. (2009). The Dodo Bird verdict–controversial, inevitable and important: a commentary on 30 years of meta-analyses. *Clinical Psychology & Psychotherapy*, 16(6), 510–522. https://doi.org/10.1002/cpp.648

Buhrmester, M. D., Blanton, H., & Swann, W. B. (2011). Implicit self-esteem: nature, measurement, and a new way forward. *Journal of Personality and Social Psychology*, 100(2), 365–385. https://doi.org/10.1037/a0021341

Burns. D. D. (1993). *Ten days to self-esteem*. New York: William Morrow Paperbacks.

Buss, A. T., & Spencer, J. P. (2014). The emergent executive: a dynamic field theory of the development of executive function. *Monographs of the Society for Research in Child Development*, 79(2), vii. https://doi.org/10.1002/mono.12096

Buss, D. M. (2009). How can evolutionary psychology successfully explain personality and individual differences? *Perspectives on Psychological Science*, 4(4), 359–366. https://doi.org/10.1111/j.1745-6924.2009.01138.x

Byrne, D & Uprichard, E. (2012). Useful complex causality. In H. Kincaid (ed.), *The Oxford handbook of philosophy of social science* (pp. 109–129). Oxford: Oxford University Press. https://doi.org/10.1093/oxfordhb/9780195392753.001.0001

Campbell, R. (2010). The emergence of action. *New Ideas in Psychology*, 28(3), 283–295. https://doi.org/10.1016/j.newideapsych.2009.09.004

Campbell, R. (2015). *The metaphysics of emergence*. New York: Springer. https://doi.org/10.1057/9781137502384

Cannon, E. N., & Woodward, A. L. (2012). Infants generate goal-based action predictions. *Developmental Science*, 15(2), 292–298. DOI: 10.1111/j.1467-7687.2011.01127.x

Carlson, G. N., & Pelletier, F. J. (eds.). (1995). *The generic book*. Chicago, IL: University of Chicago Press.

Cartwright, N. (2001). Modularity: it can–and generally does–fail. In M. C. Galavotti, P. Suppes, & D. Costantini (eds.), *Stochastic causality* (pp. 65–85). Chicago, IL: University of Chicago Press.

Cartwright, N. (2002). Against modularity, the causal Markov condition, and any link between the two: comments on Hausman and Woodward. *The British Journal for the Philosophy of Science*, 53(3), 411–453. https://doi.org/10.1093/bjps/53.3.411

Cartwright, N. (2006). From metaphysics to method: comments on manipulability and the causal Markov condition. *The British Journal for the Philosophy of Science*, 57(1), 197–218. https://doi.org/10.1093/bjps/axi156

Cartwright, N. (2007a). Are RCTs the gold standard? *BioSocieties*, 2(1), 11–20. http://dx.doi.org/10.1017/S1745855207005029

Cartwright, N. (2007b). *Hunting causes and using them: approaches in philosophy and economics*. Cambridge, UK: Cambridge University Press.

Cartwright, N. (2011). A philosopher's view of the long road from RCTs to effectiveness. *The Lancet*, 377(9775), 1400–1401. https://doi.org/10.1016/S0140-6736(11)60563-1

Cartwright, N., & Hardie, J. (2012). *Evidence-based policy: a practical guide to doing it better*. Oxford: Oxford University Press. https://doi.org/10.1093/acprof:osobl/9780199841608.001.0001

Cartwright, N., & Munro, E. (2010). The limitations of randomized controlled trials in predicting effectiveness. *Journal of Evaluation in Clinical Practice*, 16(2), 260–266. https://doi.org/10.1111/j.1365-2753.2010.01382.x

Carvalho, J. P. (2013). On the semantics and the use of fuzzy cognitive maps and dynamic cognitive maps in social sciences. *Fuzzy Sets and Systems*, 214, 6–19. https://doi.org/10.1016/j.fss.2011.12.009

Caspi, A., Houts, R. M., Belsky, D. W., et al. (2014). The p factor: one general psychopathology factor in the structure of psychiatric disorders? *Clinical Psychological Science*, 2(2), 119–137. https://doi.org/10.1177/2167702613497473

Castelnau, P., Albert, G., Chabbi, C., et al. (2017). Self-esteem reinforcement strategies in ADHD: comparison between hypnosis and art-therapy. *European Journal of Paediatric Neurology*, 21(suppl 1), 143. https://doi.org/10.1016/j.ejpn.2017.04.1290

Chakravartty, A. (2017). *Scientific ontology: integrating naturalized metaphysics and voluntarist epistemology*. Oxford: Oxford University Press. https://doi.org/10.1093/oso/9780190651459.001.0001

Chang, H. (2017). Is pluralism compatible with scientific realism? In J. Saatsi (ed.), *The Routledge handbook of scientific realism* (pp. 176–186). London: Routledge.

Chang, H. (2019). Relativism, perspectivism and pluralism. In M. Kusch (ed.), *The Routledge handbook of philosophy of relativism* (pp. 398–406). Abingdon: Routledge.

Chen, C. (2004). Searching for intellectual turning points: progressive knowledge domain visualization. *Proceedings of the National Academy of Sciences*, 101(suppl 1), 5303–5310. https://doi.org/10.1073/pnas.0307513100

Choi, S., & Fara, M. (2021). Dispositions. In E. N. Zalta (ed.), *The Stanford encyclopedia of philosophy*. Stanford, CA: Stanford University Press. https://plato.stanford.edu/archives/spr2021/entries/dispositions/.

Chomsky, N. (1966). *Cartesian linguistics: a chapter in the history of rationalist thought*. New York: Harper & Row.

Christensen, W. D., & Bickhard, M. H. (2002). The process dynamics of normative function. *The Monist*, 85(1), 3–28. www.jstor.org/stable/27903755

Chung, J. M., Hutteman, R., van Aken, M. A. G., & Denissen, J. J. A. (2017). High, low, and in between: self-esteem development from middle childhood to young adulthood. *Journal of Research in Personality*, 70, 122–133. https://doi.org/10.1016/j.jrp.2017.07.001

Cigman, R. (2004). Situated self-esteem. *Journal of Philosophy of Education*, 38(1), 91–105. https://doi.org/10.1111/j.0309-8249.2004.00365.x

Clayton, P., & Davies, P. (2011). *The re-emergence of emergence: the emergentist hypothesis from science to religion*. Oxford: Oxford University Press. https://doi.org/10.1093/acprof:oso/9780199544318.001.0001

Clearfield, M. W., Diedrich, F. J., Smith, L. B., & Thelen, E. (2006). Young infants reach correctly in A-not-B tasks: on the development of stability and perseveration. *Infant Behavior and Development*, 29(3), 435–444. https://doi.org/10.1016/j.infbeh.2006.03.001

Cohen, D. (2010). Probabilistic epigenesis: an alternative causal model for conduct disorders in children and adolescents. *Neuroscience & Biobehavioral Reviews*, 34(1), 119–129. http://doi.org/10.1016/j.neubiorev.2009.07.011

Cohen, S. M., & Reeve, C. D. C. (2020). Aristotle's metaphysics. In E. N. Zalta (ed.), *The Stanford Encyclopedia of Philosophy* (Winter 2020 Edition). https://plato.stanford.edu/archives/win2020/entries/aristotle-metaphysics/

Contreras, A., Nieto, I., Valiente, C., Espinosa, R., & Vazquez, C. (2019). The study of psychopathology from the network analysis perspective: a systematic review. *Psychotherapy and Psychosomatics*, 88(2), 71–83. https://doi.org/10.1159/000497425

Cook, J. (2020). A different view of the Lorenz system. Posted on 26 January 2020 www.johndcook.com/blog/2020/01/26/lorenz-system/

Corradini, A., & O'Connor, T. (eds.). (2010). *Emergence in science and philosophy* (vol. 6). Abingdon and New York: Routledge.

Cottrell, L. S. (1941). The case-study method in prediction. *Sociometry*, 4(4), 358–370. https://doi.org/10.2307/2785139

Cozman, F. (2013). Imprecise and indeterminate probabilities. In A. Hájek & C. Hitchcock (eds.), *The Oxford handbook of probability and philosophy* (pp. 296–309). Oxford: Oxford University Press. DOI: 10.1093/oxfordhb/9780199607617.001.0001

Cramer, A. O., Van Borkulo, C. D., Giltay, E. J., et al. (2016). Major depression as a complex dynamic system. *PloS One*, 11(12), e0167490. https://doi.org/10.1371/journal.pone.0167490

Cramer, A. O., Waldorp, L. J., Van der Maas, H. L., & Borsboom, D. (2010). Comorbidity: a network perspective. *Behavioral and Brain Sciences*, 33(2–3), 137. DOI: 10.1017/S0140525X09991567

Crocker, J., & Cooper, M. L. (2011). Addressing scientific fraud. *Science*, 334(6060), 1182. doi:10.1126/science.1216775

Curran, P. J., & Hussong, A. M. (2009). Integrative data analysis: the simultaneous analysis of multiple data sets. *Psychological Methods*, 14(2), 81. doi: 10.1037/a0015914

d'Entreves, M. P. (2019). Hannah Arendt. In E. N. Zalta (ed.), *The Stanford Encyclopedia of Philosophy* (Autumn 2019 Edition). https://plato.stanford.edu/archives/fall2019/entries/arendt/

Dafermos, M. (2015). Rethinking the crisis in social psychology: a dialectical perspective. *Social and Personality Psychology Compass*, 9(8), 394–405. https://doi.org/10.1111/spc3.12187

Dafermos, M. (2020). The metaphysics of psychology and a dialectical perspective. *Theory & Psychology*, 31(3), 355–374. https://doi.org/10.1177/0959354320975491

Dalal, F. (2018). *CBT: The cognitive behavioural Tsunami: managerialism, politics and the corruptions of science*. London and New York: Routledge.

Dale, R., & Duran, N. D. (2013). Dealing with complexity differently: from interaction-dominant dynamics to theoretical plurality. *Ecological Psychology*, 25(3), 248–255. https://doi.org/10.1080/10407413.2013.810099

Dale, R., & Spivey, M. J. (2006). Unraveling the dyad: using recurrence analysis to explore patterns of syntactic coordination between children and caregivers in conversation. *Language Learning*, 56, 391–430. https://doi.org/10.1111/j.1467-9922.2006.00372.x

Damm, L., Varoqui, D., De Cock, V. C., Dalla Bella, S., & Bardy, B. (2020). Why do we move to the beat? A multi-scale approach, from physical principles to brain dynamics. *Neuroscience & Biobehavioral Reviews*, 112, 553–584. https://doi.org/10.1016/j.neubiorev.2019.12.024

Danziger, K. (1990). *Constructing the subject*. Cambridge, UK: Cambridge University Press. https://doi.org/10.1017/CBO9780511524059

Davidson, M. (2017). Vaccination as a cause of autism–myths and controversies. *Dialogues in Clinical Neuroscience*, 19(4), 403. doi: 10.31887/DCNS.2017.19.4/mdavidson

De Bordes, P. F., Cox, R. F., Hasselman, F., & Cillessen, A. H. (2013). Toddlers' gaze following through attention modulation: intention is in the eye of the beholder. *Journal of Experimental Child Psychology*, 116(2), 443–452. DOI: 10.1016/j.jecp.2012.09.008

De Carvalho, E. M., & Rolla, G. (2020). An enactive-ecological approach to information and uncertainty. *Frontiers in Psychology*, 11. https://doi.org/10.3389/fpsyg.2020.00588

De Felice, G., Giuliani, A., Halfon, S., et al. (2019). The misleading Dodo Bird verdict. How much of the outcome variance is explained by common and specific factors? *New Ideas in Psychology*, 54, 50–55. https://doi.org/10.1016/j.newideapsych.2019.01.006

De Greene, K. B. (1993). *A systems-based approach to policymaking*. New York: Springer Science & Business Media. https://doi.org/10.1007/978-1-4615-3226-2

De Jaegher, H. (2013). Rigid and fluid interactions with institutions. *Cognitive Systems Research*, 25, 19–25. https://doi.org/10.1016/j.cogsys.2013.03.002

De Jaegher, H., & Rohde, M. (2010). *Enaction: toward a new paradigm for cognitive science*. Cambridge, MA: MIT Press.

De Jesus, P. (2018). Thinking through enactive agency: sense-making, bio-semiosis and the ontologies of organismic worlds. *Phenomenology and the Cognitive Sciences*, 17(5), 861–887. https://doi.org/10.1007/s11097-018-9562-2

De Ruiter, N. M. P., Den Hartigh, R. J. R., Cox, R. F. A., Van Geert, P. L. C., & Kunnen, E. S. (2015). The temporal structure of state self-esteem variability during parent–adolescent interactions: more than random fluctuations. *Self and Identity*, 14(3), 314–333. https://doi.org/10.1080/15298868.2014.994026

De Ruiter, N. M. P., & Gmelin, J.-O. H. (2021). What is real about 'real time' anyway? A proposal for a pluralistic approach to studying identity processes across different timescales. *Identity*, 21(4), 289–308. https://doi.org/10.1080/15283488.2021.1969937

De Ruiter, N. M. P., Hollenstein, T., Van Geert, P. L. C., & Kunnen, E. S. (2018). Self-esteem as a complex dynamic system: intrinsic and extrinsic microlevel dynamics. *Complexity*, 2018, 1–19. https://doi.org/10.1155/2018/4781563

De Ruiter, N. M. P., Van Geert, P. L. C., & Kunnen, E. S. (2017). Explaining the 'how' of self-esteem development: the self-organizing self-esteem model. *Review of General Psychology*, 21(1), 49–68. http://dx.doi.org/10.1037/gpr0000099

De Ruiter, N. M., Van der Steen, S., Den Hartigh, R. J., & Van Geert, P. L. (2017). Capturing moment-to-moment changes in multivariate human experience. *International Journal of Behavioral Development*, 41(5), 611–620. DOI: 10.1177/0165025416651736

De Weerth, C., & Van Geert, P. (2001). Changing patterns of infant behavior and mother–infant interaction: intra-and interindividual variability. *Infant Behavior and Development*, 24(4), 347–371. https://doi.org/10.1016/S0163-6383(02)00083-8

De Weerth, C., Van Geert, P., & Hoijtink, H. (1999). Intraindividual variability in infant behavior. *Developmental Psychology*, 35(4), 1102. DOI: 10.1037//0012-1649.35.4.1102

De Wolf, T., & Holvoet, T. (2004). Emergence versus self-organisation: different concepts but promising when combined. In S. A. Brueckner, G. Di Marzo Serugendo, A. Karageorgos, & R. Nagpal (eds.), *International workshop on engineering self-organising applications* (pp. 1–15). Berlin and Heidelberg: Springer.

Deaton, A., & Cartwright, N. (2018). Understanding and misunderstanding randomized controlled trials. *Social Science & Medicine*, 210, 2–21. https://doi.org/10.1016/j.socscimed.2017.12.005

DeFife, J. A., Peart, J., Bradley, B., et al. (2013). Validity of prototype diagnosis for mood and anxiety disorders. *JAMA Psychiatry*, 70(2), 140–148. doi:10.1001/jamapsychiatry.2013.270

Delignières, D., Fortes, M., & Ninot, G. (2004). The fractal dynamics of self-esteem and physical self. *Nonlinear Dynamics Psychology and Life Sciences*, 8(4), 479–510.

Delmas, E., Besson, M., Brice, M. H., et al. (2019). Analysing ecological networks of species interactions. *Biological Reviews*, 94(1), 16–36. https://doi.org/10.1111/brv.12433

Den Hartigh, R. J. R., Cox, R. F., & Van Geert, P. L. (2017). Complex versus complicated models of cognition. In L. Magnani, & T. Bertolotti (eds.), *Springer handbook of model-based science*. (pp. 657–669). Cham: Springer. https://doi.org/10.1007/978-3-319-30526-4

Den Hartigh, R. J. R., Gernigon, C., Van Yperen, N. W., Marin, L., & Van Geert, P. L. (2014). How psychological and behavioral team states change during positive and negative momentum. *PloS One*, 9(5), e97887. https://doi.org/10.1371/journal.pone.0097887

Den Hartigh, R. J. R., Van Dijk, M. W., Steenbeek, H. W., & Van Geert, P. L. (2016). A dynamic network model to explain the development of excellent human performance. *Frontiers in Psychology*, 7, 532. https://doi.org/10.3389/fpsyg.2016.00532

Deventer, R., Denzler, J., & Niemann, H. (2002). Application of Bayesian controllers to dynamic systems. In A. Abraham & M. Köppen (eds.), *Hybrid information systems* (pp. 555–569). Berlin and Heidelberg: Springer. https://doi.org/10.1007/978-3-7908-1782-9

Di Paolo, E. (2009). The social and enactive mind. *Phenomenology and the Cognitive Sciences*, 8(4), 409–415. DOI: 10.1007/s11097-009-9143-5

Di Paolo, E. A. (2005). Autopoiesis, adaptivity, teleology, agency. *Phenomenology and the Cognitive Sciences*, 4(4), 429–452. DOI: 10.1007/s11097-005-9002-y

Di Paolo, E. A., Cuffari, E. C., & De Jaegher, H. (2018). *Linguistic bodies: the continuity between life and language*. Cambridge, MA: MIT Press. https://doi.org/10.7551/mitpress/11244.001.0001

Di Paolo, E. A., Rohde, M., & De Jaegher, H. (2010). Horizons for the enactive mind: values, social interaction, and play. In H. De Jaegher & M. Rohde (eds.), *Enaction: toward a new paradigm for cognitive science* (pp. 33–89). Cambridge, MA: MIT Press.

Didonato, M. D., England, D., Martin, C. L., & Amazeen, P. G. (2013). Dynamical analyses for developmental science: a primer for intrigued scientists. *Human Development*, 56(1), 59–75. https://doi.org/10.1159/000342936

Donnellan, B. M., Kenny, D. A., Trzesniewski, K. H., Lucas, R. E., & Conger, R. D. (2012). Using trait-state models to evaluate the longitudinal consistency of global self-esteem from adolescence to adulthood. *Journal of Research in Personality*, 46(6), 634–645. https://doi.org/10.1016/j.jrp.2012.07.005

Dotterer, H. L., Beltz, A. M., Foster, K. T., Simms, L. J., & Wright, A. G. (2019). Personalized models of personality disorders: using a temporal network method to understand symptomatology and daily functioning in a clinical sample. *Psychological Medicine*, 1–9. doi: 10.1017/S0033291719002563

Douven, I. (2021). Abduction. In E. N. Zalta (ed.), *The Stanford Encyclopedia of Philosophy* (Summer 2021 edition). https://plato.stanford.edu/archives/sum2021/entries/abduction/

Dowe, P. (2000). *Physical causation*. Cambridge, UK: Cambridge University Press. https://doi.org/10.1017/CBO9780511570650

Dowe, P. (2007). Causal processes. *Stanford Encyclopedia of Philosophy*. https://stanford.library.sydney.edu.au/archives/sum2010/entries/causation-process/

Dowe, P. (2009). Causal process theories. In H. Beebee, C. Hitchcock, & P. Menzies (eds.), *The Oxford handbook of causation*. Oxford: Oxford University Press. DOI: 10.1093/oxfordhb/9780199279739.001.0001

Dowe, P. (2018). Causal processes. In E. N. Zalta (ed.), *The Stanford Encyclopedia of Philosophy* (Summer 2018 Edition). https://plato.stanford.edu/archives/sum2018/entries/causation-process/

Dreyfus, H. L. (2005). How Heidegger defends the possibility of a correspondence theory of truth with respect to the entities of natural science. In T. R. Schatzki, K. K. Cetina, & E. Von Savigny (eds.), *The practice turn in contemporary theory* (pp. 159–171). Abingdon and New York: Routledge. https://doi.org/10.4324/9780203977453

Duckworth, A. L., Quinn, P. D., Lynam, D. R., Loeber, R., & Stouthamer-Loeber, M. (2011). Role of test motivation in intelligence testing. *Proceedings of the National Academy of Sciences*, 108(19), 7716–7720. https://doi.org/10.1073/pnas.1018601108

Dumas, G., de Guzman, G. C., Tognoli, E., & Kelso, J. S. (2014). The human dynamic clamp as a paradigm for social interaction. *Proceedings of the National Academy of Sciences*, 111(35), E3726–E3734. https://doi.org/10.1073/pnas.1407486111

Dupré, J., & Nicholson, D. J. (2018). A manifesto for a processual philosophy of biology. In Nicholson, D. J. & Dupré, J. (eds.). *Everything flows: towards a processual philosophy of biology* (pp. 4–45). Oxford: Oxford University Press. DOI:10.1093/oso/9780198779636.001.0001

Eagly, A. H., & Riger, S. (2014). Feminism and psychology: critiques of methods and epistemology. *American Psychologist*, 69(7), 685–702. doi: 10.1037/a0037372

Edwards, D. (2005). Discursive psychology. In K. L. Fitch & R. E. Sanders (eds.), *Handbook of language and social interaction* (pp. 257–273). Hove, UK: Psychology Press.

Elgaard Jensen, T. (2019). Exploring the knowledge practices of psychology: reflections on a field study. *Theory & Psychology*, 29(4), 466–483. https://doi.org/10.1177/0959354319853630

Ellis, G. (2016). *How can physics underlie the mind: top-down causation in the human context*. Berlin and Heidelberg: Springer-Verlag. https://doi.org/10.1007/978-3-662-49809-5

Ellis, G. F. (2005). Physics, complexity and causality. *Nature*, 435(7043), 743–743.

Emmeche, C., Køppe, S., & Stjernfelt, F (2000). Levels, emergence, and three versions of downward causation. In P. B. Andersen, C. Emmeche, N. O. Finnemann, & P. V. Christiansen (eds.), *Downward causation: minds, bodies and matter* (pp. 13–34). Aarhus: Aarhus University Press.

English, L. Q. (2017). *There is no theory of everything: a physics perspective on emergence*. Cham: Springer. https://doi.org/10.1007/978-3-319-59150-6

Érdi, P. (2008). *Complexity explained*. Berlin and Heidelberg: Springer-Verlag. https://doi.org/10.1007/978-3-540-35778-0

Erikson, E. H. (1968). *Identity, youth, and crisis*. New York: Norton.

Erol, R. Y., & Orth, U. (2011). Self-esteem development from age 14 to 30 years: a longitudinal study. *Journal of Personality and Social Psychology*, 101(3), 607–619. https://doi.org/10.1037/a0024299

Eronen, M. I. (2020). Causal discovery and the problem of psychological interventions. *New Ideas in Psychology*, 59, 100785. https://doi.org/10.1016/j.newideapsych.2020.100785

Eronen, M. I., & Bringmann, L. F. (2021). The theory crisis in psychology: how to move forward. *Perspectives on Psychological Science*, 16(4), 779–788. https://doi.org/10.1177/1745691620970586

Fanelli, D., Costas, R., & Ioannidis, J. P. A. (2017). Meta-assessment of bias in science. *Proceedings of the National Academy of Sciences*, 114, 3714–3719. https://doi.org/10.1073/pnas.1618569114

Fearon, D. (2004). The bond threat sequence: discourse evidence for the systematic interdependence of shame and social relationships. In C. Leach & L. Tiedens (eds.), *The social life of emotions* (pp. 153–206). Cambridge, UK: Cambridge University Press. https://doi.org/10.1017/CBO9780511819568

Felmlee, D. H., & Greenberg, D. F. (1999). A dynamic systems model of dyadic interaction. *The Journal of Mathematical Sociology*, 23(3), 155–180. https://doi.org/10.1080/0022250X.1999.9990218

Ferguson, C. J., & Heene, M. (2012). A vast graveyard of undead theories: publication bias and psychological science's aversion to the null. *Perspectives on Psychological Science*, 7(6), 555–561. https://doi.org/10.1177/1745691612459059

Fischer, K. W. (2008). Dynamic cycles of cognitive and brain development: measuring growth in mind, brain, and education. In A. M. Battro, K. W. Fischer, & P. Léna (eds.), *The educated brain* (pp. 127–150). Cambridge, UK: Cambridge University Press. https://doi.org/10.1017/CBO9780511489907

Fischer, K. W., & Van Geert, P. (2014). Dynamic development of brain and behavior. In P. C. M. Molenaar, R. M. Lerner, & K. M. Newell (eds.), *Handbook of developmental systems theory and methodology* (pp. 287–315). New York: Guilford Press.

Fish, J. M. (2000). What anthropology can do for psychology: facing physics envy, ethnocentrism, and a belief in 'Race'. *American Anthropologist*, 102(3), 552–563. https://doi.org/10.1525/aa.2000.102.3.552

Fisher, A. J., Medaglia, J. D., & Jeronimus, B. F. (2018). Lack of group-to-individual generalizability is a threat to human subjects research. *Proceedings of the National Academy of Sciences*, 115(27), E6106–E6115. https://doi.org/10.1073/pnas.1711978115

Flora, D. B. (2020). Thinking about effect sizes: From the replication crisis to a cumulative psychological science. *Canadian Psychology/Psychologie Canadienne*, 61(4), 318. doi:10.1037/cap0000218

Flyvbjerg, B. (2001). *Making social science matter: why social inquiry fails and how it can succeed again*. Cambridge, UK: Cambridge University Press. https://doi.org/10.1017/CBO9780511810503

Forrester, J. W. (1993). System dynamics and the lessons of 35 years. In K. B. De Greene (ed.), *A systems-based approach to policymaking* (pp. 199–240). New York: Springer Science & Business Media. https://doi.org/10.1007/978-1-4615-3226-2

Fortes, M., Delignières, D., & Ninot, G. (2004). The dynamics of self-esteem and physical self: between preservation and adaptation. *Quality & Quantity*, 38, 735–751. DOI: 10.1007/s11135-004-4764-9

Fortis, J.-M. (2015). Family resemblance and semantics: the vagaries of a not so new concept. *History and Philosophy of the Language Sciences*. https://hiphilangsci.net/2015/10/13/family-resemblance-and-semantics-the-vagaries-of-a-not-so-new-concept

Frances, A. (2013). *Saving normal: an insider's revolt against out-of-control psychiatric diagnoses, DSM-5, Big Pharma, and the medicalization of ordinary life*. New York: William Morrow.

Franck, E., & De Raedt, R. (2007). Self-esteem reconsidered: unstable self-esteem outperforms level of self-esteem as vulnerability marker for depression. *Behaviour Research and Therapy*, 45(7), 1531–1541. https://doi.org/10.1016/j.brat.2007.01.003

Fried, E. I., Epskamp, S., Nesse, R. M., Tuerlinckx, F., & Borsboom, D. (2016). What are 'good' depression symptoms? Comparing the centrality of DSM and non-DSM symptoms of depression in a network analysis. *Journal of Affective Disorders*, 189, 314–320. doi: 10.1016/j.jad.2015.09.005

Fried, E. I., van Borkulo, C. D., Cramer, A. O., et al. (2017). Mental disorders as networks of problems: a review of recent insights. *Social Psychiatry and Psychiatric Epidemiology*, 52(1), 1–10. doi: 10.1007/s00127-016-1319-z

Friston, K. J. (2003). Learning and inference in the brain. *Neural Networks*, 16, 1325–1352. doi: 10.1016/j.neunet.2003.06.005.

Friston, K. J., & Ao, P. (2012). Free energy, value, and attractors. *Computational and Mathematical Methods in Medicine*, 2012(937860), 27. https://doi.org/10.1155/2012/937860

Friston, K. J., Kilner, J., & Harrison, L. (2006). A free energy principle for the brain. *Journal of Physiology*, 1–3, 70–87. https://doi.org/10.1016/j.jphysparis.2006.10.001

Friston, K. J., Moran, R., & Seth, A. K. (2013). Analysing connectivity with Granger causality and dynamic causal modelling. *Current Opinion in Neurobiology*, 23(2), 172–178. http://doi.org/10.1016/j.conb.2012.11.010

Friston, K. J., Preller, K. H., Mathys, C., et al. (2017). Dynamic causal modelling revisited. *NeuroImage*, 199, 730–744. http://doi.org/10.1016/j.neuroimage.2017.02.045

Galatzer-Levy, I. R., & Bryant, R. A. (2013). 636, 120 ways to have posttraumatic stress disorder. *Perspectives on Psychological Science*, 8(6), 651–662. doi: 10.1177/1745691613504115.

Galavotti, M. C. (2017). The interpretation of probability: still an open issue? *Philosophies*, 2(3), 20. https://doi.org/10.3390/philosophies2030020

Ganglmayer, K., Attig, M., Daum, M. M., & Paulus, M. (2019). Infants' perception of goal-directed actions: a multi-lab replication reveals that infants anticipate paths and not goals. *Infant Behavior and Development*, 57, 101340. https://doi.org/10.1016/j.infbeh.2019.101340

Gardner, H. E. (2011). *Frames of mind: the theory of multiple intelligences.* Hachette, UK.

Gardner, M. K. (2013). Theories of intelligence. In M. A. Bray & T. J. Kehle (eds.), *The Oxford handbook of school psychology* (pp. 79–102). Oxford: Oxford University Press. DOI: 10.1093/oxfordhb/9780195369809.001.0001

Gergen, K. J. (2009). *Realities and relationships: soundings in social construction.* Cambridge, MA: Harvard University Press.

Gernigon, C., Den Hartigh, R. J. R., Vallacher, R. R., & Van Geert, P. L. C. (2021). On the accumulation of small (and other) effects: will psychological science ever exorcise laplace's demon? Submitted.

Geukes, K., Nestler, S., Hutteman, R., et al. (2017). Puffed-up but shaky selves: state self-esteem level and variability in narcissists. *Journal of Personality and Social Psychology*, 112(5), 769–786. https://doi.org/10.1037/pspp0000093

Gibb, S., Hendry, R. F., & Lancaster, T. (eds.). (2019). *The Routledge handbook of emergence*. Abingdon and New York: Routledge.

Gibson, E. J., & Walk, R. D. (1960). The 'visual cliff'. *Scientific American*, 202(4), 64–71. https://doi.org/10.1038/scientificamerican0460-64

Gibson, J. J. (1966). *The senses considered as perceptual systems*. Boston, MA: Houghton Mifflin.

Gibson, J. J. (1979). *The ecological approach to visual perception*. Boston, MA: Houghton Mifflin.

Gigerenzer, G., Multmeier, J., Föhring, A., & Wegwarth, O. (2020). Do children have Bayesian intuitions? *Journal of Experimental Psychology: General*. Advance online publication. https://doi.org/10.1037/xge0000979

Gilden, D. L. (2001). Cognitive emissions of 1/f noise. *Psychological Review*, 108(1), 33–56. doi:10.1037/0033-295x.108.1.33

Gill, M. L. (2003). Aristotle's distinction between change and activity. In J. Seibt (ed.), *Process theories: crossdisciplinary studies in dynamic categories* (pp. 23–55). Dordrecht: Kluwer Academic Publishers. https://doi.org/10.1007/978-94-009-0553-5

Gillies, D. (2016). The propensity interpretation. In A. Hájek & C. Hitchcock (eds.), *The Oxford handbook of probability and philosophy* (pp. 406–422). Oxford: Oxford University Press. DOI: 10.1093/oxfordhb/9780199607617.001.0001

Gillon, B. S. (1990.) Bare plurals as plural indefinite noun phrases. In H. E. Kyburg Jr. et al. (eds.), *Knowledge representation and defeasible reasoning* (pp. 119–166). Dordrecht: Kluwer Academic Publishers. https://doi.org/10.1007/978-94-009-0553-5

Gilmore, R. (1993). *Catastrophe theory for scientists and engineers*. North Chelmsford, MA: Courier Corporation.

Giorgi, A. (2009). *The descriptive phenomenological method in psychology: a modified Husserlian approach*. Pittsburgh, PA: Duquesne University Press.

Glanzberg, M. (2004). Quantification and realism. *Philosophy and Phenomenological Research*, 69(3), 541–572. DOI: 10.1111/j.1933-1592.2004.tb00518.x

Glymour, C. N. (2001). *The mind's arrows: Bayes nets and graphical causal models in psychology*. Cambridge, MA: MIT Press.

Goldstein, J. (1999). Emergence as a construct: history and issues. *Emergence*, 1(1), 49–72. DOI: 10.1207/s15327000em0101_4

Gollwitzer, M., & Schwabe, J. (2021). Context Dependency as a Predictor of Replicability. Review of General Psychology, in press, https://journals.sagepub.com/doi/pdf/10.1177/10892680211015635

Gona, J. K., Newton, C. R., Rimba, K., et al. (2015). Parents' and professionals' perceptions on causes and treatment options for autism spectrum disorders (ASD) in a multicultural context on the Kenyan coast. *PloS One*, 10(8), e0132729. https://doi.org/10.1371/journal.pone.0132729

Gopnik, A., Glymour, C., Sobel, D. M., et al. (2004). A theory of causal learning in children: causal maps and Bayes nets. *Psychological Review*, 111(1), 3. doi: 10.1037/0033-295X.111.1.3

Gopnik, A., Schulz, L., & Schulz, L. E. (eds.). (2007). *Causal learning: psychology, philosophy, and computation.* Oxford: Oxford University Press. DOI:10.1093/acprof:oso/9780195176803.001.0001

Gopnik, A., Sobel, D. M., Schulz, L. E., & Glymour, C. (2001). Causal learning mechanisms in very young children: two-, three-, and four-year-olds infer causal relations from patterns of variation and covariation. *Developmental Psychology*, 37(5), 620. https://doi.org/10.1037/0012-1649.37.5.620

Gordon, S. (1991). *The history and philosophy of social science.* London: Routledge.

Gottman, J. M. (2003). *The mathematics of marriage: dynamic nonlinear models.* Cambridge, MA: MIT Press.

Götz, F. M., Gosling, S. D., & Rentfrow, P. J. (2021). Small effects: the indispensable foundation for a cumulative psychological science. *Perspectives on Psychological Science*, PsyArXiv Preprints. https://doi.org/10.31234/osf.io/hzrxf

Goudsmit, A. L. (1989). *Self-organization in psychotherapy.* Berlin and New York: Springer-Verlag. https://doi.org/10.1007/978-3-642-48704-0

Gould, S. J. (1996). *The mismeasure of man (revised and expanded version).* New York and London: W. W. Norton & Company.

Gräbner, C. (2018). How to relate models to reality? An epistemological framework for the validation and verification of computational models. *JASSS*, 21(3). http://doi.org/10.18564/jasss.3772

Graham, D. W. (2008). Heraclitus: flux, order, and knowledge. In P. Curd & D. W. Graham (eds.), *The Oxford handbook of presocratic philosophy* (pp. 169–188). Oxford: Oxford University Press. DOI: 10.1093/oxfordhb/9780195146875.001.0001

Greenberg, D. M., Warrier, V., Allison, C., & Baron-Cohen, S. (2018). Testing the empathizing–systemizing theory of sex differences and the extreme male brain theory of autism in half a million people. *Proceedings of the National Academy of Sciences*, 115(48), 12152–12157. https://doi.org/10.1073/pnas.1811032115

Greenier, K. D., Kernis, M. H., McNamara, C. W., et al. (1999). Individual differences in reactivity to daily events: examining the roles of stability and level of self-esteem. *Journal of Personality*, 67(1), 185–208. https://doi.org/10.1111/1467-6494.00052

Grice, J. W. (2011). *Observation-oriented modeling: analysis of cause in the behavioral sciences.* Cambridge, MA: Academic Press.

Grice, J. W. (2015). From means and variances to persons and patterns. *Frontiers in Psychology*, 6, 1007. doi: 10.3389/fpsyg.2015.01007

Grice, J. W., Barrett, P. T., Schlimgen, L. A., & Abramson, C. I. (2012). Toward a brighter future for psychology as an observation oriented science. *Behavioral Sciences*, 2(1), 1–22. doi: 10.3390/bs2010001

Grimm, V., & Calabrese, J. M. (2011). What is resilience? A short introduction. In G. Deffuant, & N. Gilbert (eds.), *Viability and resilience of complex systems: concepts, methods and case studies from ecology and society* (pp. 3–13). Berlin: Springer. https://doi.org/10.1007/978-3-642-20423-4

Grush, R., & Springle, A. (2019). Agency, perception, space and subjectivity. *Phenomenology and the Cognitive Sciences*, 18(5), 799–818. DOI: 10.1007/s11097-018-9582-y

Guastello, S. J. (2013). *Chaos, catastrophe, and human affairs: applications of nonlinear dynamics to work, organizations, and social evolution.* Hove, UK: Psychology Press.

Guevara, M., Cox, R. F., Van Dijk, M., & Van Geert, P. (2017). Attractor dynamics of dyadic interaction: a recurrence based analysis. *Nonlinear Dynamics Psychology and Life Sciences*, 21(3), 289–317.

Ha, S., Sohn, I. J., Kim, N., Sim, H. J., & Cheon, K. A. (2015). Characteristics of brains in autism spectrum disorder: structure, function and connectivity across the lifespan. *Experimental Neurobiology*, 24(4), 273–284. doi: 10.5607/en.2015.24.4.273

Hacking, I. (1995a) The looping effects of human kinds. In D. Sperber, D. Premack, & A. J. Premack (eds.), *Causal cognition: a multidisciplinary approach* (pp. 351–394). Oxford: Clarendon Press. DOI:10.1093/acprof:oso/9780198524021.001.0001

Hacking, I. (1995b). *Rewriting the soul: multiple personality and the sciences of memory.* Princeton, NJ: Princeton University Press. DOI:10.1086/233676

Hacking, I. (2007). Natural kinds: rosy dawn, scholastic twilight. *Royal Institute of Philosophy Supplements*, 61, 203–239. https://doi.org/10.1017/S1358246100009802

Hacking, I. (2013). Lost in the forest. Review of DSM-5: diagnostic and statistical manual of mental disorders (5th ed.). *London Review of Books*, 35(15), 7–8.

Haig, B. (2021). Understanding replication in a way that is true to science. *Review of General Psychology*, advance publication, https://journals-sagepub-com.proxy-ub.rug.nl/doi/pdf/10.1177/10892680211046514

Haig, B. D., & Borsboom, D. (2012). Truth, science, and psychology. *Theory & Psychology*, 22, 272–289. https://doi.org/10.1177/0959354311430442

Haig, B. D., & Borsboom, D. (2018). Scientific realism with correspondence truth: a reply to Asay (2018). *Theory & Psychology*, 28(3), 398–404. https://doi.org/10.1177/0959354318766718

Haimovici, A., Tagliazucchi, E., Balenzuela, P., & Chialvo, D. R. (2013). Brain organization into resting state networks emerges at criticality on a model of the human connectome. *Physical Review Letters*, 110(17), 178101. doi: 10.1103/PhysRevLett.110.178101

Hájek, A. (1997). 'Mises Redux'–Redux: fifteen arguments against finite frequentism. *Erkenntnis*, 45, 209–227. DOI:10.1007/978-94-011-5712-4_5

Hájek, A. (2009). Fifteen arguments against hypothetical frequentism. *Erkenntnis*, 70(2), 211–235. https://doi.org/10.1007/s10670-009-9154-1

Hájek, A. (2019). Interpretations of probability. In E. N. Zalta (ed.), *The Stanford Encyclopedia of Philosophy* (Autumn 2019 Edition). https://plato.stanford.edu/archives/fall2019/entries/probability-interpret/

Haken, H. (1992). Synergetics in psychology. In W. Tschacher, G. Schiepek, & E. J. Brunner (eds.), *Self-organization and clinical psychology: empirical approaches to synergetics in psychology* (vol. 58, pp. 32–54). Berlin and Heidelberg: Springer. https://doi.org/10.1007/978-3-642-77534-5

Haken, H. (2007). Synergetics. *Scholarpedia*, 2(1), 1400. www.scholarpedia.org/article/Synergetics

Hall, B. K. (2012). Evolutionary developmental biology (Evo-Devo): past, present, and future. *Evolution: Education and Outreach*, 5(2), 184–193. DOI:10.1007/s12052-012-0418-x

Halley, J. D., & Winkler, D. A. (2008). Classification of emergence and its relation to self-organization. *Complexity*, 13(5), 10–15. DOI: 10.1002/cplx.20216

Halsey, L. G. (2019). The reign of the p-value is over: what alternative analyses could we employ to fill the power vacuum? *Biology Letters*, 15(5), 20190174. https://doi.org/10.1098/rsbl.2019.0174

Hamaker, E. (2012). Why researchers should think 'within-person': a paradigmatic rationale. In M. Csikszentmihalyi (ed.), *Handbook of research methods for studying daily life* (pp. 43–61). New York: Guilford Press.

Harman, G. (2009). *Prince of networks: Bruno Latour and metaphysics*. Melbourne: Re-press.

Harré, R. (1979). *Social being*. Oxford: Blackwell.

Hartelman, P. A., Van der Maas, H. L., & Molenaar, P. C. (1998). Detecting and modelling developmental transitions. *British Journal of Developmental Psychology*, 16(1), 97–122. https://doi.org/10.1111/j.2044-835X.1998.tb00751.x

Harter, S., & Whitesell, N. R. (2003). Beyond the debate: why some adolescents report stable self-worth over time and situation, whereas others report changes in self-worth. *Journal of Personality*, 71(6), 1027–1058. https://doi.org/10.1111/1467-6494.7106006

Haslam, N. (2014). Natural kinds in psychiatry: conceptually implausible, empirically questionable, and stigmatizing. In H. Kincaid & J. A. Sullivan (eds.), *Classifying psychopathology: mental kinds and natural kinds* (pp. 11–28). Cambridge, MA: MIT Press. https://doi.org/10.7551/mitpress/8942.001.0001

Haslam, N. (2016). Looping effects and the expanding concept of mental disorder. *Journal of Psychopathology*, 22, 4–9.

Haslam, N., & Kvaale, E. P. (2015). Biogenetic explanations of mental disorder: the mixed-blessings model. *Current Directions in Psychological Science*, 24(5), 399–404. https://doi.org/10.1177/0963721415588082

Hausman, D. M., & Woodward, J. (1999). Independence, invariance and the causal Markov condition. *The British Journal for the Philosophy of Science*, 50(4), 521–583. https://doi.org/10.1093/bjps/50.4.521

Hausman, D., & Woodward, J. (2004). Manipulation and the causal Markov condition. *Philosophy of Science*, 71(5), 846–856. https://doi.org/10.1086/425235

Hawley, K., & Bird, A. (2011). What are natural kinds? *Philosophical Perspectives*, 25, 205–221. http://www.jstor.org/stable/41329468

Hayes, A. M., & Andrews, L. A. (2020). A complex systems approach to the study of change in psychotherapy. *BMC Medicine*, 18(1), 1–13. https://doi.org/10.1186/s12916-020-01662-2

Hayes, A. M., Feldman, G. C., Beevers, C. G., et al. (2007a). Discontinuities and cognitive changes in an exposure-based cognitive therapy for depression. *Journal of Consulting and Clinical Psychology*, 75(3), 409. DOI: 10.1037/0022-006X.75.3.409

Hayes, A. M., Laurenceau, J. P., Feldman, G., Strauss, J. L., & Cardaciotto, L. (2007b). Change is not always linear: the study of nonlinear and discontinuous patterns of change in psychotherapy. *Clinical Psychology Review*, 27(6), 715–723. doi: 10.1016/j.cpr.2007.01.008

Heinzel, S., Tominschek, I., & Schiepek, G. (2014). Dynamic patterns in psychotherapy-discontinuous changes and critical instabilities during the treatment of obsessive compulsive disorder. *Nonlinear Dynamics Psychology and Life Sciences*, 18(2), 155–176.

Helmich, M. A., Wichers, M., Olthof, M., et al. (2020). Sudden gains in day-to-day change: revealing nonlinear patterns of individual improvement in depression. *Journal of Consulting and Clinical Psychology*, 88(2), 119. doi: 10.1037/ccp0000469

Hennessy, S., Howe, C., Mercer, N., & Vrikki, M. (2020). Coding classroom dialogue: methodological considerations for researchers. *Learning, Culture and Social Interaction*, 25, 100404. https://doi.org/10.1016/j.lcsi.2020.100404

Herbert, J. D., & Padovani, F. (2015). Contextualism, psychological science, and the question of ontology. *Journal of Contextual Behavioral Science*, 4(4), 225–230. https://doi.org/10.1016/j.jcbs.2014.11.005

Hesp, C., Steenbeek, H. W., & Van Geert, P. L. (2019). Socio-emotional concern dynamics in a model of real-time dyadic interaction: parent-child play in autism. *Frontiers in Psychology*, 10, 1635. https://doi.org/10.3389/fpsyg.2019.01635

Hibberd, F. J. (2014). The metaphysical basis of a process psychology. *Journal of Theoretical and Philosophical Psychology*, 34(3), 161–186. https://doi.org/10.1037/a0036242

Hilgers, M. (2009). Habitus, freedom, and reflexivity. *Theory & Psychology*, 19(6), 728–755. https://doi.org/10.1177/0959354309345892

Hilgevoord, J., & Uffink, J (2016). The uncertainty principle. In E. N. Zalta (ed.), *The Stanford Encyclopedia of Philosophy* (Winter 2016 Edition). https://plato.stanford.edu/archives/win2016/entries/qt-uncertainty/

Hitchcock, C. (2021). Probabilistic causation. In E. N. Zalta (ed.), *The Stanford Encyclopedia of Philosophy* (Spring 2021 Edition). https://plato.stanford.edu/archives/spr2021/entries/causation-probabilistic/

Hladký, V., & Havlíček, J. (2013). Was Tinbergen an Aristotelian? Comparison of Tinbergen's four whys and Aristotle's four causes. *Human Ethology Bulletin*, 28(4), 3–11.

Hoffman, J., & Rosenkrantz, G. R. (1997). *Substance: its nature and existence*. London and New York: Routledge.

Hofmann, S. G., Curtiss, J., & McNally, R. J. (2016). A complex network perspective on clinical science. *Perspectives on Psychological Science*, 11(5), 597–605. DOI: 10.1177/1745691616639283

Hogan, J. A., & Bolhuis J. J. (2008). Tinbergen's four questions and contemporary behavioral biology. In J. J. Bolhuis & S. Verhulst (eds.), *Tinbergen's legacy: function and mechanism in behavioral biology* (pp. 25–34). Cambridge, UK: Cambridge University Press.

Hohn, R. E. (2020). Intransigence in mainstream thinking about psychological measurement. In J. T. Lamiell & K. L. Slaney (eds.), *Problematic research practices and inertia in scientific psychology: history, sources, and recommended solutions* (pp. 39–54). Abingdon: Routledge.

Holden, J. G., Van Orden, G. C., & Turvey, M. T. (2009). Dispersion of response times reveals cognitive dynamics. *Psychological Review*, 116(2), 318–342. doi: 10.1037/a0014849

Holden, M. T., & Lynch, P. (2004). Choosing the appropriate methodology: understanding research philosophy. *The Marketing Review*, 4(4), 397–409. https://doi.org/10.1362/1469347042772428

Holland, J. H. (2000). *Emergence: from chaos to order*. Oxford: Oxford University Press.

Holland, J. H. (2014). *Complexity: a very short introduction*. Oxford: Oxford University Press. DOI: 10.1093/actrade/9780199662548.001.0001

Hollenstein, T. (2007). State space grids: analyzing dynamics across development. *International Journal of Behavioral Development*, 31, 384–396. https://doi.org/10.1177/0165025407077765

Hollenstein, T. (2012). Using state space grids for understanding processes of change and stability in adolescence. In E. S. Kunnen (ed.), *A dynamic systems approach to adolescent development* (pp. 73–89). Hove, UK: Psychology Press.

Hollenstein, T. (2013). *State space grids: depicting dynamics across development*. Boston: Springer. https://doi.org/10.1007/978-1-4614-5007-8

Hollenstein, T., Lichtwarck-Aschoff, A., & Potworowski, G. (2013). A model of socioemotional flexibility at three timescales. *Emotion Review*, 5(4), 397–405. https://doi.org/10.1177/1754073913484181

Hooker, C. (2011). *Handbook of the philosophy of science, vol. 10: philosophy of complex systems*. Amsterdam: Elsevier BV. https://doi.org/10.1016/C2009-0-06625-2

Howe, M., & Lewis, M. D. (2005). The importance of dynamic systems approaches for understanding development. *Developmental Review*, 25(3–4), 247–251. https://doi.org/10.1016/j.dr.2005.09.002

Howell, J. L., Collisson, B., & King, K. M. (2014). Physics envy: psychologists' perceptions of psychology and agreement about core concepts. *Teaching of Psychology*, 41(4), 330–334. https://doi.org/10.1177/0098628314549705

Howell, J. L., Sosa, N., & Osborn, H. J. (2019). Self-esteem as a monitor of fundamental psychological need satisfaction. *Social and Personality Psychology Compass*, 13(8), e 12492. https://doi.org/10.1111/spc3.12492

Hruschka, D. (2018). *You can't characterize human nature if studies overlook 85 percent of people on Earth*. https://theconversation.com/you-cant-characterize-human-nature-if-studies-overlook-85-percent-of-people-on-earth-106670

Hume, D. (1960). *A treatise of human nature*. Oxford: Oxford University Press (first published in 1739).

Humphreys, P. (2016). *Emergence: a philosophical account*. Oxford: Oxford University Press. DOI:10.1093/acprof:oso/9780190620325.001.0001

Hutt, A. (2020). Synergetics: an introduction. In A. Hutt & H. Haken (eds.), *Synergetics. A volume in the encyclopedia of complexity and systems science* (2nd ed.) (pp. 1–3). New York: Springer US. https://doi.org/10.1007/978-1-0716-0421-2

Hutt, A., & Haken, H. (eds.). (2020). *Synergetics: a volume in the encyclopedia of complexity and systems science* (2nd ed.). New York: Springer US. https://doi.org/10.1007/978-1-0716-0421-2

Hutteman, R., Nestler, S., Wagner, J., Egloff, B., & Back, M. D. (2015). Wherever I may roam: processes of self-esteem development from adolescence to emerging adulthood in the context of International Student Exchange. *Journal of Personality and Social Psychology*, 108(5), 767–783. https://doi.org/10.1037/psppoooo015

Hüttemann, A. (2013). A disposition-based process theory of causation. In S. Mumford & M. Tugby (eds.), *Metaphysics and science* (pp. 101–122). Oxford: Oxford University Press.

Hyde, D. (2016). *Vagueness, logic and ontology*. Abingdon: Routledge.

Hyman, S. E. (2010). The diagnosis of mental disorders: the problem of reification. *Annual Review of Clinical Psychology*, 6, 155–179. https://doi.org/10.1146/annurev.clinpsy.3.022806.091532

Ihlen, E. A., & Vereijken, B. (2010). Interaction-dominant dynamics in human cognition: beyond 1/$f\alpha$ fluctuation. *Journal of Experimental Psychology: General*, 139(3), 436. https://doi.org/10.1037/a0019098

Ingthorsson, R. (2002). Causal production as interaction. *Metaphysica*, 3(1), 87–119.

Ioannidis, J. P. (2005). Why most published research findings are false. *PLoS Medicine*, 2(8), e124. https://doi.org/10.1371/journal.pmed.0020124

Jablensky, A. (2005). Categories, dimensions and prototypes: critical issues for psychiatric classification. *Psychopathology*, 38(4), 201–205. https://doi.org/10.1159/000086092

Jackman, S. (2009). *Bayesian analysis for the social sciences*. Chichester: John Wiley & Sons.

Jansen, B. R., Raijmakers, M. E., & Visser, I. (2007). Rule transition on the balance scale task: a case study in belief change. *Synthese*, 155(2), 211–236. https://doi.org/10.1007/s11229-006-9142-9

Jason, J. Y., Berrios, J., Newbern, J. M., et al. (2015). An autism-linked mutation disables phosphorylation control of UBE3A. *Cell*, 162(4), 795–807. https://doi.org/10.1016/j.cell.2015.06.045

Jeronimus, B. F., Riese, H., Sanderman, R., & Ormel, J. (2014). Mutual reinforcement between neuroticism and life experiences: a five-wave, 16-year study to test reciprocal causation. *Journal of Personality and Social Psychology*, 107(4), 751. https://doi.org/10.1037/a0037009

Jörg, T. (2011). *New thinking in complexity for the social sciences and humanities: a generative, transdisciplinary approach*. Berlin and Heidelberg: Springer Science & Business Media. https://doi.org/10.1007/978-94-007-1303-1

Joseph, J. (2018). Autism aetiology: the journey of discovery from the 'refrigerator mother' to the neurodevelopmental hypothesis. *Journal of Child and Adolescent Psychology*, 2(02), 1–2.

Juarrero, A. (1999). *Dynamics in action: intentional behavior as a complex system*, Cambridge, MA: MIT Press. https://doi.org/10.7551/mitpress/2528.001.0001

Juarrero, A. (2000). Dynamics in action: intentional behavior as a complex system. *Emergence*, 2(2), 24–57. https://doi.org/10.1207/S15327000EM0202_03

Kahn, C. H. (1979). *The art and thought of Heraclitus*. Cambridge, UK: Cambridge University Press. https://doi.org/10.1017/CBO9780511627392

Kamphuis, J. H., & Noordhof, A. (2009). On categorical diagnoses in DSM-V: cutting dimensions at useful points? *Psychological Assessment*, 21(3), 294–301. https://doi.org/10.1037/a0016697

Kazdin, A. E. (2007). Mediators and mechanisms of change in psychotherapy research. *Annual Review of Clinical Psychology*, 3, 1–27. https://doi.org/10.1146/annurev.clinpsy.3.022806.091432

Kazdin, A. E. (2009). Understanding how and why psychotherapy leads to change. *Psychotherapy Research*, 19(4–5), 418–428. https://doi.org/10.1080/10503300802448899

Kello, C. T., Brown, G. D., Ferrer-i-Cancho, R., et al. (2010). Scaling laws in cognitive sciences. *Trends in Cognitive Sciences*, 14(5), 223–232. https://doi.org/10.1016/j.tics.2010.02.005

Kelly, R., Desiree, K., & Stephen, P. (2015). Self-esteem, personality, and gender self-perception. *Frontiers in Psychology*, 6. https://doi.org/10.3389/conf.fpsyg.2015.66.00021

Kelso, J. A. S. (1995). *Dynamic patterns: the self-organization of brain and behavior*. Cambridge, MA: MIT Press.

Kelso, J. A. S. (2001). How the brain changes its mind: metastable coordination dynamics. The emergence of the mind. *Fondazione Carlo Erba*, Milano, 93–101.

Kelso, J. A. S. (2005). The complementary nature of coordination dynamics: toward a science of the in-between. In R. R. McDaniel & D. J. Driebe (eds.), *Uncertainty and surprise in complex systems* (pp. 77–85). Berlin and Heidelberg: Springer. https://doi.org/10.1007/b13122

Kelso, J. A. S. (2008). Haken-Kelso-Bunz model. *Scholarpedia*, 3(10), 1612.

Kelso, J. A. S. (2013). Coordination dynamics. In R. A. Meyers (ed.), *Encyclopedia of complexity and system science* (pp. 1537–1564). Berlin and Heidelberg: Springer. https://doi.org/10.1007/978-3-642-27737-5_101-3

Kelso, J. A. S., & Engstrom, D. (2006). *The complementary nature*. Cambridge, MA: MIT Press.

Kelso, J. A. S., Holt, K. G., Rubin, P., & Kugler, P. N. (1981). Patterns of human interlimb coordination emerge from the properties of non-linear, limit cycle oscillatory processes: Theory and data. *Journal of Motor Behavior*, 13, 226–261. http://dx.doi.org/10.1080/00222895.1981.10735251

Kemp, J. J., Lickel, J. J., & Deacon, B. J. (2014). Effects of a chemical imbalance causal explanation on individuals' perceptions of their depressive symptoms. *Behaviour Research and Therapy*, 56, 47–52. https://doi.org/10.1016/j.brat.2014.02.009

Kendig, C. (ed.). (2015). *Natural kinds and classification in scientific practice*. Abingdon: Routledge. https://doi.org/10.4324/9781315619934

Kernis, M. H. (2005). Measuring self-esteem in context: the importance of stability of self-esteem in psychological functioning. *Journal of Personality*, 73(6), 1569–1605. https://doi.org/10.1111/j.1467-6494.2005.00359.x

Kernis, M., Bruce, H., Grannemann, B. D., & Barclay, L. C. (1992). Stability of self-esteem: assessment, correlates, and excuse making. *Journal of Personality*, 60(3), 621–644. https://doi.org/10.1111/j.1467-6494.1992.tb00923.x

Kernis, M., Cornell, D., Sun, C., Berry, A., & Harlow, T. (1993). There's more to self-esteem than whether it is high or low: the importance of stability of self-esteem. *Personality Processes and Individual Differences*, 65(6), 1190–1204. https://doi.org/10.1037/0022-3514.65.6.1190

Kernis, M., Grannemann, B., & Barclay, L. (1989). Stability and level of self-esteem as predictors of anger arousal and hostility. *Journal of Personality and Social Psychology*, 56(6), 1013–1022. https://doi.org/10.1037/0022-3514.56.6.1013

Kincaid, H., & Sullivan, J. A. (eds.). (2014). *Classifying psychopathology: mental kinds and natural kinds*. Cambridge, MA: MIT Press. https://doi.org/10.7551/mitpress/8942.001.0001

Klein, O., Doyen, S., Leys, C., et al. (2012). Low hopes, high expectations: expectancy effects and the replicability of behavioral experiments. *Perspectives on Psychological Science*, 7(6), 572–584. https://doi.org/10.1177/1745691612463704

Koopmans, M. (2014). Change, self-organization and the search for causality in educational research and practice. *Complicity: An International Journal of Complexity and Education*, 11(1). https://doi.org/10.29173/cmplct19523

Kosko, B. (1993). *Fuzzy thinking: the new science of fuzzy logic*. New York: Hyperion. https://doi.org/10.1080/03081079408928570

Koutroufinis, S. A. (2017). Organism, machine, process: towards a process ontology for organismic dynamics. Organisms. *Journal of Biological Sciences*, 1(1), 23–44. https://doi.org/10.13133/2532-5876/13878

Kouwer, B. J. (1963). *Spel der persoonlijkheid*. Utrecht: Bijleveld.

Kraut, R. (2018), Aristotle's Ethics. In E. N. Zalta (ed.), *The Stanford Encyclopedia of Philosophy*. Summer 2018 Edition. https://plato.stanford.edu/archives/sum2018/entries/aristotle-ethics/

Krifka, M., Pelletier, F. J., Carlson, G., et al. (1995). In G. N. Carlson & F. J. Pelletier (eds.), *The generic book* (pp. 1–124). Chicago, IL: University of Chicago Press.

Kristjánsson, K., Fowers, B., Darnell, C., & Pollard, D. (2021). Phronesis (practical wisdom) as a type of contextual integrative thinking. *Review of General Psychology*, 25(3), 239–257. https://doi.org/10.1177/10892680211023063

Krueger, R. F., & Piasecki, T. M. (2002). Toward a dimensional and psychometrically-informed approach to conceptualizing psychopathology. *Behaviour Research and Therapy*, 40(5), 485–499. https://doi.org/10.1016/s0005-7967(02)00016-5

Kunnen, E. S. (2012). The art of building dynamic systems models. In E. S. Kunnen (ed.), *A dynamic systems approach to adolescent development* (pp. 99–116). Abingdon: Routledge. https://doi.org/10.4324/9780203147641

Kunnen, E. S. (2017). Why computer models help to understand developmental processes. *Journal of Adolescence*, 57, 134–136. DOI: 10.1016/j.adolescence.2017.04.007

Kunnen, E. S., & Bosma, H. A. (2000). Development of meaning making: a dynamic systems approach. *New Ideas in Psychology*, 18(1), 57–82. https://doi.org/10.1016/S0732-118X(99)00037-9

Kunnen, S. E. (ed.). (2012). *A dynamic systems approach to adolescent development*. London: Psychology Press. https://doi.org/10.4324/9780203147641

Kuorikoski, J., & Pöyhönen, S. (2012). Looping kinds and social mechanisms. *Sociological Theory*, 30(3), 187–205. https://doi.org/10.1177/0735275112457911

Kwiatkowska, M., & Kielan, K. (2013). Fuzzy logic and semiotic methods in modeling of medical concepts. *Fuzzy Sets and Systems*, 214, 35–50. https://doi.org/10.1016/j.fss.2012.03.011

Labrell, F., Van Geert, P., Declercq, C., et al. (2014). 'Speaking volumes': a longitudinal study of lexical and grammatical growth between 17 and 42 months. *First Language*, 34(2), 97–124. https://doi.org/10.1177/0142723714526573

Ladyman, J., & Wiesner, K. (2020). *What is a complex system?* New Haven, CT: Yale University Press. https://doi.org/10.12987/9780300256130

Lamiell, J. T. (2003). *Beyond individual and group differences.* Thousand Oaks, CA: SAGE Publications. http://dx.doi.org/10.4135/9781452229317

Lamiell, J. T., & Slaney, K. L. (eds.). (2020). *Problematic research practices and inertia in scientific psychology: history, sources, and recommended solutions.* Abingdon: Routledge.

Latour, B. (1987). *Science in action: how to follow scientists and engineers through society.* Cambridge, MA: Harvard University Press.

Latour, B. (1996) Om aktor-netvaerksteroi. Nogle fa afklaringer og mere end nogle fa forviklinger. *Philosophia* (vol. 25 No 3 et 4, pp. 47–64); (article written in 1990). version anglaise (English version) in *Soziale Welt* (vol. 47, pp. 369–381), 1996; downloadable from www.bruno-latour.fr/sites/default/files/P-67%20ACTOR-NETWORK.pdf

Latour, B. (2005). *Reassembling the social: an introduction to actor-network-theory.* Oxford and New York: Oxford University Press.

Latour, B., & Woolgar, S. (1979). *Laboratory life: the construction of scientific facts.* Princeton, NJ: Princeton University Press.

Law, J. (2004). *After method: mess in social science research.* Abingdon and New York: Psychology Press.

Law, J. (2017). STS as method. In U. Felt, R. Fouché, C. A. Miller, & L. Smith-Doerr (eds.), *The handbook of science and technology studies* (4th ed., pp. 31–57). Cambridge, MA: MIT Press.

Leary, M. R. (1999). Making sense of self-esteem. *Current Directions in Psychological Science*, 8(1), 32–35. https://doi.org/10.1111/1467-8721.00008

Leary, M. R., Tambor, E. S., Terdal, S. K., & Downs, D. L. (1995). Self-esteem as an interpersonal monitor: the Sociometer Hypothesis. *Journal of Personality and Social Psychology*, 68(3), 518–530. https://doi.org/10.1037//0022-3514.68.3.518

Lebowitz, M. S., & Ahn, W. K. (2014). Effects of biological explanations for mental disorders on clinicians' empathy. *Proceedings of the National Academy of Sciences*, 111(50), 17786–17790. https://doi.org/10.1073/pnas.1414058111

Lee, A. S., & Baskerville, R. L. (2003). Generalizing generalizability in information systems research. *Information Systems Research*, 14(3), 221–243. https://doi.org/10.1287/isre.14.3.221.16560

Legg, S., & Hutter, M. (2007). A collection of definitions of intelligence. *Frontiers in Artificial Intelligence and Applications*, 157, 17–24.

Leonelli, S. (2015). What counts as scientific data? A relational framework. *Philosophy of Science*, 82(5), 810–821. https://doi.org/10.1086/684083

Levy, D. A. (2019). The 'Self-Esteem' Enigma: a critical analysis. *North American Journal of Psychology*, 21(2), 305–338.

Lewin, K. (1936). *Principles of topological psychology*. New York: McGraw-Hill.

Lewis, M. D., & Granic, I. (1999). Self-organization of cognition–emotion interactions. In T. Dalgleish & M. J. Power (eds.), *Handbook of cognition and emotion* (pp. 683–701). New York: John Wiley & Sons. https://doi.org/doi:10.1002/0470013494

Libet, B. (1985). Unconscious cerebral initiative and the role of conscious will in voluntary action. *Behavioral and Brain Sciences*, 8, 529–539. https://doi.org/10.1017/S0140525X00044903

Lichtwarck-Aschoff, A., Kunnen, S. E., & Van Geert, P. L. (2009). Here we go again: a dynamic systems perspective on emotional rigidity across parent–adolescent conflicts. *Developmental Psychology*, 45(5), 1364. https://doi.org/10.1177/0743558410367953

Lichtwarck-Aschoff, A., Kunnen, S. E., & Van Geert, P. (2010). Adolescent girls' perceptions of daily conflicts with their mothers: within-conflict sequences and their relationship to autonomy. *Journal of Adolescent Research*, 25(4), 527–556. https://doi.org/10.1177/0743558410367953

Lichtwarck-Aschoff, A., Van Geert, P., Bosma, H., & Kunnen, S. (2008). Time and identity: a framework for research and theory formation. *Developmental Review*, 28(3), 370–400. https://doi.org/10.1016/j.dr.2008.04.001

Lickliter, R. (2018). An intelligent guide to human intelligence: it's all about development. *Human Development*, 61(2), 126–129. http://doi.org/10.1159/000486465

Link, B. G., & Phelan, J. C. (2013). Labeling and stigma. In C. S. Aneshensel, J. C. Phelan, & A. Bierman (eds.), *Handbook of the sociology of mental health* (pp. 525–541). Dordrecht: Springer.

Lipton, P. (2000). Inference to the best explanation. In W. H. Newton-Smith (ed.), *A companion to the philosophy of science* (pp. 184–193). Oxford: Blackwell.

Liu, S., Ullman, T. D., Tenenbaum, J. B., & Spelke, E. S. (2017). Ten-month-old infants infer the value of goals from the costs of actions. *Science*, 358(6366), 1038–1041. https://doi.org/10.1126/science.aag2132

Lobo, L., Heras-Escribano, M., & Travieso, D. (2018). The history and philosophy of ecological psychology. *Frontiers in Psychology*, 9, 2228. https://doi.org/10.3389/fpsyg.2018.02228

Lowie, W., & Verspoor, M. H. (2019). Individual differences and the ergodicity problem. *Language Learning*, 69, 184–206. https://doi.org/10.1111/lang.12324

Ma, H., Aihara, K., & Chen, L. (2014). Detecting causality from nonlinear dynamics with short-term time series. *Scientific Reports*, 4(1), 1–10.

MacBride, F. (2013). The particular-universal distinction: a dogma of metaphysics? *Mind*, 114(455), 565–614. https://doi.org/10.1093/mind/fzi565

MacBride, F. (2020). Truthmakers. In E. N. Zalta (ed.), *The Stanford Encyclopedia of Philosophy* (Spring 2020 Edition). https://plato.stanford.edu/archives/spr2020/entries/truthmakers/

MacDougall-Shackleton, S. A. (2011). The levels of analysis revisited. *Philosophical Transactions of the Royal Society B: Biological Sciences*, 366(1574), 2076–2085. doi: 10.1098/rstb.2010.0363

Madsen, E. B., & Aagaard, K. (2020). Concentration of Danish research funding on individual researchers and research topics: patterns and potential drivers. *Quantitative Science Studies*, 1. https://doi.org/10.1162/qss_a_00077

Magnus, P. D. (2018). Taxonomy, ontology, and natural kinds. *Synthese*, 195(4), 1427–1439. https://doi.org/10.1007/s11229-015-0785-2

Magnusson, D. (2003). The person approach: concepts, measurement models, and research strategy. In S. C. Peck & R. W. Roeser (eds.), *New directions for child and adolescent development. Person-centered approaches to studying development in context* (pp. 3–23). San Francisco, CA: Jossey-Bass.

Magro, S. W., Utesch, T., Dreiska̎mper, D., & Wagner, J. (2019). Self-esteem development in middle childhood: support for sociometer theory. *International Journal of Behavioral Development*, 43(2), 118–127. DOI: 10.1177/0165025418802462

Mahlan, J. R. (2019). Aristotle on secondary substance. *Apeiron*, 52(2), 167–197. https://doi.org/10.1515/apeiron-2017-0068

Maiers, W. (2021). Replication crisis – just another instance of the replication of crises in psychology? Historical retrospections and theoretical-psychological assessments. *Review of General Psychology*, advance publication. https://journals-sagepub-com.proxy-ub.rug.nl/doi/pdf/10.1177/10892680211033915

Malafouris, L. (2013). *How things shape the mind: a theory of material engagement.* Cambridge, MA and London: MIT Press.

Mallet, J. (2013). Species, concepts of. In S. A. Levin (ed.), *Encyclopedia of biodiversity* (2nd ed., pp. 679–691). New York: Academic Press. https://doi.org/10.1016/B978-0-12-384719-5.00131-3

Mane, K. K., & Börner, K. (2004). Mapping topics and topic bursts in PNAS. *Proceedings of the National Academy of Sciences*, 101(suppl 1), 5287–5290. https://doi.org/10.1073/pnas.0307626100

Mangalam, M., & Kelty-Stephen, D. G. (2021). Point estimates, Simpson's paradox and nonergodicity in biological sciences. *Neuroscience & Biobehavioral Reviews*, 125, 98–107. https://doi.org/10.1016/j.neubiorev.2021.02.017

Marcia, J. E. (1980). Identity in adolescence. In J. Edelson (ed.). *Handbook of adolescent psychology* (pp. 159–187). New York: Wiley.

Mari, A., Beyssade, C., & Del Prete, F. (eds.). (2012). *Genericity* (vol. 43). Oxford: Oxford University Press. DOI:10.1093/acprof:oso/9780199691807.001.0001

Markowitz, D., & Hancock, J. T. (2014). Linguistic traces of a scientific fraud: the case of Diederik Stapel. *PLoS One*, 9(8), e105937. https://doi.org/10.1371/journal.pone.0105937

Markowitz, F. E., Angell, B., & Greenberg, J. S. (2011). Stigma, reflected appraisals, and recovery outcomes in mental illness. *Social Psychology Quarterly*, 74(2), 144–165. https://doi.org/10.1177/0190272511407620

Marshall, M. (2020). The hidden links between mental disorders. *Nature*, 581(7806), 19. doi: 10.1038/d41586-020-00922-8

Marshall, P. J. (2016). Embodiment and human development. *Child Development Perspectives*, 10(4), 245–250. https://doi.org/10.1111/cdep.12190

Martin, S., Deffuant, G., & Calabrese, J. M. (2011). Defining resilience mathematically: from attractors to viability. In G. Deffuant & N. Gilbert (eds.), *Viability and resilience of complex systems: concepts, methods and case studies from ecology and society* (pp. 15–36). Berlin and Heidelberg: Springer. https://doi.org/10.1007/978-3-642-20423-4

Marwan, N., Romano, M. C., Thiel, M., & Kurths, J. (2007). Recurrence plots for the analysis of complex systems. *Physics Reports*, 438(5–6), 237–329. https://doi.org/10.1016/j.physrep.2006.11.001

Mascolo, M. (2020). A relational conception of emotional development. *Emotion Review*, 12 (4), 212–228. https://doi.org/10.1177/17540739209307

Mascolo, M. F., & Fischer, K. W. (2015). Dynamic development of thinking, feeling, and acting. In R. Lerner (series ed.) and W. Overton (vol. ed.), *Handbook of Child Development and Developmental Science, Vol. 1: Theory and Method* (pp. 113–161). New York: John Wiley.

Maton, K. (2008). Habitus. In M. Grenfell (ed.), *Pierre Bourdieu: key concepts* (pp. 49–62). Stockfield, UK: Acumen.

Maturana, H. R., & Varela, F. J. (1980/2012). *Autopoiesis and cognition: the realization of the living* (vol. 42). Berlin, Heidelberg, and New York: Springer Science & Business Media.

Matzler, K., Bauer, F. A., & Mooradian, T. A. (2015). Self-esteem and transformational leadership. *Journal of Managerial Psychology*, 30(7), 815–831. https://doi.org/10.1108/JMP-01-2013-0030

Maul, A. (2013). On the ontology of psychological attributes. *Theory & Psychology*, 23(6), 752–769. https://doi.org/10.1177/0959354313506273

McClelland, J. L. (2010). Emergence in cognitive science. *Topics in Cognitive Science*, 2(4), 751–770. https://doi.org/10.1111/j.1756-8765.2010.01116.x

McDaniel, R. R., & Driebe, D. (eds.). (2005). *Uncertainty and surprise in complex systems: questions on working with the unexpected.* Berlin, Heidelberg, and New York: Springer Science & Business Media. https://doi.org/10.1007/b13122

McMullin, J. A., & Cairney, J. (2004). Self-esteem and the intersection of age, class, and gender. *Journal of Aging Studies*, 18(1), 75–90. https://doi.org/10.1016/j.jaging.2003.09.006

McNally, R. J., Robinaugh, D. J., Wu, G. W., et al. (2015). Mental disorders as causal systems: a network approach to posttraumatic stress disorder. *Clinical Psychological Science*, 3(6), 836–849. https://doi.org/10.1177/2167702614553230

Medaglia, J. D., Ramanathan, D. M., Venkatesan, U. M., & Hillary, F. G. (2011). The challenge of non-ergodicity in network neuroscience. *Network*, 22(1–4), 148–153. doi: 10.3109/09638237.2011.639604

Meehl, P. (1993). Four queries about factor reality. *History and Philosophy of Psychology Bulletin*, 5(2), 4–5.

Meiss, J. (2007). Dynamical systems. *Scholarpedia*, 2(2), 1629.

Menzies, P. (2005). Causation, further themes. In E. Craig (ed.), *Routledge Encyclopedia of Philosophy Online* (pp. 125–129). London and New York: Routledge.

Menzies, P. (2007). Causation in context. In H. Price & R. Corry (eds.), *Causation, physics, and the constitution of reality: Russell's republic revisited* (pp. 191–223). Oxford: Oxford University Press on Demand.

Merlone, U., Panchuk, A., & Van Geert, P. (2019). Modeling learning and teaching interaction by a map with vanishing denominators: fixed points stability and bifurcations. *Chaos, Solitons & Fractals*, 126, 253–265. DOI: 10.1016/j.chaos.2019.06.008

Michaels, C. F. (2003). Affordances: four points of debate. *Ecological Psychology*, 15(2), 135–148. DOI: 10.1207/S15326969ECO1502_3

Michell, J. (1997). Quantitative science and the definition of measurement in psychology. *British Journal of Psychology*, 88(3), 355–383. https://doi.org/10.1111/j.2044-8295.1997.tb02641.x

Michell, J. (2021). Representational measurement theory: is its number up? *Theory & Psychology*, 31(1), 3–23. https://doi.org/10.1177/0959354320930817

Michotte, A. (1946). *The perception of causality*, translated from the French by R. Miles and E. Miles, 1963. London: Methuen.

Mitchell, M. (2009). *Complexity: a guided tour*. Oxford: Oxford University Press.

Molenaar, P. C. M. (2008). On the implications of the classical ergodic theorems: analysis of developmental processes has to focus on intra-individual variation. *Developmental Psychobiology*, 50(1), 60–69. DOI: 10.1002/dev.20262

Molenaar, P. C. M. (2004). A manifesto on psychology as idiographic science: bringing the person back into scientific psychology, this time forever. *Measurement*, 2(4), 219–247. https://doi.org/10.1207/s15366359mea0204

Molenaar, P. C. M. (2015). On the relation between person-oriented and subject-specific approaches. *Journal for Person-Oriented Research*, 1(1–2), 34–41. https://doi.org/10.17505/jpor.2015.04

Molenaar, P. C. M., & Campbell, C. G. (2009). The new person-specific paradigm in psychology. *Current Directions in Psychological Science*, 18(2), 112–117. https://doi.org/10.1111/j.1467-8721.2009.01619.x

Molenaar, P. C. M., Sinclair, K. O., Rovine, M. J., Ram, N., & Corneal, S. E. (2009). Analyzing developmental processes on an individual level using nonstationary time series modeling. *Developmental Psychology*, 45(1), 260–271. DOI: 10.1037/a0014170

Monty Python. (1972). *International Philosophy sketch*, commonly referred to as the Philosophers' Football Match.

Moosa, I. A. (2018). *Publish or perish: perceived benefits versus unintended consequences*. Cheltenham: Edward Elgar Publishing.

Morawski, J. (2021). How to true psychology's objects. *Review of General Psychology*, 108926802110465, 108926802110465–108926802110465. https://doi.org/10.1177/10892680211046518

Morgan, S., & Winship, C. (2012). Bringing context and variability back into causal analysis. In H. Kincaid (ed.), *Oxford handbook of the philosophy of the social sciences* (pp. 319–354). Oxford: Oxford University Press. DOI: 10.1093/oxfordhb/9780195392753.001.0001

Mumford, S., & Anjum, R. L. (2011). *Getting causes from powers*. Oxford: Oxford University Press. DOI:10.1093/acprof:oso/9780199695614.001.0001

Nakash, O., Nagar, M., & Westen, D. (2019). Validity and clinical utility of DSM and empirically derived prototype diagnosis for personality disorders in predicting adaptive functioning. *Personality Disorders: Theory, Research, and Treatment*, 10(2), 105. DOI: 10.1037/per0000293

Nathan, P. E., Stuart, S. P., & Dolan, S. L. (2000). Research on psychotherapy efficacy and effectiveness: between Scylla and Charybdis? *Psychological Bulletin*, 126(6), 964–981. doi: 10.1037/0033-2909.126.6.964.

Nelson, L. D., Simmons, J., & Simonsohn, U. (2018). Psychology's renaissance. *Annual Review of Psychology*, 69, 511–534. https://doi.org/10.1146/annurev-psych-122216-011836

Newell, K. M., Liu, Y. T., & Mayer-Kress, G. (2003). A dynamical systems interpretation of epigenetic landscapes for infant motor development. *Infant Behavior and Development*, 26(4), 449–472. https://doi.org/10.1016/j.infbeh.2003.08.003

Newen, A., De Bruin, L., & Gallagher, S. (eds.). (2018). *The Oxford handbook of 4E cognition*. Oxford: Oxford University Press. DOI: 10.1093/oxfordhb/9780198735410.001.0001

Newstead, S. E. (1994). Do verbs act as implicit quantifiers? *Journal of Semantics*, 11(3), 215–230. https://doi.org/10.1093/jos/11.3.215

Nguyen, H. T., Walker, C. L., & Walker, E. A. (2018). *A first course in fuzzy logic*. Boca Raton, FL: CRC Press.

Nickel, B. (2012). Dutchmen are good sailors: generics and gradability. In A. Mari, C. Beyssade, & F. del Prete (eds.), *Genericity* (pp. 390–405). Oxford: Oxford University Press. DOI:10.1093/acprof:oso/9780199691807.001.0001

Nickel, B. (2016). *Between logic and the world: an integrated theory of generics*. Oxford: Oxford University Press. DOI:10.1093/acprof:oso/9780199640003.001.0001

Nicolis, G. & Rouvas-Nicolis, C. (2007), Complex systems. *Scholarpedia*, 2(11), 1473. doi:10.4249/scholarpedia.1473

Ninot, G., Fortes, M., & Delignières, D. (2005). The dynamics of self-esteem in adults over a 6-month period: an exploratory study. *The Journal of Psychology*, 139(4), 315–330. https://doi.org/10.3200/JRLP.139.4.315-330

Noonan, H., & Curtis, B. (2018). Identity. In E. N. Zalta (ed.), *The Stanford Encyclopedia of Philosophy* (Summer 2018 Edition). https://plato.stanford.edu/archives/sum2018/entries/identity/

Norcross, J. C., Koocher, G. P., & Garofalo, A. (2006). Discredited psychological treatments and tests: a Delphi poll. *Professional Psychology: Research and Practice*, 37(5), 515–522. DOI: 10.1037/0735-7028.37.5.515

Nosek, B. A., Hardwicke, T. E., Moshontz, H., et al. (2021). Replicability, robustness, and reproducibility in psychological science. *Annual Review of Psychology*, PsyArXiv Preprints. https://doi.org/10.31234/osf.io/ksfvq

Nosek, B. A., Spies, J. R., & Motyl, M. (2012). Scientific utopia: II. Restructuring incentives and practices to promote truth over publishability. *Perspectives on Psychological Science*, 7(6), 615–631. https://doi.org/10.1177/1745691612459058

Nowak, M. A., Komarova, N. L., & Niyogi, P. (2001). Evolution of universal grammar. *Science*, 291(5501), 114–118. doi: 10.1126/science.291.5501.114

Nuijten, M. B., Deserno, M. K., Cramer, A., & Borsboom, D. (2016). Mental disorders as complex networks: an introduction and overview of a network approach to psychopathology. *Clinical Neuropsychiatry*, 13(4/5), 68–76.

O'Connor, T. (2020). Emergent properties. In E. N. Zalta (ed.), *The Stanford Encyclopedia of Philosophy* (Autumn 2020 Edition). https://plato.stanford.edu/archives/fall2020/entries/properties-emergent/

Olthof, M., Hasselman, F., & Lichtwarck-Aschoff, A. (2020a). Complexity in psychological self-ratings: implications for research and practice. *BMC Medicine*, 18(1), 1–16. https://doi.org/10.1186/s12916-020-01727-2

Olthof, M., Hasselman, F., Strunk, G., et al. (2020b). Critical fluctuations as an early-warning signal for sudden gains and losses in patients receiving psychotherapy for mood disorders. *Clinical Psychological Science*, 8(1), 25–35. https://doi.org/10.1177/2167702619865969

Olthof, M., Hasselman, F., Wijnants, M., & Lichtwarck-Aschoff, A. (2020c). Psychological dynamics are complex: a comparison of scaling, variance, and dynamic complexity in simulated and observed data. In K. Viol, H. Schöller, & W. Aichhorn (eds.), *Selbstorganisation–ein Paradigma für die Humanwissenschaften* (pp. 303–316). Wiesbaden: Springer. https://doi.org/10.1007/978-3-658-29906-4

Oosterwegel, A., Field, N., Hart, D., & Anderson, K. (2001). The relation of self-esteem variability to emotion variability, mood, personality traits, and depressive tendencies. *Journal of Personality*, 69(5), 689–708. doi: 10.1111/1467-6494.695160

Open Science Collaboration. (2015). Psychology: estimating the reproducibility of psychological science. *Science*, 349(6251), aac4716. DOI: 10.1126/science.aac4716

Orth, U., Maes, J., & Schmitt, M. (2015). Self-esteem development across the life span: a longitudinal study with a large sample from Germany. *Developmental Psychology*, 51(2), 248–259. https://doi.org/10.1037/a0038481

Ostertag, G. (2020). Emily Elizabeth Constance Jones. In E. N. Zalta (ed.), *The Stanford Encyclopedia of Philosophy* (Autumn 2020 Edition). https://plato.stanford.edu/archives/fall2020/entries/emily-elizabeth-constance-jones/

Overton, W. F. (1975). General systems, structure and development. In K. F. Riegel & G. C. Rosenwald (eds.), *Structure and transformation: developmental and historical aspects* (pp. 61–81). New York: Wiley.

Overton, W. F. (1991). The structure of developmental theory. *Advances in Child Development and Behavior*, 23, 1–37. https://doi.org/10.1016/s0065-2407(08)60019-1

Overton, W. F. (2013a). A new paradigm for developmental science: relationism and relational-developmental systems. *Applied Developmental Science*, 17(2), 94–107. https://doi.org/10.1080/10888691.2013.778717

Overton, W. F. (2013b). Relationism and relational developmental systems: a paradigm for developmental science in the post-Cartesian Era. *Advances in Child Development and Behavior*, 44, 21–64. https://doi.org/10.1016/B978-0-12-397947-6.00002-7

Overton, W. F. (2015). Processes, relations and relational-developmental-systems. In W. F. Overton & P. C. M. Molenaar (eds.), *Theory and method, volume 1 of the handbook of child psychology and developmental science* (7th ed., pp. 9–62). Editor-in-Chief: Richard M. Lerner. Hoboken, NJ: Wiley.

Owadally, M. I., Zhou, F., & Wright, I. D. (2018). The insurance industry as a complex social system: competition, cycles, and crises. *Journal of Artificial Societies and Social Simulation*, 21(4), 2. DOI: 10.18564/jasss.3819

Paoletti, M. P., & Orilia, F. (eds.). (2017). *Philosophical and scientific perspectives on downward causation*. New York and Oxford: Routledge.

Parry, R. (2020). Episteme and techne. In E. N. Zalta (ed.), *The Stanford Encyclopedia of Philosophy* (Autumn 2020 Edition). https://plato.stanford.edu/archives/fall2020/entries/episteme-techne/

Paulhus, D. L. (2002). Socially desirable responding: the evolution of a construct. In H. Braun, D. N. Jackson, & D. E. Wiley (eds.), *The role of constructs in psychological and educational measurement* (pp. 49–69). Hillsdale, NJ: Erlbaum.

Pearl, J. (2018). Challenging the hegemony of randomized controlled trials: a commentary on Deaton and Cartwright. *Social Science & Medicine*, 210, 60–62. https://doi.org/10.1016/j.socscimed.2018.04.024

Pearl, J., & Mackenzie, D. (2018). *The book of why: the new science of cause and effect*. New York: Basic Books.

Pelletier, F. J. (ed.). (2009a). *Kinds, things, and stuff: mass terms and generics*. Oxford: Oxford University Press. DOI:10.1093/acprof:oso/9780195382891.001.0001

Pelletier, F. J. (2009b). Generics: a philosophical introduction. In F. J. Pelletier (ed.), *Kinds, things, and stuff: mass terms and generics*. Oxford: Oxford University Press. https://doi.org/10.1093/acprof:oso/9780195382891.001.0001

Pereira, A. F., Smith, L. B., & Yu, C. (2014). A bottom-up view of toddler word learning. *Psychonomic Bulletin & Review*, 21(1), 178–185. DOI: 10.3758/s13423-013-0466-4

Piaget, J. (1954/2013). *The construction of reality in the child* (vol. 82). Abingdon: Routledge. https://doi.org/10.1037/11168-000

Piaget, J. (1976). Piaget's theory. In B. Inhelder, H. H. Chipman, & C. Zwingmann (eds.), *Piaget and his school* (pp. 11–23). Berlin and Heidelberg: Springer. https://doi.org/10.1007/978-3-642-46323-5

Piaget, J. (1997). *The principles of genetic epistemology* (vol. 7). Abingdon: Routledge.

Piccirillo, M. L., & Rodebaugh, T. L. (2019). Foundations of idiographic methods in psychology and applications for psychotherapy. *Clinical Psychology Review*, 71, 90–100. https://doi.org/10.1016/j.cpr.2019.01.002

Picione, R. D. L. (2015). The idiographic approach in psychological research. The challenge of overcoming old distinctions without risking to homogenize. *Integrative Psychological and Behavioral Science*, 49(3), 360–370. DOI: 10.1007/s12124-015-9307-5

Pike, H. (2019). It's time to talk about ditching statistical significance. *Nature*, 567(7748), 283. DOI: 10.1038/d41586-019-00874-8

Pilgrim, D. (2019). *Critical realism for psychologists*. London and New York: Routledge. https://doi.org/10.4324/9780429274497

Plana-Ripoll, O., Pedersen, C. B., Holtz, Y., et al. (2019). Exploring comorbidity within mental disorders among a Danish national population. *JAMA Psychiatry*, 76(3), 259–270. doi: 10.1001/jamapsychiatry.2018.3658

Plato, Cratylus. 401e and 402a. http://data.perseus.org/citations/urn:cts:greekLit:tlg0059.tlg005.perseus-eng1:402a

Ploeger, A., & Galis, F. (2011). Evolutionary approaches to autism: an overview and integration. *McGill Journal of Medicine: MJM*, 13(2). https://doi.org/10.26443/mjm.v13i2.231

Polani, D., Sporns, O., & Lungarella, M. (2006). How information and embodiment shape intelligent information processing. In *50 years of artificial intelligence: essays dedicated to the 50th anniversary of artificial intelligence. Proceedings of the 50th anniversary summit of artificial intelligence* (pp. 9–14). Ascona, Switzerland: Springer. https://doi.org/10.1007/978-3-540-77296-5

Pomagalska, D. (2005). The reification of self-esteem: grammatical investigations into scientific and popular texts. *Doctoral dissertation*, The University of Adelaide. https://digital.library.adelaide.edu.au/dspace/bitstream/2440/37812/10/02whole.pdf

Popper, K. R. (1990). *A world of propensities: two new views on causality*. Bristol: Thoemmes.

Potochnik, A., & De Sanches, O. G. (2020). Patterns in cognitive phenomena and pluralism of explanatory styles. *Topics in Cognitive Science*, 12(4), 1306–1320. https://doi.org/10.1111/tops.12481

Pratten, S. (2013). Critical realism and the process account of emergence. *Journal for the Theory of Social Behaviour*, 43(3), 251–279. DOI: 10.1111/jtsb.12017

Price, H., & Corry, R. (2007). *Causation, physics, and the constitution of reality: Russell's republic revisited*. Oxford: Clarendon Press.

Prigogine, I. (1980). *From being to becoming*. San Francisco, CA: Freeman.

Prigogine, I., & Stengers, I. (1979). *La nouvelle alliance: Métamorphose de la science*. Paris: Gallimard/ English translation Prigogine, I., & Stengers, I. (1997). The end of certainty. New York: Simon and Schuster.

Proulx, S. R., Promislow, D. E., & Phillips, P. C. (2005). Network thinking in ecology and evolution. *Trends in Ecology & Evolution*, 20(6), 345–353. https://doi.org/10.1016/j.tree.2005.04.004

Puga-Gonzalez, I., Hildenbrandt, H., & Hemelrijk, C. K. (2009). Emergent patterns of social affiliation in primates, a model. *PLoS Computational Biology*, 5(12), e1000630. https://doi.org/10.1371/journal.pcbi.1000630

Quetelet, A. (1869). *Physique sociale, ou essai sur le développement des facultés de l'homme* (vol. 2). Bruxelles: C. Muquardt.

Quine, W. V. O., & Ullian, J. S. (1978). *The web of belief* (2nd ed.). New York: Random House.

Rabinovich, M. I., Friston, K. J., & Varona, P. (eds.). (2012). *Principles of brain dynamics: global state interactions*. Cambridge, MA: MIT Press.

Racine, E., Waldman, S., Rosenberg, J., & Illes, J. (2010). Contemporary neuroscience in the media. *Social Science & Medicine*, 71(4), 725–733. https://doi.org/10.1016/j.socscimed.2010.05.017

Rączaszek-Leonardi, J., Nomikou, I., Rohlfing, K. J., & Deacon, T. W. (2018). Language development from an ecological perspective: ecologically valid ways to abstract symbols. *Ecological Psychology*, 30(1), 39–73. https://doi.org/10.1080/10407413.2017.1410387

Rad, M. S., Martingano, A. J., & Ginges, J. (2018). Toward a psychology of Homo sapiens: making psychological science more representative of the human population. *Proceedings of the National Academy of Sciences*, 115(45), 11401–11405. https://doi.org/10.1073/pnas.1721165115

Radder, H., & Meynen, G. (2013). Does the brain 'initiate' freely willed processes? A philosophy of science critique of Libet-type experiments and their interpretation. *Theory & Psychology*, 23(1), 3–21. https://doi.org/10.1177/0959354312460926

Raeff, C. (2010). Self constructing activities. *Theory & Psychology*, 20(1), 28–51. https://doi.org/10.1177/0959354309345646

Raeff, C. (2016). *Exploring the dynamics of human development: an integrative approach*. Oxford: Oxford University Press. DOI:10.1093/acprof:oso/9780199328413.001.0001

Raeff, C. (2019). From objects to acting: repopulating psychology with people who act. *Theory & Psychology*, 29(3), 311–335. https://doi.org/10.1177/0959354319844603

Ragin, C. C. (2009). *Redesigning social inquiry: fuzzy sets and beyond*. Chicago, IL: University of Chicago Press.

Ramos, R. T., Sassi, R. B., & Piqueira, J. R. C. (2011). Self-organized criticality and the predictability of human behavior. *New Ideas in Psychology*, 29(1), 38–48. doi:10.1016/j.newideapsych.2009.12.001

Ramsden, S., Richardson, F. M., Josse, G., et al. (2011). Verbal and non-verbal intelligence changes in the teenage brain. *Nature*, 479(7371), 113–116. https://doi.org/10.1038/nature10514

Reed, E. S. (1996). *Encountering the world: toward an ecological psychology*. Oxford: Oxford University Press. DOI:10.1093/acprof:oso/9780195073010.001.0001

Rennie, D. L. (2012). Qualitative research: a matter of hermeneutics and the sociology of knowledge. *Using Qualitative Methods in Psychology*, 3–14. https://doi.org/10.4135/9781452225487.n1

Rescher, N. (1996). *Process metaphysics: an introduction to process philosophy*. New York: SUNY Press.

Rescher, N. (2000). *Process philosophy: a survey of basic issues*. Pittsburgh, PA: University of Pittsburgh Press.

Resnik, M. D. (2007). Quine and the web of belief. In S. Shapiro (ed.), *The Oxford handbook of philosophy of mathematics and logic* (pp. 412–436). Oxford: Oxford University Press. DOI: 10.1093/oxfordhb/9780195325928.001.0001

Reutlinger, A. (2013). The interventionist theory of causation. In A. Reutlinger (Ed.), *A theory of causation in the social and biological sciences* (pp. 25–70). London: Palgrave Macmillan. https://doi.org/10.1057/9781137281043

Reuzel, E., Embregts, P. J., Bosman, A. M., et al. (2013). Conversational synchronization in naturally occurring settings: a recurrence-based analysis of gaze directions and speech rhythms of staff and clients with intellectual disability. *Journal of Nonverbal Behavior*, 37(4), 281–305. DOI: 10.1007/s10919-013-0158-9

Revelle, W., & Wilt, J. (2013). The general factor of personality: a general critique. *Journal of Research in Personality*, 47(5), 493–504. doi: 10.1016/j.jrp.2013.04.012

Richardson, K. (2000). *The making of intelligence*. New York: Columbia University Press.

Richardson, K. (2002). What IQ tests test. *Theory & Psychology*, 12(3), 283–314. https://doi.org/10.1177/0959354302012003012

Richardson, K. (2017). *Genes, brains, and human potential: the science and ideology of intelligence*. New York: Columbia University Press.

Richardson, M. J., Shockley, K., Fajen, B. R., Riley, M. A., & Turvey, M. T. (2008). Ecological psychology: six principles for an embodied–embedded approach to behavior. In P. Calvo & T. Gomila (eds.), *Handbook of cognitive science: an embodied approach* (pp. 159–187). New York: Elsevier.

Richardson, R. C. (2006). Explanation and causality in self-organizing systems. In B. Feltz, M. Crommelinck, & P. Goujon (eds.), *Self-organization and emergence in life sciences* (pp. 315–340). Berlin and Heidelberg: Springer. https://doi.org/10.1007/1-4020-3917-4

Rietveld, E., & Kiverstein, J. (2014). A rich landscape of affordances. *Ecological Psychology*, 26(4), 325–352. https://doi.org/10.1080/10407413.2014.958035

Riley, M. A., & Turvey, M. T. (2001). The self-organizing dynamics of intentions and actions. *American Journal of Psychology*, 114(1), 160–169. DOI:10.2307/1423388

Ritchie, S. (2015). *Intelligence: all that matters*. London: Hoer Stoughton.

Robins, R. W., Trzesniewski, K. H., Tracy, J. L., Gosling, S. D., & Potter, J. (2002). Global self-esteem across the life span. *Psychology and Aging*, 17(3), 423–434. https://doi.org/10.1037//0882-7974.17.3.423

Robinson, B. F., & Mervis, C. B. (1998). Disentangling early language development: modeling lexical and grammatical acquisition using and extension of case-study methodology. *Developmental Psychology*, 34(2), 363–375. DOI: 10.1037//0012-1649.34.2.363

Robinson, H. (2016). An argument for the existence of mental substance. In H. Robinson (ed.), *From the knowledge argument to mental substance: resurrecting the mind* (pp. 233–247). Cambridge, UK: Cambridge University Press. https://doi.org/10.1017/CBO9781316092873.016

Robinson, H. (2020). Substance. In E. N. Zalta (ed.), *The Stanford Encyclopedia of Philosophy* (Spring 2020 Edition). https://plato.stanford.edu/archives/fall2021/entries/substance/

Robinson, W. S. (1950). Ecological correlations and the behavior of individuals. *American Sociological Review*, 15(3), 351–357. https://doi.org/10.2307/2087176

Rohde, M. (2010). *Enaction, embodiment, evolutionary robotics: simulation models for a post-cognitivist science of mind* (vol. 1). Berlin and Heidelberg: Springer.

Romeijn, J.-W. (2017). Philosophy of statistics. In E. N. Zalta (ed.), *The Stanford Encyclopedia of Philosophy* (Spring 2017 Edition). https://plato.stanford.edu/archives/spr2017/entries/statistics/

Roochnik, D. (2009). What is theoria? Nicomachean ethics book 10.7–8. *Classical Philology*, 104(1), 69–82. https://doi.org/10.1086/603572

Rosen, R. (2000). *Essays on life itself.* New York: Columbia University Press.
Rosenberg, M. (1965). *Society and the adolescent self-image.* Princeton, NJ: Princeton University Press.
Rosenberg, M. (1986). Self-concept from middle childhood through adolescence. In J. Suls & A. G. Greenwald (eds.), *Psychological perspectives on the self* (vol. 3) (pp. 107–135). Hillsdale, NJ: Erlbaum.
Rosqvist, J., Thomas, J. C., & Truax, P. (2011). Effectiveness versus efficacy studies. In J. C. Thomas & M. Hersen (eds.), *Understanding research in clinical and counseling psychology* (pp. 319–354). Abingdon: Routledge and Taylor & Francis Group.
Rouse, J. (1996). The dynamics of scientific knowing: understanding science without reifying knowledge. In J. Rouse (ed.), *Engaging science: how to understand its practices philosophically* (pp. 179–204). Ithaca, NY: Cornell University Press. https://doi.org/10.7591/9781501718625
Russell, B. (1912–1913). On the notion of cause. *Proceedings of the Aristotelian Society,* 13(1), 1–26. https://doi.org/10.1093/aristotelian/13.1.1
Ruzich, E., Allison, C., Chakrabarti, B., et al. (2015). Sex and STEM occupation predict autism-spectrum quotient (AQ) scores in half a million people. *PLoS One,* 10(10), e0141229. https://doi.org/10.1371/journal.pone.0141229
Ryan, R. M., & Brown, K. W. (2003). Why we don't need self-esteem: on fundamental needs, contingent love, and mindfulness. *Psychological Inquiry,* 14(1), 71–76.
Sabat, S. R., Fath, H., Moghaddam, F. M., & Harré, R. (1999). The maintenance of self-esteem: lessons from the culture of Alzheimer's sufferers. *Culture and Psychology,* 5(1), 5–31. https://doi.org/10.1177/1354067X9951001
Salatino, A. A., Osborne, F., & Motta, E. (2017). How are topics born? Understanding the research dynamics preceding the emergence of new areas. *PeerJ Computer Science,* 3, e119. https://doi.org/10.7717/peerj-cs.119
Salmon, W. C. (1998). *Causality and explanation.* Oxford: Oxford University Press. DOI:10.1093/0195108647.001.0001
Salvatore, S. (2020). How to avoid throwing the baby out with the bathwater: abduction is the solution to pseudo-empiricism. In T. G. Lindstad, E. Stänicke, & J. Valsiner (eds.), *Respect for thought* (pp. 181–194). Cham: Springer. https://doi.org/10.1007/978-3-030-43066-5
Salvatore, S., & Valsiner, J. (2010). Between the general and the unique: overcoming the nomothetic versus idiographic opposition. *Theory & Psychology,* 20(6), 817–833. https://doi.org/10.1177/0959354310381156
Samuelson, L. K., Jenkins, G. W., & Spencer, J. P. (2015). Grounding cognitive-level processes in behavior: the view from dynamic systems theory. *Topics in Cognitive Science,* 7(2), 191–205. http://doi.org/10.1111/tops.12129
Samuelson, L. K., Kucker, S. C., & Spencer, J. P. (2017). Moving word learning to a novel space: a dynamic systems view of referent selection and retention. *Cognitive Science,* 41(suppl 1), 52–72. doi: 10.1111/cogs.12369
Samuelson, L. K., Schutte, A. R., & Horst, J. S. (2009). The dynamic nature of knowledge: insights from a dynamic field model of children's novel noun generalization. *Cognition,* 110(3), 322–345. DOI: 10.1016/j.cognition.2008.10.017

Santa Fe Institute (2021). Emergence. www.complexityexplorer.org/explore/glossary/414-emergence

Savin-Williams, R. C., & Demo, D. H. (1983). Situational and transituational determinants of adolescent self-feelings. *Journal of Personality and Social Psychology*, 44(4), 824–833. https://doi.org/10.1037/0022-3514.44.4.824

Sawyer, J. E., & Stetsenko, A. (2018). Revisiting Marx and problematizing Vygotsky: a transformative approach to language and speech internalization. *Language Sciences*, 70, 143–154. https://doi.org/10.1016/j.langsci.2018.05.003

Sawyer, R. K. (2002). Emergence in psychology: lessons from the history of non-reductionist science. *Human Development*, 45(1), 2–28. https://doi.org/10.1159/000048148

Sawyer, R. K. (2004). The mechanisms of emergence. *Philosophy of the Social Sciences*, 34(2), 260–282. https://doi.org/10.1177/0048393103262553

Schaffer, J. (2001). Causes as probability raisers of processes. *Journal of Philosophy*, 98(2), 75–92. https://doi.org/10.2307/2678483

Schaffhuser, K., Allemand, M., & Schwarz, B. (2017). The development of self-representations during the transition to early adolescence: the role of gender, puberty, and school transition. *Journal of Early Adolescence*, 37(6), 774–804. https://doi.org/10.1177/0272431615624841

Scheff, T. (2015). Three scandals in psychology: the need for a new approach. *Review of General Psychology*, 19(2), 203–205. https://doi.org/10.1037/gpr0000047

Scheff, T. J., & Fearon, D. S. (2004). Cognition and emotion? The dead end in self-esteem research. *Journal for the Theory of Social Behaviour*, 34(1), 73–90. https://doi.org/10.1111/j.1468-5914.2004.00235.x

Schermuly-Haupt, M.-L., Linden, M., & Rush, A. J. (2018). Unwanted events and side effects in cognitive behavior therapy. *Cognitive Therapy and Research*, 42(3), 219–229. https://doi.org/10.1007/s10608-018-9904-y

Schiepek, G. (2009). Complexity and nonlinear dynamics in psychotherapy. *European Review*, 17(2), 331–356. DOI: 10.1017/S1062798709000763

Schiepek, G., & Aichhorn, W. (2013). Real-time monitoring of psychotherapeutic change processes. *Psychotherapie, Psychosomatik, medizinische Psychologie*, 63(1), 39–47.

Schiepek, G., Aichhorn, W., Gruber, M., et al. (2016). Real-time monitoring of psychotherapeutic processes: concept and compliance. *Frontiers in Psychology*, 7, 604. https://doi.org/10.3389/fpsyg.2016.00604

Schiepek, G., Aichhorn, W., & Schöller, H. (2017). Monitoring change dynamics: a nonlinear approach to psychotherapy feedback. *Chaos and Complexity Letters*, 11(3), 355–375.

Schiepek, G., Gelo, O., Viol, K., et al. (2020). Complex individual pathways or standard tracks? A data-based discussion on the trajectories of change in psychotherapy. *Counselling and Psychotherapy Research*, 20(4), 689–702. https://doi.org/10.1002/capr.12300

Schiepek, G., & Perlitz, V. (2020). Self-organization in clinical psychology. In A. Hutt & H. Haken (eds.), *Synergetics: a volume in the encyclopedia of complexity and systems science* (2nd ed., pp. 263–285). New York: Springer US. https://doi.org/10.1007/978-1-0716-0421-2

Schiepek, G., Schöller, H., Carl, R., Aichhorn, W., & Lichtwarck-Aschoff, A. (2019a). A nonlinear dynamic systems approach to psychological interventions. In E. S. Kunnen, N. M. De Ruiter, B. F. Jeronimus, & M. A. Van der Gaag (eds.), *Psychosocial development in adolescence: insights from the dynamic systems approach* (pp. 51–68). Abingdon: Routledge.

Schiepek, G., Stöger-Schmidinger, B., Kronberger, H., et al. (2019b). The therapy process questionnaire-factor analysis and psychometric properties of a multi-dimensional self-rating scale for high-frequency monitoring of psychotherapeutic processes. *Clinical Psychology & Psychotherapy*, 26(5), 586–602. DOI: 10.1002/cpp.2384

Schiff, B. (2017). *A new narrative for psychology*. Oxford: Oxford University Press. https://doi.org/10.1093/oso/9780199332182.001.0001

Schiraldi, G. R. (2001). *The self-esteem workbook*. Oakland, CA: New Harbinger Publications.

Schlesinger, M., & Parisi, D. (2001). The agent-based approach: a new direction for computational models of development. *Developmental Review*, 21(1), 121–146. https://doi.org/10.1006/drev.2000.0520

Schlicht, T., & Starzak, T. (2019). Prospects of enactivist approaches to intentionality and cognition. *Synthese*, 1–25. https://doi.org/10.1007/s11229-019-02361-z

Schmittmann, V. D., Cramer, A. O., Waldorp, L. J., et al. (2013). Deconstructing the construct: a network perspective on psychological phenomena. *New Ideas in Psychology*, 31(1), 43–53. https://doi.org/10.1016/j.newideapsych.2011.02.007

Schneegans, S., & Schöner, G. (2008). Dynamic field theory as a framework for understanding embodied cognition. In P. Calvo & T. Gomila (eds.), *Handbook of cognitive science: an embodied approach* (pp. 241–271). New York: Elsevier.

Schöner, G., & Spencer, J. P. (2016). *Dynamic thinking: a primer on dynamic field theory*. Oxford: Oxford University Press. DOI:10.1093/acprof:oso/9780199300563.001.0001

Schraube, E. (2015). Why theory matters: analytical strategies of critical psychology. *Estudos de Psicologia (Campinas)*, 32, 533–545. https://doi.org/10.1590/0103-166X2015000300018

Schuhmacher, N., Ballato, L., & Van Geert, P. (2014). Using an agent-based model to simulate the development of risk behaviors during adolescence. *Journal of Artificial Societies and Social Simulation*, 17(3), 1. DOI: 10.18564/jasss.2485

Seibt, J. (1997). Existence in time: from substance to process. In J. Faye, U. Scheffler, & M. Urchs (eds.), *Perspectives on time* (pp. 143–182). Dordrecht: Kluwer Academic Publishers. https://doi.org/10.1007/978-94-015-8875-1

Seibt, J. (2002). 'Quanta,' tropes, or processes: ontologies for QFT beyond the myth. In M. Kuhlmann, H. Lyre, & A. Wayne (eds.), *Ontological aspects of quantum field theory* (pp. 53–98). Singapore: World Scientific.

Seibt, J. (2004). Free process theory: towards a typology of occurrings. *Axiomathes*, 14(1), 23–55. DOI: 10.1023/B:AXIO.0000006787.28366.d7

Seibt, J. (2018). Ontological tools for the process turn in biology. In D. J. Nicholson & J. Dupré (eds.), *Everything flows: towards a processual philosophy of biology* (pp. 113–136). Oxford: Oxford University Press. https://doi.org/10.1093/oso/9780198779636.001.0001

Seibt, J. (2020). Process philosophy. In E. N. Zalta (ed.), *The Stanford Encyclopedia of Philosophy* (Summer 2020 Edition). https://plato.stanford.edu/archives/sum2020/entries/process-philosophy/

Sekścińska K., Jaworska, D., & Rudzinska-Wojciechowska, J. (2021). Self-esteem and financial risk-taking. *Personality and Individual Differences*, 172, 110576 https://doi.org/10.1016/j.paid.2020.110576

Seth, A. (2007). Granger causality. *Scholarpedia*, 2(7), 1667.

Shaw, R., & Bransford, J. (eds.). (2017). *Perceiving, acting and knowing: toward an ecological psychology* (vol. 27). London: Routledge.

Shen, C. C., Hu, L. Y., & Hu, Y. H. (2017). Comorbidity study of borderline personality disorder: applying association rule mining to the Taiwan national health insurance research database. *BMC Medical Informatics and Decision Making*, 17(1), 8. https://doi.org/10.1186/s12911-016-0405-1

Shen, M. D., Li, D. D., Keown, C. L., et al. (2016). Functional connectivity of the amygdala is disrupted in preschool-aged children with autism spectrum disorder. *Journal of the American Academy of Child & Adolescent Psychiatry*, 55(9), 817–824. DOI: 10.1016/j.jaac.2016.05.020

Shrout, P. E., & Rodgers, J. L. (2018). Psychology, science, and knowledge construction: broadening perspectives from the replication crisis. *Annual Review of Psychology*, 69(1), 487–510. https://doi.org/10.1146/annurev-psych-122216-011845

Siegler, R. S. (1996). *Emerging minds: the process of change in children's thinking*. New York: Oxford University Press.

Silberstein, M., & Chemero, A. (2011). Dynamics, agency and intentional action. *Humana Mente*, 4(15), 1–19.

Siler, W., & Buckley, J. J. (2005). *Fuzzy expert systems and fuzzy reasoning* (pp. 29–54). Hoboken, NJ: Wiley. DOI:10.1002/0471698504

Simpson, E. H. (1951). The interpretation of interaction in contingency tables. *Journal of the Royal Statistical Society, Series B*, 13(2), 238–241. https://www.jstor.org/stable/2984065

Simpson, T., Carruthers, P., Laurence, S., & Stich, S. (2005). Introduction: nativism past and present. In P. Carruthers, S. Laurence, & S. Stich (eds.), *The innate mind: structure and contents* (pp. 3–19). Oxford: Oxford University Press. DOI:10.1093/acprof:oso/9780195179675.001.0001

Sloman, S. (2005). *Causal models: how people think about the world and its alternatives*. Oxford: Oxford University Press. DOI:10.1093/acprof:oso/9780195183115.001.0001

Smit, H., & Hacker, P. (2014). Seven misconceptions about the mereological fallacy: a compilation for the perplexed. *Erkenntnis*, 79(5), 1077–1097. https://doi.org/10.1007/s10670-013-9594-5

Smith, B. (1997). On substances, accidents and universals: in defence of a constituent ontology, *Philosophical Papers*, 26(1), 105–127. https://doi.org/10.1080/05568649709506558

Smith, B. (2003). Objects and their environments: from Aristotle to ecological ontology. In J. P. Cheylan, A. Frank, & J. Raper (eds.), *Life and motion of socio-economic units: GISDATA volume 8*. CRC Press.

Smith, E. R., & Conrey, F. R. (2007). Agent-based modeling: A new approach for theory building in social psychology. *Personality and Social Psychology Review*, 11(1), 1–18. https://doi.org/10.1177/1088868306294789

Smith, G. T., Atkinson, E. A., Davis, H. A., Riley, E. N., & Oltmanns, J. R. (2020). The general factor of psychopathology. *Annual Review of Clinical Psychology*, 16, 75–98. https://doi.org/10.1146/annurev-clinpsy-071119-115848

Smith, L. B. (1999). Do infants possess innate knowledge structures? The con side. *Developmental Science*, 2(2), 133–144. https://doi.org/10.1111/1467-7687.00062

Smith, L. B., Jones, S. S., Landau, B., Gershkoff-Stowe, L., & Samuelson, L. (2002). Object name learning provides on-the-job training for attention. *Psychological Science*, 13(1), 13–19. https://doi.org/10.1111/1467-9280.00403

Smith, L. B., Thelen, E., Titzer, R., & McLin, D. (1999). Knowing in the context of acting: the task dynamics of the A-not-B error. *Psychological Review*, 106(2), 235–260. DOI: 10.1037/0033-295x.106.2.235

Smits, M. L., Feenstra, D. J., Bales, D. L., et al. (2017). Subtypes of borderline personality disorder patients: a cluster-analytic approach. *Borderline Personality Disorder and Emotion Dysregulation*, 4(1), 1–15. https://doi.org/10.1186/s40479-017-0066-4

Sorensen, R. (2018). Vagueness. In E. N. Zalta (ed.), *The Stanford Encyclopedia of Philosophy* (Summer 2018 Edition). https://plato.stanford.edu/archives/sum2018/entries/vagueness/

Sparkes, A. C. (2007). Embodiment, academics, and the audit culture: a story seeking consideration. *Qualitative Research*, 7(4), 521–550. https://doi.org/10.1177/1468794107082306

Spencer, J. P. (2017). Models at play: using dynamic field theory to understand looking and learning in dyadic interactions. *Multidisciplinary Digital Publishing Institute Proceedings*, 1(3), 181. https://doi.org/10.3390/IS4SI-2017-04100

Spirtes, P., Glymour, C. N., Scheines, R., & Heckerman, D. (2000). *Causation, prediction, and search*. Cambridge, MA: MIT Press.

Spirtes, P., & Scheines, R. (2004). Causal inference of ambiguous manipulations. *Philosophy of Science*, 71(5), 833–845. DOI:10.1086/425058

Spivey, M. (2008). *The continuity of mind*. Oxford: Oxford University Press. https://doi.org/10.1093/acprof:oso/9780195170788.001.0001

Spivey, M. J. (2013). The emergence of intentionality. *Ecological Psychology*, 25(3), 233–239. https://doi.org/10.1080/10407413.2013.810475

Sripada, C., Kessler, D., & Jonides, J. (2016). Sifting signal from noise with replication science. *Perspectives on Psychological Science*, 11(4), 576–578. https://doi.org/10.1177/1745691616652875

Stamovlasis, D., & Tsaparlis, G. (2012). Applying catastrophe theory to an information-processing model of problem solving in science education. *Science Education*, 96(3), 392–410. https://doi.org/10.1002/sce.21002

Stasiulis, N. (2019). The transformation of modern causality in Heidegger's thought. *Filosofija. Sociologija*, 30(1), 27–36. https://doi.org/10.6001/fil-soc.v30i1.3913

Stedman, J. M., Kostelecky, M., Spalding, T. L., & Gagné C. (2016). Scientific realism, psychological realism, and Aristotelian-thomistic realism. *The Journal of Mind and Behavior*, 37(3–4), 199–218. https://www.jstor.org/stable/44631770

Steel, D. (2008). *Across the boundaries: extrapolation in biology and social science*. Oxford: Oxford University Press. https://doi.org/10.1093/acprof:oso/9780195331448.001.0001

Steel, D. (2010). Cartwright on causality: methods, metaphysics and modularity-hunting causes and using them. Approaches in philosophy and economics, Nancy Cartwright. Cambridge University Press, 2008, x + 270 pages. *Economics & Philosophy*, 26(1), 77–86. https://EconPapers.repec.org/RePEc:cup:ecnphi:v:26:y:2010:i:01:p:77-86_00

Steele, J. S., & Ferrer, E. (2011). Latent differential equation modeling of self-regulatory and coregulatory affective processes. *Multivariate Behavioral Research*, 46(6), 956–984. https://doi.org/10.1080/00273171.2011.625305

Steenbeek, H. W., & Van Geert, P. L. (2007). A theory and dynamic model of dyadic interaction: concerns, appraisals, and contagiousness in a developmental context. *Developmental Review*, 27(1), 1–40. https://doi.org/10.1016/j.dr.2006.06.002

Steenbeek, H., & Van Geert, P. (2008). An empirical validation of a dynamic systems model of interaction: do children of different sociometric statuses differ in their dyadic play? *Developmental Science*, 11(2), 253–281. https://doi.org/10.1111/j.1467-7687.2007.00655.x

Steenbeek, H., & Van Geert, P. (2013). The emergence of learning-teaching trajectories in education: a complex dynamic systems approach. *Nonlinear Dynamics Psychology and Life Sciences*, 17(2), 233–267.

Steenbeek, H., Van der Aalsvoort, D., & Van Geert, P. (2014). Collaborative play in young children as a complex dynamic system: revealing gender related differences. *Nonlinear Dynamics Psychology and Life Sciences*, 18(3), 251–276.

Steenbeek. H., & Van Geert, P. (2007). A dynamic systems approach to dyadic interaction in children: emotional expression, action, dyadic play, and sociometric status. *Developmental Review*, 27(1), 1–40. https://doi.org/10.1080/17405620544000020

Stengers, I. (2015). *In catastrophic times: resisting the coming barbarism*. London: Open Humanities Press. http://openhumanitiespress.org/books/download/Stengers_2015_In-Catastrophic-Times.pdf

Sternberg, R. J. (2003). A broad view of intelligence: the theory of successful intelligence. *Consulting Psychology Journal: Practice and Research*, 55(3), 139. https://doi.org/10.1037/1061-4087.55.3.139

Stevens, S. S. (1946). On the theory of scales of measurement. *Science*, 103(2684), 677–680. https://dx.doi.org/10.4135/9781412961288.n292

Stokoe, E., Hepburn, A., & Antaki, C. (2012). Beware the 'Loughborough School' of social psychology? Interaction and the politics of intervention. *British Journal of Social Psychology*, 51(3), 486–496. https://doi.org/10.1111/j.2044-8309.2011.02088.x

Strandell, J. (2017). Self-esteem in action: from direct causality to motive and mediator of self-performative action. *Culture and Psychology*, 23(1), 74–87. https://doi.org/10.1177/1354067X16650835

Strle, T. (2018). Looping minds: how cognitive science exerts influence on its findings. *Interdisciplinary Description of Complex Systems: INDECS*, 16(4), 533–544. https://doi.org/10.7906/indecs.16.4.2

Sturm, T., & Mülberger, A. (2012). Crisis discussions in psychology—new historical and philosophical perspectives. *Studies in History and Philosophy of Science Part C: Studies in History and Philosophy of Biological and Biomedical Sciences*, 43(2), 425–433. https://doi.org/10.1016/j.shpsc.2011.11.001

Sugarman, J., & Martin, J. (2020). *A humanities approach to the psychology of personhood*. London and New York: Routledge. https://doi.org/10.4324/9780429323416

Swenson, R., & Turvey, M. T. (1991). Thermodynamic reasons for perception–action cycles. *Ecological Psychology*, 3(4), 317–348. https://doi.org/10.1207/s15326969eco0304_2

Tafarodi, R. W., & Ho, C. (2006). Implicit and explicit self-esteem: what are we measuring? *Canadian Psychology*, 47(3), 195–202. https://doi.org/10.1037/cp2006009

Talbott, W. (2016). Bayesian epistemology. In E. N. Zalta (ed.), *The Stanford Encyclopedia of Philosophy* (Winter 2016 Edition). https://plato.stanford.edu/archives/win2016/entries/epistemology-bayesian/

Te Molder, H. (2015). Discursive psychology. In K. Tracy, C. Ilie, & T. Sandel (eds.), *The international encyclopedia of language and social interaction* (1st ed., pp. 257–273). New York: Wiley & Sons. https://doi.org/10.4324/9780429356032-4

Tellings, A. (2020). Diagnosis pressure and false positives: toward a non-reductionist, polytomic approach of child mental problems. *Philosophical Psychology*, 33(1), 86–101. https://doi.org/10.1080/09515089.2019.1698021

Teo, T. (1998). Klaus Holzkamp and the rise and decline of German critical psychology. *History of Psychology*, 1(3), 235. https://doi.org/10.1037/1093-4510.1.3.235

Teo, T. (2017). From psychological science to the psychological humanities: building a general theory of subjectivity. *Review of General Psychology*, 21(4), 281–291. https://doi.org/10.1037/gpr0000132

Thelen, E., & Smith, L. (1994). *A dynamic systems approach to the development of cognition and action*. Cambridge, MA: MIT Press.

Thom, R. (1989). *Structural stability and morphogenesis: an outline of a general theory of models*. Reading, MA: Addison-Wesley. https://doi.org/10.2307/2065330

Thompson, E. (2007). *Mind in life*. Cambridge, MA: Harvard University Press.

Tillas, A., Vosgerau, G., Seuchter, T., & Caiani, S. Z. (2017). Can affordances explain behavior? *Review of Philosophy and Psychology*, 8(2), 295–315. https://doi.org/10.1007/s13164-016-0310-7

Tinbergen, N. (1963). On aims and methods of ethology. *Zeitschrift für Tierpsychologie*, 20(4), 410–433. https://doi.org/10.1111/j.1439-0310.1963.tb01161.x

Tognoli, E., & Kelso, J. S. (2014). The metastable brain. *Neuron*, 81(1), 35–48. https://doi.org/10.1016/j.neuron.2013.12.022

Tognoli, E., Zhang, M., Fuchs, A., Beetle, C., & Kelso, J. S. (2020). Coordination dynamics: a foundation for understanding social behavior. *Frontiers in Human Neuroscience*, 14. https://doi.org/10.3389/fnhum.2020.00317

Tonello, L., Giacobbi, L., Pettenon, A., et al. (2018). Crisis behavior in autism spectrum disorders: a self-organized criticality approach. *Complexity*, 2018. https://doi.org/10.1155/2018/5128157

Tracy, J., Robins, R., & Sherman, J. (2012). The practice of psychological science in social personality research: are we still a science of two disciplines? In R. W. Proctor & E. J. Capaldi (eds.), *Psychology of science: implicit and explicit processes*. Oxford Scholarship Online. https://doi.org/10.1093/acprof:oso/9780199753628.003.0014

Trendler, G. (2019). Conjoint measurement undone. *Theory & Psychology*, 29(1), 100–128. https://doi.org/10.1177/0959354318788729

Trull, T. J., & Durrett, C. A. (2005). Categorical and dimensional models of personality disorder. *Annual Review of Clinical Psychology*, 1, 355–380. https://doi.org/10.1146/annurev.clinpsy.1.102803.144009

Trzesniewski, K. H., Donnellan, M. B., & Robins, R. W. (2003). Stability of self-esteem across the life span. *Journal of Personality and Social Psychology*, 84(1), 205–220. https://doi.org/10.1037/0022-3514.84.1.205

Trzesniewski, K. H., Donnellan, M. B., & Robins, R. W. (2016). Stability of self-esteem across the life span. *Journal of Personality and Social Psychology*, 84(1), 205–220. https://doi.org/10.1037/0022-3514.84.1.205

Tschacher, W., Dauwalder, J. P., & Haken, H. (2003). Self-organizing systems show apparent intentionality. In W. Tschacher & J. P. Dauwalder (eds.), *The dynamical systems approach to cognition: concepts and empirical paradigms based on self-organization, embodiment, and coordination dynamics* (vol. 10, pp. 183–199). Singapore: World Scientific. https://doi.org/10.1142/5395

Tschacher, W., & Haken, H. (2007). Intentionality in non-equilibrium systems? The functional aspects of self-organized pattern formation. *New Ideas in Psychology*, 25(1), 1–15. https://doi.org/10.1016/j.newideapsych.2006.09.002

Tschacher, W., & Haken, H. (2019). *The process of psychotherapy: causation and chance*. Cham: Springer International Publishing. https://doi.org/10.1007/978-3-030-12748-0

Tschacher, W., & Haken, H. (2020). Causation and chance: detection of deterministic and stochastic ingredients in psychotherapy processes. *Psychotherapy Research*, 30(8), 1075–1087. https://doi.org/10.1080/10503307.2019.1685139

Tschacher, W., Schiepek, G., & Brunner, E. J. (eds.). (2012). *Self-organization and clinical psychology: empirical approaches to synergetics in psychology* (vol. 58). Berlin and Heidelberg: Springer Science & Business Media. https://doi.org/10.1007/978-3-642-77534-5

Turvey, M. T. (2004). Impredicativity, dynamics, and the perception-action divide. In V. K. Jirsa & J. S. Kelso (eds.), *Coordination dynamics: issues and trends* (pp. 1–20). Berlin and Heidelberg: Springer. https://doi.org/10.1007/978-3-540-39676-5

Turvey, M. T., & Carello, C. (1981). Cognition: the view from ecological realism. *Cognition*, (10), 313–321. https://doi.org/10.1016/0010-0277(81)90063-9

Valentine, K. (2010). A consideration of medicalisation: choice, engagement and other responsibilities of parents of children with autism spectrum disorder. *Social Science & Medicine*, 71(5), 950–957. https://doi.org/10.1016/j.socscimed.2010.06.010

Vallacher, R. R., & Nowak, A. (1997). The emergence of dynamical social psychology. *Psychological Inquiry*, 8, 73–99. https://doi.org/10.1207/s15327965pli0802_1

Valsiner, J. (2007). *Culture in minds and societies: foundations of cultural psychology*. London: SAGE Publications. http://dx.doi.org/10.4135/9788132108504

Valsiner, J. (2019). Generalization in science: abstracting from unique events. In C. Højholt & E. Schraube (eds.), *Subjectivity and knowledge: generalization in the psychological study of everyday life* (pp. 79–97). Cham: Springer. https://doi.org/10.1007/978-3-030-29977-4

Van de Leemput, I. A., Wichers, M., Cramer, A. O., et al. (2014). Critical slowing down as early warning for the onset and termination of depression. *Proceedings of the National Academy of Sciences*, 111(1), 87–92. https://doi.org/10.1073/pnas.1312114110

Van der Gaag, M. A., & Van den Berg, P. (2017). Modeling the individual process of career choice. In W. Jager, R. Verbrugge, A. Flache, G. De Roo, L. Hoogduin, & C. Hemelrijk (eds.), *Advances in social simulation* (vol. 528, pp. 435–444). Berlin and Heidelberg: Springer. https://doi.org/10.1007/978-3-319-47253-9

Van der Gaag, M. A., van den Berg, P., Kunnen, E. S., & Van Geert, P. L. (2020). A simulation model shows how individual differences affect major life decisions. *Palgrave Communications*, 6(1), 1–9. https://doi.org/10.1057/s41599-020-0446-z

Van der Maas, H. L. J., Kolstein, R., & Van der Pligt, J. (2003). Sudden transitions in attitudes. *Sociological Methods & Research*, 32, 125–152. https://doi.org/10.1177/0049124103253773

Van der Maas, H. L. J., & Molenaar, P. C. M. (1992). Stagewise cognitive development: an application of catastrophe theory. *Psychological Review*, 99, 395–417. https://doi.org/10.1037/0033-295X.99.3.395

Van der Maas, H. L., Dolan, C. V., Grasman, R. P., et al. (2006). A dynamical model of general intelligence: the positive manifold of intelligence by mutualism. *Psychological Review*, 113(4), 842. https://doi.org/10.1037/0033-295X.113.4.842

Van der Maas, H. L., Kan, K. J., & Borsboom, D. (2014). Intelligence is what the intelligence test measures, seriously. *Journal of Intelligence*, 2(1), 12–15. https://doi.org/10.3390/jintelligence2010012

Van der Maas, H. L., Kan, K. J., Marsman, M., & Stevenson, C. E. (2017). Network models for cognitive development and intelligence. *Journal of Intelligence*, 5(2), 16. https://doi.org/10.3390/jintelligence5020016

Van der Sluis, J. K., Van der Steen, S., Stulp, G., & Den Hartigh, R. J. R. (2019). Visualizing individual dynamics: the case of a talented adolescent. In E. S. Kunnen, N. N. P. De Ruiter, B. F. Jeronimus, & M. A. E. Van der Gaag (eds.), *Psychosocial development in adolescence: insights from the dynamic systems approach* (pp. 209–222). (Studies in Adolescent Development). Abingdon: Routledge.

Van der Steen, S., Steenbeek, H., Van Dijk, M., & Van Geert, P. (2014). A process approach to children's understanding of scientific concepts: a longitudinal case study. *Learning and Individual Differences*, 30, 84–91. https://doi.org/10.1016/j.lindif.2013.12.004

Van der Veer, R., & Valsiner, J. (1991). *Understanding vygotsky: a quest for synthesis*. Blackwell Publishing.

Van Heugten-Van Der Kloet, V., & Van Heugten, T. (2015). The classification of psychiatric disorders according to DSM-5 deserves an internationally standardized psychological test battery on symptom level. *Frontiers in Psychology*, 6, 1108.

Van Dijk, M., & Van Geert, P. (2005). Disentangling behavior in early child development: interpretability of early child language and its effect on utterance length measures. *Infant Behavior and Development*, 28, 99–117. https://doi.org/10.1016/j.infbeh.2004.12.003

Van Dijk, M., & Van Geert, P. (2007). Wobbles, humps and sudden jumps: a case study of continuity, discontinuity and variability in early language development. *Infant and Child Development*, 16(1), 7–33. https://doi.org/10.1002/icd.506

Van Dijk, M., & Van Geert, P. (2011). Heuristic techniques for the analysis of variability as a dynamic aspect of change. *Infancia y Aprendizaje*, 34(2), 151–167. https://doi.org/10.1174/021037011795377557

Van Dijk, M., & Van Geert, P. (2014). The nature and meaning of intraindividual variability in development in the early life span. In M. Diehl, K. Hooker, & M. J. Sliwinski (eds.), *Handbook of intraindividual variability across the life span* (pp. 57–78). Abingdon: Routledge.

Van Dijk, M., Hunnius, S., & Van Geert, P. (2009). Variability in eating behavior throughout the weaning period. *Appetite*, 52(3), 766–770. https://doi.org/10.1016/j.appet.2009.02.001

Van Dijk, M., Hunnius, S., & Van Geert, P. (2012). The dynamics of feeding during the introduction to solid food. *Infant Behavior and Development*, 35(2), 226–239. https://doi.org/10.1016/j.infbeh.2012.01.001

Van Dijk, M., Van Geert, P., Korecky-Kröll, K., et al. (2013). Dynamic adaptation in child–adult language interaction. *Language Learning*, 63(2), 243–270. https://doi.org/10.1111/lang.12002

Van Fraassen, B. C. (1980). *The scientific image*. Oxford: Oxford University Press. https://doi.org/10.1093/0198244274.001.0001

Van Geert, P., & Van Dijk, M. (2002). Focus on variability: new tools to study intra-individual variability in developmental data. *Infant Behavior & Development*, 25, 340–374. https://doi.org/10.1016/S0163-6383(02)00140-6

Van Geert, P. (1991). A dynamic systems model of cognitive and language growth. *Psychological Review*, 98, 3–53. https://doi.org/10.1037/0033-295X.98.1.3

Van Geert, P. (1994). *Dynamic systems of development. Change between complexity and chaos*. London and New York: Harvester-Wheatsheaf.

Van Geert, P. (1998). A dynamic systems model of basic developmental mechanisms: Piaget, Vygotsky and beyond. *Psychological Review*, 105(4), 634–677. https://doi.org/10.1037/0033-295X.105.4.634-677

Van Geert, P. (2000). The dynamics of general developmental mechanisms: from Piaget and Vygotsky to dynamic systems models. *Current Directions in Psychological Science*, 9(2), 64–68. https://doi.org/10.1111/1467-8721.00062

Van Geert, P. (2002). Developmental dynamics, intentional action, and fuzzy sets. In N. Granott & J. Parziale (eds.), *Microdevelopment: transition processes in development and learning* (pp. 319–343). Cambridge, UK: Cambridge University Press. https://doi.org/10.1017/CBO9780511489709

Van Geert, P. (2008). Nonlinear-complex-dynamic-systems in developmental psychology. In S. Guastello, M. Koopmans, & D. Pincus (eds.), *Chaos and complexity in psychology: the theory of nonlinear dynamical systems* (pp. 242–281). Cambridge, UK: Cambridge University Press.

Van Geert, P. (2011). The contribution of complex dynamic systems to development. *Child Development Perspectives*, 5(4), 273–278. https://doi.org/10.1111/j.1750-8606.2011.00197.x

van Geert, P. (2014a). Dynamic modeling for development and education: from concepts to numbers. *Mind, Brain, and Education*, 8(2), 57–73. https://doi.org/10.1111/mbe.12046

Van Geert, P. (2014b). Group versus individual data in a dynamic systems approach to development. *Enfance*, 3(3), 283–312. https://doi.org/10.4074/s0013754514003061

Van Geert, P. (2019). Dynamic systems, process and development. *Human Development*, 63(3–4), 153–179. https://doi.org/10.1159/000503825

Van Geert, P., & Steenbeek, H. (2004). A model of behavior modification: the suppression of undesirable behavior. www.paulvangeert.nl/dynamic%20growth%20models/Model%20of%20behavior%20modification.doc

Van Geert, P., & Steenbeek, H. (2005a). Explaining after by before: basic aspects of a dynamic systems approach to the study of development. *Developmental Review*, 25(3–4), 408–442. https://doi.org/10.1016/j.dr.2005.10.003

Van Geert, P., & Steenbeek, H. (2005b). The dynamics of scaffolding. *New Ideas in Psychology*, 23(3), 115–128. https://doi.org/10.1016/j.newideapsych.2006.05.003

Van Geert, P., & Van Dijk, M. (2003). Ambiguity in child language: the problem of interobserver reliability in ambiguous observation data. *First Language*, 23(3), 259–284. https://doi.org/10.1177/01427237030233001

Van Geert, P., & Fischer, K. W. (2009). Dynamic systems and the quest for individual-based models of change and development. In J. P. Spencer, M. S. C. Thomas, & J. McClelland (eds.), *Toward a new grand theory of development? Connectionism and dynamic systems theory reconsidered*. Oxford: Oxford University Press. https://doi.org/10.1093/acprof:oso/9780195300598.001.0001

Van Orden, G. C., & Holden, J. G. (2002). Intentional contents and self-control. *Ecological Psychology*, 14(1–2), 87–109. https://doi.org/10.1207/S15326969ECO1401&2double_5

Van Orden, G. C., Kloos, H., & Wallot, S. (2009). Living in the pink: intentionality, wellbeing, and complexity. In C. Hooker (ed.), *Handbook of the philosophy of science, vol. 10: philosophy of complex systems* (pp. 639–683). Amsterdam: Elsevier BV.

Van Orden, G. C., Holden, J. G., & Turvey, M. T. (2003). Self-organization of cognitive performance. *Journal of Experimental Psychology: General*, 132(3), 331–350. https://doi.org/10.1037/0096-3445.132.3.331

Varela, F. J., Thompson, E., & Rosch, E. (2016). *The embodied mind: cognitive science and human experience* (Revised ed.). Cambridge, MA: MIT Press. https://doi.org/10.29173/cmplct8718

Vella, J. (2008). *Aristotle: a guide for the perplexed*. New York: Continuum.

Vogel, J. (1998). Inference to the best explanation. *Routledge encyclopedia of philosophy*. Taylor and Francis. https://doi.org/10.4324/9780415249126-P025-1

Volkmar, F. R., Reichow, B., & McPartland, J. (2012). Classification of autism and related conditions: Ppogress, challenges, and opportunities. *Dialogues in Clinical Neuroscience*, 14(3), 229. https://doi.org/10.31887/DCNS.2012.14.3/fvolkmar

Von Wachter, D. (2009). *The tendency theory of causation*. www.generativescience.org/papers/nature/Wachter-_2009-1-31.pdf

Vostal, F. (2016). *Accelerating academia: the changing structure of academic time*. Berlin and Heidelberg: Springer. https://doi.org/10.1057/9781137473608

Vostal, F., Benda, L., & Virtová, T. (2019). Against reductionism: on the complexity of scientific temporality. *Time & Society*, 28(2), 783–803. https://doi.org/10.1177/0961463X17752281

VSNU, NFU, KNAW, NWO, and ZonMw (2019). *Room for everyone's talent: toward a new balance in the recognition and rewards of academics*. The Hague. www.nwo.nl/en/position-paper-room-everyones-talent

Vygotsky, L. S. (1997). The historical meaning of the crisis of psychology. In R. W. Rieber & J. Wollock (eds.), *The collected works of L. S. Vygotsky: problems of the theory and history of psychology* (vol. 3, pp. 233–344). New York: Plenum Press.

Waddington, C. H. (1957). *The strategy of the genes*. London: Allen & Unwin. https://doi.org/10.1007/978-1-4615-5893-4

Wagenmakers, E. J., Van der Maas, H. L. J., & Molenaar, P. C. M. (2005). Fitting the cusp catastrophe model. In B. Everitt & D. Howel (eds.), *Encyclopedia of behavioral statistics* (vol. 1, pp. 234–249). New York: Wiley. DOI: 10.1002/0470013192

Wagenmakers, E. J., Wetzels, R., Borsboom, D., Van der Maas, H. L., & Kievit, R. A. (2012). An agenda for purely confirmatory research. *Perspectives on Psychological Science*, 7(6), 632–638. https://doi.org/10.1177/1745691612463078

Wagner, A. (1999). Causality in complex systems. *Biology and Philosophy*, 14(1), 83–101. https://doi.org/10.1023/A:1006580900476

Wagner, C. H. (1982). Simpson's paradox in real life. *The American Statistician*, 36(1), 46–48.

Wagner, J., Lüdtke, O., & Trautwein, U. (2016). Self-esteem is mostly stable across young adulthood: evidence from Latent STARTS models. *Journal of Personality*, 84(4), 523–535. https://doi.org/10.1111/jopy.12178

Wallot, S., & Kelty-Stephen, D. G. (2018). Interaction-dominant causation in mind and brain, and its implication for questions of generalization and replication. *Minds and Machines*, 28, 353–374. https://doi.org/10.1007/s11023-017-9455-0

Walpole, M. (2003). Socioeconomic status and college: how SES affects college experiences and outcomes. *The Review of Higher Education*, 27(1), 45–73. https://doi.org/10.1353/rhe.2003.0044

Wampold, B. E., & Imel, Z. E. (2015). *The great psychotherapy debate: the evidence for what makes psychotherapy work*. Abingdon: Routledge.

Wasserstein, R., & Lazar, N. A. (2016). The ASA statement on p-values: context, process, and purpose. *The American Statistician*, 70(2), 129–133. https://doi.org/10.1080/00031305.2016.1154108

Weisstein, E. W. (2020). Dynamical system. From MathWorld – A Wolfram Web Resource. https://mathworld.wolfram.com/DynamicalSystem.html

Wertsch, J. V. (1991). A sociocultural approach to socially shared cognition. In L. B. Resnik, J. M. Levine, & S. D. Teasley (eds.), *Perspectives on socially shared cognition* (pp. 85–100). Washington, DC: American Psychological Association. https://doi.org/10.1037/10096-004

Wertsch, J. V. (2010). Vygotsky and recent developments. In P. Peterson, E. Baker, & B. McGaw (eds.), *International encyclopedia of education* (3rd ed., pp. 231–236), New York: Elsevier. https://doi.org/10.1016/B978-0-08-044894-7.00490-5

Westen, D. (2012). Prototype diagnosis of psychiatric syndromes. *World Psychiatry*, 11(1), 16–21. doi: 10.1016/j.wpsyc.2012.01.004

Westen, D., Shedler, J., & Bradley, R. (2006). A prototype approach to personality disorder diagnosis. *American Journal of Psychiatry*, 163(5), 846–856. https://doi.org/10.1176/appi.ajp.163.5.846

Whitehead, A. N. (1929). *Process and reality: an essay in cosmology*. New York: Macmillan Company.

Wichers, M., Groot, P. C., Psychosystems, E. S. M., & EWS Group. (2016). Critical slowing down as a personalized early warning signal for depression. *Psychotherapy and Psychosomatics*, 85(2), 114–116. https://doi.org/10.1159/000441458

Wiggins, S. (2016). *Discursive psychology: theory, method and applications*. London: SAGE Publications. http://dx.doi.org/10.4135/9781473983335

Wiggins, S., & Potter, J. (2008). Discursive psychology. In W. Carla & S.-R. Wendy (eds.), *The SAGE handbook of qualitative research in psychology* (pp. 73–90). SAGE Publications. https://doi.org/10.4135/9781848607927

Wilkinson, S. (1986). *Feminist social psychology: developing theory and practice*. Milton Keynes: Open University Press.

Willems, J. C. (2007). The behavioral approach to open and interconnected systems. *IEEE Control Systems Magazine*, 27(6), 46–99. https://doi.org/10.1109/MCS.2007.906923

Williamson, J. (2009). Probabilistic theories of causality. In H. Beebee, C. Hitchcock, & P. Menzies (eds.), *The Oxford handbook of causation* (pp. 185–212). Oxford: Oxford University Press. https://doi.org/10.1093/oxfordhb/9780199279739.001.0001

Wilson, J. (2021). Determinables and determinates. In E. N. Zalta (ed.), *The Stanford encyclopedia of philosophy*. Stanford, CA: Stanford University Press. https://plato.stanford.edu/archives/spr2021/entries/determinate-determinables/.

Winters, A. M. (2017). *Natural processes: understanding metaphysics without substance.* London: Palgrave Macmillan. https://doi.org/10.1007/978-3-319-67570-1

Withagen, R., Araújo, D., & De Poel, H. J. (2017). Inviting affordances and agency. *New Ideas in Psychology*, 45, 11–18. https://doi.org/10.1016/j.newideapsych.2016.12.002

Withagen, R., De Poel, H. J., Araújo, D., & Pepping, G. J. (2012). Affordances can invite behavior: reconsidering the relationship between affordances and agency. *New Ideas in Psychology*, 30(2), 250–258. https://doi.org/10.1016/j.newideapsych.2011.12.003

Witherington, D. C. (2011). Taking emergence seriously: the centrality of circular causality for dynamic systems approaches to development. *Human Development*, 54(2), 66–92. https://doi.org/10.1159/000326814

Witherington, D. C., & Heying, S. (2015). The study of process and the nature of explanation in developmental science. *Review of General Psychology*, 19, 345–356. https://doi.org/10.1037/gpr0000033

Witherington, D. C., Overton, W. F., Lickliter, R., Marshall, P. J., & Narvaez, D. (2018). Metatheory and the primacy of conceptual analysis in developmental science. *Human Development*, 61(3), 181–198. https://doi.org/10.1159/000490160

Witkiewitz, K., Van der Maas, H. L., Hufford, M. R., & Marlatt, G. A. (2007). Nonnormality and divergence in posttreatment alcohol use: reexamining the Project MATCH data 'another way'. *Journal of Abnormal Psychology*, 116(2), 378. https://doi.org/10.1037/0021-843X.116.2.378

Wittgenstein, L. (2006). *Philosophical investigations.* Oxford: Blackwell (originally published in 1953).

Wolf, M., & Weissing, F. J. (2012). Animal personalities: consequences for ecology and evolution. *Trends in Ecology & Evolution*, 27(8), 452–461. https://doi.org/10.1016/j.tree.2012.05.001

Wong, A. E., Vallacher, R. R., & Nowak, A. (2014). Fractal dynamics in self-evaluation reveal self-concept clarity. *Nonlinear Dynamics Psychology and Life Sciences*, 18(4), 349–369.

Wong, A. E., Vallacher, R. R., & Nowak, A. (2016). Intrinsic dynamics of state self-esteem: the role of self-concept clarity. *Personality and Individual Differences*, 100, 167–172. https://doi.org/10.1016/j.paid.2016.05.024

Woods, W. C., Arizmendi, C., Gates, K. M., et al. (2020). Personalized models of psychopathology as contextualized dynamic processes: an example from individuals with borderline personality disorder. *Journal of Consulting and Clinical Psychology*, 88(3), 240. https://doi.org/10.1037/ccp0000472

Woodward, J. (2005). *Making things happen: a theory of causal explanation.* Oxford: Oxford University Press. https://doi.org/10.1093/0195155270.001.0001

Woodward, J. (2016). Causation and manipulability. In E. N. Zalta (ed.), *The Stanford Encyclopedia of Philosophy* (Winter 2016 Edition). https://plato.stanford.edu/archives/win2016/entries/causation-mani/

Wurzman, R., & Giordano, J. (2009). Explanation, explanandum, causality and complexity: a consideration of mind, matter, neuroscience, and physics. *NeuroQuantology*, 7(3). https://doi.org/10.14704/nq.2009.7.3.239

Xu, T. L., De Barbaro, K., Abney, D. H., & Cox, R. F. (2020). Finding structure in time: visualizing and analyzing behavioral time series. *Frontiers in Psychology*, 11, 11. https://doi.org/10.3389/fpsyg.2020.01457

Ylikoski, P. (2013). Causal and constitutive explanation compared. *Erkenntnis*, 78(2), 277–297. https://doi.org/10.1007/s10670-013-9513-9

Zadeh, L. A. (1975). Fuzzy logic and approximate reasoning. *Synthese*, 30, 407–428. https://doi.org/10.1007/BF00485052

Zadeh, L. A. (1978). Fuzzy sets as a basis for a theory of possibility. *Fuzzy Sets and Systems*, 100(1), 3–28. https://doi.org/10.1016/S0165-0114(99)80004-9

Zadeh, L. A. (2006). Generalized theory of uncertainty (GTU) – principal concepts and ideas. *Computational Statistics & Data Analysis*, 51, 15–46. https://doi.org/10.1057/9780230305687_6

Zahnoun, F. (2020). Explaining the reified notion of representation from a linguistic perspective. *Phenomenology and the Cognitive Sciences*, 19(1), 79–96. https://doi.org/10.1007/s11097-018-9603-x

Zeigler-Hill, V. (2011). The connections between self-esteem and psychopathology. *Journal of Contemporary Psychotherapy*, 41(3), 157–164. https://doi.org/10.1007/s10879-010-9167-8

Zeigler-Hill, V. (2013). The importance of self-esteem. In V. Zeigler-Hill (ed.), *Self-esteem* (pp. 1–20). Psychology Press. https://doi.org/10.4324/9780203587874

Zwaan, R. A., Etz, A., Lucas, R. E., & Donnellan, M. B. (2018). Making replication mainstream. *Behavioral and Brain Sciences*, 41, E120. https://doi.org/10.1017/S0140525X17001972

Index

4E, 91, 238, 294

abduction, 263, 264
ability, xi, 3, 13, 21, 22, 26, 37, 51, 55, 74, 111, 115, 117–119, 121–123, 131, 132, 144, 157, 158, 163, 174, 177, 195, 197, 199, 201–208, 213, 214, 217, 220–222, 224, 225, 227, 229, 237, 238, 242, 246, 248, 249
academic, x, xii, 45, 48–51, 62, 73, 76, 272, 273, 277, 279, 285
A-causes-B, 187
acceleration, 272, 273, 281
accordance, 116, 218, 236, 253, 274
accountability, 50
accumulation, 1, 46, 264, 273, 285
achievement, 209, 210, 212
    versus-investment, 210
actant, 54, 57, 60
action
    perception, 123, 129, 136, 167, 168, 210, 211
actor, 4, 54, 55, 261
actuality, 21, 22, 46, 121, 206, 220, 223, 226, 292, 297, 299
    potentiality, 206
acyclic, 144
adaptation, 8, 30, 102, 118, 172, 175, 211, 221, 227, 242, 270, 282
addiction, 148, 169
additivity, 26, 43, 182, 183, 190, 212, 238, 239, 255
ADHD, 10, 63
adolescence, viii, ix, 29, 80, 81, 97, 98, 103, 106, 107, 110, 167, 222
adulthood, 110, 131, 158, 168, 198, 227, 247
affordance, 99, 164, 192, 292
    effectivities, 163
age, 61, 73, 75, 80, 115, 116, 118, 119, 121, 129–131, 137, 143, 178, 199, 203
ageing, 252
agency, 143, 144, 175
agent, 15, 48, 54–57, 60, 118, 124–129, 136, 143–145, 159, 166, 167, 174, 175, 195, 246, 267–270, 274–278, 282, 284, 285, 288, 289, 291, 292
    based, 159, 174, 175
aggregation, 295
aggression, 152
allies, 55, 281, 282
Alzheimer, 94
ambiguity, 21–33, 133, 216, 218, 227, 229, 230, 232–234, 236–239, 244, 245, 248, 297, 299
American Psychological Association, 1, 279
amygdala, 154, 155
anorexia nervosa, 63
A-not-B error, 37, 135, 257
anthropology, 78
anxiety, 48, 233
APA, 230
appraisal, 91, 111
Arendt, H, 4, 47, 49, 50, 273, 277, 291
ARIMA, 101
Aristotle, 21, 22, 44–47, 52, 65, 66, 86, 133, 137, 153, 154, 155, 157, 163–165, 167, 169, 206, 223, 273, 292, 295
ASD, 245
Asperger, 133
assessment, 56, 71, 87, 100, 137, 138, 154, 196, 226, 231, 233, 236, 241, 245, 249, 281, 284, 285
Athenian, 19, 49, 119
athlete, 203–205
atomism, 20, 23
attention, 40, 63, 76, 80, 93, 113, 153, 215, 227
attitude, 53, 94, 187
attractor, viii, ix, 6, 28, 33–36, 56, 105, 106, 109–111, 166, 171, 179, 182–186, 235, 267, 274, 281–284, 286–288, 292
    deep, 183
    shallow, 183, 186
    wide, viii, 35, 36
Autism Spectrum Disorder, 121, 122, 133, 134, 154, 156, 157, 158, 231, 232, 244, 245, 255, 258

353

autonomy, viii, 33, 97, 98, 103, 104, 109, 167, 177, 274, 291
  limited, 33
autopoiesis, 164, 169, 175, 209
Auto-Regressive-Intregration-Moving-Average, 101
avoidance, 20, 157

baby, 115–117, 129, 254
basin of attraction, 35, 183, 184, 292
Bayesian statistics, 242, 243
becoming, 12, 16, 17, 20, 23, 48, 59, 85, 89, 91, 112, 156, 176, 187, 188, 230, 235, 237, 249
Bickhard, M, 7, 9, 13, 23, 25, 31, 32, 39, 66, 79, 87, 88, 91, 95, 102, 113, 159, 166, 175, 192, 209, 277, 290, 297
biology, 2, 13, 22, 33, 78, 79, 157, 291
birth, 50, 255
Borderline personality disorder, 233
Borsboom, D, 163, 179, 196, 228, 233, 234, 236, 252, 260, 283
Bourdieu, P, 1
Bracketing, 10, 18
brain, 30, 40, 41, 57, 58, 78, 154, 157, 161, 166, 167, 182, 210, 213, 217, 221, 235, 299

Campbell, R, 8, 32, 39, 76, 149, 175, 201, 276
capitalism, 272, 273, 281
career, x, xi, xii, 29, 43, 51, 79
Cartesian-split, 11, 271, 279
Cartwright, N, 142, 143, 146, 152, 153
case study, 5, 63, 86, 91, 114, 137, 194, 262, 263, 278, 285
catastrophe flags, 186
catastrophe theory, 40
category, 5, 6, 57, 97, 117, 119, 121, 122, 125, 128, 129, 133, 134, 147, 159, 180, 191, 198, 215, 218, 228, 230–234, 236, 237, 245, 248, 249, 254, 255, 258, 290, 294, 297, 301
  categorization, 56, 70, 121, 133, 144, 154, 230, 244, 273
causal, 144, 146, 153, 160, 164, 168, 174, 181, 271
  agent, 132
  cause-and-effect, 26, 76, 139, 141, 146, 157, 161, 163, 164, 171, 187, 188, 271, 275, 289, 290, 293
  effect, 151
  explanation, 5, 11, 114, 120, 154, 155, 156, 157, 161, 162, 169, 171, 172, 175, 187, 272
  loop, 181
  model, 5, 75, 142, 144, 146, 174
causality, 5, 8, 26, 26, 37, 41, 57, 75, 76, 87, 100, 106, 134, 137–144, 146–148, 150, 153–155, 157, 161–167, 169–171, 173, 175–177, 180–184, 187, 188, 193, 196, 203, 205, 206, 210, 222, 227, 228, 232, 233, 261, 271, 272, 274, 275, 280, 289, 290, 293–299, 302
  billiard-ball, 163, 188, 192
  circular, viii, ix, 105, 157, 164, 165, 293, 298
  downward, 105, 272, 293, 294, 295
  formal, 154
  horizontal, 297, 298
  intervention, 5, 152, 155, 156, 173, 183, 188, 297, 298
  manipulation/intervention, 181
  process, vi, 7, 159, 163, 164, 171, 177, 297
  token, 147
  type, 147–149, 151, 152
  upward, 302
  vertical, 302
causation
  self, 164, 168, 177, 187
central tendency, 70, 75, 77, 81, 82, 84, 85, 96, 100, 129, 259, 283
centrality, 16, 74, 277
chaos, 79, 128
children, ix, x, 10, 27, 29, 40, 41, 43, 51, 57, 69, 80, 90, 115, 119, 121, 124, 126, 128, 130, 133, 142, 144, 148, 154, 158, 163, 172, 174, 176, 178, 185, 188, 193, 199, 226, 227, 231, 232, 236, 237, 240, 243–249
  child care, xi
  parent relationship, 172, 226, 244
Chomsky, N, 279
classification, 120, 121, 133, 134, 231, 232, 244–246, 249, 298
classroom, 1, 30, 57, 188
co
  co-acting, 156
  co-adaptation, 226
  co-constructing, 94, 175, 238, 278, 299
  coexistence, xii, 16, 31, 55, 56, 102, 234–237, 288, 293
coding, 56, 97, 156, 226, 227
cognition, 30, 40, 57, 59, 87, 90, 91, 157, 159, 173, 182, 184, 187, 202, 237, 238, 279, 294, 295, 301
Cognitive Behavioral Therapy, 137–141, 145, 146
community, 4, 49, 50, 51, 52, 60, 62, 136, 211, 267, 288, 299
comorbidity, 233, 234
complementarity, xii, 22, 24, 46, 235, 236, 245, 250, 292
complex, x, 4, 5, 6, 12, 13, 14, 23–27, 30–34, 36, 38, 39, 43, 44, 49, 52, 60, 67, 94, 100, 105, 113–117, 119, 134, 137, 138, 152, 153, 155, 159, 161, 163–166, 168, 171, 173, 174, 178, 179, 181–183, 187–189, 195, 204, 215, 218, 221–224, 228, 230, 232, 234–237, 239, 246, 249, 251, 252, 254, 261, 262, 267, 270, 276, 278, 281, 282, 286, 288, 290, 293, 298, 301

complexity, 3, 15, 25, 30, 36, 37, 90, 117, 141, 157, 161, 172, 209, 211, 214, 216, 235, 237, 246, 249, 254, 264, 284, 290, 293–295
component, ix, 8, 10, 26, 29–33, 36–39, 56, 84, 90, 95, 96, 100, 101, 104, 105, 120, 145, 162, 164–167, 170, 179–181, 206, 212, 213, 234, 235, 238, 256, 267, 268, 274, 280, 292, 293, 295, 298, 302
component-dominance, 256
conditionality, 7
consciousness, 57
constraint, viii, 8, 9, 34, 37, 50, 54, 56, 59, 61, 79, 93, 105, 106, 110, 117, 123, 156, 162, 164–168, 171, 175, 177, 197, 204, 206, 217, 219, 220, 222, 223, 246, 250, 262, 266, 272–274, 277, 289, 293
constructivism, 11, 12, 52–54, 62, 267
contex, 75, 88, 197, 206
context, 6 (also see 4E), 291
    dependent, 3, 70, 153, 248, 260, 261, 264, 265, 281
    determined, 123
    specific, 197, 207, 208, 254, 261, 289
conversation analysis, 93
counterfactualism, 139, 148, 154, 156, 176, 298
counterforce, 36
coupling, 161, 164, 173, 179, 181, 209, 213, 214, 268, 292
covariation, 144, 145, 192
COVID, x, 55, 174
creation, 160
creativity, x, 277, 284, 285
critical state, 41, 294
criticality, viii, 41, 42, 169, 171, 185, 244, 294, 301
curiosity, 273, 277
cusp, viii, 40, 41
    catastrophe, viii, 40, 41
cybernetics, 173

data
    mining, 103
De Ruiter, N., x, xi, 9, 11, 40, 69, 71, 83, 96, 97, 101–106, 109, 261
deduction, 97, 263
deficit, 64, 154, 231, 245
depression, 3, 22, 34, 52, 141, 146, 148, 153, 163, 171, 179, 187, 228, 231, 233, 245, 281, 293
depth perception, 115–119, 121–123
determinable, 216, 217, 220, 223, 239, 243
deterministic, 171, 183, 280, 291
detrended, 101
Detrended
    Fluctuation Analysis, 101

developmental
    psychology, xi, xii, 11, 72, 116, 136, 167, 279, 284
    system, 156
Di Paolo, E., 59, 221
diagnosis, 138, 141, 158, 230, 245, 249, 280
differential equation, 12, 159, 207
directionality, 7
    uni, 5, 141, 155, 157, 159, 270, 297, 298
discipline, 257, 274
    cross, 263
discontinuity, 31, 39, 40, 41, 172, 184, 228, 229, 231, 233, 236, 242, 244
disequilibrium, 168
disorder, 121, 140, 154, 166, 180, 230–236, 245, 246, 280
disposition, 16, 22, 26, 70, 71, 122, 123, 129, 131, 135, 176, 197, 221, 224, 235, 238, 242, 246
Dowe, Ph, 172
DSM, 56, 133, 154, 230, 232, 236, 245
    -V, 56, 133, 154, 230, 232, 236, 245
dualism, 11
dunamis, 21, 224, 299
Dupré, J., 7, 8, 9, 12, 13, 22, 79, 88, 95, 113
dynamic
    field, 182, 238
    network, 1, 56, 179, 213, 234, 238
    system, x, 4–6, 12, 13, 24, 25, 27, 28, 30, 33, 34, 36, 39, 41, 100, 113, 114, 138, 155, 161, 169, 171, 173, 176, 178, 179, 182, 194, 204, 206, 207, 218, 221–223, 228, 229, 234, 235, 244, 250, 254, 261, 267, 270, 276–278, 281, 282, 286, 288, 290, 292, 296, 298, 301

ecological fallacy, 294, 301
economics, 124, 125, 173
education, 40, 50, 51, 62, 63, 78, 80, 211, 249, 255, 284
embodiment
    (also see 4E), x, 91, 92, 136, 211, 213, 238, 279, 294, 299, 300
emergence, 1, 3, 5, 6, 8, 9, 15, 24, 29, 31–34, 36–39, 55, 58–60, 62, 95, 96, 100, 104–106, 111, 117, 136, 141, 156, 162, 164, 167, 168, 175, 187, 189, 194, 210, 212, 213, 222, 234, 236, 238, 250, 256, 261, 262, 266, 267, 269–272, 274, 281, 282, 286, 288–290, 293–297, 299–301
    soft, 37, 38
    strong, 38
emergent properties, 31, 33, 37, 38, 167, 175, 270–272, 281, 293, 294
emotion, 11, 13, 90–93, 95, 100, 111, 183, 190, 191, 237, 299

enactivism
  (also see 4E), xii, 2, 6, 58–63, 65, 66, 68, 72, 77–79, 81, 82, 84, 86, 89, 91, 100, 108, 112, 113, 119, 123, 124, 129, 137, 142, 149, 153, 175, 193, 194, 196, 198, 200, 202, 214, 259, 260, 265, 266, 270, 274, 278, 281, 295, 298, 299
ensemble, 138, 147–149, 151, 200–202, 240, 296
entity, 7, 26, 37–39, 52, 55, 65, 66, 69–73, 76, 77, 80, 82, 83, 86, 88, 91, 95, 100, 112, 113, 121, 122, 123, 127, 132, 135, 136, 163, 191, 197, 198, 206, 211, 213, 228, 232–234, 237, 256, 260, 271, 281, 295, 297, 302
entrenchment, 7, 35, 36, 77, 95, 106, 110, 150, 171, 202, 247, 266, 267, 281, 283
epidemiology, 176
epigenetic, 33, 150, 292, 295, 299
  landscape, 33, 292, 295, 299
epiphenomena, 37, 38, 271, 272
episteme, 46, 47, 273
epistemic
  (also see epistemology), 15, 19, 86, 87
epistemological
  (also see epistemological), 13–16, 19, 59, 61, 68, 130–132, 242, 256, 265
epistemology, 2, 64, 81, 290
equilibrium, 42, 274, 275
ergodic
  see ergodicity, 74, 200, 296
ergodicity, 6, 73, 81, 82, 108, 135, 149, 171, 198, 200, 234, 241, 261, 283, 294, 296, 301
essence
  (also see essentialism), 10, 13, 14, 20–22, 68, 69, 82, 84, 113, 117, 134, 143, 150, 159, 229, 235
essence interpretation
  (also see essentialism), 134
essentialism, 158, 228, 231
ethics, 46
ethology, 157
etiology, 180, 233
etymology, 10, 26, 258
eudaimonia, 46
evolution
  rule, 29, 171, 174, 207, 244, 297
existentialism, 45
experience sampling, 56, 138, 228
experiment, 5, 6, 54, 55, 74, 78, 79, 105, 115–119, 122, 124, 126–132, 138, 143, 150–153, 181, 191, 203, 257, 258, 260, 289
extensional, 123
  set, 122, 133, 297

factor analysis, 198
feedback, xi, 36, 111, 121, 139, 181, 274, 275, 280
feminism, 288

Fischer, K., 227, 237, 262
fitness, 157, 158
  enhancing, 158
  reducing, 158
Flyvbjerg, B., 47
fractal, 101, 102, 218, 276
  dynamics, 102
frequentist, 239, 240
Friston, K, 161, 166, 173, 274

Gardner, H., 196, 212
Gaussian, 43, 294
gender, 50, 73, 148, 190, 201
  bias, 190
gene, 149, 150, 154, 157, 289
  (also see genetic), 14, 78, 145, 146, 156, 158
gene-based
  (also see gene), 150, 157
generality, 211
generalizability, 146, 201, 254, 255, 257, 260, 261
generalization, 2, 3, 81, 93, 117, 125, 131, 144, 146, 149, 172, 176, 198, 240, 255–260, 262–265, 271, 273, 285, 289
  to specific, 151, 198, 201, 202
generic
  (also see genericity), 134
  truth, 132
generic term, 297
genericity, 124
genetic, 134, 150, 156, 158, 159
g-factor, 179, 234
Gibson, J.J.
  (also see Gibsonian), 115, 118, 163
Gibsonian, 91, 175, 192, 269
goal
  achievement, 209–211, 213
Grice, J., 177, 180
group, 81, 82, 108–110, 112, 113, 200, 201, 288, 289, 294
  averages, 81, 113, 142
  differences, 80, 108, 151
growth curve, 71, 72

Hacking, I, 120, 121, 279
Haken, H., 38, 39, 40, 161, 165, 168, 176, 183, 184, 187, 266, 272, 302
Hausman, D., 139, 144, 146
Hegelian, 24
Heraclitus, 6, 20, 264
hermeneutic, 25
h-index, 46
history
  dependence, 278, 279, 281, 297, 299
  historicity, 102, 278
holism, 11, 123, 144, 180

Holland, J., 30, 32
Hollenstein, T., 96, 97, 103, 177, 282–284
homogeneity, 62
homology, 149, 202
homomorphism, 190, 192
humanities, 2, 94, 291
Hume, D., 143
hysteresis, 297

identity, 9, 20, 29, 89, 92, 104, 199, 202, 230, 295
ideology, 272, 274, 281
idiographic, 59, 128, 262
idiosyncratic
  (also see idiographic), 123, 126, 141, 150, 167, 180, 183, 201, 202, 211, 212, 234, 241
individualization, 81, 85, 129, 149
Indo-European, 10
infancy
  (also see children), vi, 37, 38, 86, 115–119, 121–132, 134–136, 167, 168, 178
innate, 159
innovation, x, 50, 51, 157, 158, 277, 279, 284, 290, 291
inscription, 56, 67, 90, 292
  (also see inscription device), 4, 56, 57, 60, 67, 68, 78, 97, 117, 118, 194, 226, 227, 249, 272
inscription device, 5, 56, 57, 60, 67, 68, 78, 97, 117, 118, 194, 226, 227, 249, 272
instrument
  (also see inscription device), 55, 56, 92, 123, 191, 195, 254, 264, 290, 292
instrumentalist, 47
intelligence, 2, 6, 10, 22, 26, 52, 53, 56, 122, 158, 179–190, 193–200, 202, 203, 205, 206, 208–214, 216, 217, 220, 223, 224, 234, 238, 239, 241, 248
  qua-substance, 197
  quotient, 190
intensional, 122, 296, 297, 298
interaction, viii, ix, 8, 14, 18, 20–25, 29–33, 36–39, 48, 51, 53–60, 62, 69, 85, 87, 88, 91, 94–106, 111, 113, 118, 121, 133, 135, 138, 150, 154, 157–159, 164–170, 172–174, 176, 178, 181, 183, 187, 192, 193, 198, 204, 206, 209–211, 213, 222, 225–227, 234, 235, 238, 239, 244, 249, 258, 260, 261, 266, 267, 270–272, 274–277, 279–284, 288–290, 292–295, 297, 299–302
  dominant, 100–102, 211
interactionist, 23
interactive, 8, 38, 53, 167, 175
interactivism, 8, 38, 53, 167, 175
interconnection, 3, 9, 18, 47, 54, 127, 266, 270, 281, 293, 300
interdependence, 174, 241, 299

interindividual, 81, 116, 131, 196, 198, 200, 201, 203, 205, 234, 239, 258, 283, 296
interventionism, ix, 3, 5, 24, 33, 34, 46, 75, 80, 130, 134, 138, 140, 141, 143, 144, 146, 148, 150–157, 161, 169–171, 173, 181, 183, 185, 187, 188, 245, 249, 289, 297, 298
intra-individual, 283, 115
intransitivity, 14, 15, 59, 297
Intrinsic, 100, 109
invariance, 43, 257
invariant
  (also see invariance), 43, 77, 254–256, 259, 260, 262
IQ, 43, 53, 193, 199, 202, 208, 212, 223, 238, 239, 241, 249
  test, 53, 208, 212, 241
irreducibility, 57
Item Response Theory, 241
iteration
  (also see iterativity), 50, 102, 171
iterativity, 8, 27, 48, 101, 164, 171, 172, 177, 204, 206, 213, 238, 243, 279, 294, 297, 299

Juarrero, A., 30, 39, 164, 166, 167, 221

Kelso, J., 24, 31, 36, 39, 40, 161, 169, 176, 186, 225, 235, 237, 244, 276, 294
Kernis, M., 70, 71, 100, 109, 262
knowledge, 1–5, 15, 19, 45–47, 52, 53, 55, 57–63, 68, 69, 79, 85, 94, 99, 108, 109, 113, 128, 132, 135, 141, 180, 195, 199, 201, 208, 215, 222, 229, 235, 237, 244, 246, 249, 254, 259, 266, 273, 276, 279, 284, 285, 290, 300
  construction, 2, 52, 55, 59, 62, 79, 108, 109, 266, 276, 284, 290
  use, 5

label, 120, 134, 280
labor, 47, 50
laboratory, 55, 68, 78, 89
Lamiell, J., 254
landscape, 33, 34, 36, 56, 166, 182–185, 274, 285–288, 290, 296
language, 10, 15, 22, 27, 29, 76, 104, 115, 118, 124, 133, 162, 172, 173, 184, 211, 226, 236, 237, 239, 242, 246, 248
  use, 118, 124, 236
Latour, B, 4, 52–58, 60, 194, 195, 251, 261, 267, 281, 282
leaders, 285
leadership, 63
learning, 30, 62, 118, 161, 163, 164, 168, 169, 172, 173, 182, 197, 204, 205, 210, 212, 227, 242, 243, 248
  and-teaching, 30, 173

level
- meso, 282, 283
- micro, 9, 150, 161, 164, 199, 282, 283, 285, 290, 300
- multi, 82, 83

lexicon, 176, 187
lifespan, 11, 72, 199
lifetime, 206, 211, 233
linear, 31–33, 43, 182, 242, 276
linearity, 43, 62
linguistic, 64, 66, 89, 118, 123–127, 134, 207, 226, 236, 237, 242, 244, 245, 272, 279, 288
Lockean, 70
logic, 54, 66, 79, 90, 127, 138, 163, 215, 243–245, 248, 250, 283
logistic function, 128, 176
longitudinal, 200
loop, 18, 35, 118, 123, 129, 136, 167, 168, 181, 204, 210, 274, 275, 280
looping, 121, 279–281, 290

macro, 9, 182, 282, 284, 285, 290, 300
- developmental, 182
- level, 9, 282, 284, 285, 290, 300
- scopic, 150, 164, 165, 170, 176, 192, 193

manipulability, 146, 156
manipulating
- (also see manipulation), 78–80, 145, 147, 227, 256

manipulation, 2, 5, 75, 142, 143, 150–152, 175, 191, 253, 298
Marxist, 159
mathematics, 28, 40, 148, 159, 182, 185, 207, 233, 239
Maturana, H, 155, 164, 209
meaning, 5, 7, 10, 12, 20, 22, 29, 39, 45, 52, 54, 57, 58, 66, 81, 85, 92, 112, 120, 121, 125, 126, 128–130, 132, 134, 147, 148, 149, 164, 165, 191, 192, 203, 204, 230, 250, 252, 256
measurable
- (also see measurement), 38, 73, 95, 123, 196, 212, 214, 216, 221, 224

measure, 5, 16, 57, 67–69, 72, 78, 79, 83, 84, 93, 95, 99, 100, 142, 191–193, 195, 196, 215–217, 225, 256, 277
measurement, xiii, 2, 5, 6, 14, 18, 21, 33, 56–58, 63, 64, 66–69, 77, 78, 83, 84, 88, 89, 92, 95, 96, 99, 100, 112–115, 123, 130, 131, 180, 189–201, 203, 206, 208, 211, 212, 214–229, 241, 248, 249, 254–256, 265, 271–273
mechanics, 192
mechanism, 6, 9, 109, 145, 156–158, 161, 172, 176, 185, 227, 257, 280, 281, 296, 297
mechanistic, 11, 163, 271
memory, 31, 136, 182, 278
mentalist, 167

mereological, 57
meso, 9, 282, 283, 290, 300
meta theory, x, 4, 13, 14, 16, 25, 29, 97, 113
metaphysics, 1, 2, 4, 12, 20, 21, 23–25, 62, 85, 95, 132, 133, 194, 197, 253, 265, 288, 298, 300
metastability, 235, 237, 244
method
- (also see methodology), xiii, 4, 5, 25, 52, 61, 76, 78, 79, 81, 84, 88, 90–94, 97, 98, 102, 103, 106, 181, 210, 226, 250, 262, 264, 265, 270, 273, 275, 277, 278, 281, 283, 285, 288–290, 295, 296

methodology, 1, 4, 6, 12, 16, 24, 25, 26, 46, 60–62, 64, 70, 77, 78, 80, 82, 83, 91, 92, 94, 100, 113, 119, 138, 146, 150, 153, 231, 251, 253, 254, 260, 263, 264, 266, 267, 273–275, 277, 283, 285, 288–290

micro
- events, 150, 161, 164

micro processes, 162
microscopic, 161, 165, 193
mindset, 284
model, 4, 5, 13, 27, 29, 65, 78, 81–83, 88, 105, 114, 124, 128, 142, 146, 155, 159–161, 163, 172–181, 182, 185–187, 195, 198, 200, 201, 203, 213, 222, 225, 237, 238, 243, 244, 249, 263, 264, 271, 272, 276, 281, 283, 289, 290, 293, 296–298
modernity, 119, 285
modifiers, 244, 245
modularity, 144, 152, 298
Molenaar P., 40, 81, 149, 184, 187, 200, 201, 276, 283
mother, xi, 115–117, 119
motion, 118
motivation, x, 40, 66, 85, 162, 169, 197, 203
motor, 38, 40, 154, 157, 162, 164, 167, 174, 182, 204, 276
movement, 34–36, 39, 87, 96, 108, 117, 118, 143, 154, 155, 162, 167, 204, 211, 276
Möwenlied, 189
multi
- plicity, 6, 229, 234, 237
- stability, 105, 177, 286, 288, 299
- systemic, 152
- variate, 27

narrative, 9, 89, 98, 99, 105, 278, 280
natality, 50, 51, 277
nativism, 158, 159
natural kind, 5, 53, 73, 119–123, 127–129, 131–135, 148, 150, 151, 191, 198, 201, 232, 236, 240, 242, 249, 254–256, 259, 294, 298
natural science, 77–79, 274
- envy, 77, 78, 190

naturalistic, 134
nature, xi, 1, 3, 8, 11, 12, 14, 18–21, 23, 24, 36, 39, 51–55, 57, 58, 60, 61, 63, 68, 70, 75, 82, 83, 86, 87, 89, 91, 92, 95–97, 99, 100, 101, 105, 108, 113, 118, 121, 128, 140, 141, 147, 151, 159, 172, 175, 176, 180, 187, 188, 191, 194, 199, 205, 207, 212–214, 217, 219, 232, 234, 236, 239, 243, 248, 254, 256–262, 265–267, 269, 270, 273, 275, 276, 278–280, 282, 288, 290, 297, 298, 302
nested timescale, 31
Netherlands, 128, 285
network, x, 4, 29, 30, 52–56, 58, 60, 104, 106, 133, 137, 141, 144, 145, 152, 159, 170, 178–181, 195, 211, 212, 227, 234, 237, 259, 260, 267–271, 275–277, 282–285, 288, 289, 291, 297, 298
neuro
   biology, 173
   cognition, 40, 157
   logical, 57, 134, 167
   science, 39
neurons, 30, 31
newborn
   (also see infancy), 51
node, 29, 144–146, 179, 267–269, 276, 277, 283–285, 298
noise, 14, 70, 100, 101, 130, 183, 212, 257, 266
   pink, 102
nominalization, 125, 135
nomothetic, 63
nonlinear, 13, 31, 43, 72, 228, 297
novelty, 38, 236, 282, 290, 295
novice, 4, 11, 62, 161, 162
NWO, 285

object
   concept, 38, 135, 136, 163
   like, 295
   search, 38
objectivism, 11, 68, 87, 258
observation, 10, 18, 45, 53, 55, 65, 91, 93, 129, 130, 138, 151, 160, 177, 178, 193, 197, 202, 217–219, 221, 226, 227, 229, 243, 273, 278, 285
   oriented, 177
observer, 13, 15, 18, 216–219, 221, 222, 224, 225, 236, 243
ontogenetic, 158, 159
ontology, 1–4, 11, 13–15, 18, 23, 24, 26, 51, 52, 58, 60, 61, 63–67, 69, 70, 75, 79–81, 83, 85–87, 91, 108–110, 112, 113, 123, 124, 129–132, 136, 137, 141, 143, 149, 150, 153, 158, 159, 189, 191, 193, 194, 196–198, 206, 214, 217, 218, 221, 229, 234, 249, 256, 258, 265–267, 269, 270, 274, 279, 284, 288–290, 295, 297–301

process, 3, 4, 6, 11, 12, 24, 58, 60, 63, 64, 79, 83, 85–88, 90, 91, 95, 97, 99–101, 108, 110, 112, 113, 191, 202, 204, 267, 274, 275, 298, 301
substance, 2–4, 6, 11, 22, 24, 52, 60–66, 68–72, 76–82, 84–86, 89, 90, 99, 108–110, 112, 113, 118, 123, 141, 142, 147, 153, 158, 200–202, 214, 220, 221, 229, 232, 234, 235, 237, 239, 249, 256, 258, 259, 265, 266, 269, 271, 274–276, 278, 279, 281–283, 286, 287, 289, 296, 301
operationalization, 5, 261
optimality, 210, 211
optimization, 166, 183, 208–213
organicism, 13
organism, 9, 22, 39, 91, 118, 122, 150, 158, 159, 192, 205, 209–211, 213, 214, 238, 269, 292, 294, 295
   -environment, 91, 150, 210, 211, 213, 214, 238, 292
Overton, W., 4, 7, 11–13, 25, 79, 91, 132, 144, 163, 169, 269, 271
oxytocin, 273

pandemic, 174
paradigm, 98, 276
paradox
   Sorites, 231
parameter, 41, 172, 177, 185, 186, 286, 287, 297, 299
   control, 40, 41, 172, 177, 184–186, 282, 284, 286, 287, 297
   order, 176, 177, 183
   space, 299
parent, x, 1, 69, 97, 103, 104, 106, 109, 145, 146, 167, 172, 177, 178, 188, 223, 226, 227, 241, 244, 248
   and adolescent, 104, 177, 223
   and child, 69, 98, 103
   and infant, 178
participant, 50, 56, 60, 68, 70, 84, 89, 92, 93, 97–99, 104, 151, 193, 225, 260, 281
participation, 226, 243, 244
particular, xiii, 2, 3, 8, 10, 13, 16, 20–23, 26, 27, 30–34, 36, 38, 46–48, 51–54, 56, 57, 59, 60, 62, 65, 72–74, 78, 84, 85, 89, 92, 93, 113, 117, 119–122, 124–126, 128–134, 137, 138, 140–143, 145–147, 149, 152–154, 156–159, 161–165, 167, 168, 171, 172, 174, 176, 182–184, 186, 192–194, 197, 199, 203, 204, 206–208, 210–212, 215, 219, 221, 223–229, 231, 233, 235–242, 245, 246, 248, 255, 257–262, 266, 268–270, 272, 274, 275, 278–281, 289, 292, 294, 295, 297, 299–301
particularist, 202

patient, 139, 233
pattern, 8, 9, 13, 20, 23, 31, 36–39, 42, 62, 83, 94, 95, 97, 100–105, 110–112, 162, 164–166, 168, 169, 176–178, 183, 186, **188**, 200, 203–205, 210, 212, 218, 219, 222, 228, 237, 262, 270, 276, 278, 293, 299, 300
PDD-NOS, 133, 232
Pearl, J, 144, 146, 153
peers, 88, 151, 206
perception, 8, 11, 20, 37, 40, 59, 96, 116, 117, 121–123, 136, 143, 161, 162, 164, 165, 168, 172, 182, 210, 235, 280
    action, 161, 162, 164, 235
    action loop, 235
perceptual (also see perception), 118, 174, 182, 211, 213, 218
performance, 10, 30, 40, 41, 136, 179, **188**, 193, 194, 196, 197, 199, 203, 205–208, 210, 212, 213, 216, 217, 220, 221, 234, 238, 242, 248, 252, 262
    related, 213
performative, 92, 93
person
    environment, 213, 223, 238
    oriented, 12, 239, 275
personality, 13, 51, 52, 73, 80, 98, 158, 173, 189, 194, 200, 201, 230, 232–234, 237, 238, 276
person-dependent
    (also see idiographic), 281
person-specific
    (also see idiographic), 75, 108, 179, 180, 201, 203, 206, 212, 213, 225, 233, 234, 239, 248, 273
perturbation, 5, 6, 35, 102, 109, 110, 168, 169, 171, 177, 181, 184, 185, 187, 210, 275, 276, 282–286, 290, 294, 296
p-factor, 234
PhD, xii, 36, 51, 272
phenomenology, 18, 118, 279, 280, 288
philosopher, 3, 7, 19–23, 44, 45, 47, 53, 66, 119, 137, 142, 143, 231, 263, 279
philosophy, 1, 12, 13, 19, 21–23, 44, 45, 57, 61, 85, 87, 117, 133
phronesis, 46, 48, 50, 273
phylogeny, 158
physicalism, 167
physicist, 194, 195
physics, 2, 13, 23, 78, 79, 192, 194, 201, 222, 291
Piaget, J., 41, 135, 159, 172, 199, 275, 283, 297
Plato, 19, 21, 44, 251
play, 4, 29, 116, 151, 161–164, 168, 169, 171, 174, 184, 226, 248, 278, 282, 283
pluralism, 4, 11, 12, 14–16, 19, 24, 64, 85, 88, 180, 300
poeisis, 48

poiesis, 46, 47, 50
polarization, 174, 288
policy, 40, 47, 80, 140, 143, 147, 153, 280
population, 2, 149, 231
    based, 135
    focused, 85
    generalization, 273
    versus individual, 202
positivism, 14, 59, 73, 190, 278, 299, 300
positivity, xi
potential, 3, 21, 22, 33, 34, 94, 97, 104, 140, 142, 147, 148, 166–168, 183, 186, 223, 224, 242, 248, 270, 282, 294, 295, 299, 300, 301
potentialities, 214, 223–226, 229, 235, 240
potentiality, 21, 22, 206–208, 220–223, 242, 292, 299
power, 2, 4, 42, 43, 55, 62, 79, 138, 141, 143, 147, 150, 153, 160, 172, 176, 177, 212, 223, 252, 256, 263, 271–273, 278, 284, 294, 296, 299
    law, 42, 43, 278, 294
    structure, 4, 299
practise
    practitioners, 23, 60, 153, 193
praxis, xii, 1–6, 23–26, 38, 44, 45, 47–58, 60, 62, 63, 65, 69, 76–80, 82, 84–88, 92, 97, 99–101, 108, 112–114, 119, 121, 124, 129, 133, 134, 137, 141, 147, 150, 151, 154, 158, 163, 167, 172, 175, 182, 187, 191, 193–199, 208, 215, 219, 226, 230–233, 239, 246, 249, 251, 254, 258, 259, 265–267, 269–272, 274–279, 281–284, 286–288, 290, 291, 299
    ontology, 124
predictability, 79, 119
prediction, 74–77, 81, 84, 112, 143, 160, 203, 207, 208, 215, 220, 243, 244, 264, 273
prejudice, 66, 263
pre-Socratic, 21, 23, 279
Prigogine, I., 12, 23, 39, 161, 166, 209
privilege, 25, 83, 113, 132, 258, 278
probabilistic, 121, 129, 130, 131, 139, 140, 144, 146, 148, 151, 156, 171, 183, 187, 242, 243
probability, 6, 19, 43, 71, 117, 121, 128, 130, 131, 132, 140, 144, 146–149, 171, 182, 203, 239–242
process, x, xii, 2–27, 29, 31, 32, 37–42, 49, 52–58, 60–64, 67, 76, 78, 79, 81–83, 85–102, 105, 108–116, 118, 119, 123, 125, 128, 129, 135, 136, 138, 141, 149, 150, 156–159, 161–174, 176, 177, 179–182, 186–188, 191–193, 200–206, 208–214, 221–223, 226–230, 234–238, 241, 243, 249, 251–253, 256–264, 266, 267, 269–271, 273–284, 286–291, 293–302
    approach, 3–5, 9, 12, 14–16, 18, 19, 25, 26, 85, 87, 88, 114, 123, 159, 163, 169, 170, 256, 257, 259, 263, 267, 271, 276, 277, 284, 288, 290

based, 17, 96
branch, 21
dependent, 159
oriented, 4, 6, 24, 38, 85–87, 90, 92, 100–102, 108, 109, 112, 113, 116, 141, 156, 161, 194, 202, 260, 261, 266, 275, 276, 279, 283, 284, 286, 287, 290, 291
questions, 261
processual
(also see processualism), x, 3–6, 13, 14, 16, 17, 24, 25, 57, 60, 85–88, 91, 95–98, 100, 104, 105, 110, 113, 114, 123, 129, 135, 136, 141, 144, 155–159, 171, 173, 188, 192, 199, 202, 206, 208, 209, 212, 214, 216, 220–222, 226, 228, 229, 232, 235, 237, 238, 243, 249, 257, 262, 266, 273, 275, 283, 285, 289, 290
processualism, 4, 9, 11, 12, 14, 16, 20, 135, 300
product, 1, 46–48, 51, 213
production, 46–48, 50, 51, 115, 124, 150, 157, 158, 179, 180, 209, 248, 271–273, 299
company, 115
productivity, 60, 284
propensity, 40, 70, 176, 239, 241, 242, 246
property, viii, 2, 8, 12, 13, 15, 17, 21, 26, 27, 30–35, 37–40, 50, 57, 65, 66, 68–70, 72, 73, 75, 76, 82, 84, 85, 87, 95, 96, 100, 102, 104, 105, 109–111, 120, 121, 123, 125–134, 137, 140, 141, 143, 148–149, 151, 153–155, 157–159, 162, 164, 165, 169, 171, 172, 176, 177, 180, 182, 189, 191, 193–202, 204, 211–214, 216, 217, 220–227, 229, 230, 233, 234, 237–242, 244, 246, 249, 251, 252, 256, 259, 261, 262, 266, 269–272, 274, 278, 281, 283, 284, 286, 288, 290, 292–301
psychoeducation, 80
psychological, 10, 12, 14–16, 18, 22–24, 26, 32, 33, 36–38, 40, 47–49, 51, 52, 56–63, 65, 69, 72, 74, 77–79, 82, 86, 88, 94, 102, 108, 111, 114, 118, 120–122, 129, 130, 134, 135, 137, 138, 141, 143, 147, 153, 156, 161, 163, 169, 172, 175, 176, 185, 187–191, 194, 196–198, 200–203, 206, 214–217, 221–224, 226, 230–232, 236–240, 242, 246, 249, 251, 252, 254, 256, 257, 259, 260, 264, 266, 267, 269–284, 286–292, 295, 296, 301
science, 5, 6, 9, 10, 15, 16, 24, 26, 48, 49, 51, 52, 56–60, 62, 63, 74, 78, 79, 121, 224, 259, 264, 266, 267, 269–272, 274–284, 286–291
psychologist, 10, 12, 14, 16, 23, 26, 32, 37, 48, 51, 53, 58, 59, 61, 66, 74, 78–80, 82, 122, 143, 188, 193, 197, 199, 214, 220, 225, 250, 263, 272, 277
psychology, x–xiii, 1–7, 9, 10, 12–16, 21–26, 30, 32, 39, 40, 46, 49, 51, 52, 54, 56–59, 62, 63, 67, 78, 79, 94, 113, 115, 118–120, 122, 124, 143, 155, 157, 158, 163, 173, 175, 180, 187, 189–196, 200, 204, 211, 214, 216, 218, 238, 239, 245, 250–252, 254, 257, 258, 260, 264, 265, 269–271, 273, 275, 276, 278, 279, 281, 287, 291, 292, 296–298
researchers, 260
psychometric, 194, 196, 200, 203, 208, 211, 214
psychopathology, 13, 22, 180, 201, 228, 232–234, 236, 238
psychotherapist, 138, 139
psychotherapy, 40, 51, 137, 138, 141, 171, 183, **187**, 293
PTSD, 233
p-value, 151, 276

Quetelet, A., 128, 130, 202

Raeff, C., 3, 8, 10, 67, 78, 80, 82, 88, 91, 270
Randomized Control Trial, 150, 152, 153
rank, 72
rationalism, 16, 300
reactivity, 68, 89, 109, 282
real time, 156, 212, 223, 269
realism, vi, 11, 61, 294, 297, 300
anti, 14, 300
critical, v, 4, 14–16, 24, 47, 53, 54, 59, 61, 64, 264, 269, 288, 294, 300
deflationary, 53
naïve, 14
scientific, 53, 300
realist, 15, 64, 87, 197
reality, 1, 2, 4, 12, 14–16, 18, 19, 21, 23, 48, 49, 51–54, 57–59, 61, 63, 68, 76–78, 80, 82, 83, 85, 87, 108, 113, 118–119, 120, 121, 124, 128, 134, 147, 150, 219, 235, 256, 260, 261, 265, 266, 279, 290, 297–300
reciprocity, 163, 231
recurrence, 8, 36, 38, 96, 97, 102–105, 106, 110, 133, 138, 212, 222, 265, 279, 293–301
recursiveness, 101, 102, 104, 274
reducibility, 32, 57
reductionism, 18, 22, 57
anti, 57
reflective, xii, 262
reflexivity, 63, 64, 280, 300
regression, 182, 259, 301
regularity, 125, 236, 292
reification, 66, 76, 167, 231, 281
relational, 11, 25, 91, 156, 278
developmental, 91
relationalism, 12, 13

relationship, viii, 5, 11, 14, 28, 29, 31, 50–53, 55, 57, 64, 65, 73–75, 77, 78, 80, 81, 84, 85, 93, 96, 97, 106, 108, 112, 113, 124, 139, 141, 143–146, 149–152, 163, 166, 168, 173, 177–179, 187, 190, 195, 210, 223, 229, 234, 235, 237, 240, 251, 253, 255, 256, 258, 259, 264, 265, 268, 269, 281, 283, 290, 293, 297
relativism, 15, 19, 59, 68
reliability, 68, 143, 147, 191, 203, 207, 226, 240, 254, 264
repellor, 105, 184, 288
replicability, 6, 119, 172, 251–256, 259, 260, 263–265, 273
representation, viii, ix, 12, 13, 29, 37, 37, 59, 111, 176, 179, 181–183, 185, 190, 207, 208, 219, 221, 222, 227, 246–248, 268, 269, 295, 296
representative, 73, 122, 123, 126, 135, 147, 198–202, 211, 240, 255, 261, 295, 296, 298
reproducibility, 6, 79, 132, 251, 253–256, 258–261, 264, 265, 273, 285
  crisis, 6
  of-results, 259
Rescher, N., 4, 7, 8, 11–13, 16, 20, 22, 23, 87
research, 120, 260, 264, 272, 291
  activities (also see research practices), 269
  efficacy, 138
  practices, 1, 5, 65–67, 84, 202, 270, 277, 289
  psychological, ix, 5, 9, 23, 24, 40, 62, 72, 73, 78, 118, 120–122, 129, 134, 143, 147, 174, 191, 201, 214, 215, 221, 226, 230, 231, 239, 240, 249, 251, 252, 257, 276, 279–281, 288
resilience, 168
resistance, 14, 110, 169, 241, 276, 286
resonance, 263, 269, 270
resource, 134, 165, 174, 176, 183, 209–212, 252
response, 36, 45, 56, 70, 78, 92, 109, 151, 157, 203, 225, 227, 228, 265, 275, 282
responsibility, 49, 51
retrieval, 37, 163
review, 12, 47, 69, 70, 74, 275
reward, 124, 127, 197, 285
RGB, 216–219, 224
rhythm, 165, 169
Richardson, K., 165, 195, 204, 209, 211, 238
risk, 29, 51, 61, 73, 77, 79, 174, 277
  taking, 73, 277
rivalry, 20
river, x, 1, 3, 6, 12, 19–22, 251, 260, 264
rule, 1, 27, 29, 58–60, 63, 69, 96, 127, 139, 166, 171, 174, 190, 194, 198, 207, 253, 292, 294

safety, 18, 116, 117
Salmon, W, 172
sample, 62, 63, 73, 82, 85, 120, 122, 123, 126–130, 134, 141, 147–149, 151, 171, 175, 198–202, 208, 219, 228, 239, 240, 252, 254, 255, 257, 260–262, 273, 296, 298
Sapiens, 158
scaffolding, 29, 173
scale, 9, 33, 43, 67–69, 84, 89, 90, 92, 96, 99, 134, 159, 191, 213, 237, 257, 258, 274, 279, 282, 285
  large, 31, 63, 79, 81, 82, 134, 283, 275, 278, 283–285, 289, 290
scatterplot, 74
scheme, 4, 11, 12, 65, 97, 154, 155, 157, 159, 163–165, 180, 182, 188, 226
Schiepek, G., 40, 141, 180, 187, 228
scholars, xii, 12, 13, 50, 76, 87, 94, 275, 279
scholarship, 7, 275
Schöner, G., 182, 238
school, 7, 52, 62, 75, 91, 193, 200, 207, 239, 240, 242, 243
science, xi, 4–6, 10, 11, 13, 21–25, 45–48, 51–54, 57, 59, 60, 66, 78–80, 85, 120, 139, 142, 147, 148, 155, 171, 174, 180, 187, 190, 195, 251, 254, 258, 264–266, 267, 271, 275, 277, 278, 281, 284, 285, 290, 294
  action, 52
  -and-technology-studies, 258
scientific
  statements, 129
  understanding, 3, 146
scientist, 14, 55, 58, 61, 62, 78, 267, 276, 278, 281
score, 67, 68, 72, 77, 81, 82, 100, 196–199, 203, 222–224, 229
Seibt, J., 7, 8, 11, 20, 21, 23
self, xi, xii, 2, 5, 9, 11, 12, 16, 17, 21, 22, 24, 26, 31–34, 37–42, 48, 52, 55, 56, 60, 61, 63–102, 104–113, 118, 121, 134–136, 142, 155, 158, 164–169, 171, 173, 177, 183, 185, 187, 189, 191, 194, 195, 197, 199, 201, 204, 209, 210, 213, 219, 222, 229, 230, 238, 239, 244, 249, 252, 257, 261, 270–276, 279–282, 284, 286, 288, 290, 292, 294, 295, 299–301
  actualization, 22
  affect, viii, 97, 98, 103, 104
  amplifying, 274
  as-object, 85, 89, 99, 111, 112
  as-process, 111, 112, 275
  concept, 11, 68, 88, 92, 287
  confidence (also see self-esteem), 59
  confidence also see self-esteem, xi
  enhancement, 71
  esteem, vi, viii, 2, 5, 16, 21, 26, 40, 55, 56, 60, 63–72, 92–113, 118, 121, 134, 135, 142, 187, 189, 191, 194, 222, 238, 239, 257, 262, 275, 276, 279, 281, 288, 295
  esteem-research, 69

evaluations (also see self-esteem), 68, 98–100, 104
experience, 88, 95, 100, 102, 110–112, 261
feelings, 70
fulfilling, 249, 272
governed, 166
help, 76
maintenance, 12, 31, 34, 38, 95, 96, 100, 102, 104, 105, 158, 164, 172, 177, 183, 185, 262, 270, 271, 282, 284, 292, 299–301
narrations, 104
organization, viii, 5, 37–42, 95, 102–105, 110, 136, 141, 155, 164–166, 169, 171, 177, 183, 185, 187, 194, 204, 210, 213, 244, 270, 271, 295, 301
organized criticality, 301
perceptions, 77
perpetuating (also see self maintenance), 24
preservation, 166
reflection, 66, 88, 92, 93, 97, 261, 290
reinforcing, 272, 288
report, 77, 87, 90, 92, 93, 99, 101, 262
similarity, 72, 276
sustaining (also see self maintenance), 9, 32, 33, 38, 39, 168, 282, 286
worth also see self-esteem, 67, 68, 87, 89, 93, 94, 109, 111
self-organization, 177, 286
semantics, 133, 134
self-organization, 177, 286
semantics, 133, 134
semiotic, 55
sensory-motor, 118, 161, 162, 164
sentence, 8, 125, 142
SES, 239, 240, 243
  low, 239
set, 4, 33, 55, 63, 69, 83, 97, 101, 121, 122, 127, 128, 141, 149, 161, 162, 178, 189, 190, 193, 196, 239, 240, 245, 255, 257, 259, 291, 296, 298, 301, 302
sexes
  (also see gender), 152
shame, 93, 139
significance, 16, 38, 62, 120, 136, 151, 161, 276, 284
simulation, 175, 244, 263
single case
  (also see idiographic), 241, 262
slope, 34, 36, 184, 185, 203, 204
Smith, L., 10, 12, 36, 38, 57, 96, 118, 130, 135, 136, 156, 158, 174, 176, 212, 227, 234, 238, 274, 281, 290
social
  science, 278
  support, 152
social constructionism, 87, 288

society, 1, 9, 10, 50, 158, 213, 235, 252, 269, 272, 273, 285, 289, 300
socioeconomic status, 195, 197
sociologist, 128
sociology, 1, 78
Sociometer, 71
soft-assembly, 38, 96, 97, 111, 136, 194, 212, 237, 301
software, 175, 181
Sorites, 231
specialization, 205
species-specific, 213
specificity, 253, 254
Spencer, J., 182
spoon feeding, 115
SSG, 106
stability, ix, 1, 2, 3, 4, 9–13, 16, 18, 21, 32, 36, 38, 40, 65, 68, 70, 71, 72, 82–84, 87, 95, 100–102, 104, 105, 109, 110, 123, 139, 140, 158, 164–166, 176, 178, 183–185, 203, 222, 235–237, 242, 275–277, 280, 286, 288, 293, 295, 296, 298, 300
stadium, 44
stage, xi, 41, 172, 186, 200, 236, 237, 258, 260
  theory, 41
standard deviation, 129, 231
stasis, 11
state space, viii, ix, 27–29, 97, 106, 107, 172, 179, 182, 207, 216, 223, 224, 246, 283, 296, 299, 301, 302
state-of-the-world, 216
stationarity, 200, 242
statistician, 128, 202, 276, 283, 284
statistics, 25, 56, 62, 63, 79, 82, 85, 101, 138, 145, 151, 172, 175, 197, 200, 201, 207, 239, 242, 243, 257–259, 261, 273, 276, 278, 283, 284, 294, 296, 301
Stengers, I., 56, 116, 209
stimulus, 56
strength-of-beliefs, 224
stress, 14, 15, 57, 64, 233, 266
structural equation modeling, 145
student, viii, xii, 1, 10, 28, 36, 51, 62, 73, 78, 118, 149, 182, 207, 239, 240, 267, 268, 301
subjectivism, 11, 15, 88, 242
subjectivity, 291
substance, iv, 1–4, 6, 7, 9–11, 13–18, 20–24, 52, 56, 58, 60, 61, 63–70, 71–73, 75–87, 89, 90, 99, 108, 109, 110, 112, 113, 117, 121, 123, 125, 141, 142, 147–149, 153, 158, 191, 194, 197, 198, 200–202, 206, 211, 212, 214, 220, 221, 228, 229, 232–235, 237, 239, 249, 256, 258–260, 265, 266, 269–271, 274–276, 278, 279, 281–284, 286–289, 291, 295, 296, 298, 301
  entity, 149, 194

substance (cont.)
  primary, 65–67, 69, 72, 147, 148, 198, 295
  secondary, 65, 66, 71–73, 75, 84, 86, 87, 108, 141, 148, 150–153, 163, 198, 201, 202, 233, 295
substantialism, 4, 5, 9, 10, 12, 14, 16, 79, 87, 101, 129, 132, 135, 163, 153, 158, 276, 301
substare, 10
substrate, 221, 228
suicide, 139, 226
supervenience, 263
supervision, xii
supervisor, 128
swarm, 19, 95, 96
Sweden, 152
symptom, ix, 22, 138–141, 145, 153, 154, 163, 171, 179, 187, 228, 230, 232–234, 236, 248, 293
synchronize, 269
syndrome, 245
synergetics, 39, 39, 40, 266, 294, 301
system, v, vii, viii, ix, 4, 8, 25–32, 34–36, 38–40, 43, 48, 56, 63, 79, 91, 95–97, 99, 100, 102, 104, 105, 109, 118, 144, 152, 155, 156, 159–166, 168–171, 175–177, 179, 180, 182–185, 187, 188, 190, 192, 193, 204, 206, 207, 209, 210, 211, 213, 221, 224, 225, 226–238 , 244–246, 261, 265, 266, 267, 270, 271, 272, 274, 277–279, 282–286, 288, 290–297, 299, 301
  dynamics, 175, 180
  level, 296

talent, xi, 52, 206
teacher, viii, 1, 28, 174, 182, 205
teaching, 63, 118, 226
  learning, 226
team, 18
techne, 46, 47, 50, 51
technology, 51, 52, 53, 264
teleological, 115, 155
telescopes, 160
temporality, 7, 8, 10, 17, 18, 24, 31, 37, 52, 91, 100–102, 104, 106, 151, 158, 173, 176, 177, 199, 212, 212, 222, 272, 287, 275, 276, 278, 283, 229, 302
tenure, 46, 48, 79
  track, 48, 79
test, 22, 51, 56, 62, 72, 78, 126, 127, 185, 193, 194, 196–201, 203, 207, 208, 211, 217, 222–224, 226, 241, 248, 256, 257, 276
  retest, 72
testability, 79
Thelen, E., 12, 36–38, 95, 130, 135, 212, 238, 274, 281, 290
theorem, 206
theorist, 7, 13, 23, 206

theory, xi, 4, 13, 15, 25, 29, 30, 36, 39, 40, 44, 54, 57, 60, 62, 64, 87, 105, 108, 131, 134, 141, 143, 152–155, 159, 161, 163, 172, 175, 178, 182, 195, 196, 200, 209, 212, 213, 216, 224, 235, 238, 250, 253, 254, 256, 259, 261, 263–265, 267, 275, 276, 288, 290, 298
  of mind, 36, 163
therapist, 138, 139, 141, 150
  and client, 150
therapy, ix, 3, 51, 62, 63, 87, 138–142, 145–147, 150, 152, 171, 228, 245, 249
thermodynamics, 21, 23
Thom, R., 40, 244
time, i, ix, x, xi, xii, 3, 6, 7, 9, 11, 12, 15, 17, 18, 20, 21, 27, 28, 31, 34, 41, 45, 48, 54, 55–58, 60, 62, 69, 70–72, 82–85, 95–103, 107, 110, 113, 118–120, 122, 127–131, 142, 144, 145, 148, 150, 151, 156, 160, 162–166, 172–175, 178, 179, 181–183, 185, 186, 194–196, 198, 200, 202, 204, 206–208, 212, 216, 217, 222, 224, 227, 229, 231, 235, 236, 240, 241, 244, 246, 256, 257, 259–261, 263, 264, 267–269, 272, 275–278, 281–285, 287, 288, 293, 294, 296, 297, 300, 302
  bound, 194
  dependence, 202, 206, 224, 260, 278, 300
  evolution, 27, 244, 302
  intensive, 278
  scale, 9, 33, 43, 63, 67–69, 84, 89, 90, 92, 96, 99, 134, 159, 191, 213, 237, 257, 258, 274, 279, 282, 285
  series, 82, 95, 97–101, 103, 104, 166, 172, 207, 229, 236, 257, 276, 285
  specific, 206
  varying, 194
Tinbergen, N., 8, 157–159
toddler
  (also see children), 143
totalitarianism, 47
trait, iii, 3, 14, 21, 63, 70, 71, 75, 77, 82, 83, 84, 93, 101, 105–107, 158, 159, 201, 203, 275, 266
transferability, 146, 152
transmission, 172
treatment, 63, 120, 138–140, 169, 180, 228, 231, 260, 263, 280
truth, 46, 47, 53–56, 58, 62, 63, 124, 125, 131, 132, 134, 135, 149, 151, 201, 224, 240, 243, 252–256, 258–260, 262, 274, 297
  maker, 77, 252, 253
  making (also see truth maker), 252, 253
  statement, 132
Tschacher, W., 40, 164, 168, 183, 184, 187
Turvey, M., 39, 150, 163–167, 204, 211, 212
typicality, 246, 248

uncertainty, 6, 130, 215, 217–229, 238–240, 242–244, 249, 250, 266, 290
universality, 5, 65, 71, 72, 73, 113, 150, 151, 159, 202, 259, 295
university, i, iv, xi, xii, 44, 143, 277
unwrapping, 22
utilitarian, 48
utility, 4, 45, 124, 132
  theoretic, 124

validity, 16, 71, 76, 89, 114, 191, 203, 276
Vallacher, R, 40, 98, 254, 261, 265, 287
valorization, 299
value
  laden, 44, 267
  oriented, 47
values, 1, 4, 25, 41, 43, 47–49, 51, 52, 60, 62, 67, 74, 86, 129–132, 172, 173, 178, 184, 216, 224, 239, 234, 246, 249, 258, 269, 271, 275, 277, 278, 299
Van der Maas, H., 40, 184, 187, 213, 260
van Dijk, M., 29, 131, 206, 212
Van Fraassen, B., 155
Van Geert, P., i, iii, iv, x, xi, 12, 20, 29, 36, 40, 41, 69, 71, 74, 83, 96, 97, 103–105, 131, 172–174, 176–178, 181, 184, 206, 212, 225, 227, 230, 236, 237, 244–246, 248, 254, 260–262, 265, 290
Van Orden, G., 38, 101, 151, 163, 165, 167, 184, 212
Varela, F., 58, 59, 91, 151, 164, 209
variability, 3, 6, 9, 21, 32, 34, 35, 39, 69, 71, 82, 83, 87, 100, 101, 105, 106, 108, 109, 110, 116, 123, 186, 198–201, 212, 222, 228, 258, 265, 266, 283, 286, 290, 293, 296, 300
variable
  intervening, 80, 130, 173, 188
  latent, 163, 196, 203, 206, 226, 228, 232
variable-centred
  (also see variable oriented), 73, 74
variable-focused
  (also see variable-oriented), 76
variable-oriented, 63, 273, 281
virtue, 4, 33, 46, 49, 50, 52–55, 110, 253, 266, 268
visual cliff, 155, 116–119, 122, 123
visual-motor, 123
vita
  activa, 47
  contemplativa, 47
Vygotskian, 172
Vygotsky, L.S., 159, 172, 213, 265

Waddington, C, 33
Whitehead , A.N., 13, 23
Wiener-Granger (also see causality Wiener-Granger), 173
Witherington, D., 12, 23, 37, 39, 132, 156, 159, 163, 164, 167, 272
women, 46, 80, 83, 119, 121, 152, 198, 202, 255
Woodward, J., 139, 143, 144, 146
worldview, 25, 269, 271, 281

Zadeh, L, 215, 244

For EU product safety concerns, contact us at Calle de José Abascal, 56–1°,
28003 Madrid, Spain or eugpsr@cambridge.org.

www.ingramcontent.com/pod-product-compliance
Ingram Content Group UK Ltd.
Pitfield, Milton Keynes, MK11 3LW, UK
UKHW022248220326
469255UK00019B/424